Glend
1013
Wilm., Del.
302-478-5246

p. 210 Renzulli model

Defensible
Programs
for the Gifted

Editorial Board

C. June Maker

Critical Issues in

Gifted

Education

Defensible Programs
for the Gifted

Edited by
C. June Maker

With special assistance by
Michelle Ellis-Schwabe

VOLUME I

Printed in the United States of America

Library of Congress Cataloging in Publication Data

Defensible programs for the gifted.

(Critical issues in gifted education, v. 1)
Includes bibliographies and index.
1. Gifted children—Education—United States. I. Maker, C. June.
II. Series.
LC 3993.9.D44   1986   371.9'5'0973   86-17345
ISBN 0-89079-194-5
(Formerly 0-87189-377-0)

8700 Shoal Creek Boulevard
Austin, Texas 78758

10   9   8   7   6   5   4   3   2   1   88   89   90   91   92

To my teachers,
who have made me think
and have given me food for thought
and
To my students,
who continue to challenge my thinking
and push me to develop new answers
and new questions.

TABLE OF CONTENTS

ACKNOWLEDGMENTS

Without the advice, encouragement, patience, and assistance of many people, the development of this book would have been impossible. I cannot recognize everyone but will thank those who have been most significant.

The idea for this series was originated and shaped through conversations with a very special person, Curt Whitesel, education editor at Aspen. Curt's suggestions and his respect for my ideas kindled my excitement for the possibilities of such a series and developed my commitment to the ideas we generated. Curt's death, and my difficulties in generating enthusiasm without his spark, caused a three-year delay in the project. Thanks to Aspen's commitment to me as an author, along with the guidance and patience of a new editor, Margaret Quinlin, the idea did not die.

Ken Seeley, a good friend and an author of one of the lead articles, played an important part in shaping the concept and organization of this volume. Of course, many of us would not have voiced our concerns about "defensibility" of programs for the gifted were it not for Joe Renzulli's emphasis on that concept. Thanks to Ken and to Joe for that inspiration.

The editorial board for the series has provided me personal support as well as professional advice in the development of this volume. The suggestions from this board have also helped to develop the topics for future volumes.

Most important, I wish to express my sincere appreciation to all the authors of lead chapters and critiques. Their professionalism, their thoughtfulness, their creativity, and finally, their *patience* have made my task as editor much more pleasurable than it could have been.

A special thanks goes to my students, who have listened to my ideas, shared my enthusiasm, and asked many thoughtful questions. Some of the authors in this volume are also my students, and they deserve an extra "thanks": Shirley Schiever, Anne Udall, Ned Levine, Michelle Ellis-Schwabe and Kay Klausmeier.

Some very special friends provided the support, encouragement, and challenge that made this and other projects possible: Jim Gilmer, Doug Hammond, Darrell Anderson, Diane Madden, and Steve MacDougal. They too have listened to my ideas, shared my enthusiasm, bolstered my ego, and stimulated my thinking.

No acknowledgments would be complete without giving credit to those who provided me support in producing a readable version of the manuscript. Ann Ferraro has typed and corrected several versions of this and other manuscripts with her flying fingers, and my secretary, Mary Kord, has been the best supporter—and loyal friend—that anyone could ever hope to have.

Finally, and *certainly* not least in importance, I wish to thank Michelle Ellis-Schwabe for her valuable help as assistant editor. She has taken much of the responsibility for technical editing, corresponding with authors, and collecting materials. She has also contributed significantly to the content of one of the chapters. All this was accomplished while working on a dissertation. Thanks, Michelle, for responding to urgent requests, working hard, thinking creatively, and for being my friend.

PREFACE

This book is the first volume in a series entitled *Critical Issues in Education of the Gifted*. The series was conceived and designed as an alternative to establishing a new journal since a book series could provide a forum for the consideration of issues in greater depth than could a journal.

The purpose of the series is to critically examine timely and controversial issues in the field of education of the gifted. This undertaking shall have as its goals the following:

- to rethink old issues
- to challenge the status quo
- to present conflicting opinions
- to generate a dialogue in print
- to analyze trends and directions
- to critique theory, practice, and research
- to provide not just a summary, but a true synthesis and transformation of ideas
- to develop awareness and understanding of new issues and new trends
- to provide new answers to old questions
- to ask new questions

The issues to be examined shall be related to all aspects of education of the gifted, and shall include, but not be limited to, program development, curricula, teaching strategies, the nature of giftedness and talent, staff selection and training, sociological perspectives, psychological development, counseling approaches, parent education, research, affective needs, and various subgroups of gifted or talented children.

In each volume, the central issue will be examined from a multidisciplinary, multifaceted point of view in the attempt to develop a comprehensive understanding of the various questions involved. Theories relating to the central issue, the research and evaluation data, and practical applications/educational implications shall be examined in each volume. The underlying philosophy is that comprehensive understanding requires that answers be given based on past experience and empirical data, but that unanswered questions and new perspectives accompany these answers.

Contributing authors shall be selected who represent a variety of disciplines and a variety of points of view, including theoreticians, researchers, and practitioners.

The task of the editor shall be to reflect upon the different perspectives, identify areas of agreement among the authors, and call attention to other points of view not included in the articles. Finally, the editor's responsibility is to provide a synthesis of various perspectives and suggest possible new directions.

INTRODUCTION

Organization and Structure of Volume I

Individuals involved in research and practice were asked to present a point of view and to defend it as strongly and forcefully as possible with research evidence, philosophical statements, and/or logic. Other individuals, selected because of their differing background, experience, or perspective, were asked to react to a particular individual's viewpoint and to present a different perspective if they wished to do so. After critiques were received, authors of lead chapters were given an opportunity to respond to the critique by writing a reaction. The editor attempted to summarize, synthesize, and present the implications of the theories and practices advocated. The emphasis has been on clarification and understanding of the issue rather than on reconciliation of any differences of opinion or points of view.

In each section, lead chapters are usually followed by a critique and/or presentation of a different point of view. However, in a few instances, the editor deviated from this format to accommodate differences in content, author preferences and strengths, or to enable a better examination of the topic. For example, Silverman's article on gifted females is followed by critiques by both a man and a woman because the reactors may come from different perspectives. (In addition, I did not want to be labeled "sexist" by either sex!) The curriculum section contains two lead chapters, one critique, and a third "critique" that discusses the approaches of the two authors of lead chapters and outlines the implications of these approaches for teachers. The section on program evaluation contains two "lead" chapters and one critique that contrasts the two points of view and presents a synthesis of ideas regarding the subject.

As a courtesy to the authors of lead chapters, and as a way to stimulate further thought on the subjects, authors of lead chapters were invited to make a brief response to the critiques. Some chose to respond. Others did not. In some cases, more thought could have been generated by inviting those who wrote critiques to respond to the response! However, the process must end somewhere, and this is where the editor chose to stop.

Following are the major sections along with brief descriptions of the content and the rationale for inclusion of the section.

Qualitatively Different: Is It a Key Concept in Defining Giftedness?

An idea central to the development of defensible programs for the gifted has been that gifted students' thought processes, behaviors, and perceptions are "qualitatively different" from those of nongifted students. In this section, the concept was to be examined in seven chapters:

1. The Individual
2. Critique
3. Response
4. The Gifted Girl
5. Critique
6. Critique
7. Response

Qualitatively Different: Is It a Key Concept in Developing Curricula?

Because gifted students have been viewed as having qualitatively different learning characteristics, and because of a need to design curricula and teaching strategies that are identifiably different from the usual educational program, the concept "qualitatively different" has been central to discussions of curricula for gifted students. The concept as it applies to curriculum will be examined in five chapters:

8. The Curriculum
9. Critique
10. Response
11. Content and Process
12. Implications for Teachers

Enrichment Versus Acceleration: Is This a Continuing Controversy?

Although it is impossible to completely separate the concepts of enrichment and acceleration, certain philosophies and practices contain more of one approach than the other. In making decisions about the curriculum and the program, individuals must consider what kind of balance to establish between "the same concepts developed faster" and "different concepts developed." The issue is examined in five chapters:

13. Acceleration
14. Critique
15. Enrichment
16. Critique
17. Response

Policies, Program Development, and Evaluation: What Can We Defend, and How Should It Be Defended?

In the process of developing a program for gifted students that can be defended as appropriate and different, certain policies and procedures must be established that will facilitate and evaluate the program's success. Issues and practices related to program development and assessment are examined in six chapters:

18. Policies and Procedures for Program Development
19. Critique
20. Evaluation
21. Evaluation: A Second View
22. Critique
23. Response

Defensible Programs: What Are They?

The purpose of this section is to summarize and synthesize the points of view that have been presented—to review the similarities, point out the differences, and provide some directions for the field. This final analysis will be an attempt to achieve closure on certain of the issues while raising new questions and presenting new challenges.

Defensible Programs for the Gifted

The purpose of this volume is to examine a central issue in the education of the gifted: How can institutions develop programs that can be defended as

xviii   DEFENSIBLE PROGRAMS FOR THE GIFTED

appropriate for gifted students and *different* enough from the program for all children to justify the expenditure of additional funds or reallocation of existing resources? Within this general purpose, different points of view are examined with the hope that discussion will lead to a better understanding of the differences and similarities in the various perspectives as well as a further refinement of ideas central to the understanding and implementation of a certain approach.

As Seeley has noted in his article, the word "defensible" implies more than accountability, the term usually employed in educational circles. Defensibility also implies "guarding against attack," and suggests that educators of the gifted attend to the development of programs that are not vulnerable to attack because they have such a solid foundation, because we have built impenetrable fortresses around them, or because we have convinced our would-be attackers that their efforts are not necessary or would be fruitless.

Programs for the gifted are often under scrutiny, and even attack, by various individuals and groups: administrators who are concerned about the expense of the program, parents whose children were not accepted into the gifted program, teachers who were not chosen to staff the program, teachers who resent the bright children being taken out of their classrooms, and many individuals who simply do not believe we should be establishing special programs for those who already have certain advantages over other children. Much of this discussion results from what Jim Gallagher calls our "love-hate" relationship with the gifted. As a society, we seem to have difficulty resolving the issue of equality versus excellence. As John Gardner stated in his classic book, *Excellence,* too much emphasis on excellence puts the country in danger of creating elitism, while too much emphasis on equality causes us to ignore human differences and outstanding potential. As a society, we need the achievements of the gifted for survival and we believe in the need for all to have opportunities to develop their potential abilities. However, we also do not want to create an elite group. Thus, there will always be those who remind us, for various reasons and at unexpected times, that too much attention is being paid to the gifted.

Programs for the gifted are also under scrutiny by those who have legitimate complaints: parents whose children do not want to be in the gifted program because the activities are boring or because the other children "make fun" of them; teachers or administrators who see no relationship between the "fun and games" in the gifted program and the content taught in the regular curriculum; and researchers or evaluators who see no relationship between the stated goals and objectives of the program, theories about how children learn, and what actually takes place in the program. These "attackers" have legitimate complaints because we have not attended to the need to develop programs that are accountable, appropriate, and/or different. Unfortunately, there are many examples of our neglect described in the chapters that follow. We simply have not taken our "guardianship" role seriously enough.

I suspect, however, that Seeley also is correct when he suggests that many of our problems are due to having taken our guardianship function *too seriously*. In our efforts to guard against attack, we have protected practices that have little or no defensibility. We have failed to question our customs and the reasons why they were initiated.

Therefore, the purpose of this volume is to examine current practices in programs for the gifted to gain a better perspective on the issue of defensibility. Certain key questions have guided both the editor and the chapter authors:

- Is "qualitatively different" a key concept in defining defensible programs for the gifted?
- Are gifted individuals qualitatively different from individuals who are not gifted?
- Must one conclude that gifted individuals are qualitatively different to justify the provision of a qualitatively different curriculum?
- What constitutes a qualitatively different curriculum?
- To justify a program for the gifted, must we be able to state that the curriculum would not be good for, or could not be used with, students who are not gifted?
- What makes acceleration a defensible approach in a program for the gifted?
- What makes enrichment a defensible approach in the education of the gifted?
- How does one justify the expenditure of additional funds or reallocation of existing resources for a program for gifted students?
- What policies, procedures, and arrangements will facilitate or inhibit the development of a program for the gifted that can be defended?
- How can the continued operation of a program for gifted students be justified?

These questions, and others generated by the authors, may not be answered completely for the reader, but it is my hope that future responses to the questions will be more thoughtful—and defensible—than the responses made before reading this book.

Qualitatively Different:

is it a key concept in defining giftedness?

M any of the assailants of programs for the gifted question the need for different teaching methods or curricula for the gifted. Educators in the field have defended their practices and explained their rationale by developing the concept of *qualitatively different*. Some educators of the gifted have suggested that one can justify the provision of special services by arguing that because gifted students are qualitatively different from students who are not gifted, we must provide a curriculum that is qualitatively different. However, research evidence seems to favor the conclusion that gifted people show differences of magnitude (e.g., more rapid learning, advanced development) rather than kind (e.g., learning differently, developing differently). Qualitatively different implies that there are differences in kind.

This section examines the question of whether there are qualitative differences in gifted and nongifted individuals. William Foster explores possible answers to this question from both a biological (hereditary) and environmental point of view. He analyzes the lives and traits of individuals across a life span rather than concentrating on an individual at a particular point in time and describes qualitative differences as being observable only in adults who have made outstanding contributions. David Berliner disagrees with Foster on this point and suggests a mathematical model as further explanation of qualitative differences between gifted and nongifted learners.

Linda Silverman presents a rather controversial idea in her lead article: men and women view giftedness differently. She makes a provocative argument for her perspective, advancing the idea that women see giftedness in a developmental perspective—focusing on the gifted child as one who needs specialized services because he or she learns differently or possesses certain traits. According to Silverman, men, on the other hand, equate giftedness with productivity and innovation. It is interesting to note, too, that Foster has contributed one more set of data to support her claim. Foster states "The qualitatively different individual is defined through the realization of a life of outstanding innovation and production. The phenomenon under study is this qualitatively distinct productivity. . . ." However, Berliner and Borland seem to hold a "female" point of view, lending support to Borland's suggestion that we not label definitions along sex lines.

Lynn Fox makes a plea for avoiding "polarization" of the field into male and female perspectives, and addresses some psychometric issues brought out by Silverman's discussion. Certainly, I agree with Fox in her desire to avoid such divisions, but I must add that Silverman's ideas are supported by results of other research showing a general difference between girls and boys and between men and women in their orientation toward process and product. Men tend to focus on products while women concentrate on processes. Borland's and Fox's points about labeling these orientations as male versus female, however, are important to consider, and Silverman does so in her response: Many men hold a "female" point of view, while many women have a "male" orientation; and all of us have some degree of "maleness" and "femaleness." The problem, according to Borland, lies in the labels used for each perspective, and not in the concepts behind them.

I will now fit into the "female" profile (or, as I prefer to call it, a developmental orientation) by suggesting that what is missing from both essays on the individual is a discussion of how gifted children, or more specifically, gifted learners, differ from children or learners who are not gifted. It seems to me, as Berliner discusses, that if one is to justify the development of a qualitatively different curriculum for the gifted, one would need to describe the learner as being different now (as well as having different needs because he or she will become different as an adult). Thus, giftedness would be defined as "developmental differences" or some similar term related to current behaviors or characteristics. The major problem with viewing giftedness as "qualitatively distinct productivity" is that in this view, children are not gifted. They are only "potentially" gifted. In the identification process, then, we are looking not for something that exists, but for characteristics that suggest something might develop in a particular individual! Quite a different task. We must use retrospective studies of individuals who have been outstanding innovators or producers and infer that they possessed certain characteristics when they were young (e.g., above-average ability, creativity, and task commitment, as proposed by Renzulli). There is a significant fallacy in this approach, as Borland notes: children are not miniature adults. A second problem with such studies is that it is impossible to know whether the individual's success caused the characteristics that were observed or whether the characteristics of the individual caused the person's success. The usual inference is that the characteristics caused the success, but one cannot be certain that this inference is correct.

There is, of course, a second approach to defining the characteristics of giftedness, as Ward suggests in the next section. One could identify certain characteristics (such as high IQ) that are believed to be prerequisites of adult productivity, as Terman did, select a group of children with these characteristics, and study them over a lifetime to see if they do, in fact, turn out to be outstanding in their innovation and production. The early traits of those who became productive could be contrasted with the early traits of those who did not, providing indicators to use in selecting children with the potential to become productive. Even though this approach seems more defensible, there is an important fallacy in it, as Borland also notes: the traits necessary for or predictive of outstanding accomplishments at one time in history may not be the same as those that predict this productivity at a later period of time. A second problem with this approach is that no one knows whether or not an entirely different group of individuals with a different set of important but unstudied characteristics became more productive than those who were studied!

As we return to the question of how to justify the provision of a qualitatively different curriculum or program for the gifted, another perspective must be examined. Many will suggest that the best (or perhaps the *only*) way to justify the expenditure of public funds on special education for (potentially) gifted students is to remind the public of contributions that gifted individuals have made to society. Essentially, by providing special services for a small number of children, we have gained benefits for an entire society. Very few people seem to realize, however, that special education for the handicapped does not need to be justified in this way. In fact, it is not. We establish special programs for the handicapped for the sake of individuals—to enable them to become participating members of society and to enable them to reach their individual potentials. It seems reasonable to suggest that the same line of reasoning can be used in defense of the need for special programs for the gifted. This kind of defense, in contrast with the "contribution" line of reasoning, is more consistent with a democratic philosophy that purports to advocate an individual's right to choose a line of work that interests him or her rather than one that "pays back" a debt owed to the society for providing an appropriate education.

One's view of giftedness as differences in the traits of children versus the productive accomplishments of adults has implications not only for the identification process but also for curriculum development and program evaluation.

If learners are viewed as "potential producers," the focus of a program should be on preparing them to produce, and the curriculum should be designed with this as a goal. The ultimate test of the program's success would be the number of participants who actually became innovative producers. If learners instead are viewed as "children and youth who learn differently or need different experiences," the curriculum and instructional strategies need to be designed to enhance or accommodate these different learning characteristics, as Berliner states so well. The test of effectiveness would be the growth of the students and the match of the curriculum to student learning needs.

Obviously, the question of how to define giftedness will not be answered in this volume. Indeed, the discerning reader will note that I have chosen to present only a few questions (which I hope are provocative) and to avoid a "head-on collision" with the question of who to serve in a program for the gifted. Some questions are generated by contributions in this book: "Should we choose and serve those who are judged to need services because of their present learning characteristics, or should we select and program for those we predict will become productive as adults? Which decision is most defensible? Which decision is morally and ethically more appropriate?" At the risk of being labeled a coward, I will choose not to provide answers to those questions, but to end this discussion after presenting a few quick thoughts and questions. However, since I do not like to be considered cowardly, I must hasten to propose that the issue of who to serve is too complex a topic to examine in appropriate depth as a subpart of "defensibility," and promise to examine it in depth in a later volume.

1

Giftedness: The Mistaken Metaphor

William Foster, Ph.D.
Rutgers: The State University of New Jersey

A t one time or another, each of us has received a gift that has caused us to believe ourselves to be different from those around us, special in some particular way. These fleeting moments of distinction are most easily found in our childhood memories, in some experience recalled from over the expanse of years. Perhaps it was that new bicycle that raced like the wind, the check received from a kind aunt that temporarily bulged our bank account to a formative two digits, or a book that gave us access to vistas none of our friends ever imagined. In that moment each of us stood out from the rest. We were special, provided with a quality that set us apart. Perhaps that is the magic of the well-chosen gift. It offers the recipient a sense of his or her distinctiveness and uniqueness. But when the personal experience of gift getting is reified into a metaphor and employed as the intellectual centerpiece of a model of differential capacity, setting some persons apart as peculiar, endowed with qualitative capacities or gifts, transcendent over mundane humanity, a grave mistake has been made.

As individuals we differ from one another. Certainly this is true, at least in terms of how much of something we have. Some of us are taller, some are more talkative, and some more energetic. Also, there is little debating the assertion that each person's life experience is unique in character, both in terms of individual personality and personal experience. In the construction of these personal particulars it is clear, when we look at the unfolding of individual lives, that each of us uses the various, general human capacities and available situational resources to weave our own personal histories. In this sense we are all qualitatively distinct. Yet, any intrinsic differences among individuals in initial psychological potential are best understood to be quantitative rather than qualitative in character.

The qualitative differences that distinguish each individual life develop from that unique weaving of quantitative capacity, environmental opportunity, and specific learning that each of us experiences. At times the personal achievements represented in an individual life are of such substance that we think of that person as the embodiment of a special quality—talent, eminence, or genius. And then we seek this quality's origins. In the process of resolving this question, we frequently attribute the cause of such a special life to another qualitative state, giftedness. We now explain the cause of the unique person and his or her attendant productivity through a simple metaphor, suggestive of an original, innate, qualitatively distinct capacity. But I suggest we are mistaken when we do so. The metaphor of giftedness is inadequate and unnecessary to explaining the evolution of a life of innovation and productive accomplishment.

Some Things Remembered

My early life as a boy growing up in rural Maine during the late '40s and early '50s seems, upon reflection, to have bridged two worlds. One was the world of the future, the world to come. The other was the world of the past, a world that had been.

David, a close friend up the road, had just gotten a television. Because we had no set of our own I would trudge through the heaviest of snows to watch with him as a new world unfolded before us. We sat transfixed as Walt Disney swept us through a fantasyland of comic book characters and frontier figures; Howdy and Buffalo Bob taught us how to be happy no matter what the circumstance; and Mr. Wizard left us spellbound by the magic of modern science.

About the same time, my dad gave up old Route 1 as the best way to get to Boston. Instead he turned onto a black expanse of tar he called the "four lane." We no longer stopped to eat at one of the many Route 1 diners or inns I had always enjoyed so much. We now pulled in at a place with an orange roof. It was the only one on the "four lane." No more decisions about where to eat. This new world sure was simple, but its simplicity was deceptive. I found that upon further inspection it could be much more complex than the older one of inns, two-lane roads, and radio programs. When, at the end of the meal, I was confronted by 28 flavors of ice cream from which to choose, I began to wonder how much I was really going to like this new world. Too much contemplation of the joys of raspberry ripple as compared with the mysteries of butter pecan can overload a seven-year-old boy's circuits. Over at the general store Mr. Glidden's routine query of "What'll it be, Billy, vanilla, chocolate, or strawberry?" had not prepared me for such things. So much for the simple life.

But as inadequate as that old world was in preparing me to deal with many of the nuances of my new orange-roof, four-lane, video-tube existence, it did offer me some perspectives that spanned the gap. They still give guidance today. One of these is Mr. Dunn's proverb of the linchpin.

Across the road from my house was the Dunn farm. Mr. and Mrs. Dunn had worked that farm for many years. It was not a large place; no farms are in Maine. They are usually just big enough to live off. The Dunns were old. Their farm was old. Things were falling down. The barn roof leaked, so in a big rain the hay got wet. Then a wonderful smell filled the air and Blindy whinnied louder than usual for his food.

The hay he called for was hay he had helped gather. He would pull the cutting bar and the hay rake as Mr. Dunn and I, sweaty and itching, pitchforked the golden rows up onto a wooden-wheeled wagon. Then Blindy tugged it to the barn. We unloaded and went back for more. As the harvest proceeded Mr. Dunn guided him along with a series of whistles and clucks, as Blindy could not see for himself.

One hot August afternoon as we whistled, clucked, and pitched our way along the rows, Mr. Dunn pointed to the tongue of the haywagon and said I should always remember to check the linchpin before I left the barn. If I didn't check I might forget the pin and everything would fall apart. The wagon would go one way and Blindy would go the other. Then he went on to say that life was sort of like that. You always had to check the linchpin in whatever you were doing or things were apt to fall apart.

I always listened to Mr. Dunn and I usually remembered what he had to say. After all, he was a town selectman and he chewed tobacco. Either of these accomplishments should have been enough to make me attentive. But to ensure his status in my eyes I only had to remind myself that his maiden sister was my teacher. Given this, I thought it only prudent to listen and remember. So Mr. Dunn's linchpin proverb stayed with me over the years. It has served me well as I have tried to focus on the key part of some situation or theory confronting me in today's complex world. I always start by checking for the linchpin.

The Linchpin for a Construct

So, as I began to consider the theoretical framework supporting the conceptualization of the gifted individual and how that framework related to the notion of qualitative difference and its relation to the gifted movement, I thought of Mr. Dunn and the linchpin. What he said about all things having a linchpin appears to have some useful application to a discussion of qualitative differences among individuals. The gifted metaphor seems to be a conceptual linchpin holding together the framework supporting one explanation of qualitative differences among individuals. Without this metaphor in its proper place the framework of the gifted movement begins to teeter. Then any effort to explain individual talent, eminence, or genius must turn to a complex explanation based on differences of magnitude, timing, experience, and support, rather than differences in initial qualities.

What are the particulars of this relationship among the hypothetical construct of qualitative difference, the metaphor of giftedness, and individual experience? It is not that this relationship has not been discussed previously; it has (Hollingworth, 1942; Pressey, 1955; Montour, 1977). However, such discussions have tended to assume the utility of the gifted metaphor and the existence of a causal connection among these three factors. An implicit line of reasoning is involved.

An Endowment Emphasis

There is an initial presumption that some of us are endowed with a gift. This gift sets such people apart from others, who are not so endowed, giving the recipient a special kind of individuality. This special brand of individuality is different not only because the gifted have more of what others have, a quantitative distinction, but because this quantitative distinction can be of such a magnitude that it establishes a new qualitative state or category. The gifted then have something beyond what others have. They are qualitatively different by reason of their respective gifts, their initial potentials.

In the extreme, this categorical thinking is as if the human race at some point had no vision. Then someone is born who has eyes. That individual's capacity for sight is the differentiating aspect of his or her individuality, setting him or her apart in a qualitative manner from the rest of humanity. This gift of sight allows the individual to experience the world on qualitatively different terms. Dramatic innovation and change become possible, change both for the individual and for the society in which he or she lives. Jean Auel's novel *The Clan of the Cave Bear* (1980) is a fictionalized representation of this perspective on qualitative difference and social change.

The assumption that this giftedness contributes to defining qualitative differences among individuals has been a linchpin idea of the gifted movement for quite some time. Its assumed validity has justified an enormous amount of effort to locate these specially endowed individuals early in life so pains can be taken to ensure that their gifts are nurtured and shaped in favorable directions (Marland, 1972). Such special development of presumed gifts in individual lives has been met with varying degrees of success (Montour, 1977).

The assumption of the existence of a special endowment in selected lives has a long tradition in speculation. In Plato's account of Socrates' dialogue with Ion (Cooper and Hamilton, 1961), we find Socrates attributing the distinctive talents of different poets to the intervention of a deific Muse:

> She first makes men inspired, and then through these inspired ones others share in the enthusiasm and a chain is formed, for the epic poets, all the good ones, have their excellence, not from art, but are inspired, possessed, and thus they utter all these admirable poems. . . therefore, each is able to do well only that to which the Muse has impelled him—one to make dithyrambs, another panegyric odes, another choral songs, another epic poems, another iambs. In all the rest, each one of them is poor, for not by art do they utter these, but by power divine. (pp. 219–220)

So, from as early as the writings of Plato we have suggested to us the notion of a gift that sets the person apart and defines him or her as qualitatively distinct as an individual. This same theme has been central to the work of theoreticians of the gifted movement.

A few examples of the importance of this linchpin idea extracted from the published works of such thinkers may be instructive in better understanding and elaborating the nature of this basic notion about the characteristics of qualitative differences among individuals.

> Hollingworth (1942): If children inherit their mental abilities through their parents . . . and if inherited ability is the prime determinant of achievement, then we shall expect to find almost all eminent persons to be born of parents above average in social status. . . . It follows that their children will be born under the conditions which they have wrought for themselves, or which they have inherited from their own parents, and that these children will be superior, as a group, if "like begets like." . . . Opportunity and eminence are not causally related, except insofar as they are both referable to a common cause—able parents. (p. 13)

> Pressey (1955): It has been well said that "in the present international tug of war, survival itself may depend upon making the most effective use of the nation's intellectual resources." . . . Superior

abilities are now generally considered so predominantly a product of innate constitution that certain "educational" factors, possibly of very great importance in the growth of such abilities are over-looked. . . . There may be ways by which more "geniuses" might be not only discovered but even, to a substantial degree, made and brought to fruition. (p. 123)

Havighurst (1961): Children become mentally superior through a combination of being born with superior potential and being raised in superior environment. . . . There is some validity to a view of the production of mentally superior people as a *processing* of human material. Some of this material is of better biological quality than other parts of it, but it all depends heavily on social processing for the quality of the final product. (p. 524)

Silverman (1983): The attainment of excellence begins with a vision—a vision of what is possible. The vision does not visit every-one; it selects the most fertile ground for its development. What criteria does it use? Inherent capability, surely. However, there must also be emotional receptivity, a willingness to embrace the vision and devote oneself to it. It only remains with those who are willing to work toward its fruition. (p. 8)

Plato's Muse and Silverman's vision seem not far apart. Both have at their disposal gifts that each may grant to certain people, supplying a quality of distinction. In Silverman's version of the event not only is the person visited, thus making him or her special, but the individual is distinctive even prior to any visitation. To be visited he or she must provide "fertile ground"—a fertility synonymous with "inherent capacity."

We now have more than gift giving involved in the a priori construction supporting this hypothetical construct of qualitative difference. A kind of genetic environmentalism comes into play through the image of the "fertile ground." The gifted individual derives his or her distinction from a kind of double, positive whammy—a gift from the Muse falling on the fertile ground of a promising genetic disposition.

It seems clear that the mystical does not visit the drab or the average, at least in this conceptualization. In whole or in part a majority of the efforts to explain qualitative difference depend upon hypothesizing a dispositional condition that differentiates the individual from his or her fellows. In the twentieth century the prime dimension of this dispositional condition has been assumed to be not divine but genetic in character. The basis for qualitative difference has become, in substantial part, physiological. DNA and RNA now have an important role to play in explaining the presumed phenomenon of initial qualitative differences among individuals.

It follows, then, that a corollary eugenics perspective must play a role in this biological model of qualitative difference. Good gene pools, when mixed, produce favorable offspring. Mating of genetically predisposed adults increases the probability of the occurrence of gifted children (Keules, 1984)

Most, if not all, advocates of a biologically based position actively acknowledge the importance of proper environmental support for and training of such promise if it is to be realized eventually in the form of mature originality and productivity. But without such a dispositional biological condition, the phenomenon of giftedness cannot exist and qualitative difference does not exist. The previous citations reveal this pattern of reasoning. Giftedness, alias biological disposition, is the linchpin metaphor for the concept of the qualitatively different individual so central to the framework of the gifted movement. Whether alone or in combination with an environmental/learning view, it serves as the primary basis for distinguishing the gifted individual as qualitatively distinct.

Consequently, the gifted movement is disposed toward an analysis of traits of personality like intelligence and creativity. Such traits fit well into this biological presumption and sponsor a preoccupation with the psychometrics of identifying specialized aspects of these general psychological states, like higher thought processes, in individuals. From this point of view, such identification must occur as early as possible in an individual's life. Late identification is problematic because, as has been noted, the effect of an unstructured environment on learning can be fatal to the mature realization of the individual's gift.

Even when pursued with vigor, the application of such an identification process may have flaws culminating in inadequate or improper identification (Richert, 1982). The first flaw in the application of the identification process, that of overlooking individuals, can result in ignoring vital raw material so necessary to the successful social engineering of our human resources (Havighurst, 1961). The second, false identification, implies a similar but converse dysfunctional circumstance—the ineffective and inefficient use of limited environmental resources such as appropriate educational services (Marland, 1972).

In summary, a significant part of the conceptual basis for the hypothetical formulation of giftedness as the significant qualitative difference between certain individuals and the general population rests on the assumption that giftedness is provided through a psychological/physiological differentiation of the elite. This qualitative state is, in part, the consequence of a distinctive biological disposition derived from good breeding or chance genetic modification or both. Given this initial, biological qualitative disposition, favorable environmental conditions facilitate the eventual realization of such difference in innovative, productive adult lives. A major task of the researcher and educator is the identification of the gifted as early as possible to ensure that appropriate familial, educational, and social resources are brought to bear on the individual in order to bring about the realization of some desirable adult outcome.

An Environmental Emphasis

The contrary adoption of an environmental or tabula rasa metaphor of the individual does not necessarily imply a simple adoption of the nurture side of the classic nature/nurture debate. Rather, it is often an attempt to resolve this dichotomy by adopting a both/and stance. From this perspective, a partial explanation of qualitative difference among individuals may lie in the positing of certain antecedent factors that are quantitative and constitutional in character, but the added assumption of a qualitative, dispositional state of giftedness is not necessary to this perspective in explaining qualitative difference. Qualitative difference is defined by life outcomes. The environmental circumstances surrounding the individual always mediate, either in favor of or against, the eventual realization of the individual's initial ability. From this perspective the qualitative difference is defined by this eventual realization in some form of adult talent, eminence, or genius.

There are some proponents of a model of qualitative life outcomes who depend only on an environmental justification for explaining such difference. Perhaps the most well known of these thinkers is B.F. Skinner. In 1972 he gave a talk entitled "A Lecture on 'Having a Poem'." Unlike Plato, Skinner does not invoke the assistance of a Muse to explain the process:

> . . . a person does not act upon the environment, perceiving it and deciding what to do about it; the environment acts upon him, determining that he will perceive it and act in special ways. . . . The poet is also a locus, a place in which genetic and environmental causes come together to have a common effect. . . . And because the poet is not aware of the origins of his behavior, he is likely to attribute it to a creative mind, an "unconscious" mind, perhaps, or a mind belonging to someone else—to a muse, for example, whom he has invoked to come and write his poem for him. . . . To wait for genius or a genie is to make a virtue of ignorance. If poetry is a good thing, if we want more of it and better, and if writing poems is a rewarding experience, then we should look afresh at its sources. . . . The task is not to think

of new forms of behavior but to create an environment in which they are likely to occur. . . . We can build a world in which men and women will be better poets, better artists, better composers, better novelists, better scholars, better scientists—in other words, better people. We can, in short, "have" a better world. (pp. 352–355)

This better world is well represented in Skinner's only novel, *Walden Two*.

As extreme as this environmentalist view may be, it is representative of a trend toward emphasizing the role of experience and learning in explaining individual excellence. Perhaps the best known current advocates of this thinking are Robert Albert and Benjamin Bloom.

Albert's (1975) writing reflects a desire to base the definition of qualitative difference squarely on the recognition of a set of circumstantial and behavioral correlates that precede the granting to an individual of the illustrious title of genius. Genius is not an a priori condition, not even in the nascent form of the prodigy. It is

> . . . not a blessing, a danger, or a fortuitous occurrence: it is not a trait, an event, or a thing. Rather it is, and always has been, a judgment overlaid with shifting values. What genius has often been based on is far more solid—behavior. What it must be based on is creative behavior, which, although highly personalized, is made public and is eventually influential over many years and often in unpredictable ways. By being both productive and influential, this behavior can be measured, its influence traced, and the factors and events underlying it better understood. Of all the qualities attributed to persons of genius the most remarkable, along with perceptiveness, are continuity, endurance, productivity, and influence. Men and women with such attributes are usually esteemed and often honored. They are almost always eminent in comparison to others. But they do not have genius. (p. 151)

Following Albert's conceptual effort, Bloom (1981; 1982) has pursued an intensive study of a sample of lives characterized by the subjects having attained a level of eminence in their field of endeavor prior to middle age. Though not viewed as a genius, each has achieved much in his or her young life. The thrust of Bloom's investigation is social-psychological in character. Apart from early and continuous opportunities to develop their interests, the antecedent conditions of the lives of the individuals in the sample do not differ significantly from the early life experiences of most middle- and upper-middle-class children in current American society (Bloom & Sosniak, 1981). Specific commitments to work hard for what they want, an often extraordinary investment of family resources in the training of the talent, and open access to exceptional instruction stand out as the key antecedents to the emergence of the individual's exceptional talent—a talent that sets the individual apart, that causes him or her to be viewed by others as qualitatively different in performance from the average person.

Assuming giftedness as a qualitative distinction or precondition for exceptional talent or genius is not an essential aspect of this environmental interaction approach to understanding and characterizing qualitatively different lives. In their efforts to explain qualitative differences among individuals, the advocates of this position focus on life outcomes and de-emphasize initial potential, whether divine or physiological in character, as the linchpin of their model. Experience, learning, and development are the essential elements.

Howe's recent statement (1982) on the development of outstanding individuals takes the same tack in analyzing how individual excellence occurs. From this perspective, the key to such outcomes lies in the life experiences of the individuals and not some organic state beyond that available to all members of the species. He does not posit a predispositional state of giftedness. Early experiences are often thought to be central to the building of exceptional lives, but this is not necessarily the case. Biographies of Darwin (Gruber, 1981) and Freud (Clark, 1980) give ample testimony to the fact that serendipitous, later life events may be the central factor in the eventual formulation of such lives of eminent achievement. Darwin's trip on the *Beagle* transformed an up-to-that-point mundane career into the realization of extraordinary contributions to biological theory. Freud's work on hysteria, which led him to the postulation of his revolutionary view of psychic life, was done at middle age. Until then he had been but an ordinary physician in the turn-of-the-century Viennese medical community. Prior to such events it would have been unreasonable to think of Darwin's and Freud's lives as predispositionally and descriptively different in character from those of their peers.

Which Is The Correct Linchpin?

Science is by definition an effort to understand naturally occurring phenomena. To achieve such understanding the first task of the investigator must be to accurately identify the phenomenon under study. Once this has been accomplished the scientist begins to elaborate the description of the event and then to speculate about the underlying dynamics of the event, particularly its causes. This chapter began with the assertion that the phenomenon under scientific review is qualitative differences among individuals. Darwin and Freud are representative of this class of events, as are Mozart and Mother

Teresa. But we have two very different conceptual definitions of the origins of such lives, each quite distinct in character.

As Kuhn (1961) has pointed out, such a situation is ideal for the working of science. The task becomes the confirmation of one or another of these models of qualitative difference:

> In scientific practice the real confirmation questions always involve the comparison of two theories with each other and with the world, not the comparison of a single theory with the world. (p. 54)

The first explanatory model defines qualitative difference by proposing it to be equal to the dispositional state called giftedness. Giftedness is understood to be synonymous with either or both a divine or biological intervention in the form of a qualitative endowment in individual lives. In this description of the phenomenon, qualitative difference becomes both the cause and effect. Qualitative difference and giftedness are equivalent constructs. Qualitative difference is said to be the result of being gifted. The logic is circular. The predisposing cause is also the effect, both the reason and the consequence. The phenomenon is its own explanation. Being qualitatively different is being gifted and being gifted is being qualitatively different. As a conceptual framework this is analogous to the snake that swallows its own tail.

The second explanation differs in at least two ways. It defines quality differently than does the first and speculates about key causes of this difference as existing outside the individual. The qualitatively different individual is defined through the realization of a life of outstanding innovation and production. The phenomenon under study is this qualitatively distinct productivity, what Albert (1975) refers to as "a life of genius." Descriptions of the antecedent life conditions of such exceptional achievement serve as the backdrop for identification of causal factors used to explain such special productivity. In this model, biological disposition may be cited as possibly one of the numerous factors that contribute to the realization of a qualitatively distinct life. More often than not, however, such inherent capacity is viewed as having limited explanatory value, since individual development is mediated by so many other, more powerful environmental variables. This definition of qualitative difference and its causal explanation is based in large measure on a combination of sociological, social-psychological, and learning theory propositions (Amabile, 1983) characteristic of a behavioral model of growth and learning. To the degree that it focuses attention on an endowment factor it does so speculatively, because the advocates of this view see such a dispositional dimension as not empirically testable, at least at this point in time. Therefore, initial disposition has little direct role to play in the empirical investigation of individual lives of outstanding productivity and must be relegated to the position of armchair speculation. Howe (1982) writes:

> The precise causes of individual excellence may be unique to each person, prohibiting any valid generalization at all. Alternatively, the effects of measurable causes, and the sheer number of contributing influences may preclude assessment of their separate effects. Also, it is conceivable that the effects of ill-understood genetic influences on individual development are too crucial to permit successful prediction and understanding of the causes of excellence until our knowledge of hereditary mechanisms is greatly extended. (p. 1071)

Using excellence in a field of endeavor as the empirical definition of qualitative difference among individuals allows those who attempt to explain this phenomenon in this manner to view giftedness, defined as a quantitative distinction, as of limited importance or to dismiss it altogether. If special genetic factors play an important role in the eventual emergence of lives of talent and genius, they must remain speculative causes as they are not measurable with today's instrumentation. Consequently, the study of the role played by environment, development, and learning in the actualization of individual achievement holds out the most promise for understanding and analysis of this qualitative difference among individuals.

A Preferred Emphasis

Thus giftedness does not stand as the sole linchpin metaphor in developing an explanatory model of the occurrence of qualitative difference among individuals. From the extreme point of view of the environmental/feedback perspective, giftedness is, in fact, an irrelevant construct.

The position defines differences of type not in terms of predispositional states but as an outcome condition resulting from the interaction of a complicated set of factors, many of which are developmental and experiential in nature. The qualitative phenomenon is outstanding life achievement rather than giftedness. The best explanation of qualitative distinctions lies in the open-ended interaction of multiple factors: general human capacity, environmental opportunity, universal patterns of human development, and intentional and accidental learning.

Giftedness, as special genetic disposition, may contribute to such an outcome, but with our limited assessment tools we have no effective procedures for measuring the presence or the impact of such an influence on the eventual life outcome.

Qualitative difference is the attainment of individual excellence in the form of an innovative, productive life of outstanding proportions—an achievement attained by few. In the extreme, such lives are lives of genius, differentiated from both the usual and the talented not just by some difference in magnitude of the life achievement, but by the quality of that achievement.

Genius is the outcome of a life of innovation and productivity that in some fashion changes the way in which we view our human condition. Such contributions of genius may be made in any field of human endeavor. Darwin and Freud exemplify this type of individual contribution. So do William Shakespeare, Norbert Wiener, Karl Marx, and Madame Curie. The life achievements of such people produce what Kuhn refers to as a paradigm shift, a change that fundamentally alters the view of reality that guides the fields in which the genius works. Such innovative, productive genius is qualitatively different in character, distinct from the productivity of the average life. Variability in average attainment is best understood in terms of differences of magnitude. The explanations of such differences of magnitude are understandable through the application of our usual models of individual difference based on nomothetic assumptions about human differences.

In summary, the notion of qualitative difference among people may be defined in two ways. Qualitative difference can be viewed as equivalent to a dispositional state of giftedness or psychological/physiological endowment. This condition is assumed to be the crucial factor in achieving an exceptional life outcome, and such an outcome is not to be attained without this initial dispositional difference. The life of genius is the outward and ultimate manifestation of this initial qualitative distinction or giftedness. Alternatively, qualitative difference can be understood to refer to a life outcome of extraordinary innovation and productivity, a life of genius. The explanation of this outcome, in contrast with the first, is that it comes from a unique weaving of general human capacities and life experiences into a pattern of psychological and vocational competence that results in, if not a life of genius, then a life of talent.

It must be noted that both positions hold that such innovation and productivity, however derived, are found in the life of the individual and are not characteristics of group actions. Groups do not exhibit talent or genius. Only individuals do. This in no way denies the contribution that others make to such lives. Individual accomplishment must be viewed as partially social in derivation. The role others play in its realization is crucial, if often very subtle (Foster, 1983). But qualitative difference, either as giftedness or life achievement, is a difference demonstrated in individual lives.

What Research Suggests

With these two perspectives on the orign and nature of qualitative difference in mind, we must turn to the results of research investigations to test the respective validity of these contrasting linchpin metaphors. In doing so we are drawn to the tentative conclusion that the data testing the environmental/ feedback approach is the more empirically persuasive of the two positions. This conclusion is reached after a comparative review of a representative sample of both the methods and findings of research on each of the two positions.

Prior to detailing the particulars of this review, we must note certain presumptions about the basic nature of the research act for each position. For example, from the perspective of the gifted model we should be able to identify quite early in individual lives some qualitatively distinct behavioral expression of giftedness. This should certainly be the case when the individual's behavior is compared with the behavior of nongifted individuals, people who are not so endowed. In addition, this endowment or gift must not derive from social origins. So, constructs like self-concept, widely understood to be an interactional, derived construct (Wylie, 1974), would be by definition unacceptable for evaluation as representative of giftedness.

Proceeding under the assumption that giftedness, as an expression of some form of organic endowment, does exist and is indirectly measurable with today's instrumentation, we might expect to see, as an addition to early chronological expression, some acceleration of or possibly skipping of developmental sequences, especially in relation to age mates. An extreme example of such developmental anomaly might be a three-year-old who successfully performs Piaget's tests for formal operational thinking.

As has already been noted, a matched sample of age mates is important for studies done to validate the gifted model, since the recognition of qualitative difference among individuals is always comparative. All such taxonomic logic and nominal scaling has this comparative character.

Therefore, our empirical review of this model must be limited to the work of investigators who carefully address their task by making comparisons between or among groups and who select constructs for investigation that are operationalized as organic or developmental variables. For such contrasting, psychological patterns to be adequately researched, the general environmental contingencies between the groups must be reasonably matched, since it is not assumed in this model that unfavorable experience is irrelevant to the realization of the gift in its mature adult form. The gifted explanation of qualitative difference in individuals does not operate from the assumption that "the cream will always rise to the top" in spite of unfavorable environmental circumstance (Foster, 1979).

Given the conceptual prerequisites that the qualitative difference dimension be organic or developmental in character, we are forced to limit our review to work on such psychological constructs as forms of cognition, types of affective sensitivity, kinds of learning style, or patterns of interpersonal processing. As such factors of personality and temperament are presumed to be more indigenous to the basic psychology of the individual than are derived dimensions of character like risk taking or self-esteem, they constitute that constellation of constructs necessarily investigated by researchers of the gifted. The gifted individual should be qualitatively distinct from the norm. In short, he or she should appear as a special type of human being if the general propositions of the model are to be substantiated by empirical investigations. Moreover, if differences either in endowment or developmental speed are found to apply in cases where environmental influences are held constant or treated as random influences, then their expression should continue across the life experiences of the gifted, maintaining the qualitative distinction between them and the normal population through the duration.

Let us proceed to a representative though not exhaustive review of the current research literature, looking for an empirical validation or refutation of this gifted viewpoint. In doing so, only studies meeting the methodological and conceptual constraints just outlined have been selected for review.

Terman's work (1925–1959) is an obvious point of departure. For Terman the variable distinguishing the gifted was the organic construct of intelligence, operationally defined as 140+ on the Stanford-Binet Intelligence Test. His longitudinal study of some 1,500 individuals distinguished by this score was comparative in nature, and the life progress of his sample was constantly evaluated in relation to the normative progress of matched groups of individuals from the general population. Therefore, Terman's work meets all the requirements of our methodological and conceptual standards of review.

This vast research effort has been discussed extensively in other reviews (Sears, 1977). The most current of these is a summative reevaluation of the Terman data done by Feldman (1984). Feldman's primary purpose was to follow up the very high IQ subjects in the Terman sample. This is ideal, as such a selective analysis of the extremes of the Terman sample should accentuate the overt effect of the dispositional trait of exceptional intelligence. If the gifted hypothesis is adequate to the task of defining qualitative difference, this data should evidence the fact.

As Feldman has suggested (Eby, 1983):

> Ever since Lewis Terman developed the first IQ test as a systematic way of identifying gifted children, the concept of giftedness as an

innate, largely unchangeable quality bestowed on certain people has become firmly entrenched as an educational fact. It is impossible to calculate the full impact of Terman's view of giftedness on educational policy and practice, but giftedness and genius came to be defined in IQ terms not just among educational researchers but in the public mind as well. (p. 30)

In his reanalysis of the Terman sample, Feldman divided the pool of subjects into two subsamples. He compared the life outcomes of that group of individuals who scored around the 150 IQ mark with a group of individuals whose IQ scores were at or above 180. The total number of subjects in the two groups was 52, 26 in the first and 26 in the second, the sample size being limited by the number of subjects in the original study who scored at or above 180. The comparison between the two samples ranged across a number of behavioral dimensions including patterns of education, career, and marriage. At the outset, Feldman assumed, because of the 30-point IQ spread, that his comparative study would result in differences similar to those presumed to exist between a sample of the general population and the whole Terman group.

Following his analysis of the available data, however, Feldman was forced to conclude that the 180 IQ group was not substantially different in character from the 150 IQ sample. None of the dimensions surveyed distinguished between the two groups, even though the initial arithmetic difference between the two IQ groupings, 30 to 40 points, was substantially the same as the difference between the general population and the lower gifted group. If an exceptionally high IQ score is assumed to be an accurate representation of the innate trait of qualitatively distinct intelligence, and if having such a high order of intelligence does not distinguish an individual subject qualitatively from his or her less intelligent peers in terms of specific behavioral patterns or general life outcomes, then the validity of a strict gifted/qualitative difference hypothesis is drawn into question.

But does an endowment of a 140 + IQ distinguish an individual from his or her more average peers in some qualitative fashion? Such IQ differences are certainly differences of magnitude, but are they truly differences of type? To review evidence regarding this question, we must look to Terman's own work (Terman & Oden, 1959). His youth and mid-life follow-ups on the original sample demonstrate evidence of difference between the 140 + group and the general population. But what kind of differences are involved?

In commenting on the differences evident between the sample of gifted individuals and the norm at a point in late childhood and early youth, Terman concluded:

The deviation of gifted children from the generality is in the upward direction for nearly all traits; there is no law of compensation whereby the intellectual superiority of the gifted is offset by inferiorities along non-intellectual lines. (1959, p. 24)

It appears that the positive differences are general, not limited to particular areas.

As for the review of the group's experience at mid-life,

[t]he follow-up for three and one-half decades has shown that the superior child, with few exceptions, becomes the able adult, superior in nearly every aspect to the generality. (1959, p. 1)

From these findings it is reasonable to conclude that high levels of intelligence, as measured in childhood, seem a good predictor of a continuing positive discrepancy between high IQ groups and the general population. This is, however, a discrepancy based on amount, not type. That is to say, such outcomes are quantitatively rather than qualitatively distinct from the general population. In their reviews of Terman's findings, Gallagher (1975), Sears (1977), and Feldman (1984) all comment on this fact, pointing out that no persons of qualitative distinction have emerged from this group of individuals. Feldman's conclusions following his review of the 180+ subsample of the Terman group, the subsample showing the greatest difference of magnitude in relation to the general population, must give us pause regarding our confidence in the qualitative endowment model based on the central metaphor of giftedness. As Feldman notes:

On the whole, one is left with the feeling that the above-180 IQ subjects were not as remarkable as might have been expected. . . . While 180 IQ suggests the ability to do academic work with relative ease, it does not signify a qualitatively different organization of the mind. It also does not suggest the presence of "genius" in its common-sense meaning, i.e., transcendent achievement in some field. (p. 522)

Drawing the conclusion that initial, differential levels of intelligence, as measured by IQ, are any more than simple indicators of a difference of magnitude with limited life implications seems unwarranted, whether the IQ is exceptional as in the 180+ group or moderate as in the 150+ group.

Though the Terman studies are instructive for gaining a fuller appreciation of the life experiences of individuals who have exceptionally high IQ scores, we are unable to conclude from them that such presumed endowment differentiates these individuals from the generality in any fashion other than on such outcome variables as amount of economic status, level of educational attainment, and degree of career achievement. No indications of genius are evident. The inevitable question is whether or not an assumed special endowment of intelligence, operationalized as IQ, even at the 180+ level, is evidence of qualitative difference among individuals.

It is arguable that the gift of the 140+ IQ may not have resulted in lives of genius because of environmental conditions. We should not forget that the gifted model does not assume that the endowment carries with it its own necessary realization in some form of exceptional achievement. In fact, the advocates of this stance take just the opposite position.

Then we ought to look at the environmental and experiential aspects of these lives to see if we can identify certain shared constraints on their experience that might explain their pleasant but moderate attainments. Upon inspection it is evident that these people as a group are representatives of a privileged social class, having had access to numerous opportunities for experience and training in early life. However, being from the middle and upper middle socioeconomic strata of American society is not a sufficient condition unto itself to ensure the realization of full evolution of the initial gift. By itself such a social context is too passive.

Perhaps Terman's people, though having access to opportunity, did not receive sufficient adult counsel and assistance in realizing their gift's full utility? Regarding this question Feldman's review is again helpful. He points out that rather than remaining a detached scientific observer of his sample's life experience, Terman often intervened to provide them access to the best possible academic or social experiences. He was very much an active advocate for his subjects' growth. Given this, advocacy and recognizing the preferred social status of the Terman group, it is difficult to assert that the context in which these individuals grew or the opportunities for development they shared were in some manner unfavorable to their growth. The opposite assertion is the more reasonable.

When all is said and done, intelligence, even when present in extreme amounts and aided by a favorable experience, does not appear to be a meaningful determiner of later life experience. The most ubiquitous characteristic of the gifted individual, a high score on an IQ test, can not be viewed, based on an adult outcome criterion, as an indicator of a significant qualitative difference in the person even when favorable social factors coexist with the high IQ.

Intrinsic constructs other than intelligence, however, may hold the key to identifying a distinctive trait of endowment that stands as that aspect of the individual's experience constituting the defining characteristic of qualitative difference.

Dunn and Price (1980) studied learning style characteristics to see if they might discriminate the gifted from the nongifted. Using a discriminant analysis procedure they found that the gifted could be differentiated from the nongifted on the basis of 6 of 24 learning style variables. The 6 consisted of such things as responsibility, structure, and tactile-kinesthetic preference. They noted that these variables could be used to predict, with 53 percent accuracy, whether a student falls into the gifted category or not. Such a low level of predictive accuracy is unusual if a qualitative difference is involved in the person's experience. Yet even these modest findings are brought into question by certain statistical concerns endemic to Dunn and Price's analysis procedure. As the authors themselves note, though the predictive power of the 6 variables is statistically significant, the difference scores involved could well be a result of the effect of a shared error variance coming from the reduction of the number of variables from 18 to 6. Given this statistical confounding and the relatively low predictive accuracy of the general variable cluster itself, this dimension of learning style preference does not seem to be a sufficient construct for defining qualitative difference of giftedness.

Focusing on another aspect of learning, specifically paired-associates learning, Scruggs and Cohn (1983) found that verbally gifted students did not differ in any significant way from a matched nongifted sample who performed the same learning tasks. They stated:

> This investigation can offer no evidence that verbally gifted students learn in a manner that differs qualitatively from more typical individuals. . . . One major factor which seems (is assumed) to distinguish "gifted" children and youth from their age peers is the (assumed) remarkable rate at which they appear to acquire and retain information. . . . The results of the present investigation suggest that this presumption may not be true. . . . The findings of the present investigation do lend support to the notion that gifted children may not be, in a psychological sense, as "different" as they may appear. (p. 171)

Perhaps a process construct like problem solving can serve as the qualitative factor of giftedness. The findings from Ludlow and Woodrum's work (1982), however, suggest that this is not the case. Reviewing the literature on problem solving, they note that research on human problem solving has concentrated on assessing the performance of the normal learner across a number of situations and that little to no work has been done with the gifted population. Using a cutoff score of 130 IQ on the Slosson, range from 130 to 157, the researchers selected a group of gifted children and then identified a matched comparison group of youngsters who were not gifted. They asked each subject to perform a set of four problem-solving tasks and made two observations on the subjects' scores. They then calculated levels of success for each subject and categorized the type of problem-solving strategy employed by each subject. Results were equivocal. Gifted students showed higher levels of performance related to memory and attention but not in relation to measures of efficiency or strategy selection. Both groups used similar problem-solving strategies across tasks but the average group used more advanced forms of the strategies when favorable feedback conditions existed. The researchers were unable to show that the gifted sample used more advanced deductive reasoning, finding no differences in logic procedures between groups. Since it is generally assumed that the gifted use more advanced cognitive abilities or higher thought processes than their peers, the nonsignificant findings in relation to the researchers' hypothesis stand as further evidence against this specific proposition and against the metaphor of giftedness in general. In fact, Ludlow and Woodrum end their article acknowledging the probable value of instruction in realizing advanced cognitive skills in individuals:

> Opportunity to practice, if not specific instruction, may be needed for the acquisition and use of component cognitive skills and organizational strategies even by gifted students. (p. 103)

Selecting the psychologically derived, socially interactive construct of interpersonal sensitivity, Ritchie, Bernard, and Shertzer (1982) tested the qualitative difference hypothesis assuming that the gifted "possess a superior ability in interpersonal sensitivity. . . ." (108). Like the previous findings on other constitutional variables, their study's results did not support the presumption of a qualitative difference in interpersonal sensitivity in the gifted sample.

Carter and Ormrod (1982) took a somewhat different approach to the issue by considering the question of difference from a developmental viewpoint. Rather than testing for a difference on the basis of a stable dimension, such as intelligence, they began with the Piagetian proposition regarding the developmental acquisition of formal operational thinking. The research effort proceeded on the assumption that the gifted reflect a form of developmental acceleration in relation to a chronologically matched sample of nongifted individuals. The researchers also tested for the Piagetian similar sequence hypothesis to determine whether or not the gifted proceed through the same developmental sequence as did their matched sample of average youngsters.

Carter and Ormrod's work is important since, as in the Terman work, its conceptual backdrop is physiologic in character. Piaget's model of cognitive development flows from a biological foundation in that it assumes that the observed cognitive stage changes have direct correlates in specific phys-iological changes in the individual.

The results of the Carter and Ormrod work suggest that both the gifted and nongifted groups proceed through the developmental stage sequence in the same fashion, supporting the similar sequence hypothesis. However, their analysis of the data showed a temporal difference between the groups. The gifted acquired the capacity to perform in a cognitive stage earlier than the nongifted group; the gifted showed superiority in tasks related to the develop-mental stage studied; and they progressed through the stage more quickly than the average group. There was no indication, however, that the gifted group gained any absolute advantage over the nongifted group in regard to cognitive development. The nongifted achieve formal operational thinking as well as the gifted group, only at a later date. Consequently, it is unwarranted to conclude from this data that the assumed gifted/qualitative difference is a difference of type. However, Carter and Ormrod's work does support the position that, from a relative perspective, the gifted may gain access to certain ubiquitous human capacities, such as formal operational thought, earlier than average youngsters. The practical psychological or educational implications of this possibility have yet to be explored.

In summary, it appears that research designed to test for qualitative disposi-tional differences in gifted as compared with nongifted samples has produced data providing little direct support for the existence of a qualitative difference in the gifted that is representative of an intrinsic psychological or physiological endowment derived from some favorable divine or genetic intervention. There seems little support in current research findings for the gifted metaphor as the basis for explaining the existence of qualitative difference among individuals. The only significant indications regarding such a condition relate to a form of developmental acceleration, at best a transient difference eventually amelio-rated by time. As Robinson (1981) has pointed out:

> . . . when we refer to a child as a "genius," we are likely to mean that his or her development has progressed at a remarkable rate in some general sense, i.e., that the child behaves like individuals who are considerably older. Rate of development is the important compo-nent of this definition. (p. 67)

Note that use of the label "genius" by Robinson should not be confused with Albert's usage (1975), for Robinson is referring to the behavior of the prodigy while Albert is referring to a life outcome of the mature adult.

In contrast to the lack of clear empirical support for the gifted emphasis, findings of researchers working from the perspective of qualitative difference as a socially derived end state of extraordinary life outcomes show promise of supporting the model. However, work from this perspective is relatively new and therefore limited in the number of studies and the detail of their analysis. Most of the studies use eminent achievement as the empirical starting point for the design of the research. They then work backward to antecedent conditions that correlate positively with such qualitatively distinct outcomes. Certainly the most compelling of these recent studies investigating the connections between eminence and antecedent experience is Bloom's project on talent development (1981, 1982). In this study of accomplished adults, Bloom and his co-workers identified a series of situational factors that contributed to the realization of high orders of achievement. Extensive familial support, early selection of a career area, willingness to work hard, and contact with exceptional teachers proved to be significant predictors of the exceptional achievement. Each variable identified was environmental or experiential in character.

Paradoxically, Terman's work (1959) also provides support for this model. The most powerful predictors of later life achievement were not intrinsic to the individual but proved to be derived traits of adult personality emerging from the person's interaction with supportive environmental circumstances and favorable social learning. These include persistence at a task, integration of goals, and self-confidence—all learned attitudes and behaviors. The acquired motivational pattern, persistence at a task, has been identified as a key construct in so many studies of exceptional achievement that it is reasonable to suggest that it is a necessary factor for the attainment of eminence and key to attaining genius (Roe, 1952; Barron, 1969; Nicholls, 1972). This motivational trait of personality is not an endowed condition, being derived instead from sociocultural origins (Maehr & Nicholls, 1983).

VanTassel-Baska (1983) recently studied the life profiles of the Midwest Talent Search finalists to identify "contributive factors in the background experiences of these students that might have partially predicted their high level test performance" (p. 1). This study is a survey of the finalists of the Johns Hopkins University Talent Search for the north central part of the United States. Each student scored at or above 630 on SAT-M or 580 on SAT-V, or achieved a combined score of 1100 +. The project is different from the other retrospective projects cited, since the subjects were 14 years of age or less. Bloom's work sampled individuals much later in life. A significant portion of the VanTassel-Baska sample exhibited early accelerated behavior in areas such as reading and mathematics. These students also demonstrated precocious behavior in areas ranging from memory to vocabulary. No effort was made to attribute the cause of such early behavior, but it seems reasonable to assume that it is a result of relatively high intellect and a good deal of support and instruction from adults—parents and teachers.

The general findings, in fact, point in the same direction as the Bloom project. The realization of exceptional performance on the SAT examinations is highly correlated with certain activities such as extra learning experiences, academic acceleration, and extensive adult involvement. The vast majority of this talent search sample came from highly educated, professional families that appear to have spent a great deal of time supporting the intellectual develop-ment of their children.

A major limitation of studies investigating this explanation of qualitative difference among individuals is that by the nature of their retrospective design they cannot test for the specific effect of any particular environmental or experiential variable. Rather, their value lies in the descriptive presentation of those interactive aspects of environment, learning, and adult support highly correlated with qualitatively distinct achievement.

Conclusions drawn from a review of the findings of this approach to investigating qualitative difference must be considered as tentative. However, as a rule the data demonstrate the apparent impact of antecedent life experience on the outcome variable of extraordinary accomplishment. The studies lend credence to the view that qualitative difference in individuals is best defined in terms of life outcomes. And the research tends to support the proposition that such outcomes are, in large part, the consequence of environmentally based feedback and learning. They do not directly deny the import of an individual beginning the process of development with more of some inherent trait or ability than his or her peers. But they do suggest that such an endowment is only a distinction of magnitude and not of type. Qualitative difference remains to be constructed through an appropriate weaving of life experience and training.

In Conclusion

A friend and colleague of mine, Andrew Ortony, wrote an essay on meta-phor and its role in model building entitled "Why Metaphors Are Necessary and Not Just Nice" (1975). In it he argued that metaphors have great power, for they help us understand the unknown. They serve as linguistic shortcuts to knowledge, especially knowledge relevant to theory building. Most great ideas have metaphors as their conceptual centerpieces. For example, Darwin's great intellectual achievement—the dynamic of selection of the fittest—is based on the metaphor of the growth of a branching tree. Species branch off from one another to fill an emerging environmental niche. No species is, by this meta-phor, better than another, however distant or distinct it may be in character. This metaphor of the branching tree placed Darwin's thinking in direct contrast to the more accepted metaphor of the time—the ladder of biological progress with the human standing on the top rung, dominant, the ideal creation.

Both metaphors, the branching tree and the ladder, embody the essentials of a good conceptualization. Ortony (1975) specifies three primary features of this goodness—compactness, expressiveness, and vividness. Each is compact, being quick, concise, and effective. Each presents the inexpressible, allowing the user to effectively communicate aspects of the model otherwise too complex to efficiently discuss. Each is vivid, conveying meanings that are very close to the experiences all of us have shared, especially the emotional ones. Though both embody all the qualities of a good metaphor, only one is adequate to represent the reality of biological change. Darwin's is the more adequate, though it leads to the emotionally dissatisfying conclusion that humans are not inherently better than the rest of the living world—just different, suited to different ends.

The debate in this chapter is also about the comparative adequacy of metaphors. The metaphor of the gift is elegant, but like the pre-Darwinian ladder of progress, probably misguided. Little evidence exists to support the notion that giftedness defines a predispositional qualitative endowment that distinguishes certain privileged individuals from the mass of humanity.

Another metaphor is apparently more accurate in terms of mapping our human experience. That is the metaphor of the threshold. Here the presumption is that all of us begin the process of living with the same basic equipment, varying only in amount, not type. Subsequent interaction with environmental opportunity and specific learning through feedback shape the structure and outcome of individual lives to the point of a threshold moment where innate aptitudes and life experience blend in a fashion that allows some individuals to initiate the complex process of creating qualitatively different life outcomes. Some of these lives become lives of talent, eminence, and genius. The compactness, expressiveness, and vividness of this threshold metaphor are as adequate as those of the gifted metaphor. Yet this metaphor has, like Darwin's tree, the additional property of being more empirically valid in terms of what is evidenced from the investigation of individual lives.

References

Albert, R. (1975). Toward a behavioral definition of genius. *American Psychologist, 30,* 140–51.

Amabile, T. (1983). *The social psychology of creativity.* New York: Springer-Verlag.

Anderson, J. (1960). The nature of abilities. In E. Paul Torrence (Ed.), *Talent and Education.* Minneapolis: University of Minnesota Press.

Auel, J. (1980). *The clan of the cave bear.* New York: Thorndike.

Barron, F. (1969). *Creative person and creative process.* New York: Holt.

Bloom, B. (1982). Master teachers. *Phi Delta Kappan, 63,* 664–68.

Bloom, B., & Sosniak, L. (1981). Talent development and schooling. *Educational Leadership, 39,* 85–94.

Carter, K., & Ormrod, J. (1982). Acquisition of formal operations by gifted children. *Gifted Child Quarterly, 26,* 33–36.

Clark, R.W. (1980). *Freud: The man and the cause.* London: Jonathan Cape/Weidenfeld & Nicolson.

Dunn, R. & Price, G. (1980).The learning style characteristics of gifted students. *Gifted Child Quarterly, 24,* 33–36.

Eby, J. (1983). Gifted behavior: A nonelitist approach. *Educational Leadership, 41,* 30–36.

Feldman, D. (1984). A follow-up of subjects scoring above 180 IQ in Terman's "Genetic Studies of Genius." *Exceptional Children, 50,* 518–23.

Foster, W. (1979). The unfinished task: An overview of procedures used to identify gifted and talented youth. In N. Colangelo & R. Zaffram (Eds.), *New voices in counseling the gifted.* Dubuque, IA: Kendall/Hunt.

Foster, W. (1983). Self concept, intimacy and the attainment of excellence. *Journal for the Education of the Gifted, 6,* 20–29.

Gallagher, J. (1975). *Teaching the gifted child* (2nd ed.). Boston: Allyn & Bacon.

Gruber, H. (1981). *Darwin on man: A psychological study of scientific creativity* (2nd ed.). Chicago: University of Chicago Press.

Havighurst, R. (1961). Conditions productive of superior children. *Teachers College Record, 62,* 524–31.

Hollingworth, L. (1942). *Children above 180 IQ.* New York: World Book.

Howe, M. (1982). Biographical evidence and the development of outstanding individuals. *American Psychologist, 37,* 1071–1081.

Keules, D. (1984, October). Annals of eugenics. *The New Yorker,* 51–114.

Kuhn, T. (1961). The function of measurement in modern physical science. In H. Woolf (Ed.), *Quantification.* Indianapolis: Bobbs-Merrill.

Ludlow, B., & Woodrum, D. (1982). Problem solving strategies of gifted and average learners on a multiple discrimination task. *Gifted Child Quarterly, 26,* 99–104.

Maehr, M., & Nicholls, J. (1983). Culture and achievement motivation: A second look. In N. Warren (Ed.), *Studies in cross-cultural psychology* (Vol. 3). New York: Academic Press.

Marland, S. (1972). *Education of the gifted and talented* (Report to Sub-Committee on Education, Committee on Labor and Public Welfare, U.S. Senate). Washington, DC.

Montour, K. (1977). William James Sidis: The broken twig. *American Psychologist, 32,* 265–279.

Nicholls, J. (1972). Creativity in the person who will never produce anything original and useful. *American Psychologist, 27,* 717–727.

Ortony, A. (1975). Why metaphors are necessary and not just nice. *Educational Psychology, 25,* 45–53.

Pressey, S. (1955). Concerning the nature and nurture of genius. *Scientific Monthly, 81,* 123–129.

Richert, S. (1982). *National Report on Identification* (Contract #300-80-0758). Washington, DC: U.S. Department of Education.

Ritchie, A., Bernard, J., & Shertzer, B. (1982). A comparison of academically talented children and academically average children on interpersonal sensitivity. *Gifted Child Quarterly, 26,* 105–109.

Robinson, H. (1981). The uncommonly bright child. In M. Lewis & L. Rosenblum (Eds.), *The uncommon child.* New York: Plenum Publishers.

Roe, A. (1952). A psychologist examines 64 eminent scientists. *Scientific American, 187,* 21–25.

Scruggs, T., & Cohn, S. (1983). Learning characteristics of verbally gifted students. *Gifted Child Quarterly, 27,* 169–172.

Sears, R. (1977). Sources of life satisfaction of the Terman gifted men. *American Psychologist, 32,* 119–128.

Silverman, L. (1983). Personality development: The pursuit of excellence. *Journal for the Education of the Gifted, 7,* 8–19.

Skinner, B. (1972). A lecture on "having a poem." *Cumulative record: A selection of papers* (3rd ed.). Englewood Cliffs, NJ: Prentice-Hall.

Terman, L., & Oden, M. (1959). The gifted group at mid-life: Thirty-five year's follow-up of the superior child. In L. Terman (Ed.), *Genetic studies of genius.* Stanford: Stanford University Press.

VanTassel-Baska, J. (1983). *Profiles of precocity: The Midwest Talent Search finalists.* Unpublished manuscript, Northwestern University, Midwest Talent Search Project.

Wylie, R. (1974). *Self concept.* Lincoln: University of Nebraska Press.

2

Catastrophes and Interactions:

comments on "The Mistaken Metaphor"

David C. Berliner, Ph.D.
University of Arizona

D r. Foster has accomplished what every thoughtful author wants to accomplish; namely, he makes his readers pause and examine their own beliefs. I was unaware of my own beliefs about the nature of giftedness until I read Foster's analysis of the issue. He apparently believes that gifted students should *not* really be seen as qualitatively different in nature from other students. To him the gifted are people who, through the co-occurrence of fortuitous circumstances, attain an unusually productive life. Although Foster acknowledges that the quality of their work and its magnitude is exceptional, the gifted themselves need not be seen as qualitatively different in nature from the less productive/less exceptional of us, *until and unless they have a lifelong history of productivity and exceptionality.*

Another issue about which I had only vague opinions was the physiological, genetic, and social-class origins hypothesized to be causal factors in the development of giftedness. Foster apparently believes that these factors have been overemphasized and are, in fact, best ignored in thinking about etiological factors in the development of giftedness, whatever its nature.

Despite my possession of unformed and malleable opinions about the nature and origins of giftedness, Foster failed to convince me that his viewpoints were tenable. I found myself thinking of some different and even counter arguments to the ones he brought forth. Let me discuss these issues in the order I have just presented them.

The Nature of Giftedness

The belief that the gifted are "more" than the rest of us is well accepted in most societies. Most people acknowledge that the gifted are *more* intelligent, however we measure that, or *more* creative, however we measure that. They are often considered better painters, writers, problem solvers, salespersons, home-makers, etc. That is, they are seen to possess *more* of the qualities needed to be painters, writers, problem solvers, etc. Foster shares the common belief that the gifted are "more" than the rest of us, but has trouble accepting the notion that the gifted, particularly the school-age gifted, are "different" in nature from the rest of us. His reason for concern is appropriate. The "different" argument often is related to arguments about possible genetic, physiological, familial, or social-class factors as the origin of the differences. By proclaiming, for exam-ple, that the gifted are qualitatively "different," and then highlighting the positive correlation between customary measures of social-class standing and customary measures of giftedness, one can easily come to believe in the human eugenics movement, a system of beliefs that is capable of great mischief if not actual harm to members of a society. The potential dangers are real, and made clear by Foster. However, these dangers are not at all integral to the argument concerning whether or not the gifted are "different" in nature from the rest of us. They are quite distinct and separate issues.

To show the separateness of the issues of differentness and the contribution of hereditary factors, we need only totally ignore any genetic, physiological, or social-class arguments about the etiology of giftedness and embrace whole-heartedly a behavioristic approach to the origins of giftedness. An adherent of behaviorism would argue that individual competence in intelligence, curiosity, divergent thinking, and school achievement is shaped by the environment. When a certain configuration of such environmentally shaped traits occurs simultaneously, we use the term "gifted." If such a person is, indeed, "differ-ent" from other people, we have a case of difference without needing to bring in genetic, physiological, or social-class explanations of etiology. Thus, there is no logical reason that the "difference" argument must be shunned simply because of the unfortunate historical association of the "difference" argument with the genetic and social-class discussions of the etiology of giftedness.

Now, having demonstrated that one can accept the argument that the gifted are "different" without also accepting a belief in genetic or social-class etiological factors, let us move to a consideration of social policy issues related to arguments about the nature of the gifted. If we accept that the gifted are only "more" than the rest of us, as Foster does, then we might find greater concern about curriculum and school organization and less concern for instruction among those who provide services for the gifted. For example, if the nature of the gifted is that they are merely "more" than the rest of us, we might want to speed up their mastery of the basic curriculum. Their rate of learning becomes an important indicator of the quality of services provided to the gifted school child. Enrichment activities become important, also, because a student capable of "more" must be challenged by something other than the customary mathematics, the ordinary literature, the basic science, etc. Thus, when working under the "more" hypothesis, the educational planners of services for the gifted feel obliged to speed up the curriculum and make it bigger and broader. In addition, school organizational issues arise. The wide-spread agreement that the gifted are by nature "more" than the rest of us also requires rethinking of the concept of age grading in schools. It seems obvious that to accommodate to the increased speed of the gifted child, ungradedness in the area of a child's giftedness is the only organizational structure that makes any sense.

However organizational and curriculum issues are finally addressed, when only the "more" hypothesis is held, there appears to be no pressing need by educational planners to be concerned about instructional issues. This lack of concern is not viable when there is a belief that the gifted are "different" as well as "more" than the rest of us. Speed and breadth still remain appropriate concerns. But if the gifted are seen as different, then they must also be seen as requiring unique ways to be taught. Viewed in this light, the gifted, along with the learning disabled, the blind, the deaf, and the retarded are *special* children in need of *special* education by a *specially* trained teacher. Complex teacher educa-tion and teacher certification issues appear when one holds the "different" hypothesis about the nature of the gifted child. The instructional and teacher education issues are not as obvious when only the "more" argument is used to describe the gifted. Nevertheless, let it be noted that even the "more" argu-ment, without the "different" argument, has policy implications of great magnitude for the schools.

Resolving the More and Different Argument: The Nature of Catastrophes

I choose, like most others, to believe that the gifted are "more" than the rest of us, but I believe they are "different" from the rest of us as well. My limited understanding of the history of scholarship about the gifted leads me to believe my reasoning is odd, even if my conclusion is common enough. I believe the gifted are "different" from the rest of us *because* they are "more" than the rest of us. No physiological, genetic, or sociological conceptual breakthroughs need to be posited to explain the nature of the gifted. One only has to believe in catastrophes.

A catastrophe occurs when gradually changing phenomena suddenly evolve into something else. Catastrophe theory is a mathematical system to account for abrupt changes in the nature of objects. It is the invention of Rene Thom, a topological mathematician, who first published his work in 1968 while working at the Institut des Hautes Etudes Scientifique at Bures-sur-Yvette, in France. For centuries the only sophisticated mathematical models of complex events had been the differential calculus of Newton and Leibniz. As useful as the differential equations were to Newton when describing gravity, or James Clerk Maxwell when describing electromagnetism, or Einstein when describing relativity, they represent a system of mathematics that describes *only those changes that are smooth and continuous.* The world, however, particularly the world of the social and behavioral sciences, is filled also with phenomena that are discontinuous, sudden, and unpredictable. These phenomena are not differentiable. Change occurs gradually to some point, perhaps inperceptibly, and then suddenly a new state occurs. The simplest example from the physical world is the change of water into steam. As water heats, at some point (depending on pressure, volume, chemical particles, etc.), the object changes from liquid to gas. This is an example of more (heat) becoming the agent for a fundamental change in the nature of the object of study. More leads to different.

An example worked out by the behavioral scientist E.C. Zeeman (1976) is a prediction of whether a dog that is becoming more enraged and more afraid at the same time will engage in fight or flight. This event is a catastrophe, an instantaneous change of state of considerable importance, especially if you are approaching a growling dog with its ears back. Thom has shown that for processes controlled by no more than four factors there are only seven elementary catastrophe models. Let us posit one such model in verbal form (Thom's mathematical proofs are beyond my ability). Suppose our four-factor model consists of aptitude, curiosity drive, history of reward for achievement in some area (an achievement motivation variable), and history of reward for divergent thought (a creativity variable). Taken one at a time, we might talk of bright and dull people, motivated or unmotivated people, creative and noncreative people. Each person may be placed along some scale on each dimension. We might then further posit that when *more* of these attributes are possessed in some unique configuration, a catastrophe occurs—the person goes from bright to gifted, or achievement oriented to gifted, or creative to gifted. That is, at some point, a change in state occurs. This is a change in the very nature of the object, simply by the object being "more" than others on some of the dimensions. That is the point of this discussion.

Changes in quantity sometimes automatically result in changes in nature, like water to ice (a reduction of heat), or water to steam (an increase in heat). Changes in state occur when a stationary, growling animal decides to run or attack, based on more or less fear, and more or less rage. Anorexic-bulimic behavior has been the subject of catastrophe models, as behavioral scientists try to predict a sudden discontinuity from the normal state to starving or binging behavior. The models have been applied to stock market behavior (the state of bull or bear), language acquisition, and dozens of other areas where there is a discontinuous change in state.

The lesson from catastrophe theory is that a vector or factor or combined score on aptitude measures, curiosity measures, achievement motivation measures, and creativity measures might result in a state change. In short, "more" becomes "different." Nothing magic. No muses, brain physiology, genetics, social-class factors, or any other factors need be hypothesized to accept the "different" argument. Nature abounds with examples of discontinuities where "more" (or less) always becomes "different." Since Foster and most other people believe the gifted are "more," they have every reason to keep an open mind about the issue of "different," since in many cases "more" automatically means "different." In my mind, these two arguments about the nature of the gifted are not as distinguishable as they appear in the literature and in Foster's paper. Once you accept the "more" argument, I believe you have no choice but to consider seriously the "different" argument. The many examples of catastrophes in nature require attention to the "different" argument and to the social policy and instructional concerns associated with that argument, as discussed above.

At the conclusion of his paper Foster presents the only conditions under which he accepts the "different" argument. When he has a view of a person's life work, that is, when he can take a retrospective view, he believes he can discern qualitative differences among people. He would, I believe, judge the products of the Terman gifted at mid-life to be indicators that the Terman sample was "more" *and* "different" from the rest of us. If Foster had determined the educational programs for the Terman sample, would he have recommended any special treatment for the children in their schools? He probably would not have recommended any special treatment. Would that decision have been wise? Maintaining that giftedness can only be seen in retrospect is, to me, a form of educational cowardice—a failure to act. If we are to err as educators, perhaps we might want to do so in the other direction. Let us assume all, or most, children are gifted, and have the school seek maximum speed and maximum enrichment for each child as individual instructional programs are designed to accommodate each child's unique attributes. We can let exceptionality happen, and judge it later, or declare as our policy that we will seek it out and promote it as early as possible. I would opt for the latter—a position taken by the country of Venezuela, in one of the grandest social experiments of our time (Walsh, 1981). Let us now leave the "more" and "different" arguments and examine the etiology of this fascinating human characteristic called giftedness.

Etiology of Giftedness

The second major issue raised by Foster is the etiological one—What are the roots of giftedness, or talent, or ability? Is the environment the only cause? The dangers of speculation about physiological causes are clear, but my problem with Foster's strong environmental position is that there exists a very impressive scholarly work that convincingly argues that some human abilities are "hard-wired." Howard Gardner (1983) makes this point as he presents his evidence for multiple intelligences. Gardner describes six kinds of intelligence. Linguistic and logical/mathematical intelligence are described in ways similar to the ways the psychometricians have presented them throughout this century. A spatial, visual, artistic intelligence is also described, and does not depart drastically from historical conceptions of this kind of ability. But then, using the same evidential base, Gardner posits some other built-in human abilities. He talks of musical intelligence, body or kinesthetic intelligence, and personal, or self, or introspective intelligence. Gardner, however, uses a very different data base than the psychometricians to establish the existence of each form of intelligence as a distinct kind of intelligence. He studies prodigies in art, literature, athletics, self-knowledge, and mathematics; he studies idiot savants with unique mathematical or musical ability; he analyzes the behavior of brain-damaged subjects who through war, surgery, or accident have certain abilities impaired while others remain intact. The evidence from his analysis leads one to conclude that humans have within their physical brains hard-wired, built-in capabilities in at least six major areas—verbal, mathematical, musical, visual/spatial, body, and self. Gardner while taking a strong physiological position *in no way downplays the role of environment*. These hard-wired intelligences are realized *only* through interactions with the environment.

Suzuki, the great Japanese music teacher, creates an environment so that the hard-wired musical intelligence possessed by everyone can develop early. His system brings forth such intelligence in children much earlier than in other cultures, where natural contingencies shape musical ability. The kinesthetic sense, as brought out in the Chinese culture where juggling and acrobatics are selected, or the apparent selection of mathematical, engineering, and science abilities of Asians in the United States, or the apparent verbal abilities among

American Jews, speaks to both the issue of hard-wiring or aptitudes *and* cultural shaping. The fact is there is sufficient evidence to take seriously the case that half a dozen intelligences exist, as Gardner believes. Moreover, the distribution of these intelligences in different cultural groups may differ according to genetic and cultural factors, a possibility put forth by Lesser and his colleagues (Lesser, Fifer, & Clark, 1965). Despite evidence for cross-national hard-wiring of aptitudes *and* the appearance of distinct cultural differences in aptitudes, few people advocate a purely genetic etiology for intelligence or for giftedness. Nevertheless, a purely environmental approach, as Foster hopes to promote, ignores the strong evidence of these genetic and physiological influences. A resolution is possible, however.

The environmental argument is no less valid or humane when put into an interactive framework. A purely genetic or physiological approach to giftedness leaves out familial and cultural influences. A purely environmental approach to giftedness leaves out genetic or physiological factors whose influence is too strong to simply ignore. An interactive approach, to which I subscribe, recognizes *both* and places an enormous burden on schools as moderators of giftedness. If only genetic and physiological factors are considered as causal elements in the development of giftedness, then schools are irrelevant as change agents. Aptitudes, from this perspective, are seen as relatively immutable. People get to play only the deck they were handed. On the other hand, if only environmental factors are considered as causal elements in the development of the gifted, all children should be considered alike, and treated the same. "The best for everyone" is an appropriate model. Only with the interactive hypothesis about the etiological factors in giftedness is a heavy burden placed on the schools. With an interactive hypothesis in mind, the schools must accept that profound individual differences in aptitudes do exist, *and* they must also accept their responsibilities for affecting those aptitudes through instruction. Thus, school people who hold interactive views must necessarily consider adaptive, individualized, tailored instruction for each student more seriously than those school people who hold physiological or genetic views, or those that hold strictly environmental views.

It may seem as if a strong environmental hypothesis is the most "liberal" position. But that may be illusory. An interactive position about etiological factors is, I think, the only tenable position for school people to hold. It is the only position that necessarily promotes adaptive instruction, a goal of great personal value to me.

Conclusions

Foster holds that the gifted are "more" than the rest of us, and believes also that only in retrospect can one tell if the gifted are "different" from the rest of us. I believe that retrospective views of giftedness are inadequate—they lead to no necessary school policies for teaching exceptional students. Furthermore, the "more" hypothesis leads only to speed, breadth, and organizational recommendations, but does not lead schools to ask questions about how to adapt instruction to individual differences. When you believe, as I do, that "more" can easily also lead to a catastrophe, you find that more implies different, and therefore, you come to believe that educational policies must reflect a concern for individual differences among children.

With regard to etiology, also, we find evidence for a physiological basis for exceptionality in at least six major areas, and evidence for environmental influences as well. If one were to hold a strict physiological orientation to etiology, where there exist beliefs about the immutability of cognitive functioning, one would have schools designed to sort and select based on the characteristics students possess when they enter school. If one held a pure environmentalist view, as Foster does, one would have schools designed to present a single, best, program, where students must adjust to the environment offered, like that proposed in the Paideia proposal (Adler, 1982). Only when one holds an interactive view of aptitude and environment does the educational policy necessarily require concern for adapting schools to individual differences. Thus, on the basis of catastrophes and interactions, I question Foster's positions on the nature and etiology of giftedness, and I thank him for making me pause and think through my own beliefs.

References

Adler, M.J. (1982). *The Paideia proposal*. New York: Macmillan.

Gardner, H. (1983). *Frames of mind*. New York: Basic Books.

Lesser, G.S., Fifer, G., & Clark, D. (1965). Mental abilities of children from different social classes and cultural groups. *Monographs of the Society for Research in Child Development, 30*(4), no. 102.

Thom, R. (1975). Structural stability and morphogenesis. Reading, MA: Benjamin/Cummings Publishers.

Walsh, J. (1981). A plenipotentiary for human intelligence. *Science, 214,* 640–641.

Zeeman, E.C. (1976). Catastrophe theory. *Scientific American*, pp. 65–83.

3

A Response to "Catastrophes and Interactions"

William Foster

I am always surprised when educators and psychologists persist in using the gifted metaphor in their arguments in support of individualized, differentiated services for students in public schools. Giftedness need have nothing to do with it. That is, if, as the metaphor connotes, giftedness is understood to be some initial, innate, and qualitative difference that distinguishes the particular child as a distinct human type, falling into a special class denoted as "the gifted."

To me the more compelling position is that these very educational practices are justified on the basis of a careful analysis of the present capacity of children to perform in relation to the demands of the learning context in which they find themselves. If the capacity/task match (Foster, 1984) is appropriate, then the present educational activities are adequate. If the match is poor, then "more" (but, sometimes "less") and/or "different" educational activities need to be organized.

The notion that the present capacity of a child to perform is the outcome of an "interaction" between present aptitude (nature) and past opportunity (nurture) is a very credible basis for understanding the origins of those qualitative differences in performance that justify differential educational needs in individual students. But Dr. Berliner's suggestion that this differs from my perspective is in error. He and I appear to be in basic agreement as to the importance of "interaction" for the realization of qualitative difference:

The qualitative differences that distinguish each individual life develop from that unique weaving of quantitative capacity, environmental opportunity, and specific learning which each of us experiences.

If there is a difference here it is that, for me, qualitative difference is understood to be a special characterization specific to an individual's present performance as compared with some norm for that performance in the general population rather than a designation of inferred, differential endowment which can be used as a key explanatory construct in discussing the origins of that same, observed performance.

Notwithstanding Gardner's (1983) current speculations relative to qualitatively different forms of initial intelligence, I suggest that the data from studies done to characterize the nature of giftedness as an innate, qualitative difference have proved wanting. The viability of Gardner's ideas awaits the results of the long-term study of his model in which he is now engaged and the evaluation of those findings by his research peers.

Like Dr. Berliner, I think Thom's metaphor of catastrophe is instructive as it suggests why certain students come to their educational experiences with unique learning characteristics that justify differential instructional services. Renzulli (1978) has used a variant of this notion as the basis for his suggestions regarding educational practice with the exceptionally able student since his effort at redefining giftedness in the late '70s. However, as employed in Dr. Berliner's critique, Thom's model is simply a way of pointing to the outcome effect of the "interaction" process just discussed. I believe it is important to recognize that catastrophe theory does not speak to qualitative differences in initial states but rather points to certain special outcomes derived from the "interaction" of ordinarily occurring variables, i.e., H_2O and heat. It is the process of "interaction" among certain ordinary, but select factors, co-occurring in specific quantities in a system, that contributes to the realization of a set of particular qualitative outcomes, i.e., ice, water, or gas. As I noted in my chapter:

... the presumption is that all of us begin the process of living with the same basic equipment, varying only in amount, not type. Subsequent interaction with environmental opportunity and specific learning through feedback shape the structure and outcome of individual lives ... where innate aptitudes and life experiences blend in a fashion that allows some individuals to initiate the complex process of creating qualitatively different life outcomes.

I think Dr. Berliner and I agree much more than we differ. I just do not see much intellectual or practical value in the metaphor of giftedness, but he seems to think that it retains such value.

References

Foster, W. (1984). Helping a child toward individual excellence. In J. Feldhusen (Ed.), *Excellence in gifted education*. Denver: Love Press.

Gardner, H. (1983). *Frames of mind*. New York: Basic Books.

Renzulli, J. (1978). What makes giftedness? *Phi Delta Kappan, 60*, 180–184.

4

What Happens to the Gifted Girl?

*Linda Kreger Silverman,
Ph.D.
University of Denver*

" . . . caught in my struggle for higher achievements, and my search for
love that don't seem to cease . . . ."
—Joni Mitchell

The Strange Case of the Disappearing Gifted Girl

In the earliest stages of life, girls have several developmental advantages over boys: they are somewhat more robust babies (Hoffman, 1972); they learn to talk earlier (Terman & Tyler, 1954); they tend to read earlier; and they learn to count earlier than their male counterparts (Maccoby, 1966). They tend to score higher than boys on IQ tests during their preschool years (Maccoby, 1966) and are ready for formal schooling at an earlier age (Ilg & Ames, 1960). Girls have outnumbered boys in most studies of early entrants to elementary school, and the results have been judged highly successful (Callahan, 1979). They generally enjoy higher grades in elementary school (Maccoby & Jacklin, 1974), and they are less often counted among dropouts (Maccoby, 1966) or underachievers (Dowdall & Colangelo, 1982).

Yet, Richert (1982a) found that girls are disadvantaged in the identification procedures for giftedness in many school districts. Many more gifted boys are

Copyright © 1986 by Linda Kreger Silverman.

43

discovered than gifted girls, particularly in the junior and senior high school years (Fox & Turner, 1981). And the discrepancy between the number of eminent males and the number of eminent females is staggering, a fact which has often led to the belief that males are innately superior to females. Despite their early indications of promise, gifted girls fail to become eminent women.

The number of gifted females appears to decline with age. Preschool programs for the gifted have no trouble finding gifted girls. By the third grade, when many school districts begin their gifted programs, many of those "early bloomers" who appeared gifted in the earlier grades have lost their lead and demonstrate no particular advancement over their peers. By junior high school, there are clearly more gifted boys than gifted girls, and in high school the number of gifted girls continues to dwindle. College rolls contain even fewer gifted females, except in those fields that are traditionally feminine, and graduate school narrows the number even more. The gifted female is an endangered species.

What happens to the gifted girl? Why doesn't she grow up to be a gifted adult? A review of beliefs about women's abilities held until recent times may shed light on these questions.

A Historical Look at Sex Differences In Intelligence

For millennia, it was simply assumed that females were innately inferior to males in almost all respects, including intelligence. Both Eastern and Western religions promulgated the notion of the natural superiority of males; women were portrayed by various clergymen as imperfect males, defective in intelligence and moral character, intrinsically evil, lacking souls, and born to be subjugated (Walker, 1983). There was even some question as to whether they were human. Bowman (1983) reports that in the year 584, 63 clergymen (bishops and their delegates) debated this question at great length. The final vote was 32 yes, 31 no. Women were declared human by one vote!

Debates in the latter part of the nineteenth century over whether women should be admitted to higher education reveal startling views of women within the scientific community. Le Bon, the founder of social psychology, wrote:

> In the most intelligent races . . . there are a large number of women whose brains are closer in size to those of gorillas than to the most developed male brains. This inferiority is so obvious that no one can contest it for a moment; only its degree is worth discussion. All psychologists who have studied the intelligence of women, as well as

poets and novelists, recognize today that they represent the most inferior forms of human evolution and that they are closer to children and savages than to an adult, civilized male. They excel in fickleness, inconstancy, absence of thought and logic, and incapacity to reason. Without doubt there exist some distinguished women, very superior to the average man, but they are as exceptional as the birth of any monstrosity, as, for example, of a gorilla with two heads; consequently, we may neglect them entirely. . . . A desire to give them the same education, and, as a consequence, to propose the same goals for them, is a dangerous chimera. . . . (1879, pp. 61–62, as quoted in Gould, 1981, pp. 104–105)

There were few dissenters from this view until the present century. An interesting exception was John Stuart Mill, whose last work, *The Subjection of Women,* was published in 1869, the same year as Galton's *Hereditary Genius.* Galton and Mill were considered to be two of the most brilliant individuals who ever lived (Boring, 1950; Cox, 1926), yet their philosophies about women were diametrically opposed. Galton supported the beliefs of his times, furnishing "scientific proof" of the superiority of males in his initial study of intelligence. The females in his sample of 9,337 subjects were consistently outperformed by the males in every dimension (Boring, 1950; Pearson, 1924).

Mill, however, passionately decried the inequality of women under the law, proclaiming that it had no basis in nature, only in custom, and that the custom was derived from antiquated rule by the strongest. He avowed that the lot of woman was the lowest form of slavery, involving psychological as well as economic bondage, constant surveillance (even slaves had time to themselves), moral injunctions of submission and self-abnegation, no opportunities for revolt, and no legal protection—not even of their lives. The injustice of unequal treatment was compounded by the injustice of indoctrination. Although slaves had the right to resent their masters, females were assiduously taught to serve their masters gratefully and to compete for their favor. Educated from childhood to believe that they were inferior beings, that their lot in life was ordained by "divine will," most women accepted their servility as the natural order of things. Mill felt that under such repressive social circumstances women could not possibly know the true extent of their own capabilities.

Stone and Church (1973) point out that only recently have women begun to be accorded full human status, and that the process is by no means complete. The pathway from slavery to equality is education, but education was almost universally denied to women until the past century (Hollingworth, 1916; Walker, 1983). Even when women could afford to pay for private lessons, university doors were closed to them, as were most careers. The grounds for this discrimination were that these pursuits would interfere with women's major functions of childbearing and childrearing, that they were "unseemly" activities for the "fairer sex," and that women were unfit to serve in masculine roles. Walker (1983) writes:

> If women were really unable to learn medicine, law, theology, science, or any other field of endeavor, it would hardly have been necessary for men to exert such efforts to keep them from learning. The theory of feminine intellectual inferiority began to recede from view when women managed to receive education. But many men still clung to the belief that women must be less able to think than men. (p. 926)

Leta Hollingworth (1926) summarized four general theories concerning the intelligence of females that prevailed in America during the first part of this century:

> (1) girls do not belong to the same intellectual species as boys, having a different and much lower central tendency; (2) girls have the same central tendency or average intelligence as boys, but they are less variable and do not deviate as far from mediocrity in either direction; (3) girls are relatively noncompetitive and lack the zeal for struggle which is involved in eminent achievement; (4) girls are emotionally unstable and for this reason do not achieve intellectual leadership. (p. 60)

Such deeply rooted beliefs do not vanish without a struggle. Terman successfully challenged the first theory, while Hollingworth launched a life-long battle against the second. Unfortunately, the third and fourth still confront us today, waiting to be disputed. With the development of a standardized intelligence scale for children, Terman discovered that the intelligence of females is at least equal to that of males. He also fueled Hollingworth's personal war against the "variability hypothesis" with data from his longitudinal study of gifted children, since the three highest cases—with IQs above 190—were girls (Hollingworth, 1926).

When intelligence testing was first carried out in the United States, test constructors presumed that different norms would be necessary for the two sexes. To the surprise of all, not only were the distributions of intelligence similar for the sexes, but the average scores of the girls on the *Stanford-Binet Intelligence Scale* were two to three IQ points above those of the boys for all age groups up to the age of 14 (Terman, 1916). Then the situation reversed itself: from 14 to 16 boys' scores slightly exceeded those of girls. Since this news was publicly received with some measure of disbelief, Terman followed up his results with an analysis of school records and teacher judgments for nearly 1,000 students.

> The supplementary data, including the teachers' estimates of intelligence on the scale of five, the teachers' judgments in regard to the quality of the school work, and records showing the age-grade distribution of the sexes, were all sifted for evidence as to the genuineness of the apparent superiority of the girls age for age. The results of all these lines of inquiry support the tests in suggesting that the superiority of the girls is probably real even up to and including age 14, the apparent superiority of the boys at this age being fully accounted for by the more frequent elimination of 14-year-old girls from the grades by promotion to the high school.
>
> However, the superiority of girls over boys is so slight (amounting at most ages to only 2 to 3 points in terms of IQ) that for practical purposes it would seem negligible. This offers no support to the opinion expressed by Yerkes and Bridges that "at certain ages serious injustice will be done individuals by evaluating their scores in the light of norms which do not take account of sex differences." (Terman, 1916, p. 70)

The test constructors finally agreed that differences in performance between the sexes were statistically insignificant and the same norms could be applied to both groups. This finding represents an unsung landmark in establishing the equality of male and female intelligence. It is generally assumed today that the only reason males and females perform equally well on IQ tests is that the most widely used tests are carefully constructed to minimize or eliminate sex differences (Maccoby & Jacklin, 1974). In actuality, the equality of performance goes back to the earliest days of testing, well before special precautions to eliminate sex bias were instituted.

As it became clear that the average female child was at least as bright as the average male child, another theory gained popularity in the scientific community to explain the supposed differences in the sexes—the theory of greater male variability. According to the variability hypothesis, females had a much more restricted range of abilities; consequently, there would be fewer of them at either the high or low end of the spectrum. Originally proposed by Darwin (1871), who had observed greater differentiation of secondary sex characteristics in males of many species, the hypothesis had evolutionary implications. Darwin saw variation from the average as a primary means of evolution and believed that males were more advanced on the evolutionary scale than females (and therefore the superior sex).

Proponents of this view often cited as proof of their position the facts that there were more mentally defective males than females in institutional settings and fewer eminent females than males. Shields (1975) describes the significance of the hypothesis:

> The importance placed on "eminence" should not be underestimated. In that era it was believed that high ability naturally found expression in achievement of social power and prestige.
>
> The real impact of the variability hypothesis lay in its logical corollaries: If women were less likely to have above-average ability, it would not be reasonable to expect achievement from them. Their education should, therefore, be geared to preparing them for the activities in which they were more likely to engage. (p. 854)

Galton's influence is clearly seen in the above quotation (see next section). Among the individuals who proclaimed that women were only capable of average achievement was Edward L. Thorndike, Leta Hollingworth's advisor in psychology at Columbia University. In his classic text, *Educational Psychology*, Thorndike (1910) wrote:

> [In] the great achievements of the world of science, art, invention, and management, women have been far excelled by men. . . . In particular, if men differ in intelligence and energy by wider degrees than do women, eminence in and leadership of the world's affairs of whatever sort will inevitably belong oftener to men. They will oftener deserve it. (p. 35)

With remarkable courage, Hollingworth opposed her major advisor, taking it as her personal mission to set the record straight about variability in females. In 1912, the opportunity arose for her to accumulate data to refute the theory. She was hired to administer Stanford-Binet tests to charity cases at the Clearing-House for Mental Defectives in New York City. During the next two years, she assessed 1,000 individuals, and discovered a most interesting age bias (Benjamin, 1975). In the younger age groups, the males far outnumbered the females, but in the older age groups, the females outnumbered the males. Hollingworth (1914) interpreted this finding in the following manner:

> The boy who cannot compete mentally is found out, becomes at an early age an object of concern to relatives, is brought to the Clearing-House, and directed toward an institution. The girl who cannot compete mentally is not so often recognized as definitely defective, since it is not unnatural for her to drop into the isolation of the home,

> where she can "take care of" small children, peel potatoes, scrub, etc. . . . Thus, they survive *outside of institutions.* (pp. 515–516)

If social circumstances were responsible for the age differences, it is likely that women would be institutionalized at an older age, when they had become too old to be seen as "useful," and this is exactly what Hollingworth found.

In a later work, Hollingworth (1926) substantiated her position further by citing a study of the parents of feeble-minded inmates. The average IQ of the mothers was a full standard deviation below that of the fathers. It was possible to function as a housewife with an IQ of 61!

> The median IQ of the mothers was 61, which enabled them to function at housework on a noncompetitive basis (support being legally insured by the marriage contract.) The preponderance of males in institutions for mental defectives does not mean that there are more exceptional individuals among them. It is merely an index of the extent to which social-economic pressures bear more heavily upon them than upon females of an equal degree of stupidity. (p. 64)

Once she had dismantled the current credo about the greater number of intellectually inferior males, Hollingworth set about to demonstrate that there were as many intellectually superior females as males, despite the fact that few of them attained eminence. Her first attack against the concept of the natural mediocrity of women was in 1914.

> It is undesirable to seek for the cause of sex differences in eminence in ultimate and obscure affective and intellectual differences until we have exhausted as a cause the known, obvious, and inescapable fact that women bear and rear the children, and that this has had as an inevitable sequel the occupation of housekeeping, a field where eminence is not possible. (p. 529)

Many believe that Hollingworth's research on the psychology of women ended after she received her doctorate, because she devoted the rest of her life to the study of exceptional children (Benjamin, 1975; Shields, 1975); however, it was through her work with the gifted that she was most clearly able to combat the variability hypothesis. She publicized the fact that girls were at least equal to—if not more intelligent than—boys. She let the world know that the highest scorers in the Terman study were females. And she built a solid case for the scarcity of eminent women being attributable to lack of opportunity rather than lack of ability.

Although Hollingworth defeated the major form of the variability hypothesis, it has not been completely laid to rest: minor variants are still alive and well in gifted education. The current versions claim that males are more variable on the number of personality traits and in mathematical ability. Callahan (1979) summarized this body of research, providing an alternate explanation of the results.

> One of the most striking findings in the literature that focuses on differences between gifted males and females and/or differences between gifted persons and the normal population is the greater homogeneity of females as a group. Gifted boys and men appear to differ from normal males on many more traits than gifted girls and women differ from normal females. In addition, the variability of scores among males seems to be greater than among females across many cognitive and personality variables. In a study of creative women (mathematicians, architects, and college students), Helson found that, in general, there was less variability among this group on most personality traits than among men. Torrance found less variability among girls than among men on measures of fluency, flexibility, inventive level, originality, and on the *Iowa Test of Basic Ability;* and Werner and Bachtold, in comparing creative males and females, found fewer personality traits distinguishing gifted females from normal peers. More recently, the results of testing in the Study of Mathematically Precocious Youth indicate much greater variability in mathematics ability among gifted males. The lack of variability among females may be cautiously interpreted as a manifestation of desire for conformity among gifted women in order to avoid being labeled as abnormal and the risk of social rejection. (p. 409)

Callahan's conclusion implies that females are not necessarily less variable than males in actual ability; they only appear more conforming in order to avoid social rejection. Why do females prefer to conform than to differ from one another? The answer lies in the complex web of role expectations woven into the structure of our society.

Variability is more likely to occur where there is more opportunity for its expression and development. This is clearly demonstrated by the continuous record-breaking performances in the Olympics. Montague and Hollingworth (1914) described how the interaction of ability and environmental stimulation serve to enhance variability in males and inhibit it in females.

> . . . we should expect to find adult males more variable than adult females, because the males are free to follow a greater variety of

trades, professions, and industries, while women have been confined to the single occupation of housekeeping, because of the part they play in the perpetuation of the species. Thus variability has had comparatively little survival value for women. A woman of natural herculean strength does not wash dishes, cook meals, or rear children much more successfully than a women of ordinary muscle. But a man of natural herculean strength is free to abandon carpentry or agriculture and become a prize-fighter or a blacksmith, thus exercising and enhancing his native endowment. (p. 343)

This view relates to the third theory of female inferiority: that they are "noncompetitive" and "lack the zeal for struggle." Competition plays an active role in the development of variation; it stretches the talents of the talented. The "natural" conformity and noncompetitiveness of girls may have less to do with a yielding spirit and more to do with consequences girls face when they do compete and excel.

Males are taught to compete, and winning leads to glory and leadership. For females, the script is different: victory often brings defeat. Literary works (e.g., *She Stoops to Conquer*) and musicals (e.g., *Annie Get Your Gun*) conspire to give young women the impression that with achievement comes isolation. When struggle leads to gain, individuals are more likely to struggle. Within the social structure of the female world, one gains by losing and loses by winning. This is not the kind of environment that breeds achievement or rewards striving. Almost all gifted women have found it necessary to hide their abilities at some time in their lives just to survive socially.

Conformity is prized and heavily reinforced in females by parents, teachers, friends, relatives, employers, and spouses. Girls are taught from the cradle, by observing their mothers and other role models, that their function is to serve others, to place the needs and desires of others above their own. A girl who rejects this picture of reality quickly faces rejection from those closest to her.

The female peer group adds to this pressure to conform by rejecting a girl who appears too smart or too successful. There is an unwritten code against females excelling: if someone breaks the code, she is punished. The peer group serves as a powerful social agent, carefully monitoring the behavior of its members. Its main tool is ostracism, a very effective means of controlling a group with deep needs for affiliation and connection (Gilligan, 1982). If a girl-child has not learned the lessons of conformity sufficiently in her own home, they will be made painfully evident to her in her encounters with the peer group—she either conforms to the wishes of the group or she will be treated as if she ceased to exist.

This situation cannot be expected to change until full equality between the sexes is attained. Those females who challenge the traditional feminine role threaten the very fibre of society and they will be "put in their place" by well-meaning keepers of the status quo. A competitive, striving, autonomous young woman must often choose between being herself and having friends (Sanford, 1956). In her adult life, an achiever is likely to find others like herself and establish deep bonds of friendship and love, but that does not erase the loneliness and damage to self-esteem endured in her childhood.

The fourth theory, related to feminine emotionality, is based on the slowly disintegrating belief that reason is good and emotions are bad. Emotions have only recently begun to be exonerated within the psychological community (Sommers, 1982). Most of the world still believes men to be more suitable leaders because they supposedly are more "objective" than women and less emotional. The research on performance of males and females in similar tasks shows no sex differences (Deaux, 1984), but myths die hard, especially when there is such a deep emotional investment in maintaining the status quo.

Hollingworth (1914) fervently believed that women would attain equal opportunity to develop their abilities by the twenty-first century. She felt that objective scientific investigation would continue to counter the myths that erected obstacles to women's achievement. An extremely careful and conscientious researcher herself, Hollingworth was appalled at the misuse of science that paraded "tradition and opinion as scientific fact" (Shields, 1975, p. 856). Until the opportunities for females in society are equal to those of males, it will be difficult to determine the extent of any real differences that prohibit achievement.

Giftedness and Eminence

The spirit of Galton has continued to cloud our perceptions of giftedness in women. Galton's belief that men of genius inevitably rise to eminence established eminence as the quintessential evidence of giftedness. In his famous book *Hereditary Genius*, Galton (1869) attempted to demonstrate that genius runs in families (especially in his family), and that a strong genetic endowment inevitably leads to victory in the struggle for success. He traced the lineage of celebrated personalities appearing in *The Dictionary of Men of the Time*, a nineteenth-century *Who's Who*, and concluded that eminence is hereditary, that ancient Athenians were genetically superior to Europeans, and that Anglo-Saxons are superior to Blacks. He did not try to convince people that males were superior to females, since that was taken as a "given" in his time; he simply omitted females from consideration. The fact that many of the eminent families he used to validate his theory, including his own, were independently wealthy, did not enter into the picture as a causal factor. He insisted that social advantages could not create eminence and that genius would "rise from the ranks" regardless of misfortune.

> The general plan of my argument is to show that high reputation is a pretty accurate test of high ability . . . . (p. 2) By reputation, I mean the opinion of contemporaries, revised by posterity—the favourable result of a critical analysis of each man's character, by many biographers . . . .
> By natural ability, I mean those qualities of intellect and disposition, which urge and qualify a man to perform acts that lead to reputation. . . . I mean a nature which, when left to itself, will, urged by inherent stimulus, climb the path that leads to eminence, and has strength to reach the summit—one which, if hindered or thwarted, will fret and strive until the hindrance is overcome, and it is again free to follow its labour-loving instinct. It is almost a contradiction in terms, to doubt that such men will generally become eminent. . . . It follows that the men who achieve eminence, and those who are naturally capable, are, to a large extent, identical. (pp. 33–34)

Hollingworth (1926) countered Galton's argument, drawing attention to the linkage between social position and eminence:

> Those who investigate eminence agree, therefore, upon the following facts. An overwhelming majority of illustrious persons have had fathers who were far above the average in social-economic conditions—nobles, professional men, or men successfully engaged in commerce. Very few children of manual workers become eminent in high degree, either in old settled countries or in the United States. . . . Very few women can be included among those who in the world's history have achieved first rank for mental work. . . . If opportunity were indeed the prime determinant of eminence, then we should expect those who belong to socially inferior categories to be virtually excluded from it. This is just what we do find, since the uncultured, the poor, servants, and women are very seldom found to have achieved eminence. (p. 11)

After Galton suggested the equivalence of eminence and genius, Terman equated genius with giftedness, completing the linkage between giftedness and eminence. Terman believed that those students scoring in the top percentile on the *Stanford-Binet Intelligence Scale* had the most potential for attaining eminence ("genius"). Thus, he entitled his monumental study of 1,528 gifted individuals over their lifespan *Genetic Studies of Genius* (1925–1954). Alas, the prophecy was not fulfilled, and though the "Termites" were, for the most part, happy and productive in their lives, they did not achieve greatness as the world judges it. The disappointed critics rejected the intelligence test as having failed in its mission of predicting the next round of heroes.

Many today give little credence to the concept of giftedness, declaring that it is unreal, impossible to determine in children, related to too many chance factors—because they, too, equate giftedness with eminence. The true test of giftedness, as they see it—and as Galton saw it—is the attainment of widespread acclaim. However, it is within this view that women are most disadvantaged. Since the opportunities for eminence are not equally available to males and females, far fewer women are recognized for their oustanding achievements than are men.

In her attempt to draw attention to the inequality of opportunity for women, Hollingworth (1926), curiously enough, quoted Galton's description of the difficulty of married men as compared with single men in rising to the top.

> A very gifted man will almost always rise, as I believe, to eminence, but if he is handicapped with the weight of a wife and children in the race of life, he cannot be expected to keep as much to the front as if he were single. He cannot pursue his favourite subject of study with the same absorbing passion as if he had no pressing calls on his attention, no domestic sorrows, anxieties and petty cares, no yearly child, no periodical infantine epidemics, no constant professional toil for the maintenance of a large family. (Galton, 1869, p. 320)

Herein lies an apt description of the lives of most of our foremothers, and explains in no small degree why they are not listed among our most eminent figures. Hollingworth raised the question that if hereditary ability were all that were required for the attainment of eminence, what happened to all of the sisters of the great men? She also wondered what life paths awaited the gifted girls who had recently been discovered with Terman's intelligence test for children.

> It may certainly be said now, however, that mental tests have given no explanation of the great disproportion of eminence among men. If, for instance, the figures quoted . . . from Terman were ultimately proved to hold for perfectly systematic search, then on the basis of mental gifts alone we should expect for every hundred and eleven men of eminence for intellectual work one hundred women of equal eminence. Moreover, the most eminent persons should be women (since the highest IQ's found were those of girls).

As this is by no means what history reveals (though we know that intellect in childhood is predictive of intellect in maturity) we must assume that there are powerful determinants of eminence beside intellect. It will be particularly interesting to observe the development and the adult careers of little girls who test above 170 IQ. It will be of social value to observe the deflections from possible eminence which they meet, and to see how many will survive "domestic sorrows, anxieties and petty cares, a yearly child, and periodical infantine epidemics." (p. 68)

More than a half-a-century has passed and we can indeed observe what has happened to the little girls who tested above 170 IQ. According to Dowling (1981), two-thirds of them became housewives and office workers. Only one in 300 gifted women received a Ph.D. (Groth, 1969). We have lived through the feminist revolution, yet the statesmen, the judges, the mathematicians, the composers, the writers, the artists, the chefs, the pilots, the engineers, the principals, and the college presidents are still men. According to the U.S. Bureau of Labor Statistics 1983 report, only 2 percent of the electricians, 3 percent of the dentists, 6 percent of the engineers, 8 percent of the architects, 15 percent of the physicians, and 20 percent of the life and physical scientists in the United States are female. However, 99 percent of the secretarial work force are women. Where are the 100 eminent women for every 111 men? Many of them are typing papers or washing dishes.

Masculine and Feminine Conceptions of Giftedness

I believe that current perspectives of giftedness, which are essentially derived from Galton's equation of genius and eminence, impede the full recognition of giftedness in females. For the potential of gifted girls to be fully realized, a different view of giftedness is needed. Defining giftedness as developmental advancement rather than as the potential for eminence represents such a view. The concept of giftedness as developmental advancement appears to be a natural view for women, and somewhat of a departure from the views of giftedness traditionally held by men.

Over the past five years, I have assessed gifted children from over 350 families, and have found that mothers and fathers have very different conceptions of giftedness. Mothers typically call to ask about the testing service and set up the appointments, whereas fathers often appear to have acquiesced to the process reluctantly and receive the information that their children are gifted with some degree of skepticism. In my experience, the most skeptical were frequently physicians—a finding that still leaves me puzzled. One doctor wanted to believe that the margin of error in the IQ test was no less than 28 points, and he would have happily subtracted this value from his son's IQ. I hastily assured him that his belief was unjustified and that if any error in measurement had occurred, it was probably in our underestimating his son's intelligence, not overestimating it. He found this news extremely discomforting.

Cornell (1983) found that parents' perceptions of their children's giftedness varied as a function of whether or not the child had been placed in a gifted program, the birth order of the child, and, of particular relevance here, the sex of the parent.

> . . . in cases in which the parents disagree in their perception of the child, it is almost always (13 of 15 cases) the mother who perceives the child as gifted and the father who does not. . . . (p. 329)

> Anecdotally, the fathers in this study often commented skeptically on their wives' perception of their children as gifted. Both parents hinted at marital tension over their different perceptions of the child. (p. 332)

In considering the puzzle of why fathers and mothers appear to react so differently to their children's gifts, I have come to believe that there are distinct masculine and feminine perspectives of giftedness. According to the masculine view, the true test of one's abilities is the quantity, quality, and influence of one's accomplishments in adult life. The total impact of one's life on posterity is usually assessed posthumously by the number of biographies written about an individual (Galton, 1869; Goertzel & Goertzel, 1962).

A posthumous determination of giftedness, however, has rather limited utility for teachers and parents. Indeed, trying to guess which children will be the most influential adults is a bizarre game of chance. To a father, it seems like a cruel game, at best, because if his child is selected for the "potentially eminent group," the child may be being set up for failure—a life of unbearable pressures and false hopes. The father's protective reaction is therefore to deny his child's giftedness.

Mothers whose major work is homemaking live in a different world from that of their husbands. They observe on a daily basis the dynamic developmental processes of their children. They notice that their children walk earlier than others in the playgroup and that they are talking in sentences before the child's peers can combine two words. Their awareness of the developmental differences between their children and other children gradually grows into uneasiness. "Are we doing enough to nourish our child's abilities?" "Is the school program going to be adequate?" "Will our child be lonely?" Questions like these finally lead to their seeking professional guidance and assessment of their child's abilities.

In short, for a father, there is only the "potential" for giftedness in childhood; the child's giftedness has yet to be proved by means of adult achievements. For the mother, the same child has been perceived as "gifted" from infancy or from whenever the mother first observed the developmental differences between her child and others.

These differences in parental perceptions appear to be mirrored in the various definitions of giftedness proposed by many male and female writers in the field. Male writers (e.g., Feldman, Gardner, Renzulli, Witty) are most likely to define giftedness in terms of predictors of eminence, whereas female writers (e.g., Hollingworth, Hildreth, Maker, Roedell) tend to subscribe to a more developmental perspective. The masculine view places heavy weight on future achievements and productivity; the feminine view is primarily concerned with the impact of developmental differences on a child's immediate needs. From the vantage point of the first view, intelligence tests are of little value, since they do not correlate with adult achievement; from the second viewpoint, they are a valuable means of assessing advancement and discovering hidden abilities. The emphasis in the former perspective is on demonstration of talent, while in the latter perspective there is more concern for the amelioration of underachievement.

The masculine view of giftedness dominates the field at the present time. Some quotations are illustrative. In 1940, Witty presented the position that still resides as our most current view:

> It is abundantly clear that an extraordinarily high IQ in childhood is not an indicator of later attainment that may be regarded as highly or significantly creative; nor do the most remarkable test ratings in childhood warrant expectancies of adult performance which may be characterized as the work of genius. . . .
>
> If by gifted children we mean those youngsters who give promise of creativity of a high order, it is doubtful if the typical intelligence test is suitable for use in identifying them. (p. 504)

In a recent study to determine if individuals with IQ scores above 180 are "significantly more gifted" (p. 521) than those with IQs in the 150 range, Feldman (1984) concluded the following:

> On the whole, one is left with the feeling that the above-180 IQ subjects were not as remarkable as might have been expected. . . . While 180 IQ suggests the ability to do academic work with relative

ease, it . . . does not suggest the presence of "genius" in its common-sense meaning, i.e., transcendent achievement in some field. For these kinds of phenomena, IQ seems at best a crude predictor. For anything more, we will probably have to look to traditions other than the psychometric and to variables other than IQ. (p. 521)

Renzulli (1980) echoed this concern:

We simply don't know what factors cause only a miniscule number of Thomas Edisons or Langston Hugheses or Isadora Duncans to emerge while millions with equal "equipment" and educational advantages (or disadvantages) never rise above mediocrity. Why do some people who have not enjoyed the advantages of special educational opportunities achieve eminence while others who have gone through programs for the gifted fade into obscurity? (p. 601)

In contrast, a definition of developmental advancement casts a much broader net, facilitating the discovery of giftedness in females. Hildreth (1966) defined the gifted child as one whose development and behavior consistently demonstrate unusual traits, capacities, and achievements for his age. My own definition is similar:

The gifted child is defined as one who is developmentally advanced in one or more areas, and is therefore in need of differentiated programming in order to develop at his or her own accelerated pace. (Silverman, in preparation)

Developmental precocity of girls has been observed for hundreds of years, but its import has not been recognized. In 1790, Judith Sargent Murray, publicly questioning the inferior quality of women's education, wrote:

Will it be said that the judgment of a male two years old, is more sage than that of a female of the same age? I believe the reverse is generally observed to be true. But from that period, what partiality! how is the one exalted, and the other depressed, by the contrary modes of education which are adopted! the one is taught to aspire, and the other is early confined and limited. As their years increase, the sister must be wholly domesticated, while the brother is led by the hand through all the flowery paths of science. (as quoted in Kraditor, 1968, p. 32)

Belief in the inferiority of females is not just a historical artifact: women have still not attained full equality under the law. Pervasive negative views of females' abilities and their place in society has a debilitating effect on the development of giftedness in females. There is considerable evidence that socialization processes gradually constrict a girl's belief in her abilities, her aspirations, and her motivation to achieve. She has more reason to hide her abilities than to demonstrate them, and hide them she does, until she no longer believes they exist. By the third grade, when giftedness is recognized in many school districts, the giftedness of many girls may already be invisible. Defining giftedness as developmental advancement, and identifying children as gifted early in life, would enable more gifted girls to be identified and nurtured before their gifts are allowed to dwindle to the vanishing point.

Identification Practices

The current preoccupation with eminence combined with widespread disparagement of intelligence testing act to diminish the possibility of identifying the gifted girl. Gifted children are now identified in third grade or beyond, since it is believed that the performance of older children correlates to a greater degree with adult attainments. Childhood productivity and creativity are monitored, since demonstrated achievements in later childhood and adolescence appear to predict adult creativity (Albert, 1975). Identification of gifted children at younger ages is seen as irrelevant, since intelligence is presumed to be less stable in early childhood.

Intelligence testing, which constitutes one of the best methods currently available for discovering hidden talent, is viewed with a good measure of suspicion. According to Passow (1981), there is a consensus in the field today that identification procedures cannot be limited to tests of intelligence, even individual intelligence tests. However, in discovering giftedness in females, intelligence testing is enormously effective, due to its sensitivity to developmental advancement, particularly in preschool and primary-aged children. When early test results are ignored or considered no longer valid in the upper grades, girls suffer.

The necessity of finding gifted girls early in life is underscored by the fact that their advanced abilities, observable before they enter school, may be diminishing as a consequence of the educational process. Terman (1925) found that gifted girls talk approximately three weeks earlier than gifted boys. As mentioned in the previous section, it was also found that girls surpassed boys in intelligence at all age levels up to age 14 (Terman, 1916). Even the purported differences in mathematical and scientific abilities favoring the boys do not appear until the intermediate grades (Terman & Tyler, 1954). Maccoby (1966) reported that underachievement in girls usually does not appear until puberty. The progressive quality of this type of underachievement is revealing: it supports the hypothesis that females achieve less than males because they are gradually conditioned by the educational system to view themselves as less capable than males (Dweck & Bush, 1976; Dweck, Davidson, Nelson, & Enna, 1978).

Another way in which we lose gifted girls is by the misapplication of intelligence tests—specifically, repeated testing. Since gifted girls tend to demonstrate their advanced abilities much earlier in their development than do boys, and seem to taper off in ability as they get older, they can be found most accurately during the preschool years, and less easily with each passing year. Consequently, whenever "you-used-to-be-gifted but-now-you-aren't" policies are in effect, girls are affected adversely to a greater extent than boys.

Two examples serve to illustrate this point. One district in which I consulted required gifted students to be retested every three years to ensure that the right children were being served. At the preschool level, the number of girls being identified was equal to or greater than the number of boys. After the second round of tests, boys outnumbered the girls. By junior high school, the gifted classes were predominantly populated with males. It had not occurred to the psychologists that the identification procedures themselves might be partially responsible for the attrition rate among the females.

In another state which mandated education for the gifted from preschool through high school, more stringent criteria were used at the preschool level than at any other grade level. To qualify for the preschool program, children had to attain IQ scores of 148 or above; for first grade, they needed 137; and in third grade, 132. Again, retesting was required of all first and third grade candidates, whether or not they had already been tested. Many children who qualified for the preschool gifted program could not meet the entrance requirements for the first or third grade programs. The majority of the washouts were girls.

Administrators in these school districts assumed that preschool test scores were invalid and that young children initially labeled as gifted had been falsely identified. When we consider that most assessments of giftedness are under-estimates of ability because of the insufficient ceilings of most tests to capture the full range of giftedness, and that performance anxiety affects children to a greater extent as they get older, it is more likely that the later scores were less accurate than the earlier ones.

Moreover, even the Stanford-Binet, which is generally acknowledged to provide the best assessment of giftedness (Bayley, 1970; Martinson, 1974; Sattler, 1982), underestimates the abilities of gifted preschoolers. The change from the 1960 norms to the 1972 norms penalized preschool gifted children by as much as 13 IQ points, with the penalty progressively decreasing at the higher age levels. The newer norms hurt girls more than boys because of the more rapid development of girls' verbal abilities during the preschool years. Thus, a preschool girl who scored 148 on the 1972 norms of the Stanford-Binet could actually have an IQ score of 161 on the 1960 norms, four standard deviations above the mean. If such a child no longer qualifies for the gifted program by third grade, something is drastically wrong.

The use of repeated testing, which leads to attrition of females from gifted programs, stems from several misconceptions regarding IQ testing of the gifted. First, it is assumed that the most recent test is the more accurate assessment of ability. This assumption is derived from testing handicapped children, where there is ample room for test scores to show improvement upon subsequent testing. However, if a child is already at the 99th percentile on the test, where can she go from there on the next test?

Second, it is assumed that IQ scores of preschool and primary-aged children are less valid indicators of ability than scores of older students. Again, this assumption does not hold for the gifted. The younger the child, the more opportunity she has to demonstrate the full range of her developmental advancement. In addition, intelligence tests assess different attributes at different ages. At the preschool and primary levels, the tests truly differentiate advanced development from normal developmental patterns. Differences in the cognitive abilities of five-year-olds and seven-year-olds are real and observable. However, by the middle grades, the IQ tests tend to assess learning, which is more affected by socialization than is development.

Third, it is assumed that males and females have equal opportunity to succeed on tests at all age levels. The discrepancy between gifted girls' performances on tests at the primary and intermediate levels makes this assumption suspect. It seems more plausible that the lower scores are depressed than that the higher scores are exaggerated. It hardly seems possible for girls to attain higher scores than they are capable of achieving. The lower scores, on the other hand, can be attributed to a variety of causes. The penchant of girls for precision or exactness (Blackwell, 1940) may depress their scores on timed tests. Their fear of making a mistake and lack of risk-taking abilities (Gallagher, 1975) often prevent them from guessing when they are uncertain. Their low expectations of success (Dweck & Elliott, 1983; Licht & Dweck, 1984) adversely affect their test performance. There are also some questions as to sex bias in test items (Callahan, 1979) and a masculine orientation of concepts learned in the upper grades (Gilligan, in Van Gelder, 1984).

When identification of the gifted is delayed until third grade, and new proofs of giftedness are demanded at each successive level in order to qualify for services, gifted girls are systematically weeded out of programs. Girls who "used-to-be-gifted" come to believe that they were only capable when the work was easy or that they were never gifted in the first place. All practices that eliminate once-qualified students from receiving services have their most devastating effects on the self-concept of females, undermining their beliefs in their capabilities. An alternative is to define giftedness as developmental advancement, to identify giftedness in the preschool and primary grades—when gifted girls have their greatest opportunity to demonstrate advancement—and to mandate that the highest IQ score obtained on a child *at any time* be used to determine placement in gifted programs.

Sex-Role Socialization

A question arises as to whether the attrition of females from gifted programs is due to innate differences in the abilities of males and females or to socialization processes. Although there have been many claims of major differences in abilities between the sexes (Benbow & Stanley, 1983; Maccoby & Jacklin, 1974; Terman & Tyler, 1954), results of the studies are somewhat equivocal. Terman and Tyler (1954) conducted an exhaustive review of studies performed with the *Stanford-Binet Intelligence Scale* and concluded that sex differences in abilities are only apparent above the preschool and primary level. They describe one massive study of 87,000 children in Scotland in which means for males and females were almost identical in children up to 11 years of age. They also found no sex differences in abilities in mathematics and science in preschool and primary grade children.

A more recent review by Deaux (1984) indicated that sex differences actually account for only 1 to 5 percent of variance in performance on any task:

> Hyde (1981) recently analyzed those studies reported by Maccoby and Jacklin to substantiate sex differences in verbal, quantitative, and visual-spatial ability. She found that sex accounted for approximately one percent of variance in verbal ability, one percent in quantitative ability, and 4.5 percent in visual-spatial ability. Thus, although additional evidence remains to be gathered, five percent may approximate the upper boundary for the explanatory power of subject-sex main effects in specific social and cognitive behaviors.
>
> To summarize this line of research, sex-of-subject differences are less pervasive than many have thought. Main effects of sex are frequently qualified by situational interactions, and the selection of tasks plays a critical role in eliciting or suppressing differences. Furthermore, the variance accounted for by sex, even when main effects are reliable, is typically quite small. Thus, when any particular

behavior is considered, differences between males and females may be of relatively little consequence. (p. 108)

. . . when one looks for differences between women and men engaged in a specific activity, relatively few are found. (p. 114)

Thus, according to the studies cited above, there are insignificant differences in performance between gifted boys and girls in early school years and relatively minor differences in capability between males and females of any age. And yet it is still unusual to find females who become leaders in any field. If innate differences cannot account for the differences in performance between gifted males and females, then powerful environmental influences must be acting on gifted girls as their giftedness apparently slips away.

Many writers have called attention to the socialization processes that differentiate the rearing of boys from the rearing of girls. Wolleat (1979) summarizes the problem as follows:

The content of socialization differs substantially for boys and girls. The most global distinction between male and female sex roles is that set of forces which operates to socialize the male as the primary breadwinner and the female as the primary caretaker (nurturer) in the nuclear family. This basic dichotomy in adult sex roles underlies much of the observed variance in the attitudes, personality characteristics, and behavior of males and females.

Sex typing of social roles has been cited as the major contributor to the unequal achievement of adult men and women (Morse & Bruch, 1970). Whereas competence as a worker is the *sine qua non* of the male role, it has been viewed as incompatible with the traditional female role . . . . (pp. 332–333)

The major factor impeding the full development of girls is the unspoken decree in our society against female independence. Fearful for their daughters' safety, parents discourage them from risk taking, while overlooking, allowing, or encouraging the same behavior in boys. Clark (1983) told of her childhood resentment at not being allowed to climb trees, even though she was the best tree climber in her neighborhood, while the boys had no such restrictions.

The messages are subtle, but pervasive, from infancy on, and cumulatively breed feminine insecurity and self-doubt. Despite the fact that infant girls tend to be physically more robust than infant boys, parents perceive their daughters to be more fragile than they do their sons (Rubin, Provenzano, & Luria, 1974). Girl babies are touched more frequently than boy babies (Goldberg & Lewis, 1969); they are handled more gently (Stone & Church, 1973); and their cries are responded to more frequently (Hoffman, 1972). Little girls' dresses and blouses button in the back, while boys' shirts button in the front. Girls' toys promote passive behavior and imitation of mothering and house-keeping; boys' toys promote action and construction. Girls are taught to play close to home, while boys are allowed to roam over greater distances. Stone and Church (1973) contend that from toddlerhood onward, little boys are forbidden to play with girls' things, as if the parents viewed masculinity as a fragile state, easily undermined.

Once a child enters preschool, these messages are strengthened by sex-role stereotyped books, puzzles, games, and teacher behaviors. Teachers reward passivity in girls, but pay more attention to the "active" boys (Callahan, 1979; Clark, 1983). Boys participate in more active games and sports in school, while girls' energies are channeled into quieter, safer activities (Serbin, O'Leary, Kent, & Tonick, 1973). In textbooks, boys and men are more often shown doing interesting and exciting things, while girls and women are shown more often needing help and being rescued (U'Ren, 1972). Just counting the number of pictures of males versus the number of pictures of females in children's textbooks is revealing enough; analyzing their content is even more disturbing.

Many examples of the messages children receive in school could be given, but one will suffice. A "story starter" was presented in my daughter's junior high school class in which two teen-agers enter a time machine that one of them has constructed. The dialogue is classic. "Connie" is concerned with the appearance of the apparatus. "Vern" snorts and tells her that his "calculations" say it will work. She asks him how, and he replies, "I won't strain your brain with the details." He assumes she will accompany him. Her "inner voice" tells her not to go because they could be headed into trouble, but naturally she follows his lead. The dialogue ends with Connie saying, "I always thought I was nuts, and this proves it." The cast of characters is described as a "girl of any age," perhaps 12 or 13; a "boy inventor with a taste for adventure," perhaps 13 or 14; a "foxy old man" who lives on the stream of time and makes a point of helping young people in trouble; and a "beautiful woman with a problem."

The two male characters are interesting, action-oriented, courageous, and autonomous. No descriptive information is given about the two female characters, except that the woman is beautiful and has a problem. Both are dependent on the males to rescue them and so are characterized as weaker than the male figures. The "girl of any age" is almost devoid of personality and seems more like an interchangeable part. She is portrayed in a thoroughly stereotypic manner: she is the support cast rather than the initiator, frightened rather than courageous, overly concerned with looks, considered by the boy intellectually incapable of understanding his mathematical calculations, easily led against her better judgment, and insecure about her mental stability.

Ironically, my daughter wasn't paying close attention to the details and only heard the basic plot. She identified with Vern—a name she had never heard before—and assumed that "Connie" was short for Conrad. She wrote the whole story in reverse, with Vern as the competent, fearless, slightly older female protecting the sniveling younger boy. I was delighted by her error, but wondered what it would do to her grade on the assignment. Obviously, in this case, the messages did not take hold, but what of the hundreds of other subtle and not-so-subtle messages to which girls are subjected on a daily basis in school?

There is mounting evidence that despite the decade or so since the passage of Title IX banning sex discrimination in the public schools, little progress has been made toward that goal. Dr. Alice Baumgartner Papageorgiou (1982) conducted a study of 2,000 third through twelfth graders about their perceptions of sex roles. She asked each student to respond to the following question: "If you woke up tomorrow and discovered that you were a (boy) (girl), how would your life be different?" (p. 2). From their responses, she concluded that students see traditional sex roles as their only option and that sex-role stereotyping is still very pronounced in children's experiences.

> The responses from the overwhelming majority of students confirm that, as a result of sex role socialization, students see traditional sex roles as their only choice. Consequently, these students believe that their lives would change dramatically if their sex were different. The underlying themes which emerge from their descriptions of those changes highlight the damaging effects of sex role socialization. (p. 2)

> Effect #1—Females learn that it is best not to work outside the home, but if one does, one should choose from a limited number of career options. (p. 2)
> "My goal as a girl is to be nothing." (4th grader) (p. 2)

> Effect #2—Females are taught to select careers which are less rewarding than those which males are taught to select. (p. 3)
> "I want to be a nurse, but if I were male, I would probably want to be an architect." (4th grade girl) (p. 3)

> Effect #3—Females are taught that their most valuable asset is their appearance. (p. 5)
> "I wouldn't have to worry how I look." (6th grade girl) (p. 5)

> Effect #4—Males are taught that females are to be treated as sex objects; females are taught that such treatment is normal. (p. 5)

"I would have to be around other girls for safety." (11th grade male) (p. 6)

Effect #5—Males are taught to be independent, competitive, aggressive, and to use violence. (p. 6)
"If I were a boy, I'd *kill* my art teacher, instead of arguing with him as I do now." (8th grade girl) (p. 6)

Effect #6—Females are taught to be dependent, compliant, and fearful. (p. 7)
"I think I would be more outspoken and confident, but I really don't know why." (10th grade girl) (p. 7)

Effect #7—Males are taught to expect freedom; females are taught to expect restrictions. (p. 8)
"Obviously males are allowed to do more than females." (4th grade girl) (p. 8)

Effect #8—Males and females are taught that home and child care responsibilities are not to be shared equally. (p. 8)
"Life on the home front would be a lot easier. I know that for a fact since I've got a brother." (4th grade girl) (p. 9)

Effect #9—Males and females are taught only those skills which are consistent with traditional sex roles. (p. 9)
"If I were a girl, I would not be able to help my dad fix the car and truck and his two motorcycles." (6th grade boy) (p. 9)

Effect #10—Males and females exclude themselves from courses and extracurricular activities in school that develop interests and talents which are valuable to both sexes. (p. 10)
"I would drop my math class and take more classes like cooking, English and ones that would make me look good as a girl." (12th grade male) (p. 10)

Effect #11—Females receive better treatment from teachers, but males get more encouragement to achieve. (p. 11)
"If I were a boy, I'd get called on more to answer questions."
"As a boy, I would be treated with less respect." (10th grade girl) (p. 11)
"If I were a boy, I might have done better in school." (6th grade girl) (p. 12)
"Teachers expect more from guys." (11th grade girl)
"I would probably act different toward my teachers, being less cutesy and vulnerable. Boys have to make it on their own." (p. 12)

Effect #12—Both males and females are taught that being male is inherently better than being female. (p. 12)

"Girls can't do anything fun. They don't know how to do anything except play dolls." (4th grade boy) (p. 12)

"If I were a girl, I'd be stupid and weak as a string." (6th grade boy) (p. 12)

"If I were a girl, everybody would be better than me, because boys are better than girls." (3rd grade boy) (p. 12)

"If I were a girl, I'd kill myself." (p. 12)

"If I were a boy, my whole life might have been easier." (6th grade girl) (p. 13)

"My dad would respect me better than usual because I would be a boy." (4th grade girl) (p. 13)

"If I were a boy, my father would be closer because I'd be the son he always wanted." (6th grade girl) (p. 13)

"If I were a boy, my Daddy might have loved me." (3rd grade girl) (p. 13).

Effects of Sex-Role Stereotyping on Giftedness

Although the literature on the damage of sex-role stereotyping is extensive, it is not well known that gifted girls suffer this damage to a greater extent than do girls of lesser ability (Hollingworth, 1926). Gifted girls have more to lose because of their greater potential for achievement. The effects of sex biases are far-reaching, with restrictions on independence playing the heaviest role. Independence is vitally necessary for achievement, for creativity, for autonomous moral development, even for mental health (Bassoff & Glass, 1983). It is also needed for giftedness (Richert, 1982b). To the extent that independence is drummed out of little girls, these girls lose their giftedness.

Researchers have examined some of the personality factors and belief systems that prevent gifted girls from achieving to the full measure of their potential. The main factors that have emerged are lowered expectations of success, attribution of success to chance factors, and belief that success will inevitably lead to negative social consequences. Crandall, Katkovsky, and Preston (1962) discovered that as early as first grade, bright girls have unrealistically low expectations of success. They found that the higher a boy's IQ, the more successful he expected to be in learning a new task. With girls, however, the inverse was true: the brighter the girl, the less well she expected to do. Walberg (1969) obtained a similar result with teen-agers. IQ was

positively correlated with expectation of success in boys and negatively correlated in girls.

These results have recently been confirmed in a series of studies by Dweck
and her associates (Dweck & Elliott, 1983). Bright girls tend to attribute their
successes to chance factors and their failures to personality flaws, whereas boys
attribute their successes to their abilities and their failures to luck or lack of
effort (Licht & Dweck, 1984; Licht & Shapiro, 1982). Parents and teachers
appear to reinforce these beliefs in the differential feedback they give to boys
and girls. Boys are chastised for their lack of effort and admonished that they
could succeed if they really tried. Girls are often helped—encouraging greater
dependency—or given feedback that indicates that they are incapable of
succeeding (Dweck & Bush, 1976; Dweck, Davidson, Nelson, & Enna,
1978).

Horner's (1970, 1972) research on women's motivation for avoiding success is particularly relevant for understanding the complex socialization processes affecting the teen-age gifted girl. Horner found that college women fear
success because they view it as incompatible with their role expectations as
females. Anticipating that their successes will have negative social consequences, they suppress their capabilities, particularly in mixed-sex competition. Lavach and Lanier (1975) found that this motive begins to operate
during the junior high years. Throughout elementary school, girls apparently
compete freely with boys, but in seventh grade they begin to anticipate
negative consequences if they succeed. This anxiety increases from seventh to
ninth grades, with the consequence that the girls conform to role expectations
at the expense of achievement.

Junior high school is the most vulnerable period in the determination of a
gifted girl's future. Since girls surpass boys in intellectual performance during
the early years and the pattern is reversed in junior and senior high school, it is
commonly held that girls' intellectual development begins earlier than boys'
and "tapers off" sooner. However, it is likely that what appears to be a
difference in biological timetables may actually be created by powerful
socialization forces during adolescence. Adolescence is the time when girls face
the developmental task of being "feminine" (Havighurst, 1972), and if they
are shown that femininity and achievement are inconsistent, adolescence
becomes a critical turning point.

What happens to the gifted girl at 12, 13, and 14? We can gain clues by
asking the girls themselves. Casserly (1979) did exactly that, and obtained
some disconcerting responses:

"Junior high was the worst time for us—the absolute worst—with
going to a new school and a whole different social scene. And lots of

the other students thought us a bit weird—only boys had been in the pre-med club before." (p. 355)

According to two students who spoke for many others I talked with, by ninth grade (often the last year of junior high school), "the school curriculum is such that mathematics suddenly seems 'harder' for girls than for boys." Sex typing is at its peak, and it takes an unusually motivated and self-confident girl to buck it and say, "so what?" (p. 356)

Over and over again, girls remarked on the importance of girlfriends who shared "common school experiences and similar interests of similar levels" in dealing with the teasing and disapproval of the boys, which "peaked at the ninth grade." . . . (p. 355)

Many similar comments have been made by my female clients and students in recalling their junior high school experiences. One woman stated that the greatest achievement in her life was graduating third in her high school class without any of her friends knowing that she was smart. She had enjoyed being at the head of her class until seventh grade, when she faced ostracism from all the other girls for getting good grades. At that point in her life, her intellectual abilities went underground. It was too painful to be bright.

Gifted girls have more masculine interests than most other girls and they are often tormented by both boys and girls if they choose to pursue those interests. This type of abuse occurs most heavily in junior high school (Casserly, 1979), just when boys appear to surpass girls in intellectual ability.

Maccoby (1966) suggests that creativity is stifled when a bright girl suppresses her masculine interests. She points to the research of MacKinnon (1962) which indicated that creativity in men may be a function of the development of the feminine aspects of their personalities and hypothesizes that the reverse may be operating in gifted girls who choose traditionally feminine interests over achievement. She also mentions that underachievement in girls rarely develops before the onset of puberty, whereas it usually has a much earlier onset for boys. She interprets this as further evidence that declines in achievement for girls as they reach maturity are linked to the adult female sex role.

. . . it appears that the social pressures to do well or poorly in school may have a reverse time sequence for the two sexes. As noted above, the pressures on bright girls not to do as well as they can tend to be augmented in adolescence, so that correlations between ability and achievement ought to be higher during the early school years. (Maccoby, 1966, p. 31)

This does appear to be the case. Young gifted girls are closer in abilities, interests, and personality characteristics to gifted boys than are older gifted girls. The turning point is puberty. Even risk-taking abilities of girls show a marked decline with the advent of adolescence. Slovic (1966) studied the risk-taking abilities of over 1,000 children, aged 6 through 16, using a device with nine levers, eight of which yielded a spoonful of candies and one which lost all those accumulated. With each turn, the chances of pulling the "disaster" lever increased. He found no differences in risk-taking abilities of children 6 to 10 years of age, but from 11 to 16, boys were consistently better risk takers than girls.

Gilligan, author of *In a Different Voice,* also notes the deterioration of risk-taking abilities of teen-age girls, and offers an intriguing perspective on the cause of their demise.

Something happens to girls when they're about twelve. The eleven-year-old . . . will hold out for her point of view, whereas the fifteen-year-old will yield. (Gilligan, as quoted in Van Gelder, 1984, p. 38)

From her observations, Gilligan surmises that the problem may be rooted in the shift from factual knowledge to interpretive knowledge in the junior high school curriculum. Girls trust their ability to learn facts, but they do not trust their interpretive powers, largely because their own interpretations differ widely from those presented in the texts. The author contends that the interpretive level of any discipline—literature, history, psychology, biology, etc.—is oriented toward a masculine viewpoint, one that excludes the experiences of females. This erodes girls' confidence in their own perceptions and leaves them feeling that their only chance at success is through imitation of others.

And because male values are considered the norm, girls begin to see their own experience disappear from the representation of human experience. Girls begin to become aware that bringing in their own values is going to make trouble. So they start waiting and watching for other people to give them their cues as to what their values should be. And of course the irony is, that since they're very tuned in to other people, they're very good at this. (Gilligan, as quoted in Van Gelder, 1984, p. 38)

A gifted teen-ager poignantly demonstrates the profound loss of power experienced by many girls between the ages of 11 and 16. At 11, she was a brilliant achiever with an insatiable love of learning, and her future was bright.

> School became the universe I lived for—it was the bright sun I revolved around. I breathed just for another day in class, another bit of knowledge, another brain to pick . . . .
>
> I reached my intellectual peak about then, I think. I was a straight A student without ever having to try. Everything just automatically clicked. English, math, history; every subject, all day long. I constantly worked "above and beyond the call of duty" on everything and anything—I seemed to have some all-consuming need to cram in everything I could . . . . So I did every single extra credit report in the teacher's file for extra credit, read books much more difficult than my grade level called for, and so on . . . .
>
> That general age was probably the most stable time of my life; I knew who I was, where I came from, and where I was going. I was invincible—there wasn't anything I couldn't do if I really wanted to. . . .

By 17, this picture had been dramatically altered:

> I've lost that obsession to soak up and retain every miniscule grain of knowledge I can possibly gain access to. I still enjoy learning, of course, but not as much as I remember enjoying it.
>
> The future has also lost some of its sparkle. It's not a big bright field of possibilities that awaits me when I begin to reach that mystical Sometime. (Lech, 1984)

Characteristics and Concerns of Achieving Gifted Women

Several personality characteristics differentiate gifted women from their contemporaries. Studies have found that gifted females tend to score more like males than do non-gifted females on measures of interests, values, and personalities (Wolleat, 1979). Women with high ability tend to be more achievement oriented (Gjesme, 1973) and are more interested in male-dominated professions (Rezler, 1967). They are often more independent, rebellious against sex-role stereotyping, and rejecting of outside influences than are their nonachieving peers (Faunce, 1968). These "masculine" attributes often win them disfavor among their own sex.

However, gifted females also have many qualities and concerns in common with their less gifted counterparts. They feel strongly compelled to nurture others; they care deeply about relationships; they prize family life and avocations (Rodenstein & Glickauf-Hughes, 1979); they fear loneliness; and they have difficulty placing their own needs above the needs of others (Gilligan, 1982). They also bear the burden of female socialization, which manifests itself in lack of self-confidence, feelings of dependency, fear of competition, fear of hurting others, concern with their appearance, taking primary responsibility in housekeeping and childcare, needing to manage the family's social affairs, and responsiveness to others' emotional needs.

The net result is that gifted women are not really more masculine than feminine; in fact, they combine the characteristics, values, attitudes, feelings, goals, and expectations of both sexes. This blending of traits has both positive and negative consequences. On the positive side, these qualities enable gifted women to achieve to a greater degree than their less able sisters. On the negative side, the same characteristics create powerful internal pressures for these women to perform at a high level in both feminine and masculine domains. The problems that emerge are most severe where there is the greatest amount of role differentiation between the sexes—that is, when the roles and responsibilities of each sex are so clearly defined and stereotyped that a woman cannot succeed in one domain without risking serious damage to the other.

Career, Marriage, or Both?

Sex-role differentiation is becoming less acute with each generation. In previous eras, particularly before the availability of modern birth control, a bright women was usually forced to choose between marrying and actualizing her career potential. The choice to pursue a career was fraught with social perils, such as being considered a spinster, selfish, a dangerous threat to the sanctity of other people's marriages, and a profound disappointment and embarrassment to her family. An achieving woman had to have tremendous ego strength to withstand these onslaughts against her character. In addition, she had to forego the emotional support and sexual fulfillment that marriage could provide, since marriage would most likely result in childbearing. Marriage without children was rarely considered an option, and if it did exist, the sanctions against this choice were more severe than against spinsterhood. Gifted women of the past demonstrated an extraordinary degree of autonomy and resistance to socialization when they selected career over family.

Entering the male domain of the work force demanded high levels of risk taking as well. Women faced overt discrimination at every turn. There were barriers in the professions and in the educational processes to prepare women for professional careers. The deterrents in the educational system included discrimination in university admission policies, lack of scholarships for women, more stringent standards for female students, derision from male classmates and professors, and denial of doctorates to women (Russo & O'Connell, 1980). In the professional world, discrimination was encountered in obtaining positions, promotions, and salaries comparable to those of men (Committee on Education and Employment of Women in Science and Engineering, 1983). Women's creative efforts were often credited to male colleagues (Russo & O'Connell, 1980), robbing the women of recognition and making their contributions invisible. To overcome such immense odds required heroic courage and determination on the part of pioneer career women.

The choice to devote their lives to rearing children was infinitely easier and more acceptable for gifted women, but it was a path with its own profound pitfall—the silent, inexorable loss of potential. In the long run, who was better off—the career women or the homemakers?

Sears and Barbee (1977) provided some clues through their study of the life satisfaction of gifted women in the Terman sample. The 430 women, born near the turn of the century (from 1902–1924), had been originally selected for longitudinal study on the basis of Stanford-Binet scores above 135. At the time of the current study, the respondents were in their mid-60s. Based on the cultural milieu of the era in which these women were raised, the researchers predicted that women who married, had children, engaged in some income-producing work, and had higher-than-average incomes, would express the highest degree of satisfaction. The data delivered many surprises, forcing them to consider their original hypotheses "naive" (p. 32).

Looking back on their lives, the career women reported more satisfaction and fewer regrets over their life choices than did the homemakers. Women who had obtained college degrees (67 percent of the sample, despite the Depression) showed much less satisfaction with their lives on all measures if they chose to be housewives than if they were employed outside the home. Single women were the most satisfied with their work patterns, followed by married women with no children, divorced women, married women with children, and then widows. Single heads of households (single, divorced, or widowed) were generally happier than married women.

This pattern varies greatly from that of women in general:

> This is in distinct contrast to the normative samples, in which the divorced, widowed, and employed women come out lower on gen-

eral happiness than do the married housewives. We suggest that for high-IQ women, the independence from an unhappy marriage, the challenge of making one's own life alone as a widow or single person, activates over time feelings of competence rather than depression. The absence of children, with their needs for parental involvement, no doubt contributes to the ease with which this satisfaction is achieved. (Sears & Barbee, 1977, p. 57)

These results are enlightening, considering the economic and social constraints facing single women in the work force during the early part of this century, especially during the Depression. The barriers to career success that women face today are far fewer, although much more subtle in form. Since almost half of the work force is female, it is assumed that most women will work for a large part of their lives (U.S. Department of Labor, Women's Bureau, 1982). Salary discrimination is still a major issue, with women commanding 40 percent lower salaries than men in almost every field of endeavor, and promotions to administrative positions are hard to come by (U.S. Department of Labor, Women's Bureau, 1982). Moreover, the question as to whether or not to have a family looms even larger in the inner dialogue of the career woman.

Combining family and career is now more than just an acceptable option; for many women it is a necessity. Divorce rates, as well as the growing need for two incomes to support the rising cost of living, have brought many mothers into the work force. Less than a century ago, homemaking was a way of life for most women, and professional life was considered a luxury. In 1926, Hollingworth remarked that a "handful" of working mothers could be found in New York City (p. 349). Today, it is homemaking that is rapidly becoming the luxury, available only to upper-middle-class women with intact families.

Through modern birth control methods, it is now possible for a woman to determine for herself whether and when she will have children, and she can also choose to have children without a husband. These choices have replaced the dilemmas of the past as major psychological issues of today's career women. Women often feel in a double bind, wanting to have children and wanting to be successful at their careers, and not seeing how they can do both. The brighter the individual, the more career potential she has, and the more agonizing the need to choose is likely to be. When there is insufficient support, a woman is likely to believe that she must sacrifice one for the other, and being caught on the horns of this dilemma can be very painful. She may decline to make the choice, and may instead convince herself that she can handle both jobs expertly, thereby embarking upon the "Superwoman" route.

A superwoman is one who attempts to manage a full-time, demanding career while maintaining full responsibility for homemaking and childrearing.

Even if she has a kindly support staff at home, she is in charge of running all aspects of the household. She determines what meals will be prepared, what has to be used up in the refrigerator, what needs to be purchased at the store, which children need to be picked up and delivered to different places every day, who needs new clothes, when the wash will be done and when the cleaning will be picked up, who is having a birthday, how each holiday will be celebrated, and much more. In other words, she does all the worrying.

Cohen (1984) maintains that the partner who does the worrying about what needs to be done bears the real burden of responsibility, regardless of who actually performs the task. He suggests that although more men are "helping" with household chores, they are not "sharing" in the responsibilities of determining what needs to be done and seeing that they get done. They function more like children, executing tasks that they are told to do, like shopping with a list that mother has prepared.

Many of today's superwomen are gifted individuals who want the fulfillment of family life along with the fulfillment of careers. It takes unusual energy to do both (Sears & Barbee, 1977), but unusual energy is one of the characteristics of giftedness. It is also characteristic of gifted women to be perfectionistic in most aspects of their lives and to work exceptionally hard to excel. They react intensely if their own inner standards are not met, and some of the standards they set for themselves are unrealistic. They expect to succeed in a man's world according to standards set by "professional workaholics" (Russo & O'Connell, 1980, p. 20); they also aspire to be excellent mothers, alluring wives, gourmet cooks, splendid hostesses, and sympathetic counselors to their friends.

The standards for achievement that women strive to attain are not just outward manifestations of perfectionism; on the contrary, they are realistic assessments of the reward system set up in male-dominated professions. Gifted women are only seen as successful if they can compete favorably with men. The achievements of professional males are the yardsticks by which gifted women are measured and measure themselves (Shakeshaft & Palmieri, 1978). But the career paths of women are strikingly different from those of men. Ginzberg et al. (1966) found that men follow a relatively simple and straightforward pattern compared with the more complex career and life patterns of women. Much of women's work energy is siphoned off into home-related responsibilities that are not taken into account when others assess her "achievements."

Shakeshaft and Palmieri (1978) described the typical factors that diminish women's records of achievement:

> Another problem is that the energy, the creativity, and the pure time which gifted women put into the home is not counted as an

accomplishment. The gifted woman is chastised for not living up to her talents because she has not published as many papers, written as many books, or garnered as many professional titles as her male counterpart, in addition to carrying on the duties of home and family. The gifted woman or any woman, it must be remembered, does not take on a career instead of her "traditional womanly duties," she takes on a career in ADDITION to them. If the gifted woman chooses not to work, or work in the traditional manner, she is not valued at all by society. As one feminist phrased the two choices, she may either have a career and suffer from guilt/exhaustion/fulfillment or she may choose to stay at home and suffer from guilt/exhaustion/nonfulfillment. (Feshback, 1973; Shakeshaft & Palmieri, 1978, p. 474)

Superwoman takes on all of the anxieties of running the home along with all the anxieties of her professional career. Playing male and female roles simultaneously is physically and mentally exhausting, and when she is pulled in too many directions, stress mounts—sometimes to the breaking point. Some women fulfill all of their various roles at the expense of sleep, which eventually erodes their health. In order to survive their hectic life styles, they find that they must reassess their priorities and take breaks from their excessive loads. The reevaluation process is painful; it means giving up something precious or conceding to do a mediocre job in some area of their lives. Gifted women tend to view mediocrity in any area as a loss of self-esteem and the turning down of an opportunity as a loss of potential. Any hint of "I can't do it all" is experienced as a failure. But not facing these existential choices means life on a constant treadmill, with no opportunity to relax and enjoy life or share one's inner self with loved ones.

The professional superwoman can easily become resentful of the hardships of her life in comparison to the lives of her male colleagues. Russo and O'Connell (1983) summarize the problem as follows:

The woman or man who chooses less job concentration in order to devote more time to noncareer interests such as home and family must compete with the professional "workaholic," and suffers by invidious comparison. (Boring, 1951)

Thus, the norms of job concentration and the norms of marriage interact to affect the careers of both sexes. Typically, this interaction means that marriage norms work to the detriment of women's careers, while the opposite is true for married men. This is true even for women who eschew marriage in favor of single-minded job concentration, for they still lack an advantage privy to males: they still lack a wife.

In 1947, Bryan and Boring estimated that nearly all the married men but only half the married women in psychology reported marriage as helping their professional career (Bryan and Boring, 1947). The advantage of having a wife for attaining eminence . . . has not been adequately appreciated. (p. 20)

In spite of these difficulties, most gifted women prefer to try to balance these two demanding lifestyles rather than to choose between them, with potentially great rewards in personal satisfaction. Rodenstein and Glickauf-Hughes (1979) found that "Integrators" (women who combined childrearing with careers) usually derived satisfaction from their work (86 percent of the sample), from recognition of their accomplishments (82 percent), from their personal relationships (97 percent), from their children (96 percent), and from their avocations (82 percent). They enjoyed their work as much as career women, felt even more gratified by their accomplishments than did career women, gained more satisfaction from avocations than homemakers, and derived as much pleasure from their children as did the homemakers. They interpret their results to mean that it is no longer necessary for a woman to feel that she must choose between career and family.

Gratifyingly, changes are gradually coming about in society that enable women to have both. Lemkau (1983) found a trend toward fewer home responsibilities of career women educated in the '60s and '70s and exposed to feminist ideology, as compared with women who were educated in the '50s, when "homemaking was lauded as the *sine qua non* of the healthy adult woman" (p. 161). But for women to achieve their full role in society in both the home and the workplace without perpetuating the superwoman problem, this trend must be accelerated and the concept of sexual equality of responsibility must be made part of the upbringing of children of both sexes.

Of course, there is still the question of the quality of upbringing of children with two working parents. Although this topic is too lengthy to address here, this question is of major concern to modern parents. Live-in help, extended families, childcare facilities in work places, reduced work schedules of both parents, and high-quality cooperative daycare facilities are all approaches that have been effectively employed. For the gifted woman, beginning a family after her career is in place is also an alternative. It is easier to resume a blossoming career with an extensive childcare leave than it is to begin an effective career after rearing a family.

Recommendations

Women who have escaped the traditional female socialization process have a greater chance of maintaining their giftedness. Many high-achieving women avoided some of it by being an only child, the first-born in an all-girl family, or the first-born for several years before a son was born (Astin, 1969; Helson, 1971; Hennig, 1973; Lemkau, 1983; Patrick, 1973; Standley & Soule, 1974). In these cases, parents held unusually high expectations for their daughters (Kranz, 1975; Sanford, 1956). Many were "tomboys" as children, and played more with boys than with girls (Wolleat, 1979). Role models were crucial, particularly mothers who worked outside the home (Almquist & Angrist, 1971; Epstein, 1973; Ginzberg et al., 1966). Sponsors, mentors, and significant others composed a support system essential to the development of the talents of these women (Shakeshaft & Palmieri, 1978). They were encouraged by parents and teachers and tended to identify with their fathers (Astin, 1969; Fox & Richmond, 1979; Helson, 1971; Schaefer, 1970). Supportive males were more influential than supportive females in their selection of atypical professions (Lemkau, 1983).

More changes can take place to ensure that the vast potential of the gifted female population is not lost. The first of these changes should perhaps involve informing parents and prospective parents about the importance of nurturing the aspirations and abilities of their daughters. It is particularly important for fathers to be involved in parent education or counseling, since they play a vital role in the development of their daughters' talents. Lemkau (1983) reports:

> Greater involvement with a supportive father may contribute to earlier experimentation with sex-atypical activities. [Women who chose atypical professions] report, for example, paternal encouragement for their working with science projects, erector sets, and math problems, experiences that allow a young girl to assess the "goodness of fit" between her own skills and proclivities and those appropriate to atypical fields. A girl raised in such a situation would be more likely to value male activities and to feel confident in her abilities to engage in them competently. The more frequent firstborn status of [these women] may facilitate closeness with father and a less sex-typed father/daughter interaction. . . .
>
> Finally, strong support from father, male teachers, husbands, and boyfriends may provide women with the assurance that competence in "masculine" endeavors need not jeopardize heterosexual goals. Early experiences with a supportive father may "inoculate" these women against later pressures to be sex appropriate, and predispose

them to seek the companionship of males unthreatened by their unusual interests (p. 163).

Some of the aspects of a parent curriculum to enhance abilities in their daughters could include:

- holding high expectations for their daughters
- not purchasing sex-typed toys
- avoiding overprotectiveness
- encouraging high levels of activity
- allowing them to get dirty
- instilling beliefs in their capabilities
- supporting their interests
- getting them identified as gifted during preschool years
- finding gifted playmates for them to identify with and emulate
- fostering interest in mathematics outside of school
- considering early entrance and other opportunities to accelerate
- encouraging them to take every mathematics course possible
- introducing them to professional women in many occupations
- having mother acknowledge her own giftedness
- having mother work at least part-time outside the home
- spending alone-time with father in "masculine" activities
- sharing household duties equally among the parents
- assigning chores to siblings on a nonsexist basis
- discouraging the use of sexist language or teasing in the home
- monitoring television programs for sexist stereotypes and discussing these with children of both sexes
- encouraging siblings to treat each other equitably, rather than according to the traditional sex-role stereotypes they see outside the home

Preschool and primary grade teachers should be also given instruction in nonsexist activities and attitudes. Materials and books should be carefully selected to avoid sex-role stereotyping. Puzzles are now available depicting women judges, doctors, and linemen (linewomen?). Boys can be encouraged to play with dolls, with the understanding that their eventual roles as fathers will include a substantial amount of childcare. Girls should be allowed to get dirty, to play active games, and to engage in "tomboyish" behavior. There should not be two sets of norms for behavior of boys and girls. Teachers may have to work especially hard to overcome any unconscious tendencies to expect girls to be neater, quieter, and more dependent. These tendencies are the result of the teachers' upbringing, and the dependency cycle can only be broken through conscious effort.

Some elements of an inservice program for preschool and primary teachers could include

- purchasing non-sexist toys and puzzles
- encouraging both sexes to pretend they are doctors, pilots, and other interesting professionals
- encouraging both sexes to pretend they are parents and housekeepers
- encouraging early entrance for bright girls
- requiring both sexes to participate in cleaning, cooking, construction, and carrying heavy objects in the classroom
- carefully filtering books and films for sexist connotations
- encouraging independence in girls
- referring highly capable girls for diagnostic testing to establish giftedness
- allowing children to progress academically as fast as they are able

Many of the suggestions for primary grade teachers (particularly the last five items) would apply equally well to teachers at higher grade levels. In addition, elementary, middle school, and junior high school teachers can play a very active role in helping young gifted girls to expand their aspirations. Fox and Turner (1981) outline the difficulties facing girls of middle-school age and their special programming needs.

> Gifted girls do differ from gifted boys in ways that have implications for the design of programs for them. First, they have less self-confidence in their own intellectual abilities, particularly in mathematics and science. Second, they are likely to have higher social service than intellectual values. Third, they are more likely to be concerned with peer acceptance than intellectual development, particularly in adolescence. Fourth, they experience more conflict and confusion than do gifted boys with respect to their life goals. Fifth, they may need more support and encouragement for academic success and development than do gifted boys. (p. 22)

The authors conclude that the top priority for gifted girls of this age group is career counseling and life-planning counseling. They also recommend that teachers and counselors act as advocates for special classes for the gifted and that they inspire excellence in females as well as males.

The following policies are suggested for inservice training classes for classroom teachers and counselors:

- believe in girls' logico-mathematical abilities and provide many opportunities for them to practice mathematical reasoning within other subject areas
- accelerate girls through the science and mathematics curriculum whenever possible
- have special clubs in mathematics for high-achieving girls
- design co-educational career development classes in which both sexes learn about career potentialities for women
- expose boys and girls to role models of women in various careers
- discuss nontraditional careers for women, including salaries for men and women and schooling requirements
- help girls set long-term goals
- discuss underachievement among gifted females and ask how they can combat it in themselves and others
- have girls read biographies of famous women
- arrange opportunities for girls to "shadow" a female professional for a few days to see what her work entails
- discourage sexist remarks and attitudes in the classroom
- boycott sexist classroom materials and write to the publishers for their immediate correction
- discuss sexist messages in the media
- advocate special classes and after-school enrichment opportunities for the gifted
- form support groups for girls with similar interests

At the high school level, counselors, teachers, administrators, and support personnel should be involved in reclaiming the hidden talents of gifted girls. High school is a critical juncture at which highly able females make decisions that may limit their choices for the rest of their lives. Strong positive action is needed at this point to counteract the effects of sex-role socialization. Special counseling programs should be partially co-educational and partially designed for females only. Co-educational sessions are necessary to impact the attitudes of males toward the changing roles of females. Same-sex sessions are also mandatory, since girls may be unwilling to reveal some of their fears and feelings with boys present. In all sessions, the dilemma of self-actualization versus sex-role stereotyping should be approached as a societal issue that each student—male or female—must face.

Suggested features of a comprehensive program at the high school level might include:

- actively recruiting girls for Advanced Placement mathematics and science courses
- cluster grouping gifted students or cluster scheduling them so that they maintain a strong support network
- encouraging all gifted students to plan rigorous coursework programs to broaden their career options
- instituting internships, mentorships, and work/study experiences for girls to work with professional women
- making certain that the contributions of women are acknowledged in every discipline
- selecting nonsexist texts
- requiring nonsexist language in written discourse
- encouraging female students to contribute in class
- alerting male and female students to the negative effects of sex-role stereotyping
- forming support groups for gifted girls to share their concerns
- exposing students to role models of professional women with different lifestyles: professional homemakers, single career women, career women who do not plan to have children, career women/homemakers.
- discussing alternative, equitable solutions that would enable a women to combine a career and family (e.g., role reversals, sharing a position, live-in childcare)
- analyzing career paths that are autonomous (planned to actualize one's career potential) versus those which are contingent upon a mate's career (planned to actualize one's potential as a wife and mother in a mobile society)
- providing comparative information about college programs and assistance in applying for scholarships and encouraging students of both sexes to attend first-rate colleges
- actively seeking scholarships for gifted students

At the end of high school and at the beginning of college, gifted young women should be provided with special seminars to help them deal with life-planning issues that are uniquely theirs to face. Young women particularly need assistance in maintaining contact with their own inner realities while entering male-dominated educational and professional systems.

Support networks throughout undergraduate and graduate school can help women cope effectively with the multifaceted demands of their lives. At the University of Denver, we have established a support group for gifted women at the graduate level and plan to expand it to the undergraduate level. In this group, women have dealt with their own denial of or failure to recognize their giftedness, the negative messages they received from others during their childhood, and the ways in which their intense sensitivity and perfectionism have influenced their lives.

One issue that many women in graduate school face is the cyclic pattern of their work styles. They are barraged with role models of single-minded scholars who can give their undivided attention to one project at a time, and they perceive this mode to be the only one acceptable. Yet many women find themselves rotating their attention among several simultaneous pursuits and interpreting this behavior as a "lack of discipline." The nature of most women's responsibilities almost demands the ability to move easily from one project to another. Women are immensely relieved to discover that their cycling from one task to another is a normal mode for many women and an alternative path to success.

Other issues that could be addressed in seminars or support groups for gifted women are:

- dealing with multiple interests and desires
- entering a predominantly masculine profession
- deciding whether or not to marry
- deciding whether to have children
- determining how to combine a career and a family
- maintaining ego strength when their choices bring censure from family or friends
- supporting each other's achievements
- understanding the impact of keeping one's own name or taking a married name in establishing one's professional identity
- recognizing and appreciating the multipotentiality of their giftedness
- developing a big sister support system for younger gifted women
- overcoming fears of success and fears of failure
- combatting dependency and conformity
- believing in their own abilities

- learning that they can be successful without risking the loss of femininity
- learning assertiveness-training techniques
- learning to appreciate their own work cycle and to judge their accomplishments according to internal standards that take into account the many demands of their multifaceted lives.

Fox and Turner (1981) assert that being born a gifted female should be a joy, not a burden. In our era, it is a mixed blessing. There is much we can do to make the goal of self-actualization realizable for both sexes. Reviewing the world as it was at the turn of the century, we can see the progress that has been achieved through the efforts of individuals such as Leta Hollingworth. Her dream was the full flowering of children with high abilities, regardless of sex. In 1931, Hollingworth posed a challenge that is still ours to meet:

> For the first time in the history of education, we are now able to identify the highly endowed while they are in early childhood, and to educate them as we see fit. This is a serious responsibility for the intellectual guardians of youth—educators. Whether we shall choose to act as though we were ignorant of this new knowledge, or whether we shall accept the responsibility for it by experimentation, and by modification of current practice in the light of experimentation, remains to be seen. (p. 198)

References

Albert, R. (1975). Toward a behavioral definition of genius. *American Psychologist, 30,* 140–151.

Almquist, E.M., & Angrist, S.S. (1971). Role model influences on college women's career aspirations. *Merrill-Palmer Quarterly, 17,* 263–279.

Astin, H.S. (1969). *The woman doctorate in America.* New York: Russell Sage.

Bassoff, E.S., & Glass, G.V. (1983). The relationship between sex roles and mental health: A meta-analysis of twenty-six studies. *The Counseling Psychologist, 10* (4), 105–112.

Baumgartner Papageorgiou, A. (1982). *"My Daddy might have loved me": Students' perceptions of differences between being male and being female.* Denver: Institute for Equality in Education, University of Colorado at Denver.

Bayley, N. (1970). Development of mental abilities. In P.H. Mussen (Ed.), *Carmichael's manual of child psychology: Vol. 1* (3rd ed.) (pp. 1163–1209). New York: John Wiley.

Benbow, C.P., & Stanley, J.C. (1983). Sex differences in mathematical reasoning ability: More facts. *Science, 222,* 1029–1031.

Benjamin, L.T. (1975). The pioneering work of Leta Hollingworth in the psychology of women. *Nebraska History, 56,* 493–505.

Blackwell, A.M. (1940). A comparative investigation into the factors involved in mathematical abilities of boys and girls. *British Journal of Educational Psychology, 10,* 143–153, 212–222.

Boring, E.G. (1950). *A history of experimental psychology* (2nd ed.). Englewood Cliffs, NJ: Prentice-Hall.

Boring, E.G. (1951). The woman problem. *American Psychologist, 6,* 679–682.

Bowman, M. (1983, November/December). Why we burn: Sexism exorcised. *Humanist, 43,* pp. 28–29.

Bryan, A.I., & Boring, E.G. (1947). Women in American psychology: Factors affecting their professional careers. *American Psychologist, 2,* 3–20.

Callahan, C.M. (1979). The gifted and talented woman. In A.H. Passow (Ed.), *The gifted and the talented: Their education and development.* The seventy-eighth yearbook of the National Society for the Study of Education, Part I (pp. 401–423). Chicago: University of Chicago Press.

Casserly, P.L. (1979). Helping able young women take math and science seriously in school. In N. Colangelo & R.T. Zaffran (Eds.), *New voices in counseling the gifted* (pp. 346–369). Dubuque, IA: Kendall/Hunt.

Clark, B. (1983). *Growing up gifted* (2nd ed.). Columbus, OH: Charles E. Merrill.

Cohen, R. (1984, August). Sharing. *Ms., 13*(2), pp. 74–75.

Committee on the Education and Employment of Women in Science and Engineering. (1983). *Climbing the ladder: An update on the status of doctoral women scientists and engineers.* Washington, DC: National Academy Press.

Cornell, D.G. (1983). Gifted children: The impact of positive labeling on the family system. *American Journal of Orthopsychiatry, 53,* 322–336.

Cox, C.M. (1926). *The early mental traits of three hundred geniuses. Genetic studies of genius: Vol. 2.* Stanford: Stanford University Press.

Crandall, V.J., Katkovsky, W., & Preston, A. (1962). Motivational and ability determinants of young children's intellectual achievement behaviors. *Child Development, 33,* 643–661.

Darwin, C. (1871). *The descent of man.* London: Murray.

Deaux, K. (1984). From individual differences to social categories: Analysis of a decade's research on gender. *American Psychologist, 39,* 105–116.

Dowdall, C.B., & Colangelo, N. (1982). Underachieving gifted students: Review and implications. *Gifted Child Quarterly, 26,* 179–184.

Dowling, C. (1981). The Cinderella complex: Women's hidden fear of independence. New York: Pocket Books.

Dweck, C.S., & Bush, C.S. (1976). Sex differences in learned helplessness: I. Differential debilitation with peer and adult evaluators. *Developmental Psychology, 12,* 147–156.

Dweck, C.S., Davidson, W., Nelson, S., & Enna, B. (1978). Sex differences in learned helplessness: II. The contingencies of evaluative feedback in the classroom, and III. An experimental analysis. *Developmental Psychology, 14,* 268–276.

Dweck, C.S., & Elliott, E.S. (1983). Achievement motivation. In E.M. Heatherington (Ed.), *The handbook of child psychology: Vol. 4. Socialization, personality, and social development* (4th ed.) (pp. 643–691). New York: John Wiley.

Epstein, C.F. (1973). Positive effects of the multiple negative: Explaining the success of black professional women. *American Journal of Sociology, 78,* 912–935.

Faunce, P.S. (1968). Personality characteristics and vocational interests related to the college persistence of academically gifted women. *Journal of Counseling Psychology, 15,* 31–40.

Feldman, D.H. (1984). A follow-up of subjects scoring above 180 IQ in Terman's "Genetic Studies of Genius." *Exceptional Children, 50,* 518–523.

Feshback, N.D. (1973). How not to succeed in the professions without really trying or the seven stages of women. *Educational Horizons, 51,* 61–70.

Fox, L.H., & Richmond, L.J. (1979). Gifted females: Are we meeting their counseling needs? *Personnel & Guidance Journal, 58,* 256–259.

Fox, L.H., & Turner, L.D. (1981). Gifted and creative female: In the middle school years. *American Middle School Education, 4,* 17–23.

Gallagher, J.J. (1975). *Teaching the gifted child* (2nd ed.). Boston: Allyn & Bacon.

Galton, F. (1869). *Hereditary genius: An inquiry into its laws and consequences.* (London, New York: Appleton, 1870).

Gilligan, C. (1982). *In a different voice: Psychological theory and women's development.* Cambridge, MA: Harvard University Press.

Ginzberg, E., Berg, I., Brown, C., Herman, J., Yohalem, A., & Gorelick, S. (1966). *Life styles of educated women.* New York: Columbia University Press.

Gjesme, T. (1973). Achievement-related motives and school performance for girls. *Journal of Personality & Social Psychology, 26,* 131–136.

Goertzel, V., & Goertzel, M.G. (1962). *Cradles of eminence.* Boston: Little, Brown.

Goldberg, S., & Lewis, M. (1969). Play behavior in the year-old infant: Early sex differences. *Child Development, 40,* 21–31.

Gould, S.J. (1981). *The mismeasure of man.* New York: W.W. Norton.

Groth, N. (1969, March). *Vocational development for gifted girls: A comparison of Maslovian needs of gifted males and females between the ages of ten and seventy years.* Paper presented at the meeting of the American Personnel and Guidance Association, Las Vegas (ERIC Document Reproduction Service No. ED 031 747)

Havighurst, R.J. (1972). *Developmental tasks and education* (3rd ed.). New York: David McKay.

Helson, R. (1971). Women mathematicians and the creative personality. *Journal of Consulting and Clinical Psychology, 36,* 210–220.

Hennig, M. (1973). Family dynamics and the successful woman executive. In R. Knudsin (Ed.), *Women and success.* New York: Morrow, 1973.

Hildreth, G.H. (1966). *Introduction to the gifted.* New York: McGraw-Hill.

Hoffman, L. (1972). Early childhood experiences and women's achievement motives. *Journal of Social Issues, 28,* 129–155.

Hollingworth, L.S. (1914). Variability as related to sex differences in achievement: A critique. *The American Journal of Sociology, 19,* 510–530.

Hollingworth, L.S. (1916). Social devices for compelling women to bear and rear children. *The American Journal of Sociology, 22,* 19–29.

Hollingworth, L.S. (1926). *Gifted children: Their nature and nurture.* New York: Macmillan.

Hollingworth, L.S. (1931). How should gifted children be educated? *Baltimore Bulletin of Education, 50,* 195–198.

Horner, M.S. (1970). Femininity and successful achievement: Basic inconsistency. In J.M. Bardwick, M.S. Horner, & D. Gutmann (Eds.), *Feminine personality and conflict* (pp. 45–74). Belmont, CA: Brooks/Cole.

Horner, M.S. (1972). Toward an understanding of achievement-related conflicts in women. *Journal of Social Issues, 28,* 157–175.

Hyde, J.S. (1981). How large are cognitive gender differences? A meta-analysis using w^2 and d. *American Psychologist, 36,* 892–901.

Ilg, F.L., & Ames, L.B. (1960). *Child behavior.* New York: Dell.

Kraditor, A.S. (1968). *Up from the pedestal: Selected writings in the history of American feminism.* Chicago: Quadrangle Books.

Kranz, B. (1975). From Lewis Terman to Matina Horner: What happens to gifted girls. *Talents and Gifts, 17*(3), 31–36.

Lavach, J.F., & Lanier, H.B. (1975). The motive to avoid success in 7th, 8th, 9th and 10th grade high-achieving girls. *The Journal of Educational Research, 68,* 216–218.

Lech, J.A. (1984). *"Just who is this 'Jeanette' person, anyway?": Your usual answer to your usual psychology assignment.* Unpublished manuscript.

Lemkau, J.P. (1983). Women in male-dominated professions: Distinguishing personality and background characteristics. *Psychology of Women Quarterly, 8,* 144–165.

Licht, B.G., & Dweck, C.S. (1984). Determinants of academic achievement: The interaction of children's achievement orientations with skill area. *Developmental Psychology, 20,* 628–636.

Licht, B.G., & Shapiro, S.H. (1982, August). *Sex differences in attributions among high achievers.* Poster presented at the 90th annual convention of the American Psychological Association, Washington, DC.

Maccoby, E.E. (1966). Sex differences in intellectual functioning. In E.E. Maccoby (Ed.), *The development of sex differences* (pp. 25–55). Stanford: Stanford University Press.

Maccoby, E.E., & Jacklin, C.N. (1974). *The psychology of sex differences: Vol. 1.* Stanford: Stanford University Press.

MacKinnon, D. (1962). The nature and nurture of creative talent. *American Psychologist, 17,* 484–495.

Martinson, R.A. (1974). The identification of the gifted and talented. Ventura, CA: Office of Ventura County Superintendent of Schools.

Mill, J.S. (1869). *The subjection of women.* Bungay, Suffolk, Great Britain: Richard Clay.

Montague, H., & Hollingworth, L.S. (1914). The comparative variability of sexes at birth. *The American Journal of Sociology, 20,* 335–370.

Passow, A.H. (1981). The nature of giftedness and talent. *Gifted Child Quarterly, 25,* 5–10.

Patrick, T. (1973). Personality and family background characteristics of women who enter male-dominated professions. *Dissertation Abstracts International, 35/05,* p. 2396-A. (University Microfilms No. 73-24076)

Pearson, K. (1924). *Life, letters and labours of Francis Galton: Vol. 2.* Cambridge, England: University Press.

Renzulli, J.S. (1980). What we don't know about programming for the gifted and talented. *Phi Delta Kappan, 61,* 601–602.

Rezler, A. (1967). Characteristics of high school girls choosing traditional or pioneer vocations. *Personnel & Guidance Journal, 45,* 659–665.

Richert, E.S. (1982a). *National report on identification: Assessment and recommendations for comprehensive identification of gifted and talented youth.* Sewell, NJ: Educational Improvement Center-South.

Richert, E.S. (1982b). Personality patterns of gifted children, Part I. *Gifted Children Newsletter, 3*(9), 1–3, 20.

Rodenstein, J.M., & Glickauf-Hughes, C. (1979). Career and lifestyle determinants of gifted women. In N. Colangelo & R.T. Zaffrann (Eds.), *New voices in counseling the gifted* (pp. 370–381). Dubuque, IA: Kendall/Hunt.

Rubin, J.Z., Provenzano, F.J., & Luria, Z.L. (1974). The eye of the beholder: Parents' views on sex of newborns. *American Journal of Orthopsychiatry, 44*, 512–519.

Russo, N.F., & O'Connell, A.N. (1983). Models from our past: Psychology's foremothers. *Psychology of Women Quarterly, 5*, 11–54.

Sanford, N. (1956). Personality development during college years. *Journal of Social Issues, 12*(4), 3–70.

Sattler, J.M. (1982). *Assessment of children's intelligence and special abilities* (2nd ed.). Boston: Allyn & Bacon.

Schaefer, C.E. (1970). A psychological study of ten exceptionally creative adolescent girls. *Exceptional Children, 36*, 431–441.

Sears, P.S., & Barbee, A.H. (1977). Career and life satisfactions among Terman's women. In J.C. Stanley, W.C. George, & C.H. Solano (Eds.), *The gifted and the creative: A fifty-year perspective* (pp. 28–65). Baltimore: The Johns Hopkins University Press.

Serbin, L.A., O'Leary, K.D., Kent, R.N., & Tonick, I.J. (1973). A comparison of teacher responses to the preacademic and problem behavior of boys and girls. *Child Development, 44*, 796–804.

Shakeshaft, C., & Palmieri, P. (1978). A divine discontent: Perspective on gifted women. *The Gifted Child Quarterly, 22*, 468–477.

Shields, S.A. (1975). Ms. Pilgrim's progress: The contributions of Leta Stetter Hollingworth to the psychology of women. *American Psychologist, 30*, 852–857.

Silverman, L.K. (in preparation). *Gifted education*. St. Louis: C.V. Mosby.

Slovic, P. (1966). Risk-taking in children: Age and sex differences. *Child Development, 37*, 169–176.

Sommers, S. (1982). Emotionality reconsidered: The role of cognition in emotional responsiveness. *Journal of Personality & Social Psychology, 41*, 553–561.

Standley, R., & Soule, B. (1974). Women in male-dominated professions: Contrasts in their personal and vocational histories. *Journal of Vocational Behavior, 4*, 245–258.

Stone, L.J., & Church, J. (1973). *Childhood & adolescence: A psychology of the growing person* (3rd ed.). New York: Random House.

Terman, L.M. (1916). *The measurement of intelligence*. Boston: Houghton Mifflin.

Terman, L.M. (1925). *Genetic studies of genius: Vol. 1. Mental and physical traits of a thousand gifted children*. Stanford: Stanford University Press.

Terman, L.M. (Ed.). (1925–1954). *Genetic studies of genius* (Vols. 1–5). Stanford: Stanford University Press.

Terman, L.M., & Tyler, L.E. (1954). Psychological sex differences. In L. Carmichael (Ed.), *Manual of child psychology* (pp. 1064–1114). New York: John Wiley.

Thorndike, E.L. (1910). *Educational psychology* (2nd ed.). N.Y.: Teachers College, Columbia University.

U'Ren, M.B. (1972). The image of woman in textbooks. In V. Gornick & B.K. Moran (Eds.), *Women in a sexist society: Studies of power and powerlessness*. New York: Basic Books.

U.S. Department of Labor, Bureau of Labor Statistics (1983). *Employment and earnings. Household data, annual averages for 1982: Employed persons by detailed occupation, sex, and race*. Washington, DC: Author.

U.S. Department of Labor, Women's Bureau (1982). *20 facts on women workers*. Washington, DC: Author.

Van Gelder, L. (1984, January). Carol Gilligan: Leader for a different kind of future. *Ms., 12*(7), pp. 37–40, 101.

Walberg, H.J. (1969). Physics, femininity, and creativity. *Developmental Psychology, 1,* 47–54.

Walker, B.G. (1983). *The woman's encyclopedia of myths and secrets.* San Francisco: Harper & Row.

Witty, P. (1940). Contributions to the IQ controversy from the study of superior deviates. *School & Society, 51,* 503–508.

Wolleat, P.L. (1979). Building the career development of gifted females. In N. Colangelo & R.T. Zaffrann (Eds.), *New voices in counseling the gifted* (pp. 331–345). Dubuque, IA: Kendall/Hunt.

5

What Happens to Them All?

a response to "What Happens to the Gifted Girl?"

James H. Borland, Ph.D.
Columbia University

> Men have broad and large chests, and small narrow hips, and are more
> understanding than women, who have but small and narrow chests, and
> broad hips, to the end they should remain at home, sit still, keep house, and
> bear and bring up children.
>
> —Martin Luther, 1566 (cited in Berger, 1973)

Apologia

By coincidence, a few days before being asked to respond to Linda Silverman's lucid chapter "What Happens to the Gifted Girl"?, I finished Thomas Berger's provocative and disturbing novel, *Regiment of Women* (1973). The protagonist of Berger's tale is Georgie Cornell, a secretary in a publishing house. Georgie is a naive young thing who tries with mixed success to survive in the nightmare world of twenty-first-century New York City, where pollution alerts are an almost daily phenomenon, the Hudson River is a sewer separating New York from New Jersey, and a one-and-one-half-room apartment in a seedy part of town rents for $1,500 per month. Georgie, the reader learns, is primarily concerned with such things as runs in stockings, the proper use of cosmetics, the question of whether beige pumps go well with a Kelly green pleated skirt, and the best way to fend off the boss's roving hands.

91

Georgie is obviously insecure, docile to a fault, and the victim of rampant sexism. Georgie is also a man, born on the wrong side of a post-feminist gender gap that has left men in complete submission to women.

I mention *Regiment of Women* not only because it is fresh in my mind and a work of considerable merit but because it is of relevance to many of the issues Silverman raises. Moreover, I have to wonder whether I would have been as receptive to some of Silverman's points, compelling as they seem to me now, had I not experienced vicariously the vertiginous world of Georgie Cornell. Although I consider myself sympathetic to the woman's movement and reasonably sensitive to the plight of women in the workplace and the home, I am also a first-born American male who smokes cigars, drinks beer, is lost to the world during baseball season, and is insecure enough to be sure that these qualities are mentioned in a paper that deals with "women's issues." Given that no one will ever mistake me for Phil Donahue or Alan Alda, it is not unlikely that a month or so ago I would have read Silverman's paper, as I suspect many men (and some women) have, with a sense that it represents at most a tempest in a teapot. But having also read of Georgie Cornell's simpering refusal to call upon his considerable but repressed abilities, I am not so sure that this is the case.

One of the most salubrious effects of reading both *Regiment of Women* and "What Happens to the Gifted Girl?" is the realization that such phrases as "anatomy is destiny" can be used to limit the destiny of any of us. By creating a world in which male biology is seen as a liability, Berger not only exposes the specious and arbitrary nature of such patently silly and pseudoscientific assertions as the one by Luther that prefaces this chapter, but he also reinforces Silverman's contention that more plausibly scientific statements about male-female differences can be grounded in prejudice and questionable assumptions as well. It is obviously far-fetched to claim a direct line of descent from, say, Aristotle ("Women may be said to be inferior to man," cited in Berger, 1973, p. 141) to Luther to Chesterfield ("Women are only children of a larger growth," also cited in Berger, p. 222) to Galton (1869, about whom more later) to Benbow and Stanley (1983) ("Males dominate the highest range of mathematical reasoning ability before they enter adolescence," p. 1031; "It is not obvious how social conditioning could affect mathematical reasoning ability so adversely and significantly," p. 1030; "For possible endogenous influences see, for example . . ." [14 citations follow], p. 1031). Nevertheless, there is a common thread running through all of these pronouncements, an assumption that deviation from a male standard necessarily implies a failure to attain a valid criterion of excellence.

The point I am laboring to make is that giftedness as a construct is freighted with the baggage of a male-centered professional world. Moreover, we who operate more or less successfully in that world and try to give meaning to such constructs are so oblivious to this fact (as a fish is oblivious to being wet) that we are unlikely to recognize how skewed are our basic conceptions until someone points it out to us. Most important of all, we are unlikely to recognize that the unexamined assumptions that underlie our conceptions of giftedness have very real negative consequences for gifted girls and indeed for all gifted students.

That our definitions of giftedness reflect a male perspective is one of the points that comes through strongly in reading Silverman's paper, although it deals almost exclusively with the problems encountered by gifted girls and women. I hope to make this clearer by exploring some of the issues raised by this chapter, but I want first to dispose of a few cavils prompted by some of the chapter's other assertions.

Some Minor Objections

Misinterpreting Terman

The first quibble concerns what seems to be a misinterpretation of Terman's (1925–1959) major work, a problem hardly unique to this chapter. Indeed, misinterpreting Terman has become something of a cottage industry in the field of the education of the gifted (e.g., Renzulli, Reis, & Smith, 1981, pp. 24–25), and Silverman's contribution is relatively minor. However, there are two statements with which one could disagree.

Silverman states that "after Galton suggested the equivalence of eminence and genius, Terman equated genius with giftedness, completing the linkage between giftedness and eminence." This makes sense formally, but there is no evidence that this causal link is a valid one. For despite vague references to a chimerical "late Terman" (Renzulli, 1978), who supposedly forswore his belief in the IQ in favor of emphasis upon certain personality traits and who made eminence the criterion for giftedness, no such animal seems to have existed in reality. The last page of the last volume of *Genetic Studies of Genius* (1959), being posthumous, is about as late as "late Terman" gets. In the last sentence on that page, Terman and his collaborator Melita Oden pay tribute to the men in their "C" group, stating that "we might take comfort in the thought that some of the small jobs, as well as the larger ones, are being done by gifted people" (p. 152). Thus, this "C" group, the high-IQ group that failed to achieve eminence or to demonstrate "task commitment," was regarded to the end as gifted. Terman indeed equated genius (or IQ) with giftedness, but there is no credible evidence that he ever made eminence the primary criterion for validating giftedness.

Another disagreement with Silverman's interpretation of the Terman study concerns the statement that since none of the Terman group ever achieved "greatness as the world judges it," the intelligence test was rejected as a measure of giftedness. On the contrary, the life success of the Terman subjects is sometimes cited as evidence of the test's predictive validity. As Tannenbaum (1983) points out, "It would be a mistake to assume that these grown-up high-IQ individuals distinguished themselves only in rapid and high-volume mastery learning and in finding solutions to problems that others had found before, but did not distinguish themselves in innovative work of great value" (p. 112). Terman and Oden's last volume of *Genetic Studies of Genius* (1959) is replete with data that indicate that this group achieved success far beyond what could be expected for an unselected group (an estimated level of professional productivity 10 to 30 times that of the rest of the population, for example). This group did indeed fulfill the "promise of youth," and that was clearly Terman and Oden's conclusion.

The supposed failure of the Terman sample to produce an Einstein, Mozart, or Curie is frequently cited as a major failing of the study. The study is certainly flawed (see, for example, Tannenbaum, 1983, pp. 114–115), but not for this reason. Rather, it seems naive to expect a sample of this size, even a highly selected sample, to yield a genius of that magnitude. Consider the odds. Even if one pretends that the Terman sample represented all of the students in the state of California in the 1920s, not a more geographically and temporally limited group, to criticize the study for not revealing the existence of an outstanding genius is to assume too much. One must assume that any given state in the Union at any given time should have a better-than-average chance of producing such a world-renowned figure from its school-age population, and this is clearly not the case. Olympian genius may be a one-in-ten-million or a one-in-fifty-million or even a one-in-a-hundred-million phenomenon. It certainly is not as common as it would have to be for the Terman sample to have been expected to yield one.

Neither of these points is central to Silverman's argument, and my interpretations are at least subject to debate. However, these misinterpretations, if that is what they are, deserve comment because they ill serve a chapter that is very strong in most respects.

Understating the Problem

Another quibble has to do with what seems to be a case of trying to have things both ways with respect to the cognitive development of girls. Basic to

Silverman's argument is the assertion that something happens to gifted girls as they grow older, something that lowers the probability that they will be recognized as gifted women. The question is, *"What* happens?" Do girls suffer actual decrements in their abilities in certain areas as a result of various pressures to which they are subjected in school and society? Or do girls really only hide their well-developed abilities and adopt the protective coloration of the "inferior female" out of fear of rejection by males and other females? If the former is the case, as most of Silverman's chapter seems to imply, the problem is one of monumental proportions. If the latter is the case, as Silverman seems to imply in other parts of the chapter, the problem is serious but more cosmetic.

It is quite likely that it is the more serious problem that we face, that girls, who are born with cognitive potential equal to that of boys, fail to develop that potential in too many cases. One result is lowered performance on valid measures of important abilities, lowered performance that reflects, in my opinion, lowered competence. It is not probable that the results reported by such researchers as the Johns Hopkins group (e.g., Benbow & Stanley, 1983; Benbow, Stanley, Kirk, & Zonderman, 1983) are in any way illusory, although one could contest the investigators' dismissal of the possibility of environmental influences. The truth is, unfortunately, that in a number of areas in which competence is a key to success in our society, girls and women are less competent than boys and men.

This statement could be misinterpreted, so let me be very clear about what I mean. I do not mean to say that females are genetically or in any other way inherently inferior to males cognitively. I do mean to say that the problem to which feminists have been alerting us for all these years is every bit as serious as they have claimed. Real damage is being done to girls in our schools and in our society. One of the results of this damage is the frequent failure of girls to develop the abilities that they have the potential, equal to that of boys, to develop.

One possible reason that girls fail to develop these abilities is that in most of these areas there are no purely female modes of successful performance. As Silverman makes clear in one of the strongest parts of her chapter, there are "powerful internal pressures for these women to perform at a high level in both feminine and masculine domains." A man, by comparison, has it easy. To succeed in a field such as mathematics, he need not perform any contortions with respect to his sexual identity. He can simply be a man (and must, of course, be an able mathematician). A woman with similar aspirations, on the other hand, needs to be competent in two realms in addition to the mathematical if she is not to be subjected to strong social disapproval. She must do mathematics "as well as (or like) a man." But she also has to maintain what men would define as her "femininity" if she is to be happy in the mainstream of our culture. By not sustaining this dual competence, she runs the risk of being labeled "too feminine" to carry on her career or "too masculine" to be accepted by society. The ideal of the superwoman, the woman who aspires to having it all, is not the product of female hubris. It is simply an accurate interpretation of the requirement that professional women, to be successful, be convincing in both "masculine" and "feminine" roles.

It is in this sense that there are no female modes of successful behavior in certain fields. A woman, qua woman, cannot succeed; she must be like a man as well and try to succeed on terms established by men. The task of competing in these areas is greater for women than it is for men, a fact of which girls must be aware from an early age. It is understandable that comparatively few would aspire to, and that many would fail to achieve, such success. Thus, more female talent than male talent is wasted in these fields. There is certainly more to the problem, but one point that should be made is that there *is* a serious problem; girls do not develop the abilities that their equal endowments would promise.

Silverman, perhaps inadvertently, seems to gloss over the gravity of the problem in some passages. For example, she discusses the increasing disparity between IQ test scores of boys and girls as the students grow older as if it were a testing artifact. "By the middle grades, the IQ tests tend to assess learning, which is more affected by socialization than is development." What is particularly troublesome here is the distinction drawn between learning and development. Learning, the evolution of cognitive structures over time as a result of experience, is a major aspect of one's development, as Piaget (e.g., Inhelder & Piaget, 1969) and others have demonstrated. Part of human development, especially that aspect we label "cognitive development," is the growth in learning that is one result of education. Thus, to the extent that girls learn less than boys in certain domains (admittedly as a result of differential socialization experiences), their development is, by comparison, curtailed.

The general thrust of Silverman's chapter is that there are fewer gifted girls who become gifted women than there are gifted boys who become gifted men. This is a critical problem in our society and a terrible injustice. Thus, the dilemma is not simply one of how to modify the identification procedures so that more girls are admitted to programs for the gifted on the middle school and senior high school levels (although that is a worthy objective), but one of how to prevent the loss of female talent that occurs when gifted girls fail to become gifted women.

One could argue, therefore, for a stronger statement of the problem than Silverman makes in parts of her chapter and a less equivocal statement overall. However, it is not difficult to understand how even identifying the problem, if it exists, could create quite a conflict for women. If they are to state accurately the extent of the discrimination they face in our society, they have to acknowledge the inevitable results that centuries of such discrimination have wrought.

Among these, apparently, is a lower *mean* level of competence with respect to certain learned cognitive tasks. By acknowledging this, by asserting that unequal treatment of inherently equal groups results in unequal competence in some areas, one perhaps provides ammunition for those who would like to argue that women are constitutionally unsuited for certain professions or are genetically inferior. Thus, there are understandable pressures to understate the problem.

However, a problem that is not fully acknowledged is difficult to solve. I suggest, then, with the comfortable smugness of a male academic, that the problem ought to be revealed in its fullest form, that the ravages visited upon gifted girls ought to be freely acknowledged, and that the situation ought to be treated as a national disgrace. As Silverman states, "girls surpass boys in intellectual performance during the early years and the pattern is reversed in junior and senior high school . . . it is likely that what appears to be a difference in biological timetables may actually be created by powerful socialization forces during adolescence." This seems to sum up the situation succinctly. Girls start out the equals of boys, they are subjected to strong societal forces that negatively affect their cognitive development, and as a result they suffer in terms of their intellectual performance.

Perpetuating Stereotypes

My third quibble with Silverman's chapter has to do with what seems to me to be a perpetuation of sexual stereotypes. This is a bit ironic in such a context, but it is possible that Silverman assumes the existence of a situation with respect to traditional sex roles that no longer obtains, at least everywhere. It is also possible that regional differences may influence our respective perceptions and experiences. I live in New York City (the source, of course, of all that is enlightened and progressive), while the author of the chapter under consideration resides in Colorado (which, I am told, is somewhere west of the Hudson River). I must, nonetheless, draw upon my experience, however that might reflect my favored circumstances, and my experience does not confirm some of what Silverman reports with respect to mothers' and fathers' roles in rearing gifted children.

For example, Silverman writes:

> . . . mothers and fathers have very different conceptions of gifted-
> ness. Mothers typically call to ask about the testing service and set up
> the appointments, whereas fathers often appear to have acquiesced

to the process reluctantly, and receive the information that their children are gifted with some degree of skepticism.

It happens that I am the director of an experimental preschool at Teachers College (the Hollingworth Preschool, by a happy coincidence), and I receive a great many telephone calls from parents who believe that their children would benefit from such a program. It has not been my experience that the vast majority of these callers are mothers. Fathers, in the New York area at least, seem to be as concerned with their children's giftedness as are mothers.

If there is any difference in the nature of the calls received from fathers and mothers, it has to do with the degree of certainty expressed with respect to the possibility that the scion in question is exceptional. Fathers will frequently state "I have a gifted child, and I want to know how to get (him or her) tested for your program." Mothers, on the other hand, are more likely to begin with a qualifier such as, "I know all parents think their children are gifted, but. . . ." Thus, I am led to contradict another of Silverman's assertions, that "the father's protective reaction is therefore to deny his child's giftedness." Tell it to the man in the subway.

Or tell it to the man who came to my office two years ago to describe his method of teaching reading to his gifted son. For the past two months, he told me, he had been using flashcards to help this child learn to read simple phrases. I was about to suggest some more creative ways he and his son might explore the written word when the father informed me that the boy was 4 months old. How did he know that the infant was gifted? Well, when he held up a sign that read "I love you," the child smiled. My protestations that no reading comprehension was taking place, that the boy would probably smile in response to a sign that read "Ontogeny recapitulates philogeny" fell on deaf ears. This father was not one to "deny his child's giftedness" by a long shot.

Silverman's statement that "mothers whose major work is homemaking live in a different world than that of their husbands" is also problematical. It is true that there are no commas around "whose major work is homemaking," but the statement is still being made to buttress a general point, that mothers have more contact with their children and thus more concern with their daily adjustment. This assumes a state of affairs that does not seem to obtain to the extent that it used to east of the Hudson (nor, perhaps, west of the Hudson since Silverman cites the U.S. Department of Labor to the effect that almost half the work force is female). Since the two-paycheck family is increasingly becoming the norm, it is possible that what we observe in the Hollingworth Preschool—fathers dropping off and picking up their children, equal numbers of fathers and mothers at parent meetings, fathers as well as mothers bringing in their children for testing—will soon be normal elsewhere, if it is not already.

As was admitted above, this is a minor flaw in the chapter, but it does appear, ironically, to be an example of what the chapter is decrying.

Some Major Contributions

That is more than enough in the way of quibbles. I would now like to discuss three major issues that Silverman handles in a masterful manner. Her treatment of these issues reflects more accurately the quality and importance of the ideas in her chapter and constitutes, in my opinion, a major contribution to the field.

Welcome Back, Leta Hollingworth

The first issue requires little discussion, just commendation (although it will receive both). This is Silverman's effort to restore the reputation of Leta Hollingworth or, rather, to make people as aware of Hollingworth's work as they are of her name. Hollingworth is one of a triumvirate of people to whom more or less vague references are made when the history of the gifted child movement is discussed, the others being Francis Galton and Lewis Terman. Today, all three are more revered than read, and none more so than Hollingworth.

While the reputations of Terman and especially Galton could well suffer were their writings to be examined in light of today's values, Hollingworth's could only be enhanced. Galton's work virtually reeks of nineteenth-century British social Darwinism, and Terman's racial views are likely to strike today's readers as obnoxious (see Gould, 1981, for an interesting, if hardly impartial, commentary on both). Hollingworth's work, however, reveals a sensibility quite in tune with contemporary values. This comes through quite well in Silverman's chapter.

It is true that I could be accused of bias in favor of Leta Hollingworth. I am, after all, connected with both the Hollingworth Preschool and the Hollingworth Summer School, and I teach at the same institution that counted Hollingworth among its faculty. My respect for her work, however, goes beyond mere institutional loyalty, and it is shared by others.

I teach a graduate course in which the students are required to read, among other materials, three primary-source works: Galton's *Hereditary Genius* (1869), significant portions of Terman's *Genetic Studies of Genius* (1925–1959), and Hollingworth's *Children above 180 IQ* (1942). Invariably, the book that receives the most favorable reception is Hollingworth's. The same students who treat Galton with scorn and Terman with condescension react quite favorably to Hollingworth's scholarship, common sense, and humanity.

Unfortunately, I suspect that the vast majority of individuals working in the field of the education of the gifted have read none of these authors' works in their original forms. This has a number of unhappy consequences. For one, it allows some writers to force fit selective readings of past authorities into the Procrustean bed of their own theories. Were enough people sufficiently familiar with the work of Galton, Terman, and Hollingworth, this sort of abuse would be curtailed significantly.

Second, as alluded to above, the fact that the original works are seldom read allows some of our forebears to be enshrined in the Pantheon of "gifted education" without having to pay the price for some rather benighted beliefs. By making this statement, I do not mean to assert that a writer's professional output should be dismissed because of his or her views in private life. Rather, I mean that a writer such as Francis Galton, whose unfortunate conception of the abilities of women and nonwhites was part and parcel of his scientific output, should be recognized as one whose work rests on some very unenlightened assumptions, as Silverman reminds us.

Third, this disinclination to read these major works in their original forms deprives today's educators of valuable knowledge and that elusive feel for a writer and his or her times that only comes from a close reading of primary-source material. Reading Galton's *Hereditary Genius,* for example, is a fascinating experience, if only for the almost palpable sense of wonder it conveys and for the privilege of looking over the shoulder of one who is on the threshold of something that is absolutely new and without precedent.

Finally, this lack of familiarity with the primary sources of our discipline results in injustices such as the neglect into which the work of Leta Hollingworth has fallen. It is heartening, therefore, to read an essay that reflects a first-hand experience of, a familiarity with, and an appreciation for the important work of Leta Hollingworth. On this basis alone, Silverman's chapter deserves high praise.

The Definition Conundrum

Silverman's treatment of the work of Hollingworth is not the only commendable aspect of her chapter, however. Even more impressive is her discussion of definitions of giftedness. Silverman distinguishes between what she characterizes as "masculine" and "feminine" definitions. I have noticed the same underlying dichotomy as has Silverman, but it never occurred to me to interpret this as a masculine/feminine distinction. In truth, I am not very comfortable with these labels, although I think the substance of Silverman's distinction is very important.

I question the validity of splitting types of definitions along gender lines both for reasons of science (it is doubtful that empirical justification could be found for such a black-and-white division) and for reasons of politics (this could help perpetuate stereotypes of the "nurturing female" and the "demanding male" and force people into certain camps on the basis of their sex). I would like to offer another set of labels and some comments on the differences between the two types of definitions.

What Silverman calls "masculine" definitions of giftedness, I refer to as "national-resources" definitions. Writers who take this approach appear to define gifted children as a very untapped national resource that should be identified and exploited for the national good. Their definitions posit eminence or productivity as the validating criterion for giftedness, and the traits mentioned in these definitions are usually those of productive adults who have achieved eminence in the past. The entire phase of the gifted child movement that emerged from the post-Sputnik era was informed by this way of thinking (see Tannenbaum, 1979, 1983), and some current definitions, of which Renzulli's (1978) is the best known, seem to rest on this foundation.

In place of the term "feminine," I recommend the term "special-educational" to designate the second approach to defining giftedness (and to providing special programs). The term "special-educational" is apposite because the emphasis in this approach is on the child himself or herself at the present time in the real world of the school. Rather than seeking out children who may become eminent adults, this approach entails looking for those children who are exceptional in comparison with their age peers by virtue of special ability or potential, exceptional to the extent that their *educational needs* are not being met by the regular curriculum. Thus, the concept of educational need, as opposed to probability of future success, plays the determining role.

I believe that these terms are preferable to Silverman's because they are more descriptive of the nature of the definitions and the intent of the definers. They do not depend on chance associations with certain groups (male, female, or whatever) who may promulgate the definitions. Moreover, I, for one, do not relish the prospect of attacking the "masculine" definition of giftedness (although I disagree with the one so-designated by Silverman), and it is likely that others would feel themselves to be similarly boxed in by "masculine" and "feminine" labels.

There are arguments in addition to Silverman's that could be launched against the national-resources approach to defining giftedness, and some will be cited here to bolster Silverman's case for the alternative approach. One of these arguments concerns methodology. In every, or nearly every, case, the procedure followed in deriving a national-resources definition involves studying the lives and accomplishments of eminent adults (necessarily of generations that lived long before the children to whom the definition will be applied) and trying to abstract the characteristics that were most crucial to the success of those individuals. These, then, become the characteristics that enter into the definition of giftedness and, more important, the characteristics that *today's* children are required to exhibit in order to enter programs for the gifted.

What, one might ask, is wrong with this? First, there is no guarantee that the characteristics that were crucial to success in, say, Darwin's world or Edison's will be those that will be required for success in the world of tomorrow's adults. Our children are growing up in a post-industrial, post-Einsteinian age that will demand skills and traits that are perhaps beyond our power to imagine. The positivism that informed the world view of the worthies whose life histories are found in today's dictionaries of biography will probably not characterize the world view of tomorrow's adults. Giftedness, as many of our perceptive writers (e.g., Sternberg, 1984; Tannenbaum, 1983) have indicated, is at least in part determined by context. Yesterday's context could very likely not be valid for defining tomorrow's giftedness.

Second, such definitions appear to violate a basic rule of developmental psychology, the rule that states that children are not merely miniature adults or homunculi who become adults by a simple process of accretion. Children's cognition and conceptions of reality are qualitatively different from those of adults. Thus, to expect an exact isomorphism between the traits of gifted adults and "potentially gifted children" (to use Hagen's, 1980, phrase) is patently wrong. It makes almost as little sense conceptually as requiring that children, in order to demonstrate the potential for leadership, have beards since Lincoln had a beard. If we are to have a valid definition of gifted children, it must be a definition that takes into account what we have learned from developmental psychology.

Another drawback of national-resources definitions, in addition to their methodological inadequacy, is that they take us away from the source of the problem and the logical place for its remediation, the school. What we call "giftedness" usually manifests itself in response to the demands of the school curriculum, either positively or negatively. We realize that a child requires special services in a program for the gifted by interpreting his or her reaction to classroom activities, a reaction that indicates that the regular curriculum is not sufficient to meet the child's intellectual needs. This is a problem for the present, not for the future.

As educators, we are in a somewhat tenuous position when we try to predict which of our students will become eminent adults. (As a teacher, I often had difficulty predicting who would do well on Friday's quiz.) We are in an even more tenuous position when we try consciously to influence the future. However, we can affect what happens in the schools. We can modify the curriculum for those whose responses to it indicate that they are not learning what they could learn, not thinking in the ways they could think, and not producing what they could produce without such modifications. This should be the focus of our efforts as educators of the gifted, not some future that is probably beyond our capacity to predict.

Furthermore, national-resources definitions and the programs that result from them tend to favor the advantaged, the comfortable achiever, and the most-likely-to-succeed in the conventional sense. Despite protestations to the contrary, definitions such as Renzulli's (1978) and identification schemes such as his Revolving-Door Identification Model (Renzulli, Reis, & Smith, 1981) necessarily favor the well-adapted child who is working up to his or her capacity in the regular classroom, as logic, experience, and research (e.g., Kontos, Carter, Ormrod, & Cooney, 1983) have shown. The conforming behavior connoted by the term "task commitment," the nebulous quality of the term "creativity," and the disdain for the intellect implicit in the phrase "above-average ability" are such to lead school personnel, who must interpret these terms, to seek out well-motivated, well-adjusted children who are doing well in the regular classroom. The brilliant but disaffected child, the child from the "wrong" side of town who does not conform to white middle-class notions of task commitment, and the bright underachiever are all likely to go by the boards. Also affected negatively, as Silverman makes clear, are girls when they reach high school, junior high school, or even the intermediate grades.

Silverman seems to be skeptical of such supply-side definitions of giftedness that are based upon the promise of productivity or eminence. Her concept of "developmental advancement," which underlies her definition of giftedness, is compatible with the special-educational approach. Her definition of the gifted child, "one who is developmentally advanced in one or more areas, and is therefore in need of differential programming in order to develop at his or her own developmental pace," is, in fact, similar to the following one I have proposed.

> The term "gifted child" refers to those students in a given school or school district who are exceptional by virtue of markedly greater-than-average potential or ability in some area of human activity generally considered to be the province of the educational system. This exceptionality engenders educational needs that cannot be met within the confines of the regular core curriculum. (Borland, in preparation)

The focus in both definitions is on the needs of children in the schools, not on the needs of society in some indeterminate future. By making the school our focus, we are doing what we ought to be doing as educators. By placing children at the center of our definitions, we are doing what we ought to be doing as those responsible for their welfare. Thus, although I disagree with Silverman's use of the terms "masculine" and "feminine," I applaud her perceptive delineation of the dichotomy in our definitions of giftedness.

Rehabilitating the IQ

Related to the above discussion of definitions is Silverman's treatment of the IQ. The IQ test is often treated as the dark, dirty secret of the education of the gifted. Educators of the gifted decry its use in print while accepting its wholesale use in practice. Silverman acts through this hypocrisy and recommends the intelligent use of intelligence tests, making a strong case that eschewing their use will result in the identification of fewer girls than would otherwise be the case. This is a plausible argument, and it should persuade some that IQ tests have a role in identifying gifted students.

One could even go beyond Silverman's argument and state that IQ tests are exactly the sort of tool we ought to be using for definition, at least with respect to what these tests attempt to assess. I am concerned, as I suspect is Silverman, about what appears to be a strong anti-intellectual trend within the field of the education of the gifted. Although Richard Hofstadter, in his landmark work *Anti-Intellectualism in American Life* (1963), showed that the anti-intellectual impulse in this country does not abate at the schoolhouse door, it is still dismaying and ironic to sense its presence in the gifted child movement. It seems to be reflected most clearly by our collective movement away from a conception of the gifted child as one with great intellectual potential toward a conception of the gifted child as one who is likely to succeed in the conventional sense. It is doubtful that one could get a majority of the educators working in this field to subscribe to a premise stating that a major objective of gifted education is to produce intellectuals. Yet, this has historically been part of our mission. Today, however, it is favorable to disparage "lesson learners" and "test takers," just as it is socially safe during adolescence to taunt some children for being "teachers' pets" or "grinds."

The denigration of the intellect is mirrored in our abandonment of IQ tests. Admittedly, there is much that is wrong with such tests. They are not comprehensive measures of human intelligence, and they (at least) reflect society's bias against certain groups. However, they attempt to measure academic potential, and that is what we ought to be looking for in those children we label, for better or worse, "gifted." Intelligence tests are the right type of tool; they simply are not sufficient for the task by themselves. Supplemented by other instruments that take into account the diversity of groups and life styles within our society, the IQ test is a valuable measure that should be a part of our identification procedures.

When Silverman writes that "in discovering giftedness in females, intelligence testing is enormously effective, due to its sensitivity to developmental advancement, particularly in preschool and primary-aged children," one has to agree. Our experiences in the Hollingworth Preschool have repeatedly confirmed Silverman's assertion. Moreover, the IQ test is sensitive to other things as well, such as underachieving students with high intellectual potential, students who find the classroom boring but the encyclopedia fascinating, and children who are high-level thinkers but who adapt poorly to the petty restrictions of some classroom routines. It would be foolish to recommend the exclusive use of IQ tests for identifying gifted children, especially in diverse populations, but it would be equally foolish to recommend their abandonment.

Silverman is both perceptive and courageous in her remarks about the use of IQ tests. This is one more example of a case in which her principled concern for gifted girls illuminates an issue that affects all gifted children.

Conclusion

There is much to praise about the work under consideration here that I have not yet mentioned. For example, there is the graceful writing style that mixes a light and readable tone with a sure and skillful use of the language. There is the admirable combination of scholarly research and illustrative anecdote. There is the ability to make strong assertions and compelling arguments without adopting a superior attitude or a patronizing tone. Above all, there is an obvious commitment to a good cause, to making the educational system more responsive to the needs of gifted girls and all gifted students.

When June Maker asked me to write this response, she told me I would be in good company. If the chapter by Linda Silverman is any indication, I can see what she meant.

References

Benbow, C.P., & Stanley, J.C. (1983). Sex differences in mathematical reasoning ability: More facts. *Science, 222,* 1029–1031.

Benbow, C.P., Stanley, J.C., Kirk, M.K., & Zonderman, A.B. (1983). Structure of intelligence in intellectually precocious children and in their parents. *Intelligence, 7,* 129–152.

Berger, T. (1973). *Regiment of women*. New York: Delta.

Borland, J.H. (in manuscript). *The gifted child in the school*. New York: Teachers College Press.

Galton, F. (1869). *Hereditary genius*. London: Macmillan.

Gould, S.J. (1981). *The mismeasure of man*. New York: W.W. Norton.

Hagen, E. (1980). *Identification of the gifted*. New York: Teachers College Press.

Hofstadter, R. (1963). *Anti-intellectualism in American life*. New York: Vintage.

Hollingworth, L.S. (1942). *Children above 180 IQ*. Hastings-on-Hudson, NY: World Book.

Inhelder, B., & Piaget, J. (1969). *The early growth of logic in the child*. New York: W.W. Norton.

Kontos, S., Carter, K.R., Ormrod, J.E., & Cooney, J.B. (1983). Reversing the revolving door: A strict interpretation of Renzulli's definition of giftedness. *Roeper Review, 5,* 35–39.

Renzulli, J.S. (1978). What makes giftedness? *Phi Delta Kappan, 60,* 180–184, 261.

Renzulli, J.S., Reis, S.M., & Smith, L.H. (1981). *The revolving door identification model*. Mansfield Center, CT: Creative Learning Press.

Silverman, L.K. (in press). What happens to the gifted girl? In C.J. Maker (Ed.), *Defensible programs for the gifted*. Rockville, MD: Aspen Systems.

Sternberg, R.J. (1984). Toward a triarchic theory of human intelligence. *The Behavioral and Brain Sciences, 7,* 269–287.

Tannenbaum, A.J. (1979). Pre-Sputnik to post-Watergate concern about the gifted. In A.H. Passow (Ed.), *The gifted and the talented: Their education and development* (pp. 5–27). Chicago: University of Chicago Press.

Tannenbaum, A.J. (1983). *Gifted children: Psychological and educational perspectives*. New York: Macmillan.

Terman, L.M. (1925–1959). *Genetic studies of genius* (Vols. 1–5). Stanford: Stanford University Press.

6

On Finding Lost Gifted Girls:

comments on "What Happens to the Gifted Girl"

Lynn H. Fox, Ph.D.
The Harrison Group, Inc.

L inda Silverman's chapter "What Happens to the Gifted Girl?" should bring loud applause from feminists, but educators and psychologists may be critical of her intrepretations, assertions, and speculations concerning some psychometric issues. Few readers will remain neutral.

In my opinion the strength of the chapter lies in the well-documented discussion of the historical evolution of the arguments concerning the failure of women to achieve eminence in equal proportions with men in virtually every academic and/or culturally valued arena. Her choice of some direct quotes from educators and scientists such as LeBon and Thorndike are calculated to boil the blood of all but the most hardened male chauvinist. Clearly, her discussion of the barriers to women's achievement in adulthood is impressive and the implications of these barriers for counseling gifted girls must not be ignored.

Silverman, however, like others before her who have tackled the problem of gender differences in intellectually gifted populations (Fox, 1977; Callahan, 1979), can lay out only an incomplete tapestry of research on the interconnectedness of social and biological factors to cognitive functioning on tests of general or specific abilities in childhood and adolescence. Proofs of cause-and-effect relationships are much too elusive. Indeed, we are continually frustrated by the paucity of good research on gender differences within the gifted population per se and must often assume that conclusions reported about sex differences in studies of the general population will also be valid for gifted

107

populations, even though we know that gifted girls differ from other girls in several ways.

Where the Silverman chapter seems most vulnerable to attack is in the area of discussion of and recommendations for the identification of gifted children. Sometimes the discussion of sex differences in the numbers of boys versus girls identified as gifted seems confusing because the cited studies are not reported in enough detail to allow understanding or replication or the distinctions between or among the various procedures or tests used in these various studies are not fully explained. For example, Silverman discusses the greater numbers of girls than boys found in some populations of preschoolers, presumably on individual measures of intelligence such as a Stanford-Binet. She then notes that there are more males than females identified in adolescent populations and references Fox and Turner (1981). The Fox and Turner article was reporting the findings of several studies but primarily the work at The Johns Hopkins University, in which more boys than girls were identified as mathematically gifted on the basis of the Scholastic Aptitude Test-Mathematics (SAT-M) rather than a study using an individual intelligence test such as the Stanford-Binet. Indeed in the Hopkins studies approximately equal numbers of boys and girls are identified as verbally gifted on the SAT-V, a test more closely correlated with the Stanford-Binet than the SAT-M.

Even if it is true that more boys than girls are identified as gifted on an individual intelligence test at ages 6 to 13 than are identified at ages 2½ and 5½, the contention put forth by Silverman that the tests are more valid at the younger ages flies in the face of standard psychometric theory. First, the reliability of tests is typically greater for older children than for younger children. Less reliable tests are less valid. For example, the reliabilities for scores in the 140–149 range on the Stanford-Binet are as follow:

.83 (ages 2½ to 5½)
.91 (ages 6 to 13)
.95 (ages 14 to 18)

Thus, if we compare the scores of girls tested on the Stanford-Binet (S-B) at age five with those of girls tested at age eight, the common psychometric wisdom is that there is less error of measurement for the eight year olds. The contention that girls cannot score "brighter than they are" is not technically accurate. Error of measurement is assumed to operate "for" as well as "against" a testee. Indeed, on the S-B it is clear that the "weighting tends to magnify the error of measurement at the upper levels because the chance of passing or failing a single item makes a larger difference in total score at these levels than it does at the lower levels" (Anastasi, 1982, pp. 237–238), and thus the scores are less reliable at the upper levels of ability. In general, the probability of scoring above one's "true" score is equal to the probability of scoring below it. Consider the case of a child with a "true" score of 140 on the Slosson, which has an error of measurement of roughly four points. She has an equal probability of scoring 136 and 144; indeed, we would expect her to score within the range of 136 to 144 about two-thirds of the time if she were repeatedly tested. What is true but not clearly explained by Silverman is that regression to the mean is expected to operate. Thus if on the first testing the little girl scores 144, we would expect her score to be lower on a second testing.

Actually, I agree with Silverman's contention that there are as many gifted girls as boys but I would pursue some of the other possible explanations for differences in the ratio of boys to girls identified in adolescence. For example, research shows that gifted girls have less self-confidence than boys and that teachers are not necessarily positive toward the gifted girl nor as aware of her as they are of the gifted boy. Perhaps the differences in adolescence are a function, at least in part, of differential nomination of girls and self-nomination or selection of girls into some advanced programs, as in the case of Advanced Placement calculus classes in the study by Casserly (1980). For many years far more boys than girls went to college, but today we see approximately equal numbers of boys and girls entering college and a dramatic jump in the numbers of young women who are entering college as premedical or business majors. Significant sex differences are now noticeable mostly in the numbers majoring in the physical sciences and engineering and in the numbers who go farther and achieve doctorates in mathematics or science. Similarly, in the past, counselors, teachers, and parents often did not "push" girls to take algebra in the eighth or ninth grade. Now there are far fewer differences in course enrollments in mathematics in the middle and high school years, with the exception of perhaps courses like computer science and calculus.

Another important question is whether or not statistically significant differences in studies of large numbers of children are actually reflecting practical differences. Sometimes the differences are a matter of half an item on a test and do not necessarily indicate a real difference in ability to learn in the classroom. More research is needed to understand all the factors affecting the identification of girls for special programs. It may be that some of the tests are "biased." Perhaps one way to increase the number of girls identified in the upper elementary school grades and middle and high school years is to encourage the utilization of a wider variety of measures and methods for identification to ensure better representation of girls.

Finally, we must not overlook the possibility that girls are performing more poorly than boys on the tests because they are learning less at home and school. Perhaps whatever verbal advantage they may have in the preschool years is being lost because the kinds of educational experiences they encounter do not foster their spatial and quantitative reasoning skills. If it should be found that girls on the average are slightly less able to learn these skills, it is not wrong to propose some remediation, for surely a great deal of effort is now devoted to fostering the language and verbal skills of boys in the early school years. If we find that the male and female brains are organized somewhat differently it need not be that one is better. They may be merely different.

I would like to plead with Linda Silverman and others who research the field of sex differences and the gifted. Let us avoid polarization and political footballing. I feel that trying to catalogue or categorize identification models along the lines of those proposed by women as feminist and those proposed by men as male chauvinist is incorrect and potentially harmful. Silverman's own proposed definition is almost identical to one used by Julian Stanley (1977) in his studies in which far more boys than girls are identified as mathematically gifted on the basis of apparent greater readiness for accelerated learning. Nor is Renzulli's Revolving-Door Model incompatible with what Silverman proposes. Indeed, some of the most encompassing models for identification have been proposed by men: those proposed by Tannenbaum and Passow or the one by Feldman (see Fox, 1981, for a discussion of definitions).

In conclusion, let me reaffirm the time-honored truth: even when differences are found between males and females, not all males are better than all females or vice versa; indeed, sometimes differences do not bespeak superiority. Those of us who are concerned about the fair treatment of women at school and in the world of work must be extremely careful in our rebuttal to charges of male superiority so that we do not fall into the same errors of overgeneralizing from the data, or mixing opinion and evidence indiscriminately in our discussions of the issue. We must be careful to avoid error on picky points that weaken our overall credibility and to focus our energy on the really important battles. A little reminder now and then of past inequities may be necessary to maintain interest and commitment to action. In the end, however, it is the final pages of recommendations of Silverman's chapter to which we must turn our attention. Prolonged debate of the questions such as "Women in Science: Why So Few?" must give way to the development of constructive approaches to achieving educational and career equity. Overall, Silverman's chapter provides much to challenge and stimulate these efforts!

References

Anastasi, A. (1982). *Psychological testing*. New York: Macmillan.

Callahan, C.M. (1979). The gifted and talented woman. In. A.H. Passow (Ed)., *The gifted and the talented: Their education and development*. Chicago: Univ. of Chicago Press.

Casserly, P.L. (1980). Factors affecting female participation in advanced placement programs in mathematics, chemistry, and physics. In L.H. Fox, L. Brody, & D. Tobin (Eds.), *Women and the mathematical mystique*. Baltimore: The Johns Hopkins University Press.

Fox, L.H. (1977). Sex differences: Implications for programming for the academically gifted. In J.C. Stanley, W.C. George, & C.H. Solano (Eds.), *The Gifted and the creative: A fifty-year perspective*. Baltimore: The Johns Hopkins University Press.

Fox, L.H. (1981). Identification of the academically gifted. *American Psychologist, 36*, 103–111.

Fox, L.H., and Turner, L.D. (1981). Gifted and creative females: In the middle-school years. *American School Education, 4*, 17–23.

Stanley, J.C. (1977). Rationale of the Study of Mathematically Precocious Youth (SMPY) during its final five years of promoting educational acceleration. In J.C. Stanley, W.C. George, & C.H. Solano (Eds)., *The gifted and the creative: A fifty-year perspective*. Baltimore: The Johns Hopkins University Press.

7

The Psychometric Dilemma of Giftedness

Linda Kreger Silverman

I deeply appreciate Dr. Borland's thoughtful and witty review of the chapter "What Happens to the Gifted Girl?" I could not quarrel with many of his "minor objections." Not meaning to add to the cottage industry of misinterpreting Terman, I do think that the very title of his *magnum opus* implies that Terman considered the subjects of his study to be geniuses, and that he was hoping to prove his point in their adult lives. It is true that many of the Termites distinguished themselves, but recent critics (e.g., Feldman, 1984) have been rather unimpressed with the level of eminence attained by the sample.

The second issue involves whether females simply hide their abilities or actually suffer a loss of abilities. I believe that hiding one's talents eventuates in loss, simply because talents must be consciously nurtured in order to develop to their fullest.

Dr. Borland's third question was whether traditional sex roles still obtain anywhere, when they seem to have disappeared in his neck of the woods. His experience with New York City fathers is quite different from mine with Colorado fathers. The majority of the children I have tested come from middle- and upper-middle class families, in which the fathers work, and the mothers—regardless of education—stay at home to raise their children. With the cost of living east of the Hudson River, staying home with one's children is a luxury most women cannot afford. This would certainly lead to the discrepancies in our observations. To add to the irony, in 1926, Leta Hollingworth noted that there were more than a hundred women in New York City who combined child-rearing with careers. Not so long ago. My guess is that traditional sex roles still prevail in the "real" world (that is, west of the Hudson).

Dr. Fox's critique causes more difficulty in responding in the amount of space provided. I would like to address one of her major points, the psychometric issue. It is true that reliability improves with age on intelligence tests, and that reliability is a primary factor in establishing validity. However, reliability does not tell the whole story, and some subtleties in the assessment of the gifted are overlooked in this argument. If a child scores 145 at the age of 14, his score tends to be quite stable. He will probably attain a similar score at the age of 16. This does not take into account the difficulty of attaining a score of 145 at the age of 14, since the ceiling effects at that level are prohibitive.

The scores for adolescents on intelligence tests are compressed, just as they are on achievement tests, since the tests do not permit the full range of the student's abilities to be demonstrated. If a student obtained a score in the 99th percentile on a math achievement test, the chances are that she would obtain nearly the same score if she took the test a second time. The reliability would be superb. If she took the Scholastic Aptitude Test twice in a row, she might attain a score of 500 one time and 600 another time. The reliability of the SAT scores would be inferior to those obtained on the math achievement test. Which is the more valid indicator of her abilities—the math achievement test or the SAT? A test with an attenuated range will produce high reliabilities for brighter students, while underestimating the true level of their abilities.

As Stanley has repeatedly emphasized:

> The matter of "appropriate difficulty" of tests has also received less emphasis from measurement specialists than it merits. (1976, p. 4)

There is likely to be greater variability in test scores of very young children due to the difficulties in gaining their full attention and cooperation. Four-year-olds will perform for one tester and refuse to answer questions for another. This phenomenon accounts for much of the lower reliability of scores of young children. Under these circumstances, it is quite remarkable that scores for children in the 2½- to 5½-year-old range attain reliabilities of .83. This reliability coefficient is definitely within the acceptable range (Sattler, 1982). The validity of these early scores, then, does not rest upon shaky ground.

The variability in young children's attention also explains why some who attain low scores in early childhood may actually be gifted. But what about the child who receives a high score in early childhood? Can this be accidental? Is it possible for a child of five to accidentally decipher the block counting problem that was designed to stump many ten-year-olds? Is this not a real sign of giftedness that is being measured?

The intention of my chapter was not to polarize the field, but to call attention to the possibilities of a biased perspective in both the definitions of giftedness and the identification methods employed. Dr. Borland's analogy of the fish being oblivious to the fact that it is wet is precisely the point. Perhaps the terms "masculine" and "feminine" are red flags that obscure the real issues. A masculine, productivity orientation is certainly not held by all men, nor is a feminine, developmental orientation held by all women. Masculine and feminine might be better understood in the Jungian sense, as parts of us all.

The two reviews of my chapter may speak more to the appropriateness of one or the other orientation for children at different ages. For adults, or children nearing adulthood, the productivity view does seem to make sense. For preschoolers and elementary-aged children, a developmental perspective appears more appropriate. Dr. Borland, working with a preschool population, might be more inclined toward a developmental view, whereas Dr. Fox, having worked closely with junior and senior high school students, might see more of the benefits of the other perspective. I am not opposed to the marriage of these views; I simply want to see the extraordinary abilities shown by young children acknowledged as meaningful. Only by counting these early performances as evidences of giftedness can we hope to reclaim the talents of females, underachievers, and gifted-handicapped children.

References

Feldman, D.H. (1984). A follow-up of subjects scoring above 180 IQ in Terman's, "Genetic Studies of Genius." *Exceptional Children, 50,* 518–523.

Hollingworth, L.S. (1926). *Gifted children: Their nature and nurture.* New York: Macmillan.

Sattler, J.M. (1982). *Assessment of children's intelligence and special abilities* (2nd ed.). Boston: Allyn & Bacon.

Stanley, J.C. (1976). Use of tests to discover talent. In D.P. Keating (Ed.), *Intellectual talent: Research and development* (pp. 3–22). Baltimore: The Johns Hopkins University Press.

II

Qualitatively Different:

is it a key concept in developing curricula?

Sandra Kaplan, in her lead article, clarifies her concept of a differentiated curriculum for the gifted by contrasting its important elements with a description of what a differentiated curriculum should not be. She presents an interesting idea based on Popham and Baker's conception of curriculum as a relationship between means and ends. They suggest that one of two approaches could be taken to differentiate the curriculum for individual learners: (*i*) modify the objectives (ends) or (*ii*) modify the methods (means). Either or both these approaches could be used in defining the curriculum for the gifted, according to Kaplan. In light of the earlier discussion of "who is gifted," a perception of giftedness as adult productivity would seemingly necessitate a modification of the "ends," while the perception of giftedness as differences in learning traits would imply that a modification of "means" would be necessary. I would propose, however, that the most defensible practice would be first to modify both the means and the ends, to integrate as much of the regular curriculum as possible into this new curriculum (as part of the means), to strive for many of the same goals as are found in the regular program (e.g., develop skills to enable students to reach their potential), and to modify *individual performance expectations* within these general goals.

In his critique, Virgil Ward agrees with and highlights Kaplan's discussion of the need for a curriculum that is not only different but also appropriate for the gifted. He refers to certain "seminal thought" and "conceptual analyses" of the concept of a differentiated curriculum and then reminds us that these undergirding conceptual abstractions are needed, but lacking, in the field. Among the principles he proposes are these: (*i*) the scope of the content should extend into the general nature of the chief branches of knowledge, and (*ii*) instruction "should be characterized by a pace and a level of complexity that are best suited to their broader capacities, and that their school achievement shall be evaluated in terms of objectives that are equally as advanced." Implementation of this last principle would necessitate, in Popham and Baker's schema, that both the "means" and the "ends" need to be modified for the gifted.

Chapter 11 focuses on current practices in the development of curricula and expands upon the idea that the curriculum for the gifted must be not only *different*, but also *appropriate*, an idea the reader has heard before from both Kaplan and Ward, and will hear later from Klausmeier and Van Tassel-Baska. The focus of Chapter 11 is on curricula for the development of thinking, through integration of significant or meaningful content with processes. An implicit assumption is that gifted learners have a greater capacity to develop thinking skills and that educators should employ teaching strategies that challenge and extend these abilities. The emphasis on concurrent development of understanding of key concepts and principles in the various disciplines suggests that gifted learners are also being prepared for careers as leaders, producers, and innovators. Certainly, I would not deny this suggestion, but the emphasis is on the differences in the learner now. Because the gifted learner is different now, he or she has the capacity to become an innovative producer or leader in the future, and the current curriculum must provide the tools to *enable* such learners to become outstanding in an area they choose.

Shirley Schiever demonstrates clearly that the ideas presented by Kaplan, Ward, and Maker can be translated into actual classroom practice and gives an example of how this can be done if a teacher plans in advance for integration of high-level content and process development. She also compares Maker's approach with that of Kaplan, showing many similarities in the ideas of the two authors.

What none of these authors chose to address, myself included (!), is a question that was posed to all in the outline of possible contents of this volume: To justify a curriculum for the gifted, must we be able to state that the curriculum would not be good for, or could not be used with nongifted students? Renzulli (1977), in his description of the Enrichment Triad as a defensible program for the gifted, implies that to defend our programs, we must be able to prove beyond a doubt that the curriculum provided in the special program is *uniquely* appropriate for the gifted. Two types of enrichment are suggested for use in the regular classroom because they cannot be defended as only good for the gifted, while the third type is advocated for the gifted program because it is not appropriate for all children. Silverman (in preparation) contrasts the requirement that gifted programs be uniquely appropriate with requirements for other special populations. In other special education programs, the provisions for a special population need only satisfy the requirement of being appropriate for those being served. Indeed, one could argue that most of the techniques used in special education represent good teaching that would benefit all children and that the need for special provisions for any exceptional population stems from the fact that certain individual needs of students are not being met in the regular classroom. In other words, children who are not placed in special education programs do not need these "special provisions" as much as do those who are placed in the special program. Further, even though certain techniques or approaches would be good for all children (including the handicapped and the gifted), the fact is that they are *not being used*. If such approaches are essential for the special population, but are not being employed in regular classrooms, the justification for their use can simply be this: (*i*) they are essential, (*ii*) they are appropriate, and (*iii*) they are not being used in the regular classroom. As certain practices become more prevalent in a regular classroom setting (e.g., results from the current emphasis on development of thinking skills and problem-solving abilities), educators of the gifted will have to develop other ways of differentiating the curriculum (we will be challenged!) and can concentrate on other needs of gifted students.

An additional issue related to the question of justifying a curriculum for the gifted based on its being uniquely appropriate is whether or not it is *possible* to implement a particular curricular approach or teaching technique in a regular classroom setting. It seems that many of the provisions advocated in this and the following sections would be impossible to implement effectively in many regular classroom settings. Furthermore, many more of these provisions could become the domain of the program for gifted students because they can be implemented more efficiently and effectively in a setting where gifted students are grouped together. Indeed, a major consideration in the development of abstract reasoning skills is providing a setting in which students interact in discussions of significant issues with a teacher who asks appropriate challenging questions with *other students at a similar intellectual level*. Clearly, such discussions could be held in a regular classroom setting *if* there are enough gifted students at a similar intellectual level, *if* the teacher is skilled in asking questions and stimulating thinking, and *if* the teacher is skilled in the use of classroom management techniques that enable him or her to plan and implement different strategies with different groups of students. However, such discussions can be planned and carried out more efficiently and perhaps also more effectively in a special setting. Another consideration is that students who are highly gifted are less likely to find "intellectual peers" in a regular classroom setting than are those who are closer to the norm.

In summary, I would propose that the most significant criterion to use in developing defensible curricula and programs for the gifted is appropriateness. Next in importance would be differentness, and last would be unique appropriateness.

In conclusion, let us return to the notion that we should justify the development and implementation of a qualitatively different curriculum on the basis of the argument that gifted learners are qualitatively different. If this justification is necessary, some would argue that we have none, since most research, as cited earlier, supports the conclusion that the differences are in magnitude or degree rather than in kind.

I would like to submit two thoughts for your consideration. First, most of the practices we advocate for gifted students represent differences of degree or magnitude rather than kind. For instance, *more* time is spent on "higher levels of thinking" and *less* time is spent on "lower levels of thinking"; research skills are taught *earlier*; material is presented at a *faster* rate; and ideas taught are *more* complex. These differences in magnitude are matched to the different needs and characteristics of the gifted students they are designed to serve.

The second thought to consider is that gifted learners as well as gifted adults *are* qualitatively different. If, as the research indicates, intellectually gifted children and youth progress through the stages of cognitive development at a more rapid rate than those who are not gifted, and if one accepts the argument that the thinking of children at differing stages of cognitive development is qualitatively different, then one must conclude that *the thinking of gifted students is qualitatively different from the thinking of their age mates who are not gifted*. A perhaps more convincing argument is that presented by Berliner in his discussion of catastrophe theory: *the gifted learner is qualitatively different because of the many differences in degree or magnitude*. The same justification applies to the curriculum. The differences in degree result in a difference in kind.

The reader is invited to explore these provocative ideas in depth through reading the chapters that follow, through pursuing the references cited by authors, and through discussions with colleagues. Most important, readers are admonished to *think* and *question*.

References

Renzulli, J.S. (1977). *The enrichment triad: A guide for developing defensible programs for the gifted and talented*. Wethersfield, CT: Creative Learning Press.

Silverman, L.S. (in preparation). *Gifted education: Providing for gifted and talented learners*. St. Louis, MO: C.V. Mosby.

8

Qualitatively Differentiated Curricula

Sandra N. Kaplan, Ph.D.
National/State Leadership Training
Institute on the Gifted and the Talented

The concept of differentiation is not particular to the gifted. Popham and Baker (1970) refer to differentiation as a "principle of great utility in planning instructional sequences for learners." These educators also state that "differentiation is far more easily preached than practiced." The translation of an accepted concept of differentiation into practice has been the focal point of discussions by educators who plan, implement, and evaluate learning experiences for the gifted, parents who have expectations for their gifted children's advancement through the educational system, and key decision makers such as school board members and legislators who authorize and/or support educational services for the gifted.

According to Passow (1981), the major issue in education of the gifted today is no longer whether or not a need for differentiated curricula for the gifted exists, but rather how to identify what constitutes such curricula. A review of the literature related to differentiated curricula for the gifted reveals that differentiation for the gifted is not well defined, and that it is ambiguous and value laden (Clasen, 1982; Gallagher, 1981; Maker, 1982). Clasen (1982) claimed that the term "differentiated curricula" has become a shibboleth for educational provisions for the gifted because of the lack of clarity and specificity necessary to define the meaning of the term.

The current status of the differentiated curriculum is described by many educators. Ward (1980, p. ix) termed the present curricular situation in education of the gifted as "a growing miscellany of practices that exist in the absence of a comprehensive theory" to determine the appropriate modifications needed to differentiate curricula for the gifted. During the evaluation studies he conducted, Renzulli (1977) observed curricula for the gifted consisting of "fun-and-games" activities, lacking continuity, and showing little evidence of developing the abilities that led to the identification of the students as gifted individuals. Some educators attribute the low motivation and failure on the part of many gifted students to realize their abilities to differentiated curricula that are defined inappropriately. Gallagher (1981) claimed that research concerning differentiated curriculum development is the necessary prerequisite to clarifying and extending the present "minimal level" of curriculum for the gifted.

Definitions of Differentiation

Perhaps one method that can be employed to give clarity to the meaning of differentiation for the gifted is to reference such definitions against a set of descriptors that identify what differentiation for these students *should not be*. Recognition of the should nots supports the importance of the shoulds that govern the dimensions of a differentiated curriculum for the gifted (Kaplan, 1981).

Differentiated curricula for the gifted *should not* be:

1. *Exploitative Curricula*—curricula that claim as a prime objective to be personally enhancing of the gifted students' abilities while really preparing and using their abilities for community and/or school gains in the forms of rewards and ribbons from contests, fairs, and so forth. This type of curriculum is usually a byproduct of an overzealous concern to provide for the gifted without ample knowledge about their needs.

2. *Popularized Curricula*—curricula that are currently fashionable, promoted, and/or generally accessible. In the eagerness of educators and parents to appropriately educate the gifted, they become susceptible to current ideas, trends, and materials labeled as new, original, or different curricula that are often acclaimed as "the answer" to the needs of the gifted.

3. *Left-Over Curricula*—curricula that provide the gifted with those learning experiences believed to be what other types of learners cannot or do not need or want to do. Left-over curricula could be described, for example, as chapters in a textbook that are not usually taught because they are perceived to be too difficult or of minimal value for other types of students.

4. *Mismatched Curricula*—curricula that are developed in accord with a preconceived ideal of the stereotypical gifted student without an awareness and analysis of the real functioning characteristics of these learners. Usually,

such curricula are developed with an esoteric and academic subject-matter orientation and are more concerned with what the students as gifted individuals could or should learn rather than what these students are receptive to and ready to learn. Such curricula are often constructed against the ideal rather than the real understanding of giftedness and can serve to disprove rather than enhance the students' giftedness. Academic rigor and pedantic curricula are not necessarily synonymous.

5. *Disjointed Curricula*—curricula presented as learning experiences that are independent of other learning experiences. These experiences lack a focal point or organizing element that cohesively binds them into a meaningful and articulated set of mutually reinforcing learnings. Curricula that are developed in this manner do not provide the necessary comprehensiveness and continuity for learning. Such curricula are often more apt to stimulate exposure to experiences rather than to provide for the proficiency of learnings by the students.

6. *Different Curricula*—curricula that are identified as being appropriate for the gifted because they are not provided for or available within the general curriculum or to any other student population. Exclusivity cannot be utilized to justify the curricular match between learners and the learning experiences offered to them. Under the guise of being different, a variety of unusual, oft-times interesting, learning opportunities have been defined for the gifted that are not necessarily relevant for them.

7. *Self-Developed Curricula*—curricula that expect the gifted students to define their own curriculum and instruct themselves. Such curricula are often founded on the faulty assumption that independence of thought, a common characteristic of giftedness, and independence of action are correlated. They are also predicated on the erroneous idea that self-initiated or self-directed study and independent study are similar. In some cases, this form of curriculum has exonerated teachers from their responsibility toward the gifted and placed undue responsibility on gifted learners to direct their own education without adequate teacher intervention.

8. *Flamboyant Curricula*—curricula that arouse public and professional interest and support but may be short-lived. This type of curriculum is frequently selected to combat the demands of parents, community members, and educators who require evidence that gifted students are being provided for within the educational setting. Curricula developed to validate provisions for the gifted are not necessarily valueless; however, they may be one-time learning opportunities that are disassociated with a comprehensive curriculum but are conceived as separate experiences in time. The degree of notoriety attributed to a learning experience is not usually commensurate with the appropriateness or the quality of this experience for the gifted.

Regardless of the difficulties involved in defining the differentiated curriculum for the gifted, many attempts have been made to do so (Maker, 1982). A variety of perspectives has been used to conceptualize the meaning of and to provide the data sources for differentiating the curricula for the gifted:

1. A *societal* definition of the differentiated curriculum refers to that curriculum which is responsive to the societal responsibilities gifted students are expected to assume by virtue of their superior endowments (Ward, 1980) and/or the contribution to society it is anticipated that they will make as a consequence of their identification and participation in a gifted program.

2. A *programmatic* definition of the differentiated curriculum is reflected in administrative patterns such as acceleration or enrichment (Stanley, 1979) or curricular construction procedures such as vertical or horizontal modifications of the regular curriculum (Passow, 1981).

3. The *discrepancy* definition of the differentiated curriculum is related to attempts to compensate for curricular deficits or gaps in curricula originally designed for the general, average, or non-gifted students.

4. The *model-specific* definition of the differentiated curriculum uses cognitive, developmental, or procedural models such as Guilford's Structure of the Intellect or Bloom's Taxonomy of Cognitive Objectives as the basis of formulating the curriculum (Passow, 1981).

5. The *trait-related* definition of the differentiated curriculum recognizes the unique inherent and performance needs, interests, and abilities of the gifted and tries to develop curricula to complement the differing characteristics that distinguish the gifted from the non-gifted (Clark, 1979; Renzulli, 1977).

6. The *instruction-related* orientation describes differentiation as modification in the variables or elements of the curriculum such as content, process, product, and/or environmental or instructional settings (Gallagher, 1975; Maker, 1982).

In reality, there is no single definition of differentiation. All definitions could recognize and include the many perspectives that describe differentiation. It appears that a multistaged definition inclusive of many perspectives would suffice to give substance and clarity to the concept of differentiation. Each of these stages represents a source from which to *define* and *refine* the concept of differentiation.

A Stage Definition of Differentiation

Stage I—Reflective

The reflective stage is founded on statements of philosophy, beliefs, and/or values descriptive of a variety of educational, economic, political, or social contexts.

Definitions of differentiation usually emerge from and are consistent with a contextual reference. The contextual reference could be economic, social, political, personal, and/or technical in nature. Regardless of the contextual reference, definitions of what constitutes a curriculum for the gifted cannot be considered apart from or without respect for the environment(s) in which the curriculum will be designed, implemented, and evaluated.

The influences that contextual references or environments exert on curricular definitions are illustrated in Table 8–1.

It is important to note that the contextual references are interactive. For example, the economic and political references are often related. It is also interesting to ponder the fact that the curricular implications from the contex-

Table 8–1 Contextual References and the Curriculum

Contextual Reference	Current Status	Examples of Implications for Curriculum for the Gifted
Economic	• Concern over low productivity index as compared with foreign countries such as Japan, Germany • Concern for the quality of work or output—"excellence"	• Emphasis on comprehending the role and consequences of productivity and its relationship to problem solving and creativity • Emphasis on output through the generation of knowledge (new ideas) and products • Introduction of criteria to assess the quality of production • Inclusion of theoretical and practical studies of technology • Inclusion of a global perspective in studies of the social sciences
Personal Social	• Concern for achievement—recognition and grades, awards • Concern for limited space in universities	• Inclusion of discussions about the relationships between cooperation and competition • Expectations for scholarliness as opposed to stressing only scholarship
Political	• Concern for the uniqueness of the individual as self-directed, autonomous	• Inclusion of more interest-based studies through independent investigations • Differentiating between the general versus specific educational needs of students

tual references may not result in new curricula, even though they all are rooted in contemporary issues. The inference drawn from this fact is that the dimensions and expectations of curricula for the gifted may not vary greatly over time; however, it is possible that contemporary issues simply alter what is predominant versus subordinate in the curriculum for these students at any point in time. Therefore, the relegation of curricular elements to particular positions of importance might change, the aggregate of curricular elements often remains the same.

Explanations of the contexts that define and direct the nature of curricula also have been described as four viewpoints or perceptions: humanistic, social reconstructionist, technological, and academic (McNeil, 1977). Each of these belief systems could be instrumental in giving meaning to the term "qualitatively different" as it applies to curricula for the gifted. As an example, *social reconstructionism* is the belief that the individual is schooled to fulfill social responsibility and to affect social reform. For the gifted, this conceptionalization of curriculum could be translated into a curriculum that has as its purpose to prepare the "natural resource of our society"—the gifted learner who benefits the society. The principle of *social parallelism*, the idea that curricula for the gifted should reflect the needs of the society (Ward, 1980), reinforces the social reconstructionistic viewpoint. This viewpoint is noted also in the infusion of problem-solving skills and futuristics into the curriculum for the gifted. An example of the *technologists'* view is seen in curriculum that utilizes modern technical devices for teaching and learning with students. Technologists also rely heavily on the use of models and systems for designing and producing curricula. In education of the gifted, the technologists' perception is evidenced through the use of a variety of models and systems to approach curricular decision making and construction.

Stage II—Generic

The generic stage refines the statements derived from contextual references in terms of broad ends and multiple means specific to the gifted but inclusive of aspects of the regular or basic curriculum for all students.

The curriculum can be viewed as a relationship between means and ends. Two strategies to differentiate curricula are (1) modifying the objectives or ends for different students and (2) proposing different activities or means for different students (Popham & Baker, 1970). Using these strategies, differentiated curricula could retain aspects of the basic, regular, or general curriculum as the means to pursue the new or more recognized ends or objectives for the gifted. Conversely, the fundamentals of the basic, general curriculum can be maintained as integral parts of differentiated ends while specifying appropriate means that fit the unique needs, interests, and abilities of the gifted to attain these ends.

The subjective nature of curriculum decision making and construction can result in slippage in the translation from general to specific statements of intent. To avoid this curricular pitfall, the translations of the statements emanating from the contextual references into ends and means statements should be benchmarked against a set of prevailing principles that govern differentiated curricula. These principles serve to validate the appropriateness and merit of the ends and means suggested by the contextual references. There are many sets of principles that can be used for this purpose. One such set of principles was proposed by the members of the Curriculum Council sponsored by the National/State Leadership Training Institute on the Gifted and the Talented. These are summarized by Passow (1982):

1. The content of curricula for the gifted/talented should focus on and be organized to include more elaborate, complex, and in-depth study of major ideas, problems, and themes that integrate knowledge within and across systems of thought.

2. Curricula for the gifted/talented should allow for the development and application of productive thinking skills to enable students to reconceptualize existing knowledge and/or generate new knowledge.

3. Curricula for the gifted/talented should enable them to explore constantly changing knowledge and information and develop the attitude that knowledge is worth pursuing in an open world.

4. Curricula for the gifted/talented should encourage exposure to, selection, and use of appropriate and specialized resources.

5. Curricula for the gifted/talented should promote self-initiated and self-directed learning and growth.

6. Curricula for the gifted/talented should provide for the development of self-understandings and the understanding of one's relationship to persons, societal institutions, nature, and culture.

7. Evaluations of curricula for the gifted/talented should be conducted in accordance with prior stated principles, stressing higher-level thinking skills, creativity, and excellence in performance and products.

Table 8–2 illustrates the translation from philosophical statements originating during the reflective stage into ends and means, which are subsequently validated against the principles of differentiation.

Stage III—Selective

The selective stage refines broad ends and means into specific learning experiences descriptive of the nature of the gifted within a particular popula-

Table 8–2 Validation of Differentiation

Contextual Referenced Statements of Philosophy, Beliefs, Values	Proposed Ends and Means	Validation (Principles of Differentiation)
Inclusion of an understanding about the relationship between cooperation and competition	*End:* To judge the positive and negative consequences of cooperation and/or competition for various political, scientific, and social advancements of modern society. *Means:* Students will research and/or interview individuals who have collaborated to accomplish some thing (i.e., Nobel Prize, Academy Awards recipients, etc.)	The content of curricula for the gifted/talented should focus and be organized to include more elaborate, complex, and in-depth study of major ideas, problems, and themes that integrate knowledge with and across systems of thought.

tion and articulates teaching and learning options to meet these specific learning experiences for individual students.

With an understanding of the gifted population in a given district or school as a guide, curriculum planners determine the precise meaning of the broad ends and means for their group of gifted students. The primary purpose of this stage is to ensure that the ends and means of the curriculum are modified to be responsive to the specific needs of the gifted group for whom the curriculum has been designed. This stage prevents a curriculum from being prescriptive and stresses the need for it to be adapted and/or modified.

It is within this facet of curricular differentiation that the personal interests, needs, and abilities of students are considered as the focus of teaching and learning. The interests of the gifted are assessed within the parameters of differentiation, which in turn is circumscribed by the statements of ends and means. It is from this larger frame of reference that personal adjustments in the curricula are made for specific individuals.

Table 8–3 depicts how broad ends and means can be modified for individual students.

Table 8–3 Modification of Ends and Means

Proposed Ends and Means	Diagnostic Evaluation of Student Population	Curricular Adaptation
End: To judge the positive and negative consequences of cooperation and/or competition for various political, scientific, and social advancements of modern society.	Sam—Interest in political science	Sam—Evaluate the effects of leaders who have collaborated to affect governmental changes.
	Ingrid—Very competitive and has difficulty working with peers; enjoys music	Ingrid—Participate in a Buddy Study concerning individuals who have collaborated to create musical compositions.

Appropriate Curricula

In defining and assessing curricula for the gifted two questions that need clarification seem to emerge:

1. Is the curriculum *differentiated* for the gifted?
2. Is the curriculum *appropriate* for the gifted?

It is possible that the curriculum could be differentiated and yet not be appropriate for gifted learners. Differentiation of the curriculum implies a general altering of the curriculum with regard to the collective descriptors of giftedness. Appropriateness of the curriculum implies an adaptive altering of the curriculum to the individualistic needs, interests, and abilities of each gifted member of the group.

A differentiated curriculum is *appropriate* for the gifted when it meets the conditions shown in Table 8–4.

One question often posed by educators relates to how many of the above criteria need to be met before a particular curriculum designed for gifted students can qualify as appropriately differentiated for them. Although this type of quantitative approach to validating curricula for the gifted seems simple to answer, the response to this inquiry is meaningless. The criteria in and of themselves do not validate the appropriateness of a curriculum for gifted students. Each of the criteria previously listed cannot be used independently of the principles of differentiation (Passow, 1982). Whereas the criteria determine the appropriateness of the curriculum, the principles of differentia-

Table 8–4 Curricular Appropriateness

Criteria	Rationale
It is directed by a philosophical point of view and/or theory of curriculum	A curriculum cannot be developed in a vacuum, nor can it be determined by whim or fancy as opposed to wisdom.
It adheres to the principles of continuity and sequence outlined for curricular designs (Tyler, 1950).	A curriculum is a set of learning experiences that is sequenced to attain specified objectives over time. Disregard for order assumes that readiness and/or prerequisite training are not important. Disregard for continuity ignores the need for multiple opportunities to attain mastery and to extend or elaborate comprehension and skill development.

The assumption that the gifted are readily able to learn anything at any time without developing their readiness to do so is fallacious. Scoping and sequencing are vital to appropriate curricula. |
It provides for vertical and horizontal experiences without overemphasizing one type of curricular option over another.	While the issue of value between acceleration and enrichment as curricular adjustments to accommodate the needs of the gifted continue to be debated, an appropriate curriculum should provide for *both* these modes. Some gifted students will benefit from acceleration or moving through the curriculum more rapidly and others will gain greater knowledge and skills from enrichment or more of a breadth of experiences. Most gifted students will profit educationally from both types of experiences.
It integrates selectively the models and strategies that reinforce the attainment of specific objectives without compulsive or blind allegiance to one model or strategy over another.	Curriculum development can be guided by a variety of models and strategies. Curriculum development can also be *dominated* by a variety of models or strategies. The abdication of the curricular decision-making process to a model or strategy and the overdependence of the curriculum planner on a model or strategy has resulted in some curricula that represent an organized set of learning experiences focused on a particular component of curricula, such as processes, rather than a comprehensive curriculum inclusive of *all* the elements of content, process, product, and affect.
It necessitates that the teacher adapt, modify, and alter the curriculum to make it responsive to the gifted population and does not anticipate that the teacher will follow the curriculum in a lock-step manner.	A constructed curriculum is not intended to be prescriptive. Constructed curriculum refers to that curriculum that has been planned. Such a plan outlines the intent and direction of the curriculum, with the expectation that the plan is a *guide* for teaching and learning.

Table 8–4 continued

Criteria	Rationale
It accommodates the range of learning and teaching styles represented by students and teachers.	A curriculum should complement the variances in teaching and learning styles that identify the uniqueness of the individuals who participate in the teaching/learning processes. To that end, a curriculum should include teacher- *and* student-directed learning experiences, the options to learn through different modalities, a variety of resources, etc.
It provides for basic instructional variables such as motivation, reinforcement, transfer, appropriate practice, and feedback.	A curriculum that is developed for nongifted learners most often attends to all the instructional variables. Sometimes when a curriculum is developed for the gifted, these very same variables are ignored. It is assumed that the gifted are already motivated, need little or no practice opportunities, and are secure in the knowledge of their abilities so they have no need for feedback. Good instruction is not reserved for students who are not gifted.
It communicates the objectives and learning experiences in clear, precise, and concrete terms.	A curriculum should be expressed in language that articulates what is to be taught so that teacher accountability and student mastery are reinforced. A curriculum that is written in global nomenclature may be misinterpreted and/or ignored. As an example, references in a curriculum to "the development of higher-level thinking skills" were changed to define specifically which skills of critical thinking, creative thinking, problem solving, or logic were to be developed.
It recognizes and responds to the needs, interests, and abilities of each gifted learner who is a member of the total gifted group.	A curriculum that is differentiated must still be individualized or personalized. There cannot be a single differentiated curriculum that is appropriate for all gifted students. There can be an accepted common core of learning experiences from which individualizing can be initiated.

tion form the elements against which the criteria are applied. For example, one criterion to determine the appropriateness of curricula for the gifted states that curricula should be directed by a philosophical point of view and/or theory of curricula. The principles of differentiation support this criterion because they describe a curricular philosophical point of view or a theory. Another example of the way in which the principles defining differentiation and the criteria defining appropriateness work in tandem is seen in the relationship between the criterion explaining the need to accommodate the range of learning and teaching styles and the principle of differentiation that promotes the need for gifted students to engage in self-selected and self-initiated studies. The principles that define differentiated curricula for the gifted and the criterion that define the appropriateness of such curricula function to explain and/or reinforce each other. The nature of their relationship is founded on the concept that differentiation alone does not constitute appropriate curricula for the gifted.

Exhibit 8–1 is an excerpt from a curriculum developed for gifted students; it is presented to exemplify the integration of some of the principles defining differentiated curricula for the gifted with some of the criteria defining the appropriateness of such curricula for these students.

Defending Differentiation

Definitions of differentiation and the factors that determine the appropriateness of a differentiated curriculum both can be used to support the defen-

---

Exhibit 8–1 Principles and Criteria for Gifted Curricula

Learning Experience
Collect evidence to prove that artistic and personal style is an expression of beliefs and conditions.

Learning Activities	*Criterion*
—Introduce students to the methodology necessary to conduct historical research so that archival data can be used to investigate a self-selected change in artistic and personal styles.	Recognize and respond to needs, interests of students
—Develop skills to delimit a topic to investigate and outline the steps needed in studying a topic independently.	*Principle of differentiation* Establish criteria to evaluate the teaching/learning process. Develop criteria to evaluate progress and/or mastery of debating skills. Identify one's personal style. Develop self-understanding.
—Conduct large-group discussions related to the topic "Style: Individuality or Commercialism?"	*Criterion* Accommodate the range of learning and teacher styles.

sibility of a curriculum for the gifted. Knowledge and understanding of differentiation become the best sources to advocate a differentiated curriculum.

The curriculum is defensible for the gifted when it evidences the following:

1. A direct response to the nature of the real characteristics of the gifted and an attempt to develop, as well as to recognize, these traits
2. A relationship and balance between attending to the collective needs of all children and the specialized needs of the gifted
3. Substantive and valued learnings that are planned and articulated by design rather than happenstance.
4. Acknowledgment of prerequisite learnings, readiness for learning, and the cumulative effect of learning over time
5. A correlation to a philosophical and theoretical framework

Summary

Definitions of differentiated curricula are vulnerable to and dependent on the perspectives of educators, the availability of resources, and the administrative design of gifted programs. In many cases, an inappropriately differentiated curriculum for the gifted has been viewed as appropriately differentiated as a consequence of a lack of knowledge and/or poor educational consumerism.

Several factors appear to facilitate the decision-making processes which ultimately direct the definition and appropriateness of differentiated curricula:

1. Understanding of the elements that should and should not comprise a differentiated curriculum.
2. Comprehending the principles that define differentiation and serve as a foundation upon which curriculum for the gifted can be developed.
3. Applying the criteria that define appropriateness of curriculum for the gifted.
4. Translating the knowledge about the definitions of differentiation and appropriateness of curriculum for the gifted into classroom practices.

References

Barbe, W., & Renzulli, J.S. (1981). *Psychology and education of the gifted*. New York: Irvington Publishers.

Clark, B. (1979). *Growing up gifted*. Columbus, OH: Charles E. Merrill.

Clasen, D.R. (1982). *Qualitatively different programming for the gifted*. Madison, WI: University of Wisconsin-Madison Extension Course Outline.

Freehill, M.F. (1982). *Gifted children: their psychology and education*. Ventura, CA: Office of the Ventura County Superintendent of Schools.

Gallagher, J.J. (1975). *Teaching the gifted child* (2nd ed.). Boston: Allyn & Bacon.

Gallagher, J.J. (1981). An interview with . . . James J. Gallagher. *The Directive Teacher, 3*(2), 25–27.

Kaplan, S.N. (1981). The should nots and shoulds of developing appropriate curriculum for the gifted. In W.B. Barbe and J.S. Renzulli (Eds.), *Psychology and education of the gifted* (pp. 351–358). New York: Irvington Publishers.

Maker, C.J. (1982). *Curriculum development for the gifted*. Rockville, MD: Aspen Publishers, Inc.

Marland, S. (1972). *Education of the gifted and talented*. (Report to the sub-committee on education, (1977). Committee on Labor and Public Welfare, U.S. Senate). Washington, DC.

McNeil, J.D. (1977). *Curriculum—A comprehensive introduction*. Boston: Little, Brown.

Passow, A.H. (1981, August). *The four curricula of the gifted and talented: Toward a total learning environment*. Paper prepared for the Fourth World Conference on Gifted and Talented Children, Montreal, Quebec, Canada.

Passow, A.H. (1982). Differentiated curricula for the gifted/talented. In *Curricula for the Gifted*. (pp. 4–20). Ventura, CA: Office of the Ventura County Superintendent of Schools. National/State Leadership Training Institute on the Gifted/Talented.

Popham, J.W., & Baker, E.L. (1970). *Systematic instruction*. Englewood Cliffs, NJ: Prentice-Hall.

Renzulli, J.S. (1977). *The enrichment triad model: A guide for developing defensible programs for the gifted and talented*. Wethersfield, CT: Creative Learning Press.

Stanley, J.C. (1979). The study and facilitation of talent for mathematics for the gifted and talented—*The seventy-eighth yearbook of the National Society for Study of Education*. Chicago: University of Chicago Press, 169–185.

Tannenbaum, A. (1981). Pre-Sputnik to post-Watergate concern about the gifted. *Psychology and education of the gifted*. New York: Irvington Press.

Tyler, R. (1950). *Basic principles of curriculum and instruction*. Chicago: University of Chicago Press.

Ward, V. (1980). *Differential education for the gifted*. Ventura, CA: Office of Ventura County Superintendent of Schools.

9

Criterially Referenced Curricular Design:

a critique of "Qualitatively Differentiated Curricula"

Virgil S. Ward, Ph.D.
University of Virginia

Nature of the Critique

Apart from the problem of getting a firm grip upon the concept of giftedness itself, and the derivative educational necessities of identifying and placing qualified youth promisingly within the school organization, the problem of curriculum would appear to be the centralmost concern in the entire range of considerations making for Differential Education for the Gifted (DEG) (Ward, 1980). Of these two problems, the concept of giftedness on one hand, and on the other, the nature of the experience made possible for "gifted" populations, i.e., "qualitatively" differentiated instructional processes and content for learning—the literature of some two-thirds of a century on the first is voluminous, and yet still unsatisfactorily resolved; and that on the second consideration (curriculum), possibly the least satisfying, with the greatest distance yet to go toward a theoretically sound (i.e., criterially referenced) resolution.

Sandra Kaplan in the lead article to which this critique relates, has written on the subject of curriculum out of possibly as wide a background of experience and leadership as anyone in the contemporary scene. Working from a professional base with the National/State Leadership Training Institute on the Gifted and Talented, she with her Institute colleagues has given enormously influential conference lectures and training workshops in virtually every academic nook and cranny of this country since the mid-1970s. And her publications, couched in the contemporary style of thought that has characterized the gifted or talented education movement during this period, have been stimulating and helpful to thousands of teachers and program administrators across the land. The reader new to her work is assured of having her in typically good form in the chapter being reviewed; and it is trusted that this sample of her work will send all looking for more.

Under generously wide latitudes of the editor of this volume on defensible programs in the series planned on critical issues, the present reviewer of the Kaplan work immediately at hand will pursue the following approaches. First an acknowledgment helpful probably to the less experienced reader, of the positive qualities in the work will be offered. This is a kind of outsider's perspective which hopefully sheds positive light on thought which might not otherwise be recognized within the context of similar literature on curricular differentiation for positively exceptional persons. Second, the reviewer, true to his own established forms of thought over the years, under the main rubric of *Differential Education for the Gifted* (Ward, 1980), will venture certain critical commentary, of necessity bearing in part upon the work which the primary author has done, but rather as much or more, upon the thought of the entire group of us who have addressed the problem. This literature as a whole is still less than fruitful in terms of what *needs be*, and what really *could be*, given the existence of remarkably fertile advances in the arts and sciences which support the educative endeavor. Third and finally, the analyst, risking some immodesty in view of the importance of the subject, will highlight certain of his own work in the nature of criterial principles. These principles (formally set forth in the axiomatic style of propositions and corollaries), if rigorously interpreted, would appear to possess some at least of the directionality and the substantive discipline which have been needed, no less when first spelled out some three decades ago, than today.

Contributory Strength of the Lead Article

Kaplan offers to any reader, deeply experienced in the effort toward extraordinary education for extraordinary youth, or inexperienced, considerable gems of wisdom emanating almost incidentally from her own extensive immersion in the field. Three sections of the chapter stand out, however, as contributing more than what is found in the usual textbook or journal treatment, to the understanding of the critically important concept and process of curricular differentiation.

In the section, early on, where the six types of definitions, or sources for defining the qualitatively distinctive educational regimen, are presented, a compact and yet wide-ranging set of understandings is developed. Played against the preceding set of "negatives," or varieties of treatment which do *not* constitute the needed construction, this portion of the chapter deserves considerable study for anyone who wishes to look next with a critical eye at what is taking place within his or her own locale.

In the further section where Kaplan takes into account the thought of her close associates, she favors us as readers by citing a list of seven principles, previously published (National/State Leadership Training Institute on the Gifted and Talented, 1981). These principles are indeed clearly thought through, and as substantive material in re the present consideration, they constitute a very useful list of "guiding principles," not unlike the present critic's "axioms" (Ward, 1952) noted above, for the development of differentiated curricula.

Had Kaplan taken these very principles, those of her committee's or those of this critic's (to be explored in the closing section of this review), as a point of departure for her own inquiry toward a "qualitatively differentiated curriculum" much of her anguished travail over definitions and difficulties might have been foregone; and the liberty of her own imagination and reason, in consequence, might have been constructively employed toward the greatly needed objective of that firm and relatively enduring knowledge base (science, theory) which remains the centralmost obligation of the contemporary scholar in this field.

The reviewer is further impressed with the ensuing section in which Kaplan focuses (as the series editor suggested) upon the *appropriateness* factor of specific curricular constructions, acknowleding in course that not all content possible of identification is necessarily fitted to the logical requirement of relevance for the capabilities of the targeted groups. The dual columns, addressing in parallel fashion "criteria" (of appropriate material) and "rationale," provide in convenient list fashion important considerations of the problem in focus.

Taken together, these three portions of the chapter constitute thought of considerable value. However, those who, like the present commentator himself, expected basic clarifications among the subordinate issues and problems of the special curriculum, will find themselves invited to dig a bit more deeply still toward the necessary levels of analysis and resolutions which will then free up the practicing educator (teacher, curriculum specialist, researcher) to work more productively within a contextual framework that has the requisite, or *pre*requisite, ideational character.

Less Contributory Thought

But for the overriding need to arrive at some satisfying resolutions as to the central qualities of a fitting curricular structure for positively exceptional students, the reviewer could leave any kind of adverse reflections to the reader herself. It is disappointing, however, and may perhaps serve a useful function so to indicate, when a scholar of the main author's stature, lethargically engages in useless and confusing discourse. Again, delimited examples may suffice, both to caution the reader; and, contingent of course upon the perspicacity of the criticism, to chasten the author toward greater concentration as her influential work among educators continues.

General Ambiguity

None but the opening sections (introduction, background) are necessary to identify disappointing superficialities in reasoning and communicative ambiguities. To propose, for instance, that "the translation of an accepted concept of differentiation into practice" has been a pervasive focus among educators, is actually to state the situation in reverse; i.e., it is the *failure* to concentrate upon this *sine qua non* conceptual base, that has led to such inordinate superficiality, excess, and looseness in the curricular aspects of gifted education. To bemoan that progress toward defining and providing appropriately distinguishable curricula has been "quantitatively rather than qualitatively assessed" is simply to confuse the issue of what the desirable curricular quality *is*, with degrees to which this fit state is lacking. The desired hypothetical condition, when attained, will be very properly subject, of course, to quantitative estimation as are other educational "intangibles," in the hands of discerning specialists in measurement. And to cite from various other students of the problem (Clasen, et al.) as to diverse deficiencies in educational thought in re curricular activities for the gifted, with the loosely referenced pronoun "it" (literature? curriculum?) leaves this reader, at least, wondering whether it is the curricular deficiencies themselves or the thought attempting to dispel such which constitutes the problem. It lends little of sense toward clarifying the general confusion when we are invited through the citation of another prestigious figure (Gallagher) to look to the ubiquitous *research* process for clarifying ambiguities which are subject in the first place to conceptual analysis, the real missing component among the matrices of deficiencies.

Unacceptable Substantive Omissions and Distortions

Few writers who take the lead in offering thought on a given issue, can entirely escape the observation by their critics that they regrettably omitted this or that particular consideration. Beyond mere cavil, however, is Kaplan's failure to seize upon seminal thought on curricular issues and conceptual analyses of the focal problem of curricular differentiation that do exist in literature with which she should be familiar. Ausubel, Bruner, Hollingworth, Newland, and Tannenbaum are cases in point, none cited in her study.

A. Harry Passow, for instance, in a further section of the work cited above, has supplied a respectably discerning concept relating to the problem in focus, which if seized upon would have relieved Kaplan of writing in sing-song fashion of the difficulties of conceptualizing the specialized curriculum; and indeed of undertaking to discuss at the length she takes, what does and what does not qualify as *differential* in the comprehensive disarray of existing thought. Passow distinguishes among "four curricula for the gifted" as follows:

> . . . there is a specialized curriculum consisting of engagements which provide the individual with learning opportunities needed to nurture his/her particular talents. It is here that potential scientists, musicians, poets, humanitarians, and other gifted/talented individuals begin nurturing those skills, knowledges, insights, modes of thinking, and behaviors which will enable him/her (given the opportunity) to make outstanding contributions to society which, at the same time, are personally rewarding. This is what we usually think of as the differentiated curriculum, although differentiation takes place in the basic curriculum as well. (p. 35)

Nor does this passage, ostensibly in reference by Kaplan (though the reference lacks precision), sustain the interpretation given, i.e., that it implies "model specific" curricula, a la, for instance, Guilford, Terman, or Williams, which are in frequent use these days.

This distortion of meaning is accompanied by another, in regard to this reviewer's own work, namely the citation of Ward (Ward, 1980, p. 83) in support of the principle of "social parallelism," without inclusion of the most significant meaning of the concept as involving *not* the immediate *social needs* of the parent society, but rather, if needs be, values in *contradiction* to the existing normative predilections, such that (with Dewey) change can be made synonymous with progress.

Incorrect Perception of Scientific Thought

Where the principal author submits under the rubric of "mismatched curriculum" along with some negatively flavored adjectives (esoteric, pedantic, preconceived) that an ideal stereotype of giftedness constitutes an unworthy basis for the construction of special curricula, in contrast to a "real understanding" of giftedness, she (or any other writer) should return to her textbooks to recover an irresponsible remission in understanding of the nature of scientific thought and process. It was precisely for the purpose of developing a "factual prolegomenon" to education that Lewis M. Terman, a leading American psychological scientist for some 50 or 60 years, set out upon his *Genetic Studies of Genius* (1925 to date) and had produced by 1947 a "composite portrait" of the hypothetical gifted individual in mid-life. By analogy, though water to the chemist is ineluctably compounded of two parts hydrogen and one oxygen, an *ideal stereotype* indeed in that few of us have ever drunk such pure stuff and in that our bodies might have difficulty in accommodating it if we did, chemical science is predicated upon this elemental understanding, and would be plunged into chaos if it did not.

Both scientists and philosophers, as their thought is concisely and exactingly recorded in dictionaries and encyclopedias, strive to get at the pure or ideal state in nature, and at the most abstract, essential, and enduring constructs relating to the social order, knowing in each case, but not being deterred by the fact, that the observed condition usually deviates; and counting upon technologist and consumer alike to accommodate to the "unrealities" of actual conditions.

Hopeful, however, that this reluctant recital of weaknesses in Kaplan's otherwise useful thought will not suggest to the astute reader a general distrust of her writing, for this is unnecessary and would be unfortunate, it lends perspective to set these deficiencies into the class or genre of intellectually shoddy work that has gushed forth in a decade (1970s) of historically unprecedented "awareness" activity and outreach that has endangered the stabler foundations of the field through sheer mass of numbers. Eager novitiates and instant experts have thrust themselves precipitously into the action to the detriment of what might otherwise have been disciplined advance in this socially important field of professional responsibility. Renzulli, for instance, a scholar and leader of note, is cited by Kaplan as deploring a "fun and games" mentality; and Ward, along with a few others (Martinson, Newland) has over the years regretted that the field at large (DEG) has never risen to its level of importance in the affairs of humankind, or to the inherent experiential potentialities of the extraordinary educand.

Theoretically Disciplined Curricula

What is needed in this entire area of social and professional obligation (DEG) are undergirding conceptual abstractions, preferably a *set* thereof for compass, consistency, and proportion, which are mainly warranted by responsible analysis and inference, playing upon significant inquiry both in the nature of research (conceptual, empirical) and progenital thought (Binet, Dewey, Mead, Toynbee) from the past, and inside and outside the problem field itself. For practical purposes in the quest for such tested and testable foundations, nice distinctions may be bypassed as to which understandings constitute *science* (summary observations supported by empirical investigation), and which *theory* (purposive observations embodying both scientific and philosophic thought)—for this intellectually underdeveloped educational arena, ironically, has altogether little of either.

But both the necessary knowledge for such an essential set of constructs, and certain reasonably firm elements which can be incorporated into it, appear to be available, and to have been available for some time; and even isolated attempts to work out in rudimentary form an essential science and/or theory are embedded in the literature for examination by serious students, researchers, and practitioners.

Given the virtually indisputable presupposition that a subpopulation, distinguishable from the general mass of youth in today's schools, exists and is reliably identifiable through the present technologies of the psychological and social sciences; and given further the essentially undeniable proposition that *general intelligence*, apart from *specific aptitudes* (in technical terms, the "*g*" factor as distinct from multiple "*s*" factors), exists and constitutes a reasoned basis for the construction of appropriately differentiated educational experience (DEG) for the main body of gifted students, the present reviewer's own efforts toward the intellectualization of reliable information at hand as early as mid-century (early 1950s) would appear to be suggestive, then and equally so now—suggestive, that is, as to the feasibility of constructing a requisite body of thought which in form and substance constitutes both a promising point of departure for further inquiry toward the advancement of a science of DEG, and as a "head start" predicate for sound and enduring practical action. A few examples must suffice for the present occasion, thus

> That administrative adaptations of the regular school program, though perhaps incidental to the accomplishment of a largely unique program, must not constitute the uniqueness in themselves. (Ward, 1980, p. 90)

The preemptive force of this injunction, in the void of attention given to it, can be perceived through the frequency with which "acceleration," "grouping," and "enrichment," all within the established school organization, are subscribed to; with a corresponding failure to conceptualize beyond organizational form toward the teaching and learning acts which constitute a disciplined differentiation as such.

> That the instruction of the gifted should be characterized by a pace and a level of complexity which are best suited to their broader capacities, and that their school achievement shall be evaluated in terms of objectives that are equally as advanced. (Ward, 1980, p. 129)

Textual elaborations of this principle speak as clearly today as in the early 1950s of what this proposition requires by way of curriculum, e.g.

> . . . beyond the "why's" and the "how's" lie the "for what purposes" and the "to what consequences" types of thinking which lead toward the theoretical and philosophical frameworks under which the examined disciplines are subsumed.

> The poor quality in logic, the awkwardnesses in style, which might include the very usages which the serious and able student is trying to eliminate from his own writing, and the unimaginative and unsystematic quality of the development of ideas—all such concomitants to the presentation of subject matter pertain to qualitative levels of instruction.

> That in the education of the gifted child and youth the scope of the content should extend into the general nature of all the chief branches of knowledge. (Ward, 1980, p. 144)

Thus, it may be added briefly, the door is opened to direct instruction in transcendent knowledge groups—"great ideas" of the Western and Eastern Worlds; library classifications of knowledge (Bliss, Dewey, Library of Congress); and epistemological systems (Morse, Phenix), in addition to the conventionally designated school subjects scattered about in their present uneven, fragmented, and concrete nature.

Confusions begin on technical grounds, and sheer chaos evolves in the arena of practicing education, when the altogether justifiable search is begun for specific aptitudes which exist, and which stand in whatever relationship to the central core of intelligence. The manifest efforts to clarify these confusions which are embedded in the literature bearing upon the nature of human aptitudes and their potential for experiential development through formal (school, church) and informal sociocultural processes (home, community), remain as yet but inconclusively drawn for the purposes of education. It remains especially regrettable that, given the brilliant recent advances in the life sciences and in the social, that efforts to arrive at relatively reliable resolutions from these supporting sciences for the purposes of constructive developmental intervention in the futures of children remain today not a great deal further advanced than they were a quarter of a century ago.

Meanwhile, school personnel who must, willy-nilly, take action would appear to be at their accountable best as they attempt to build programs and curricula if they do so in terms of the more reliable and time-tested understand-ings—"g" factor; Q and V aptitude, interest and achievement patterns; and if they practice with corresponding caution to engage but sparingly in belief and action following (more or less blindly) upon the ubiquitous proliferation of prescriptive "guidelines," and upon the loose and suspect uncertainties herald-ing in various guises as "talents" apart from "giftedness," "learning styles," "individualized educational plans," and a host of other hastily concocted "models" and "systems" offered indiscriminantly through a burgeoning mass of publishing presses and journal outlets.

Summary Observations

Given these comments by way of both positive appraisals of Kaplan's chapter and, as was felt warrantable, candid notes as to deficiencies in this particular piece among thought customarily more than ordinarily worthwhile, certain concluding observations may now be offered, these relating to the field of DEG in general, including the curricular issue, as the problem areas have evolved, and in this critic's view, deteriorated especially during the decade of the 1970s in which political expediency appears to have taken the reins from scientific and professional integrity. Three such general observations are sub-mitted in the interest of proper and productive linkages between defensible theory and defensible practice, both of which are essential to fruitful advances in the knowledge base (science), and toward authentic forms of instruction and guidance which are in parallel phase with the experiential potentialities with which positively exceptional youth are biopsychologically endowed.

Observation 1: That contemporary thought in the field of DEG has deviated to considerable extents and in numerous ways from the purposes and the intellectual foundations upon which the gifted child movement in America was founded, to the end that the current scene (early 1980s) is in a state of degeneration and disarray characterized in substantial proportion by excessive numbers, excessive spontaneity, excessive and senseless diversity; that within this ill-begotten condition beginning students are victimized by a plethora of weakly founded, internally inconsistent, and loosely framed "approaches," "models," "plans," and "programs" all too often aggressively promoted through shameless devices, not of communication but of emotional contagion (concocted language, media, ritual, song); and that unless and until scholars and practicing educators alike—teachers, curriculum developers, program evaluators, researchers, teachers of teachers—assume responsibility and take necessary actions to restore the "common sense" (Abraham) and professional integrity (intent, logic, substance) which gave rise to the movement, continuing degeneration can but further entail: (*i*) the deprivation of qualified and intellectually underdeveloped youth of developmental experience which is their due; (*ii*) the increasing failure of programs because of unconvincing distinctions between what all children can accommodate and deserve by way of general education, and those subtleties and complexities of knowledge and cognition of which but few are functionally capable; (*iii*) the stagnation of the science (knowledge base); and in the end, as can be noted even now, the endangerment of the entire concept of DEG, rendered vulnerable, however unjustifiably, by default to vigorous and astute ideological dissent (elitist, undemocratic) and denial.

Observation 2: That historically the literature of DEG, beginning in America with the pioneer work of Terman (scientific prolegomenon) and Hollingworth (educational initiatives in New York), and continuing through the formative years of the 1930s and 1940s and into the 1950s and 1960s—in the work of people such as Hildreth, Laycock, Newland, Strang, O'Shea, Seagoe, Norris, Pregler, and Witty—has been reasonably consistent as to the logical and empirical predicates for the extraordinary education of extraordinary youth; and further that recent advances in supporting sciences such as human biology and developmental psychology, have made possible genuine and essential extensions of our earlier understandings as to the nature of individual differences; such that the contemporary student and the serious-minded practitioner do in fact have recourse to understandings requisite to a criterially meritorious accomplishment of this task.

Observation 3: That given the paucity of direct and explicit initiatives in the nature of theory in DEG—here taken to mean no more than an essentially stable body of descriptive and explanatory abstractions (constructs, resolved issues, principles, informed hypotheses) which subsume the particulars of past experience (observation, inquiry, analysis) and thereby constitute an advantageous basis for purposive planning and action in the present and future—the early conceptualizations of the present critic (see Ward, 1980, and the illustrative propositions above from this main work) appear, despite want of update in given substantive detail, to constitute in rudimentary but exemplary form the kinds of ideational sets which are desirable as an economy for study at the point of entry for students, teachers, and researchers, in the interest of a head start toward truly contributory inquiry and practice in this inordinately consequential field of democratic social obligation and professional challenge. To this observation the writer, having elsewhere identified efforts of this kind toward the deliberate construction of science and theory to be an obligation of high priority in each succeeding generation (decade) of scholarship, it can be happily added that even within the generally dissolute condition of affairs in this arena today, there is evidence (selective current publications, intriguing projects, an upturn in the quality of organizational leadership) that any number of current scholars and leaders, given the disposition, could individually and collectively contribute ably to this dire need.

References

National/State Leadership Training Institute on the Gifted and Talented (1981). *Curricula for the gifted*. Ventura, CA: Ventura County Superintendent of Schools.

Terman, L.M. (1925). *Mental and physical traits of a thousand gifted children*. Vol. 1, Genetic studies of genius. Stanford, CA: Stanford Univ. Press.

Ward, V.S. (1980). *Differential education for the gifted*. Ventura, CA: Ventura County Superintendent of Schools.

10

Response to the Review

Sandra N. Kaplan

Since the nature of writing, reading, and responding are subjective, it seems futile to engage in defensive discourse to attempt to prove or disprove another's perceptions as right or wrong. The task of further explaining what has been written seems to be a more worthy expenditure of effort. Thus, the following discourse will serve to explain rather than defend the ideas presented in the chapter.

The major purpose of the chapter was to provide educators of the gifted with alternative perspectives about differentiated curriculum. As a consequence of reading the chapter, it was intended that the reader would be able to:

1. Comprehend the range of concerns confronting curriculum planners involved in selecting, constructing, or implementing differentiated curriculum for the gifted (Section: Background)
2. Recognize the various ways by which differentiated curriculum is defined (Section: Definitions of Differentiation)
3. Recognize an approach to use in the process of defining and refining differentiated curriculum (Section: A Stage Definition of Differentiation)
4. Identify criteria to be applied to select, construct, or evaluate appropriate differentiated curricula for the gifted (Section: Appropriate Curricula)

The intended reader for this chapter is the educational consumer—the individual who is charged with the responsibility to determine suitable differentiated curricula for the gifted from the literature and presentations describing such curricula. The plight of the educational consumer is no different from that of any other consumer. As the area of gifted education expands, it makes available more alternatives from which to select definitions of appropriate curricula for the gifted and the actual samples of such curricula. Consumerism necessitates a means by which to discriminate from available alternatives. Concerns, definitions, and criteria related to differentiated curricula for the gifted have been offered to the reader as indicators to facilitate the process of decision making. Thus, the chapter was written to guide educational consumers in their search for meanings and examples of appropriately differentiated curricula for the gifted.

An analysis of any consumer report or digest reveals that the purpose for these documents is to assess the qualities of products that have been produced, not to produce new products. The purpose of the material in Chapter 8 was to clarify the state of the art with reference to differentiated curriculum; it was not to propose a new theory of differentiation. Ward's comments about anguish over definitions and superficial analysis of theory might be warranted if the goal of this chapter were to create a theory of differentiated curricula. This was not the case. The goal was to prepare readers (educational consumers) to sift through existing theory—a task that cannot be performed without prerequisite understandings of concerns, criteria, and definitions related to differentiated curriculum.

Ward reminded us that he had developed a theoretical framework for differentiated curriculum in the 1950s. Theories of curricula for the gifted written by such august educators as Ward have formed the foundation for the work of others. Still, such theories have not had as much impact as they should have. Perhaps one reason for their lack of impact can be traced to the insufficient data and inadequate readiness on the part of educational consumers to discern substantial theory affecting differentiated curriculum for the gifted from the plethora of superficial descriptors, ideas, and quasi-theories about differentiating curriculum for the gifted. Without adequate guides for decision making, the educational consumer is susceptible and vulnerable to a variety of options less appropriate for the gifted than those professed by experts. Chapter 8 proposes such guidelines.

It would be most difficult for an educator of the gifted, such as this author, who advocates critical thinking for gifted children to resent the critical thoughts of a gifted individual such as the reviewer. Too often there is a discrepancy between what educators state they believe and what they are willing to have practiced. The critical thoughts with which I, as the author, am *most concerned* are those of the reader. As a consequence of reading the chapter, it is anticipated that the reader will be able to assess more critically the qualities of an appropriately differentiated curriculum for the gifted. The merit of the chapter will ultimately be decided through the critical thinking process educational consumers apply to selecting, designing, and implementing curricula for the gifted. The ultimate test of the worth of this chapter will be in the ability of educational consumers to respond to these questions:

1. What are the concerns to be considered in defining, selecting, or constructing differentiated curriculum for the gifted?
2. What definition best accommodates the construction and/or selection of differentiated curriculum for the gifted?
3. What criteria can be applied to assess definitions and/or curricula developed for the gifted?

11

Integrating Content and Process in the Teaching of Gifted Students

C. June Maker, Ph.D.
University of Arizona

O ne of the phrases heard most often from teachers and other educators of the gifted is "I teach the children *how* to think, not *what* to think!" The individual will continue with an explanation of the importance of process and the lack of importance of content, lamenting the fact that other educators are only concerned with how much children learn about math, science, social studies, language arts, and other disciplines.

Certainly, the process is important, and it is important that children, especially those who are gifted, learn how to think as a result of their school experience. The development of high levels of reasoning has been neglected in many of our schools. One example of such neglect is the finding that only 30 percent of entering freshmen at one university in the Southwest can reason at the formal operational level (Lee, 1976). Other studies have consistently shown that only between 30 and 50 percent of late adolescents succeed at formal operational tasks (Kohlberg & Gilligan, 1971). Piaget (Piaget & Inhelder, 1969) suggested that children usually achieve this level of cognitive development between the ages of 11 and 13. Researchers have repeatedly found that even though children cannot grasp a concept from a higher stage of development if they are not yet at that level (Kohlberg & Mayer, 1978), educators can arrange an environment that will facilitate cognitive growth so that students achieve the levels they are capable of achieving (Blatt, 1969; Rest, 1974; Sullivan, 1975; Taba, 1964, 1966; Ashton, 1978). Positive change, or cognitive growth, occurs through *active* interactions with the environment. Children need opportunities to construct their own reality, organize the information they encounter, and draw their own conclusions. Gifted students need to use their advanced levels of reasoning, receive feedback and critiques from the teacher, and then improve their reasoning. The teaching techniques that develop thinking skills and aid the children in their progression from one level or stage of cognitive development to the next are generally those labeled "process" or "how to think" activities.

Although the process is important, and should continue to be emphasized, educators of the gifted have often placed so much emphasis on process that they have neglected the development of ideas/conclusions in the academic disciplines and the teaching of important concepts necessary as a foundation for further learning and creativity. One of the most extreme examples of this neglect is a program in the Southwest in which students are selected for a gifted program because of their high achievement in science. They are pulled out of the science class and placed in a class where they learn how to play chess. As one might expect, they often remain in the program for only a year because at the end of the year, they no longer qualify for the program. Their learning in the subject that initially qualified them for the program was neglected. Even though this is an extreme example, numerous similar instances could be cited in which the gifted program is criticized heavily because the children spend all their time playing thinking games, doing logic exercises, and doing creative thinking exercises that have seemingly no relationship to the learning of academic concepts. As Jim Gallagher has often stated, "gifted children need something to think *about!*"

The teaching of processes, or how to think, must be combined with the teaching of important ideas and information. Even Parnes (1966; 1967), who is known for his Creative Problem Solving Process, emphasized the importance of an information base in the development of creative products. He explains that creative behavior is a function of knowledge, imagination, and evaluation and that sophisticated, creative products are seldom, if ever, developed by those who have not achieved a high level of understanding of the area in which they are working.

When dealing with the gifted, or when attempting to develop higher levels of thinking, not just "any old content" will do. The content that forms the basis of the teaching process must be as rich and as significant as possible. Taba (1962) suggests that thinking skills can be taught through any subject matter, but that it is impossible to separate content from process. The "richness" and the significance of the content with which children work will affect the quality of their thinking as will the processes used. Taba further suggests that there are certain "thought systems" in each discipline and that these systems contain both content and process. The examination of thought systems in the various disciplines would be an important activity both for teachers in the development of teaching strategies and for students as a part of the learning process.

Requirements for Content

Maker (1982a) has established certain requirements that must be met by content that becomes a part of the curriculum for gifted students: a focus on abstract ideas and concepts, complexity of ideas and concepts, and an organization of facts and information around key concepts or ideas that facilitates economy in the learning process. With regard to the actual categories of content, she suggests a systematic sampling of major branches of knowledge in addition to the study of creative, productive people and the methods of inquiry used in the various branches of knowledge studied.

When developing the content to include in a curriculum for gifted students, it is essential that content experts be involved in reviewing and commenting on the significance, usefulness, and validity of the ideas to be taught. Teachers who must be familiar with many different disciplines cannot be experts in every area they teach, so the advice and assistance of such experts is necessary. Bruner (1960) suggests two criteria for use in making decisions about the inclusion of content: (1) when fully developed, is the concept worth being known by an adult? and (2) having known it as a child, does a person become a better adult? If the answer to either of these questions is negative or ambiguous, the material is "cluttering" the curriculum.

The following are some examples of key ideas that have been reviewed by experts and included in curriculums for the gifted:

- Language Arts
  Humans use language for a variety of purposes, including the following: to entertain, to persuade, to inform, to celebrate, to judge, and to solve problems.
- Science
  Patterns of regularity exist in our physical and living environments. Discovering, measuring, describing, and classifying these patterns is the business of science.
- Social Studies
  Science and technology are accelerating the rate of change in the world, not only generating data about the earth and human existence, but also providing an expanded range of choices available to human beings in lifestyle, ethics, medicine, environmental modifications, conflict resolu-

tion, nutrition, etc. Whether these choices will be made in the best interests of humanity depends on the ability of individuals and institutions to foresee their ramifications.

- Mathematics
  The use of mathematics is interrelated with all computation activities. Everyday situations can be translated into mathematical expressions, solved with mathematics, and the results can be interpreted in light of the initial situation.

Requirements for Process

The processes used in programs for the gifted must also meet certain requirements (Maker, 1982a). They must

- emphasize higher levels of thinking (i.e., the use rather than acquisition of information)
- be open-ended, both in the design of the activities and in the attitudes of the teacher implementing them
- develop inductive reasoning processes through discovery whenever possible
- require students to explain their reasoning as well as provide their conclusions
- permit students to choose topics to study and methods to use to the extent that students are self-directed in their learning
- encourage and permit interaction in group situations
- be paced rapidly so that students do not become bored

To maintain interest and develop a variety of thinking skills, teachers should also employ a variety of methods, including discussions, lectures, learning centers, simulations, field trips, committee work, and projects.

In the development of process plans for a curriculum for gifted students, a variety of models is available. Certain models are more appropriate than others for use in programs for the gifted because they meet many or most of the process requirements listed above (Maker, 1982b) and because they are adaptable to and compatible with each other and with the goals of programs for the gifted. These approaches include those developed by Bloom (1956), Krathwohl (Krathwohl, Bloom, & Masia, 1964), Bruner (1960), Guilford (1967; 1972), Kohlberg (1966), Parnes (1977), Renzulli (1977), Stevenson et al. (1971), Taba (Institute for Staff Development, 1971a, b, c, d), Taylor

(1968), Treffinger (1975), and Williams (1970). Other models also exist, but are less well-known and since they are not used quite as frequently [e.g., Conceptual Blockbusting (Adams, 1976), The Purdue Three-Stage Model (Kolloff & Feldhusen, 1981; Flack & Feldhusen, 1983)] there is not much information available on their effectiveness or adaptability.

The use of one particular model as a basis for the development of processes, although common, is not necessary, and is usually not desirable since no one model meets all the process requirements for programs for the gifted. The different approaches have different strengths and weaknesses, which are directly related to their purposes and reasons for development. The most effective process plans will combine several models to achieve the desired result. Use of models is strongly encouraged, rather than a "hit-or-miss" approach because models have been tested, refined, and constructed as ways to systematically and appropriately develop certain thinking skills in children. An entirely eclectic or a random approach does not have the background of research and development that can suggest its potential for success in achieving program goals related to the development of abstract reasoning skills or "how to think" in gifted students (Maker, 1982b).

In a discussion of ways to implement Taylor's (1968) multiple talent approach, Maker (1982b) gives an example in which Taylor's category of forecasting is combined with Taba's (Institute for Staff Development, 1971c) questioning strategy for application of generalizations.

> In the next activity, students are asked to extend their thinking about the present activity and to predict what might happen in a new situation based on what happened in the previous experiment: "Suppose that the volcano continues to erupt at least twice a month with about the same force as in the past. What do you think the health of the local residents will be like in five years?" After allowing the students to think for a few minutes, the teacher should ask the following questions in the order listed:
>
> Step 1. What do you think might happen to the local residents? (List all predictions, only stopping the flow to seek clarification of unclear ideas.)
>
> Step 2. Why do you think this might happen (that is, what were some of the results of your experiment that led you to believe that might happen)? (Ask for reasons for all predictions.)
>
> Step 3. What other conditions would be necessary, both before and during this time, to make this prediction come true? Why would that be necessary? (Ask for conditions and reasons for as many of the predictions as possible.)

Step 4. Suppose all the conditions you listed as necessary did happen and this prediction (select a few medium-range predictions from the list) did come true. What would happen then? (Follow the same procedures as in number three with each of the new predictions.)

Step 5. Based on this discussion and what you already know, what would you conclude would be most likely to happen to the health of the local residents in five years? How did you reach this conclusion? Why did you conclude that would be the most likely result?

During this discussion, the teacher should be an active listener, noticing the types of conditions and consequences listed by students. He or she should make certain the students consider the human element (social awareness), patterns or chains of cause-effect relationships (conceptual foresight), and possible changes that might occur that would affect the predictions (penetration).

The Taylor and Taba strategies are combined because Taylor's model presents some very good guidelines for identifying particular kinds of talent, such as forecasting, but does not provide methods for teaching questioning and a questioning sequence that has been validated as a successful way of developing abstract reasoning skills pertaining to the ability to make predictions. Essentially, the Taylor model provides the overall focus for the activity, but Taba's strategy provides the specific questions.

Meaning*less* Content versus Meaning*ful* Content

As one might expect logically, it is possible to separate content from process, but it is not possible to entirely separate process from content. If one examines the two examples given in this paper, the meaning of the above statement can become clear. The examples of content do not suggest or denote any particular kind of process to be used. However, the example of process did suggest a particular type of content. The students were asked to predict what would happen to the health of local residents if a volcano continues to erupt. The content is essentially "environmental conditions can have a strong impact on the health of humans," or, at a more abstract level, "all living organisms interact with their environment, and these interactions determine change in the organism."

Even though process activities must of necessity contain some reference to content, it is possible to design interesting, enjoyable process activities with meaningless content, and herein lies the major criticism faced by many programs for the gifted in the past. *The content of many process activities did not possess the richness, significance, and organization, or sequencing that was necessary to develop an understanding of academic disciplines while enhancing thinking skills.* Many times I have tried to defend the familiar activity to develop and test creative thinking, "What are all the uses you can think of for a tin can?"

Let me hasten to add that I believe in the usefulness of such activities. They can be very valuable as warm-up exercises to "get the creative juices flowing" and develop or measure divergent thinking without penalizing individuals because of their lack of information about a particular topic. However, such activities should not form the basis of a program for the gifted, nor should they constitute a majority of the activities in a classroom for gifted students. We should instead be designing activities that will serve the *dual* purpose of developing divergent thinking and other thinking skills and developing an understanding of major ideas and theories in the chief branch of knowledge. Following are some examples of teaching activities using meaningless content followed by the same process used with content that meets the requirements for appropriate content for the gifted.

Example 1

Our first example uses Parnes' (1967) Creative Problem Solving approach. A problem situation is either presented to the students or identified by them. The group and/or each individual goes through the identified steps to reach an acceptable solution.

Problem Situation A. Mrs. Gonzales has been having repeated visits from various religious groups who send individuals out to talk with people about their church and its viewpoints. She does not feel that she has time to talk with these people, and is not really interested. However, they are very persistent, and she is having a difficult time being rude to them.

1. *Fact-Finding.* List the facts that are known about the situation. List the information that needs to be known in order to develop a solution. Discuss possible sources for the unknown information.
2. *Problem-Finding.* Identify the underlying problem in the situation. Analyze the information and identify a problem which, if solved, would provide a solution to the major issues.

3. *Idea-Finding*. List as many possible ideas as you can think of for solving the problem. Use the rules of brainstorming and defer judgment or evaluation. Focus on quantity rather than quality of ideas.
4. *Solution-Finding*. Choose criteria for evaluating the ideas. Apply these criteria to the ideas to see which ones could be combined or modified to make them more useful.
5. *Acceptance-Finding*. Develop a plan for implementing the solution chosen. Consider all audiences who must accept the solution, make plans for answering their questions, and decide how to convince them the solution is appropriate.

Problem Situation B. Several years ago, there was a series of riots in the maximum security prison in Santa Fe, New Mexico. Many prisoners were killed by other prisoners and several guards and workers were also killed. Much damage was done to the prison as well. Since that time, the state legislature and other officials in the State of New Mexico have been struggling with the issue of whether to build another prison or to develop a new reform system and what kind of prison or system would be needed to prevent problems such as these.

1. *Fact-Finding*. List the facts that are known about the situation. List the information that needs to be known in order to develop a solution. Discuss possible sources for the unknown information.
2. *Problem-Finding*. Identify the underlying problem in the situation. Analyze the information and identify a problem which, if solved, would provide a solution to the major issues.
3. *Idea-Finding*. List as many possible ideas as you can think of for solving the problem. Use the rules of brainstorming and defer judgment or evaluation. Focus on quantity rather than quality of ideas.
4. *Solution-Finding*. Choose criteria for evaluating the ideas. Apply these criteria to the ideas to see which ones could be combined or modified to make them more useful.
5. *Acceptance-Finding*. Develop a plan for implementing the solution chosen. Consider all audiences who must accept the solution, make plans for answering their questions, and decide how to convince them the solution is appropriate.

In this example, the process is exactly the same for both situations. Groups and/or individuals complete the steps, and the teacher either leads them through the process or assists them in it. However, the complexity of Situation B is much greater as is its significance for our social system. Students can conduct research into many important issues while attempting to solve this problem and must deal with more abstract ideas that have a certain richness in their ability to stimulate thought. Although Situation A can certainly serve as a warmup and can be used to teach students how to use the creative Problem-Solving Process, the content of the majority of problem situations presented to gifted students should be of the type illustrated by Situation B.

Equally important, however, is the planning of teaching activities around a central idea or theme—a "big idea" or generalization that brings continuity and organization to the concepts and information that are presented or taught to gifted students. Problem Situation B could be one of several activities designed to develop an understanding of a bigger idea such as "Every society has had rules, written or unwritten, by which social control over the people's conduct is maintained."

Example 2

In the second example, Williams' (1972) Strategies for Thinking and Feeling, especially the strategies of *attributes* and *provocative questions* are used as the process approach. In each case, a sample list of teacher questions is included.

Question Sequence A
1. List all the qualities of this ballpoint pen.
2. How would a caveman react to this pen?
3. How is this pen like a tomato?
4. What would happen if suddenly all the ballpoint pens in the world were destroyed?

Question Sequence B
1. List all the qualities of living things.
2. List all the qualities of non-living things.
3. In what ways are living things different from non-living things?
4. In what ways are living things similar to non-living things?
5. How would/does a tree (living thing) react to a sidewalk (non-living thing)?
6. What would happen if an object or item were discovered which had the following characteristics: (Describe some of the characteristics of living things and some of the characteristics of non-living things.)?

As in the first example, question sequence B provides and requires more significant content, although Sequence A can be used as a warmup exercise and a way to develop familiarity with divergent-type questions. The process objectives are similar in both situations. Sequence B can be even more appropriate if it is part of a group of activities designed to develop an abstract concept such as "Patterns of regularity exist in our physical and living environments. Discovering, measuring, describing, and classifying these patterns is the business of science."

Summary

If programs for the gifted are to survive, educators must devise acceptable answers to some of the criticisms of our curricula. We must be ready with defensible answers and must clearly show how we are making our programs connected to, but not repetitive of, the regular curriculum. Teaching activities must be as significant and as meaningful as possible, and we must be able to demonstrate success in both the development of reasoning skills and the development of deep insights into important ideas. Integrating high-level content with processes that develop higher levels of thinking is one way to achieve these goals.

References

Adams, J.L. (1976). *Conceptual blockbusting: A pleasurable guide to better problem solving.* San Francisco: San Francisco Book Co.

Ashton, P.T. (1978). Cross-cultural Piagetian research: An experimental perspective. *Stage theories of cognitive and moral development: Criticism and applications.* Reprint No. 13. Harvard Educational Review. Montpelier, VT: Capital City Press.

Blatt, M. (1969). Studies of the effects of classroom discussion upon children's moral development. Unpublished doctoral dissertation, University of Chicago.

Bloom, B.S. (1956). *Taxonomy of educational objectives: The classification of educational goals. Handbook I: Cognitive domain.* New York: Longmans, Green.

Bruner, J.S. (1960). *The process of education.* Cambridge, MA: Harvard University Press.

Flack, J.D., & Feldhusen, J.F. (1983). Future studies in the curricular framework of the Purdue three-stage model. *G/C/T, 27,* 2–9.

Guilford, J.P. (1967). *The nature of human intelligence.* New York: McGraw-Hill.

Guilford, J.P. (1972). Intellect and the gifted. *The Gifted Child Quarterly, 16,* 175–243.

Institute for Staff Development (Eds.). (1971a). *Hilda Taba teaching strategies program: Unit 1.* Miami, FL: Author.

Institute for Staff Development (Eds.). (1971b). *Hilda Taba teaching strategies program: Unit 2.* Miami, FL: Author.

Institute for Staff Development (Eds.). (1971c). *Hilda Taba teaching strategies program: Unit 3.* Miami, FL: Author.

Institute for Staff Development (Eds.). (1971d). *Hilda Taba teaching strategies program: Unit 4.* Miami, FL: Author.

Kohlberg, L. (1966). Moral education in the schools: A developmental view. *The School Review, 74,* 1–29.

Kohlberg, L., & Gilligan, C. (1971). The adolescent as a philosopher: The discovery of the self in a postconventional world. *Daedalus, 100,* 1051–1086.

Kohlberg, L., & Mayer, R. (1978). Development as the aim of education. *Stage theories of cognitive and moral development: Criticisms and applications.* Reprint No. 13. Harvard Educational Review. Montpelier, VT: Capital City Press.

Kolloff, M.B., & Feldhusen, J.F. (1981). PACE: An application of the Purdue three-stage model. *G/C/T, 18,* 47–50.

Krathwohl, D.R., Bloom, B.S., & Masia, B.B. (1964). *Taxonomy of educational objectives: The classification of educational goals. Handbook II: Affective domain.* New York: David McKay.

Lee, N. (1976). Formal operational thought: Component skills and observational learning. Unpublished doctoral dissertation, University of New Mexico.

Maker, C.J. *Curriculum development for the gifted.* (1982a). Rockville, MD: Aspen Systems.

Maker, C.J. (1982b). *Teaching models in education of the gifted.* Rockville, MD: Aspen Systems.

Parnes, S.J. (1966). *Programming creative behavior.* Buffalo, NY: State University of New York at Buffalo.

Parnes, S.J. (1967). *Creative potential and the education experience* (Occasional Paper No. 2). Buffalo, NY: Creative Education Foundation.

Parnes, S.J. (1977). Guiding creative action. *The Gifted Child Quarterly, 21,* 460–472.

Piaget, J., and Inhelder, B. (1969). *The psychology of the child.* New York: Basic Books.

Renzulli, J.S. (1977). *The enrichment triad model: A guide for developing defensible programs for the gifted and talented.* Wethersfield, CT: Creative Learning Press.

Rest, J. (1974). Developmental psychology as a guide to value education: A review of "Kohlbergian" programs. *Review of Educational Research, 44,* 241–257.

Stevenson, G., Seghini, J.B., Timothy, K., Brown, K., Lloyd, B.C., Zimmerman, M.A., Maxfield, S., & Buchanan, J. (1971). *Project implode: Igniting creative potential.* Salt Lake City, UT: Bella-Vista Institute for Behavioral Research in Creativity.

Sullivan, E.V. (1975). *Moral learning: Some findings, issues and questions.* New York: Paulist Press.

Taba, H. (1962). *Curriculum development: Theory and practice.* New York: Harcourt, Brace.

Taba, H. (1964). *Thinking in elementary school children* (U.S.O.E. Cooperative Research Project No. 1574). San Francisco: San Francisco State College. (ERIC Document Reproduction Service No. ED003 285)

Taba, H. (1966). *Teaching strategies and cognitive functioning in elementary school children* (U.S.O.E. Cooperative Research Project No. 2404). San Francisco: San Francisco State College.

Taylor, C.W. (1968). The multiple talent approach. *The Instructor, 77,* 27, 142, 144, 146(a).

Treffinger, D.J. (1975). Teaching for self-directed learning: A priority for the gifted and talented. *The Gifted Child Quarterly, 19,* 46–59.

Williams, F.E. (1970). *Classroom ideas for encouraging thinking and feeling* (2nd ed.). Buffalo, NY: D.O.K.

Williams, F.E. (1972). *A total creativity program for individualizing and humanizing the learning process* (instructional materials). Englewood Cliffs, NJ: Educational Technology Publications.

12

Applications and Implications of the Integrated Model of Curriculum Development

Shirley W. Schiever, Ph.D.
University of Arizona

The integration of content and process in the curriculum for gifted students needs to be examined in various ways before being advocated. It is important to first determine whether Maker's integrated model results in qualitatively differentiated curricula for the gifted, as defined by experts in the field. Practical considerations are important, and the model needs to be reviewed in light of classroom applications. Since the classroom is where curricular modification meets teacher and student, the effect of such modification on the teacher and students is the ultimate test of its value. To explore the implications of Maker's integrative model in the classroom, we must ask the following questions: In what ways will implementing this model affect the teacher of the gifted? What changes must he or she make in planning, classroom organization, and teaching techniques? What differences will there be for students?

This chapter will look at Maker's integrated model in light of Kaplan's definitions of the qualitatively differentiated curriculum presented in this volume and explore the implications of the model for teachers of the gifted and their students. As another means of examining the model, Maker's modifications will be compared with the content and process modifications for gifted that Kaplan (1984) suggests, and implications of the differences between the two models will be drawn.

Differentiation

The differentiation of Maker's integrated model may be seen to have both the trait-related and curricular-related perspectives mentioned by Kaplan. That is, the modifications are in terms of modifying elements of the curriculum, but these modifications are based on the needs of the gifted, as related to their characteristics. The integrated model also has elements of several of the stages of differentiation that Kaplan mentions. It is reflective in its philosophical and theoretical base, comparative in redefining the ends and means relationship into principles that direct the curricular decision-making process, diagnostic in specifying learning experiences as indicated by characteristics of the particular group of students, and selective in recognizing the self-direction and independence needs of individual learners.

Applying Kaplan's criteria to Maker's model reveals that it satisfies all five essentials. It evidences (*i*) a response to the nature of the gifted; (*ii*) a relationship and balance between the needs of all children and the specialized needs of the gifted, (*iii*) roots in substantive learnings articulated by design, (*iv*) acknowledgment of the principles of learning, and (*v*) a correlation to its philosophical and theoretical framework. By Kaplan's definition, then, curricula designed in accordance with the principles of Maker's integrated model will be appropriate, qualitatively different, defensible curricula for the gifted.

Implications for the Teacher

Planning

Effectively integrating the necessary content modifications with the required process modifications and producing a curriculum with flow and unity requires long-range planning. To organize facts and information around concepts or ideas that facilitate economy in learning, to plan for the systematic sampling of major branches of knowledge, to include the study of creative, productive people and methods of inquiry in these branches, and to integrate specific processes, the teacher needs to make an overall plan or outline of the year's curriculum. This plan will include the major topics to be covered or generalizations to be explored, the disciplines most closely related to those topics, contact persons within the disciplines, key concepts, process objectives, and appropriate learning activities.

For example, a teacher might choose a generalization such as the following as a main focus for the year's curriculum:

Man is part of a complex ecosystem that is altered in diverse and far-reaching ways by the satisfaction of his needs and desires.

Developing this generalization into a teachable curriculum requires that experts be consulted in order to identify the key concepts, methods of inquiry, and the creative, productive people within the various related disciplines. These disciplines might include the biosciences, chemistry, agriculture, meteorology, geography, sociology, and others. If the teacher starts with topics rather than a generalization, the generalization can be developed through combining concepts to develop a world view or cosmic statement. For example, if the teacher were to start with the topic of man in his world, the following concepts might result in the development of the previously stated generalization:

Food chains
Land use
Pollution—sources and impact
"Natural" disasters related to man's impact on the environment
Urban versus rural environmental impact
Effects of overpopulation
Man's basic needs

Regardless of how the generalizations are derived, the teacher needs to evaluate their abstractness and complexity. The following criteria (Gallagher et al., 1966) may be used for evaluation:

• Two or more concepts are included.
• These concepts are interrelated either as a set of component parts in a system or as part of a larger generalization.
• The topic focus is a large idea having broad applicability, or the concepts making up the generalization do not have concrete referents.

All three of the criteria must be present in a generalization used for the development of curriculum for the gifted; each is necessary but not sufficient (Maker, 1982a). Generalizations with the same underlying principle may be stated in different degrees of abstraction (Womack, 1966); the level of abstraction can be determined by both its range of applicability and by how far it is removed from a student's concrete experience (Maker, 1982a).

Examining the sample generalization reveals that it (*i*) contains many concepts that are (*ii*) interrelated, and that (*iii*) the focus has broad applicability. The generalization is highly abstract; its concepts have wide transferability, do not have concrete referents, and are removed from a student's concrete experiences.

The generalizations, key concepts, methods of inquiry, and a list of creative/productive people within the related disciplines are the raw material from which learning experiences will be fashioned. The question is "How?"; how does one best integrate process components with this content? This requires selecting teaching/learning models that are most suitable for the students in the program and the content selected. In the current example, the Taba Teaching Strategies (Institute for Staff Development, 1971a, b, c, d), the Parnes Creative Problem Solving (1977) model, Kohlberg's Discussions of Moral Dilemmas (1966), and Bruner's Structure of a Discipline (1960) lend themselves to use with the content. It is assumed here that the characteristics of our hypothetical students indicate a need for all of the content and process modifications. If the teacher wants to explore affective issues and considerations, Krathwohl's Affective Taxonomy (Krathwohl, Bloom, & Masia, 1964) may be included. Using a variety of teaching/learning models and a variety of methods is not only stimulating for the student, but also provides accommodation for different learning styles of individual students and exposure to new ways of learning.

Teaching

Discussions based on the Taba Teaching Strategies (Institute for Staff Development, 1971a, b, c, d) incorporate process modifications such as higher-level thinking, open-endedness, proof of reasoning, group interaction, and pacing (Maker, 1982b). For example, a *concept development* discussion could be used to clarify, extend, and assess the students' concept of the sources of pollution. This strategy enables students to develop broad categories of data that are related in some way, or concepts about the data (Maker, 1982b). The first focusing question might be "From what you know and have read or observed, what are some specific sources of pollution?" After listing the data, the students group the sources and support their grouping (give proof of reasoning). Labeling the groups, regrouping and relabeling, and subsuming items under labels and labels under labels completes the exercise, thus providing a way of organizing and looking at the different relationships between the sources of pollution. This strategy and the others, *interpretation of data, application of generalizations,* and *resolution of conflict,* would have repeated application throughout the year, integrated with various content elements.

After students have developed and refined their concept of the sources and impact of pollution, the Parnes Creative Problem Solving (1977) model might be used to explore possible solutions to the problem. Here students engage in the five steps: (*i*) fact-finding, (*ii*) problem-finding, (*iii*) idea-finding, (*iv*) solution-finding, and (*v*) acceptance-finding. These activities involve higher thinking, are open-ended, allow discovery and inductive reasoning, and provide variety (Maker, 1982b).

Kohlberg's Discussions of Moral Dilemmas (1966) could be used to explore decisions regarding industrial compliance with strict environmental controls. The dilemma could center on the consequences to flora and fauna and health and economic consequences for the community. The dilemma would be presented in a personalized format, mentioning specific persons and the impact that compliance or noncompliance with the regulations would have on them. The facts of the situation would be listed, and the perspectives of the different characters explored. The group would then identify two or three major alternatives of the protagonist (e.g., the Chairman of the Board) and explore the consequences of these alternatives. Each individual would take a tentative position on the issue, and small groups would choose the best reasons supporting such a position. The last step would be a full-group discussion of conclusions and reasons supporting them. This process entails higher level thinking, open-endedness, discovery through inductive reasoning, proof of reasoning, group interaction, and pacing (Maker, 1982b).

Bruner's Structure of a Discipline (1960) might be used as a framework for helping students to design and organize independent investigations of areas or problems that are of interest to them. This requires that the student use primary sources and collect raw data; study the ideas and conclusions of others in secondary sources; and acquire, transform, and evaluate new information, in the manner of a "real" scholar. Using this model to structure independent studies provides not only higher level thinking, open-endedness, and discovery (Maker, 1982b), but freedom of choice, as well.

If the teacher wants to incorporate the exploration of affective issues and considerations related to this content area, Krathwohl's Affective Taxonomy (Krathwohl, Bloom, & Masia, 1964) might be used to design tasks to include in a learning center. An issue that lends itself to exploration of the affective component is that of land use—using land for a park versus using it for a low-cost housing development, for example.

A film or filmstrip highlighting the disadvantages and advantages of either or both uses, a visit from a city planner, or a field trip that includes time in a park and observation of a housing development under construction could be used to give the students the knowledge/experience base necessary for using the learning center. The first level of the taxonomy is *receiving*: the student is assumed to have received the information through the experience provided. Task cards for a learning center might include activities such as the following: Responding level—Write several paragraphs explaining how you feel about using land for a park (housing development) and why you feel this way. *Valuing* level—Prepare a five-minute oral presentation to the class explaining how important low-cost housing is for families. Be prepared to defend your view. *Organization* level—Design and make a mobile that illustrates how important, from most important to least, the following uses of land are: (*i*) parks, (*ii*) housing developments, (*iii*) industrial complexes, (*iv*) agriculture, (*v*) wildlife refuges, and (*vi*) schools. When your mobile is ready to hang, be prepared to explain and defend the reasons for your rankings. *Characterization by a Value or Value Complex* level—Design the ideal community, considering the need for homes, places to work, places of worship, recreation, schooling, waste disposal, natural beauty, growing food, transportation, and shopping areas. Build a model or draw a diagram of your community; include an explanation of how you provided for these needs and what makes your community ideal.

The learning center would have many choices of tasks at each level; since the taxonomy is hierarchical, students should move through the levels in sequence. Of the process modifications, this model provides only for higher-level thinking (Maker, 1982b). However, it adds an affective component to the curriculum, which is an important aspect of education for the gifted (c.f. Clark, 1979; Kaplan, 1984; Piaget, 1967; Whitmore, 1980; Williams, 1981), and used within a learning center, it also offers variety and freedom of choice. In addition, the Krathwohl model could easily be used to structure a discussion of pertinent issues.

The balance of the content modifications could be provided through a variety of experiences. Films, guest speakers, and a classroom collection of biographies could be utilized for students to learn about the lives of creative/productive people within the disciplines. Methods of inquiry might be taught by an expert, the teacher, or audiovisual materials. Public television programs related to featured disciplines are another resource either to be watched by individual students at home or videotaped and used as appropriate in the classroom.

The teacher planning this curriculum would also undoubtedly include field trips, simulations, committee work, lectures, and projects, as Maker suggests, integrating content and process in a variety of ways. Teaching/learning models other than those used here as examples and as listed by Maker could be implemented according to instructional goals and objectives, teacher preference, student needs, and content area.

Effects

Using this method of curriculum development—beginning with a generalization and integrating the related content with process models and activities—will result in a well-defined, differentiated curriculum for the gifted. Most teachers are not accustomed to approaching curriculum planning in this way and need to form new ways of conceptualizing and planning in order to incorporate and integrate the modification. The benefits to the student seem obvious—meaningful, interesting, well-organized, fast-moving content learned in a variety of exciting and challenging ways within an overarching framework that fosters the establishment and examination of complex relationships. The benefits to the teacher may be less obvious, but they are no less real. Once the overall design for the year is drawn, the teacher will discover how gratifying and exciting it is to fit in the pieces—to discover the "perfect" speaker, a great field trip, or some other resource that enhances the curriculum while helping to reach curricular objectives. The integration of content and process within this framework provides the teacher a certain security and confidence and a firm sense of the direction of the curriculum and the school year. The long-range planning also provides the luxury of incubation time for the teacher's ideas. This not only enriches the students' experiences, but the teacher's, as well. Excitement with teaching and the feeling of a job done extraordinarily well go a long way toward preventing burnout.

A Comparison

An additional perspective on Maker's suggested modifications may be gained by comparing them with those content and process modifications suggested by Kaplan (1984). These include the following: content—organization, interdisciplinarity, acquisition of generalizations, and appreciation for new scholarly areas; and process—basic skills, creative/productive thinking, and research.

Content

Kaplan, like Maker, believes that content should be organized around broad issues, problems, or themes. Her interdisciplinarity is similar to Maker's variety and complexity of content, which includes the number of disciplines to be integrated. Kaplan mentions the acquisition of generalizations. Maker does not specify that generalizations be acquired, but it may be assumed from the organization around generalizations and her principle of economy, selecting those learning experiences with the greatest potential for transfer or generalization, that such acquisition will occur. Kaplan's appreciation for new scholarly areas may be assumed by Maker because of the variety of content and disciplines to be included, but it is not specified. The content modifications of both authors, then, include the organization principle and the concept of cross-disciplinarity. Each author includes some things the other does not; Kaplan—acquisition of generalizations and appreciation for new scholarly areas; Maker—abstractness, complexity, economy, study of methods of inquiry, and the study of creative, productive people of the disciplines. Maker's modifications appear to be more developed and specific than Kaplan's, and she gives ample guidelines to those planning implementation.

Maker's approach is top-down, or concept driven, rather than bottom-up, or data driven, both in conception and implementation. The model is developed from a theoretical and philosophical position and is geared toward the needs of the learners, as indicated by their characteristics. Implementation begins with a broad, substantive generalization and works toward the learning needs of a particular group. Kaplan's model appears to be more bottom-up, beginning with the characteristics of the student and what he or she should learn, and using the principles of her content modifications to create a curriculum that matches the needs of the learner and the teaching objectives.

Process

Kaplan's process modifications include the basic skills, which for the gifted include the skills of the disciplines. An important clarification here is that the basic skills for the gifted are a means to an end rather than the end itself. For example, all children should learn to write a paragraph; for the gifted the important thing is the *use* of the skill to write an essay, story, editorial, etc. (Kaplan, 1984). Maker does not mention basic skills, but includes the skills of the disciplines in her content modification, the study of methods.

Maker's process modification, higher levels of thinking, is related to Kaplan's creative-productive thinking, which includes logic, creative and critical thinking, and problem solving—all higher-order cognitive processes.

Kaplan mentions research skills as being important for the gifted; Maker does not specify this, although research would be one of the methods of inquiry in the disciplines.

Overall, both models place an emphasis on the higher-order cognitive processes. Kaplan wants the basic skills and research skills to be taught; Maker feels that open-endedness, discovery learning, proof of reasoning, freedom of choice, group interaction, pacing, and variety are important process components that meet the needs and match the characteristics of gifted learners.

Implications

The differences between these two models have several implications for the teacher. The planning required to implement Kaplan's model in the classroom would not necessarily be as long-range as for Maker's. It is possible that planning could be done one unit of study at a time and adequately implement Kaplan's content modifications. Maker's process modifications require a student-centered classroom, with very little whole-group instruction. The teacher is more a facilitator and catalyst, encouraging student interaction and individual independence, than an instructor. The teacher in Kaplan's model would be doing more direct teaching and small and/or large group instruction, filling a more traditional role of instruction in basic skills and research, and leading the activities that teach higher level thinking skills.

Students in a classroom implementing Maker's model would be expected to be or become independent and self-directed and to show noticeable and measurable cognitive growth. The variety of content and process, and the freedom of choice will be especially appealing to gifted students. Students in a Kaplan classroom should be able to use the basic skills with great facility, carry out research projects, and exhibit the higher cognitive processes and problem solving.

Conclusion

The integration of content and process, as Maker suggests, is unfortunately a practice that has not seen extensive implementation in programs for the gifted. Weighing the advantages for student and teacher against resistance to change and objections that might be raised leaves the "cons" on the light side of the scale. A curriculum should serve the best interest of the students for whom it is used. It is clear that integrating content and process in the ways Maker suggests is not only well-grounded theoretically and supported by research, but is logically and intuitively appealing as well.

References

Bruner, J.S. (1960). *The process of education*. Cambridge, MA: Harvard University F ·ess.

Clark, B. (1979). *Growing up gifted*. Columbus, OH: Charles E. Merrill.

Gallagher, J.J., Shaffer, F., Phillips, S., Addy, S., Rainer, M., & Nelson, T. (1966). *A system of topic classification*. Urbana, IL: University of Illinois, Institute for Research on Exceptional Children.

Institute for Staff Development. (1971a). *Hilda Taba teaching strategies program: Unit 1*. Miami, FL: Author.

Institute for Staff Development. (1971b). *Hilda Taba teaching strategies program: Unit 2*, Miami, FL: Author.

Institute for Staff Development. (1971c). *Hilda Taba teaching strategies program: Unit 3*. Miami, FL: Author.

Institute for Staff Development. (1971d). *Hilda Taba teaching strategies program: Unit 4*. Miami, FL: Author.

Kaplan, S.N. (1984, September). *Curriculum modifications for the gifted*. Paper presented at the Latin American Conference on Gifted and Talented Education, Mexico City, D.F.

Kohlberg, L. (1966). Moral education in the schools: A developmental view. *The School Review*, 74, 1–29.

Krathwohl, D.R., Bloom, B.S., & Masia, B.B. (1964). *Taxonomy of educational objectives: The classification of educational goals. Handbook II: Affective domain*. New York: David McKay.

Maker, C.J. (1982a). *Curriculum development for the gifted*. Rockville, MD: Aspen Systems.

Maker, C.J. (1982b). *Teaching models in education of the gifted*. Rockville, MD: Aspen Systems.

Parnes, S.J. (1977). Guiding creative action. *The Gifted Child Quarterly, 21*, 460–472.

Piaget, J. (1967). *Six psychological studies*. New York: Random House.

Whitmore, J.R. (1980). *Giftedness, conflict, and underachievement*. Boston: Allyn & Bacon.

Williams, F.E. (1981). Models for encouraging creativity in the classroom. In W.B. Barbe & J.S. Renzulli (Eds.), *Psychology and education of the gifted*. New York: Irvington Publishers.

Womack, J.G. (1966). *Discovering the structure of social studies*. New York: Benziger Bros.

III

Enrichment
Versus
Acceleration:

is this a continuing
controversy?

A s Tannenbaum asserted over ten years ago, and I have always believed, it is "archaic and trivial" to ask which form of program design is "the best" for gifted students. As one who has never been accused of being archaic (although the label of trivial may have been applied to my ideas!), I must emphasize that real and very appropriate questions still exist about acceleration and enrichment and must be addressed in our literature, research, and practice. Perhaps the problem lies more in the desire to identify *one* approach that will be *best* for a group of diverse learners. Indeed, I would argue that three important questions must be addressed in our literature, research, and practice:

1. What kinds of accelerative practices are best for what kinds of gifted learners at what times?
2. What kinds of enrichment procedures are best for what kinds of gifted learners at what times?
3. What are the most effective ways to implement enrichment and acceleration?

The authors of articles in this section, collectively, have provided us with answers to these questions from their own perspectives, and I will not attempt to review their answers in this introduction. The different authors, without stating the obvious, seem to concur in the view that certain kinds of acceleration are important for certain gifted learners at certain times and that the same is true of enrichment. To ensure effectiveness, however, educators must select the kinds of learners who can benefit from a particular practice, and they must implement the practices appropriately. Van Tassel-Baska, in fact, describes in depth three programs illustrating acceleration "prototypes," showing how the research can best be put into practice. She also provides direct answers to the questions regarding learners for whom certain kinds of acceleration are most appropriate.

In his critique of Van Tassel-Baska's chapter, Ned Levine takes a different approach, and discusses more fully those gifted learners for whom acceleration may not be an effective approach. He also suggests that we must document more clearly the positive effects of acceleration for gifted learners rather than justifying its use by providing evidence for the lack of negative results. With regard to timing, Levine seems to be suggesting that students in high school and college might be the best candidates for most accelerative practices. From his perspective as a public school administrator, he also offers ways for decisions about accelerative practices to be made. Klausmeier reviews several approaches to enrichment and discusses the relative advantages and disadvantages of each, focusing especially on gifted learners in regular classroom settings. Collectively, the authors provide guidelines for designing effective enrichment programs and again chide those who appear to be searching for one answer that will fit all gifted learners. We must be reminded that there are varying types of giftedness and that within each type there are varying degrees of giftedness. My questions then become: What type(s) of gifted students benefit most from enrichment practices? What level (degree) of giftedness is important in determining the appropriateness of enrichment practices? and (given the complexity of the concept of enrichment and the many different definitions that exist, a more difficult question) What type of enrichment is best suited to these types and degrees of giftedness? Only further research and adequate documentation of the results of program development practices can provide definitive answers to these questions.

The chapters in this section provide a consensus of opinion that both accelerative practices and enrichment practices have been used inappropriately, and have been abused. I suspect that those who criticize either set of practices focus upon the abuses rather than the appropriate uses of the practices.

It also seems clear from a reading of the four chapters that there are many similarities in the authors' descriptions of the accelerative and enriching practices they advocate: a consideration of individual interests, individualized instruction, curricular reorganization to facilitate a focus on the structure of a discipline or inherent themes, use of a variety of teaching methods and learning strategies (to name only a few). In fact, there may be more similarities than differences between the effective practices often labeled acceleration and the effective practices labeled enrichment. Indeed, the "other intervention strategies" listed by Van Tassel-Baska as issues important in the success of accelerative approaches are often key components of definitions of enrichment.

Am I suggesting that there is no difference between acceleration and enrichment practices? Not quite. What I am suggesting, however, is that it is difficult to separate the two in any research or practice designed to compare effectiveness or demonstrate success for particular learners. Thus, we will probably never have definitive answers to the three questions proposed at the beginning of my comments. We will definitely have guidelines for decision making, however.

There does appear, though, to be a major difference between practices labeled as acceleration and those labeled enrichment. It is a difference in focus, or perhaps in *degree* of focus. Proponents of particular practices label them "acceleration" because they are focusing on the "rapid pacing of material" to meet the needs of those who learn rapidly. Proponents of other practices label them "enrichment" because they are focusing on the "teaching of different content or the use of different teaching methods" to meet the needs of learners who have different interests and different ways of learning.

Administrative versus Curricular Decisions

The differences between practices labeled with one or the other name would become more clear, I believe, if one were to consider administrative versus curricular decisions as a dimension within each category of practices labeled acceleration and enrichment. With regard to administrative decisions, there is usually a clear difference between enrichment and acceleration. If enrichment is chosen, a student remains in the current grade level placement, while the choice of acceleration implies movement (for at least a part of the day) to a higher grade level. With regard to curricular decisions, however, the lines between the categories of practice become much more fuzzy. In order to provide the most appropriate curriculum to "build upon the interests and different learning styles" of gifted learners (often a stated goal of an enrichment program), one must teach concepts or provide opportunities for learning concepts that are usually taught (or learned) at a much higher grade level (acceleration by definition). Indeed, I have been able to demonstrate in every case in which I have been asked to examine so-called enrichment programs that many, if not most, *relevant* content taught in these programs is taught at a higher level of education (often, admittedly, in college). Certainly, a great deal of irrelevant or, in Taba's terms, "insignificant" content is taught in programs for the gifted as enrichment to avoid the wrath of next year's teacher who does not want to hear "but I learned that last year in the gifted program"! The same is true of processes developed, although fewer processes are taught well in the regular curriculum. Thus, it is difficult, in a curricular sense, to separate enrichment from acceleration, but much easier to make the separation when administrative issues are the focus.

The Relationship to the Concept of Giftedness

I would now like to pose a few questions that are related to the concept of giftedness. As discussed earlier, there are two prevalent viewpoints on the issue of who is gifted. From one point of view, giftedness is equated with adult productivity, while from the other perspective, giftedness is defined in terms of the learner's differences. Adult productivity is considered a qualitative difference, while learner differences are usually considered differences in degree (quantitative), although certain writers and many teachers (myself included) believe that gifted learners are qualitatively different and that they possess differences in degree as well.

With regard to the present discussion, a frequent interpretation of research on traits of gifted individuals is that because most, if not all, of the well-documented differences between gifted learners and those who are not gifted are differences in degree, especially rate of learning, the most defensible practices are accelerative. The learners simply need to move through the existing system more rapidly and to learn the same material more quickly. If, in this viewpoint, these rapid learners have the potential to become productive as adults, acceleration offers them the chance to cover the usual curriculum more quickly and begin their productive careers earlier in life. However, since schools do not usually focus on learners as potential producers, "enrichment" practices are needed to supplement the education of these potentially gifted learners through development of skills in inquiry and problem solving and through provision of an environment that encourages motivation and facilitates inquiry. Thus, the "giftedness as productivity" concept implies the use of both accelerative and enrichment practices to fulfill the needs of the learner.

Viewing giftedness as qualitative differences between learners also requires the use of both acceleration and enrichment. Experiences usually labeled enrichment are necessary to accommodate different learning styles and interests, while experiences usually labeled acceleration may be necessary to accommodate differing interests—and certainly would be required to match the learner's rate of acquisition of concepts. I would also like to suggest, however, that appropriate instruction for gifted students also requires slowing the pace of "covering material." Gifted students often are interested in pursuing topics in much more depth than are their less able or less motivated peers. Thus, a teaching unit that was planned for a month may take three or four. Similarly, gifted students may become excited about a discussion topic and continue for hours, while their peers may have become bored after 15 minutes!

In summary, it is obvious that the issues surrounding acceleration and enrichment practices will not have been resolved in this section, nor will all the important questions have been answered. I can only hope that the questions will now be more appropriate.

13

Acceleration

Joyce Van Tassel-Baska, Ed.D.
Northwestern University

Acceleration is a word that conjures up strong feelings in those who hear it. Frequently at cocktail parties and other questionable soirees someone will be heard to remark how acceleration ruined his life and was responsible for his becoming a social outcast. It has long been my contention that certain gifted individuals who have developed atypical social behaviors need a scapegoat and that acceleration appropriately fills the bill. In addition, there are educators who view acceleration with alarm in the abstract, noting the nebulous "feeling" they have that acceleration is harmful to social-emotional development. And finally, there are well-meaning parents who feel their child may not be "ready" for this enormously significant intervention called acceleration.

From the scenarios cited above, it is clear that a great deal of mythology surrounds our common understanding of the educational practice called acceleration. Kulik and Kulik (1984) in their recent meta-analysis of the effects of acceleration note that when convincing research evidence collides with prevailing social values, social values will out. Most research reviews that have been conducted on acceleration as well as substantive individual studies have shown it to be a highly effective intervention technique with intellectually gifted learners. (Goldberg, 1958; Reynolds, Birch, & Tuseth, 1962; Begle, 1976; Gallagher, 1969; Daurio, 1980; Kulik & Kulik, 1984). Yet misunderstandings and misinterpretations persist regarding its efficacy.

This chapter will attempt to accomplish four goals: (1) present a synthesis of the research literature regarding acceleration according to age and level of schooling, (2) provide workable descriptions of types of acceleration in practice across the country, (3) delineate causes for the lack of accelerative policies and practices in our schools, and (4) outline recommendations for decision making on the issue of acceleration.

What Does the Research Literature Say about Acceleration?

There are two kinds of educational research in the field of education of the gifted. There is program practice research that tends to document what has been done with the gifted. A teacher in School A does some elective projects with the class. The projects turn out well and the teacher publishes what was done in a journal. It then becomes part of the research on the education of gifted children. That kind of "educational research" usually occurs over a short duration of time, e.g., one year, and usually does not have an experimental design or even a quasi-experimental design. In truth, it was not really intended to be a research project but a report of what went on in a particular classroom. Most research in the area of enrichment for the gifted tends to be of this type.

The second kind of research in the education of the gifted, however, attempts to show experimentally or quasi-experimentally that certain program practices produce certain effects while controlling for intervening factors. These research efforts tend to be longer, usually of at least three years duration. Many could be characterized as longitudinal efforts. This second kind of research seems to characterize the body of acceleration research.

Research on Early Entrance

There is a body of acceleration research related to early entrance procedures for gifted children. The question is, How effective is acceleration of a child into kindergarten when he or she is four years old? Three studies that characterize this research (Birch, 1954; Worcester, 1956; and Hobson, 1963) concur on three vital points: (*i*) the students who were accelerated were as academically capable or more so than their nonaccelerated equal-ability peers, (*ii*) they were socially as well adjusted or more so than their nonaccelerated age peers, and (*iii*) there were no discernible negative effects from accelerating them for one year in their studies. In addition, the Hobson research included a longitudinal study of early entrance programs and found that over time the scholastic performance increased in early entrance students, their extracurricular activities were more frequent, they received more honors and awards at high school graduation, and significantly more of them went on to college than their nonaccelerated peers.

In their review of research on the evaluation of early admittance programs, Reynolds, Birch, and Tuseth (1962) state: "It may be concluded from the research that early admission to school of mentally advanced children, who are within a year of school-entrance age and who are generally mature, is to their advantage. There are few issues in education on which the research evidence now available is so clear and so universally favorable to a particular solution." Roedell, Jackson, and Robinson (1980) working with young gifted children at the University of Washington state that "placement according to readiness rather than age facilitates learning as well as the general adjustment of the child."

Research on Elementary School Acceleration

When we turn to elementary school acceleration data, again the emerging picture continues to be positive. Beginning in the early 1890s with the rapid advancement classes in St. Louis, we began to see work in the area of content acceleration with the homogeneous grouping of gifted students. The Cleveland Major Work Program, one of the oldest gifted programs in the country, was studied by Barbe (1954), Hall (1954), and Hauck and Freehill (1972). The Cleveland Program has demonstrated its effectiveness through the success of its graduates. All were exposed to acceleration in foreign language, math, and science. Perhaps one of the crucial studies on acceleration was the Terman and Oden study (1947). These researchers reported several findings: (*i*) when they studied the intelligence factor and the linkage between intelligence and the importance of acceleration, they noted a need for students with a 135-plus IQ score to receive two years of acceleration; (*ii*) acceleration was beneficial both academically and vocationally; (*iii*) minimal socio-emotional maladjustment may have been forthcoming in some individual instances, but it proved to be of very short duration; and (*iv*) for elementary school 10-year-olds, there was almost no correlation between years spent in a subject area and the achievement in that area. This last point is interesting because studies were also done on a general school population (Learned & Wood, 1938) that showed a very modest correlation even at that level between number of years spent and achievement in a particular subject area. One last study that is important to report was conducted by Klausmeier et al. (1963) over a one-, two-, and six-year period. That study revealed no unfavorable effects in the socio-emotional area, the academic area, or the physical area for those students who had been involved in accelerated programs.

Research on High School Acceleration

The body of research on high school acceleration is all positive; at least nine studies have supported that thesis (Flesher, 1945; Pressey, 1949; Casserly, 1968–69; Benbow and Stanley, 1983; Daurio, 1979). The advanced placement approach in particular was found to be extremely positive. In fact, as reported on in *College Board Review* (Casserly, 1968–69), 90 percent of the students that were surveyed in 252 schools and 20 colleges indicated that advanced placement had raised their aspirations and increased their motivation. This idea was also echoed by the students who wrote the fine volume published by the American Association for Gifted Children called *On Being Gifted* (1978).

Research on Higher Education Acceleration

The higher education research studies on acceleration are also consistent and very supportive again of early admission to college and the accelerative possibilities for students. Pressey (1949) found that 6,000 accelerated Harvard undergraduates studied over an eleven-year period had better academic records, were accorded more honors, and had fewer disciplinary involvements than their nonaccelerated peers. An Ohio State study conducted during World War II ($N = 104$ matched pairs) found that twice as many nonaccelerates as accelerates left college without a degree, and noted that acceleration tends to reduce academic mortality among the intellectually gifted. In the Fund for the Advancement of Education study (1953) ($N = 1,350$), early admission scholars found the experience profitable, would recommend it to a friend, and felt that an early admission policy should become a part of all American college admission policies.

Research on Eminent Persons' Acceleration

Another type of research that is supportive of acceleration involves biographical case studies of eminent persons. When one examines this research (Cox, 1926; Hollingworth, 1929; Miles, 1946; Pressey, 1949; Montour, 1976), over 40 in-depth descriptions of early college entrance by age 14 are detailed. The recent Bloom study conducted over a three-year duration stressed individual student self-pacing as the hallmark of talent development; and that indeed talent development proceeds from practice and mastery of increasingly more difficult and complex skills at an individual rate (Bloom & Sosniak, 1981).

What Acceleration Prototypes Are Practiced in Schools?

In 1949 Pressey wrote an important monograph on the subject of accelera-tion. He defined acceleration very simply as "progress through an educational program at rates faster or ages younger than is considered the norm." That particular definition has held up over time and can be seen operational in all three types of acceleration currently practiced.

One type has typically been called *grade acceleration,* which in essence has been defined as having a child "skip a grade," usually at the elementary or middle school level. For example, moving from kindergarten to second grade or from seventh grade to ninth grade are two of the more common levels at which grade acceleration occurs in public school systems. If we look to program examples of grade skipping, we see as prime cases many of the early entrance programs that have been in effect around the country, some for four-year-olds who are tested and put into kindergarten programs early and others for early high school and college entrance.

A second kind of acceleration is *telescoping.* By telescoping a student covers all of the scope and sequence of a two-year curriculum but merely does it in one year. This tends to be a somewhat appealing approach to acceleration because curriculum specialists don't have to alter scope and sequence charts. They stay the same; the child merely covers material at a faster rate. An example of this kind of acceleration is the completion of high school in three years instead of four by students who nevertheless complete all the required course work that is normally associated with high school graduation. Another very popular adap-tation of telescoping is the completion of college work in three years instead of the traditional four.

The third type of acceleration is *content acceleration.* This type of acceleration allows a student to move through a content area at a rate commensurate with his or her level of attainment and capability to proceed. Program examples tend to be one of the following types: (1) Talent search programs at Hopkins, Duke, Northwestern, and Denver Universities where students at the junior high level are given the opportunity to go on to advanced mathematical work that is normally reserved for high school students. This content acceleration also occurs in verbal areas and in the sciences. (2) High school programs such as the College Board Advanced Placement Programs and the International Baccalaureate Program. (3) In-school continuous progress programs for the gifted. Cities such as Seattle, Washington, and St. Charles, Illinois, allow gifted students this flexibility of progressing through a curriculum area at their own rate, regardless of grade placement. Consequently, ten-year-olds may be doing algebra.

The following section describes one program in depth from each of the prototypes just discussed.

Prototype: Content Acceleration

Program: The Northwestern University Programs for Academically Talented
    Students

Northwestern's program for the academically talented subscribes to specific principles regarding curricular experiences for very able junior high age students. It supports the idea that students of exceptional ability in mathematical and verbal areas should have the opportunity to interact with others of similar ability in academic settings, that in-depth experiences in the core content domains of knowledge should provide the focus of the program based on a match between tested student aptitude and the specific course work content, and that a diagnostic/prescriptive approach to teaching should represent the major strategy for instruction so that each student may profit from an appropriate level of study. Thus, the summer, academic year, and correspondence programs may enable a student to achieve greater proficiency in a pre-college program and move to higher levels of course work in the home school.

Northwestern's summer, commuter, and correspondence program for Midwest Talent Search (MTS) participants represents an educational effort designed to help develop the potential of high ability students through accelerative work. Students enroll in one intensive, fast-paced course in which instruction proceeds at a rate commensurate with their ability and with appropriate depth of coverage. The goal of the learning experience is to facilitate rapid progress through traditional high school subjects at an honors level in order to prepare students for Advanced Placement coursework and other opportunities at a college level.

Summer programs. Three-week experiences are provided in the summer to talented students in nine academic areas, including mathematics, biology, chemistry, geological science, Latin, Greek, American studies, literary analysis, and expository writing. Students take the College Board Achievement Tests or comparable standardized instruments in the content area studied to demonstrate proficiency levels for school placement. Table 13–1 shows the 1984 summer students' mean scores in comparison with an older college-bound senior population. As can be seen, the talent search students equalled or exceeded their older counterparts in almost all courses.

Fast-paced academic year commuter classes. The commuter classes meet for three hours on Saturday morning for 26 weeks. Commuter courses require regular attendance and homework. The typical class size is 15–20 students. The instructors are a talented and diverse group that includes members of the Northwestern faculty, graduate students, and specially qualified public and private school teachers. Courses are available in precalculus, mathematics, computer science, Latin, and expository writing.

Letter-links learning program. The Midwest Talent Search Project currently offers four courses by mail. These are Latin, precalculus mathematics, writing for publication, and mathematics and computers. The correspondence courses are handled individually by the instructor-mentor assigned. After registering, students receive a more complete description of the course and course materials. Students send assignments directly to the instructor on a regular basis. The instructor then returns the students' work, corrected and graded. The pace

Table 13–1 A Comparison of Standardized Test Results for Northwestern University Talent Search Students and College-Bound Seniors

Course	No. of Students	Test Used	Mean Score for MTS Students	Score or % Rank for High School Population After a Full Year of the Course
Precalculus	96	Algebra Cooperative Test	Algebra I —34.5 Algebra II—27.3	97th % 85th %
Biology	24	College Board Achievement Test Series (CBAS)	530.8	544
Chemistry	36	CBAS American Chemical Society Test	562.4 30.4	569 85th %
Latin I & II	4	CBAS	570	550
Literary Analysis	27	CBAS	527	523
Expository Writing	29	CBAS	541.6	518
American Studies	22	CBAS	492.7	516

may vary somewhat depending upon the student's ability and/or prior knowledge, but every attempt is made to guide students toward proficiency at a fast pace.

It is very important that students who wish to take correspondence courses possess independent study skills. They must be capable of independent intellectual pursuit and investigation and be responsible and consistent with respect to meeting assignment deadlines in order to successfully negotiate the correspondence course offerings.

Other issues. The eligibility criteria for all Northwestern programs are based on the Scholastic Aptitude Test Verbal (SAT-V) or Mathematical (SAT-M) sections. Each course carries different SAT criteria for enrollment. In general, students must have a combined SAT score of 900 (SAT-M≥500 and SAT-V≥400) to qualify for mathematics and science programs. Verbal programs typically require SAT-V 430.

In the summer and commuter programs, parents may schedule an educational advising session with the instructor on the last day of the course. Parents and the student meet with the instructor at this time to discuss the student's progress during the program as well as long-range educational planning. Although face-to-face conferences are most desirable, telephone conferences are also held.

After the course is over, Northwestern sends an individual evaluation and recommendation for future course work to each student and the designated school official in order to help each program participant receive appropriate placement and/or credit for work completed through the Northwestern programs.

Prototype: Telescoping

Program: University High School, Urbana-Champaign, Illinois

The program at University High School begins for students in seventh grade. Successful entry to the school is based on scoring above the 90th percentile on the Secondary Schools Aptitude Test (SSAT). The nature of the program allows for 7th and 8th grade to be telescoped into one year. Thus all core curriculum areas offer the equivalent of two years in one.

A specific example of telescoping curriculum would be in the area of mathematics where the telescoped curriculum focuses on teaching algebra, mathematical logic, truth tables, and inference schemes all in grade 7. Then in grade 9 (since there is no formal grade 8 at the school) gifted students study advanced algebra, some geometry and trigonometry, elementary matrix algebra, determinants, and the analytic geometry study of conic sections. Grade 10 is devoted mainly to geometry but combines Euclidean synthetic geometry, Cartesian analytic geometry, and vector geometry. Grades 11 and 12 are reserved for a two-year in-depth study of calculus.

The philosophy of the program at University High School is to provide the telescoping mechanism for gifted students so that they may use the accrued time to best advantage in at least three ways:

1. To even out the pace and level of coursework. Typically, junior high level work is significantly easier and less complex than high school work, thus requiring a major shift in a student's study pattern and attitude toward challenging work
2. To pursue meaning, understanding, heuristics, and originality in one's approach to a curriculum area; to deal with subject matter in depth rather than superficially
3. To individualize and personalize student learning instead of presenting a prepackaged program that was designed for "average students" with no real students as the basis of the program.

In these ways the University High School program for academically talented students attempts to provide a telescoped curriculum that more readily accommodates the needs of a gifted learner over a five-year period.

Prototype: Grade Acceleration

Program: St. Charles, Illinois

St. Charles School District provides a comprehensive, articulated program for identified gifted students in grades K-12 at several attendance centers. Program philosophy stresses the growth of the whole child by involving the gifted student in differentiated instruction that stresses the use of higher-level thinking skills, divergent thinking, and the student's preferred style of learning.

Students who meet the eligibility requirements for a subject are grouped for instruction in that subject. Qualitatively different instruction is carefully planned by the teacher in reading, language arts, and mathematics (K-5); and English, mathematics, science, and social studies (6-12). In the Individualized Education Program (IEP), the teacher documents the sequentially planned major tasks that help the student achieve annual goals. Much emphasis is placed on content acceleration and developing critical and creative thinking skills. Instruction in affective education is an integral part of the program.

Grade level acceleration (K-8), and course level acceleration and/or advanced placement in college courses (9-12) may be considered as components of the student's total program. Parent involvement in program planning is actively sought. A multidisciplinary staffing is held for each student prior to his or her placement in the program. Appropriate cognitive and affective goals are discussed with parents at this staffing. An annual review is held at the end of the year to assess the student's progress and determine appropriate placement for the next year.

Articulation meetings with administrators and teachers of the gifted are held periodically throughout the year. These meetings provide opportunities for discussions not only with staff at one's grade level/subject but also other grade levels/subjects, and they help ensure a comprehensive, articulated program.

A student entering grades K-8 who meets the criteria in all academic areas may be considered for grade level(s) acceleration. A student entering grades 9-12 who meets the criteria in an academic area may be considered for course level acceleration. A student may be required to take a proficiency test, depending upon the division for which course acceleration is being considered. The school psychologist administers any additional test that may be needed (K-12). The principal schedules a staffing at which the parents, teachers, (counselor, psychologist, social worker, and student, as deemed appropriate) determine whether grade level(s) acceleration is in the best interest of the student at his particular stage of development.

Thus St. Charles represents a school district that has formally adopted a grade acceleration policy that allows for systematic review of a student's record on an annual basis to determine readiness for that type of intervention. The cooperative staffing model chosen for decision making also facilitates the likelihood of appropriate placement and follow-up services. Since several students are accelerated annually and cluster or class grouping is available at all grade levels, the "transition" period for accelerated students is made easier.

Summary

Perhaps it is worth noting that each of the programs described here provides more benefits to gifted students than just accelerative experiences. Grouping, individualization, in-depth enrichment, counseling, and discussion opportunities are also dominant factors in these programs. It is the impact of these several techniques within the framework of acceleration that makes such programs so viable.

Good accelerative programs for the gifted, then, are cognizant of and attend to the following issues:

1. The affective needs of gifted students
2. The need for peer interaction through intellectual discussions
3. Reorganization of the curriculum for the gifted according to higher-level skills and concepts to compress learning more effectively
4. Selection of materials that organize subject matter according to its structural and/or thematic nature
5. Diversity of teaching strategies and learning experiences

Consequently, it can be demonstrated through practice that acceleration is a critical aspect of effective programming for the gifted, but that it is enhanced by the inclusion of other intervention strategies as well.

The Case for Acceleration

What can we conclude are the advantages of acceleration? Based on research and effective practice, it is fair to make the following claims for the benefits of acceleration. First of all, it improves the motivation, confidence, and scholarship of gifted students. Second, it prevents the development of habits of mental laziness. Third, it allows for earlier completion of professional training, and fourth, it reduces the total cost of education particularly at the collegiate level for parents and for students themselves.

Why, then, in view of the research evidence and the many examples of successful practice, has acceleration not been widely embraced? There are at least three important reasons: (1) Acceleration goes against the current organizational structure of schools, which are geared to average students and which provide no access ramps for abnormalities, whether they be physical or mental. Schools have an age/grade obsession that is also fed by the selection of basal materials for learning. (2) Acceleration tends to challenge the purpose of the school, both in terms of perpetuating the democratic ideal (even though we forget too soon Aristotle's notion of democracy being that of treating unequal talents unequally) and the concept of socialization as being more important than the facilitation of individual learning. (3) Acceleration as a strategy is misinterpreted by schools to mean only covering more material faster, or being responsible for social-emotional maladjustment, or creating skill gaps in core areas. While neither the research literature nor effective practice supports these interpretations, they are commonly held beliefs in the schools. If educators are truly concerned about talent development, then the self-pacing mechanism of acceleration in its various forms must be the recommended framework around which schools facilitate the education of academically talented learners.

Decision Rules for the Practice of Acceleration

The exercise of educational judgment should temper any decision made about student learning experiences, the context in which they unfold, or the stage of development at which they occur. Regardless of the convincing evidence favoring educational acceleration, it still requires examining several issues with respect to individual students.

The following recommendations are meant to be general considerations, not prescriptive guidelines, that may provide clarity for administrative decision making.

1. *Consider carefully the nature of individual gifted students who are candidates for acceleration.*

What are the behavioral characteristics of the gifted that point to the need for acceleration in some form? In the cognitive area, the ability to manipulate abstract symbol systems much better than their average age peers obviates against a lock-step, incremental, part-to-whole teaching-learning process, which in essence is what often results in the regular classroom. The rate and pace of the gifted student's ability to learn material and the manner in which he or she can process large amounts of information point to the need for advanced work early. Many gifted individuals are early readers who are operationally two to six years ahead of their age peers on achievement tests. The power of intellectual thought of gifted students enables them to master concepts and systems of thought holistically rather than piecemeal, thus reducing the needed time to teach them any given topic. The general quickness and alertness of the gifted can cause boredom and frustration when they are held back in a regular classroom situation, or when they are submitted to a start-and-stop method of reaching a particular point in a set of materials and being told to wait until the rest of the class is ready to go on. Such situations become extremely problematic for them.

Affectively, there tends to be in the gifted a great impatience. When the disparity between appropriate pacing and what is actually happening in the classroom emerges, they reveal heightened frustration. A greater degree of sensitivity, even mild hyperactivity and central nervous system reaction, can cause an internal reaction against the "braking mechanism" that tends to occur in learning when they are not allowed to move ahead at their own rate.

2. *Consider the degree of giftedness of individual students and the areas in which it manifests itself in order to determine the type and extent of acceleration.*

One criterion to consider in deciding about acceleration is that the student should be in the upper 2 percent of the general population in terms of general ability. Gallagher, in *Teaching the Gifted Child* (1976), advocated acceleration of two years for any student who had an IQ of 130 and above. As we have noted, the Terman and Oden research (1947) chose to use a cutoff of 135 +. In addition to examining general inventory ability issues, it is also important to consider performance on achievement and aptitude measures. Content acceleration is feasible for students performing two or more years beyond their age peers in a given area. Many students whose aptitude levels are four or more grade levels beyond their age peers need more rapid advancement.

3. *Consider student preferences for doing accelerated work or being placed in an accelerated setting.*

The interest and motivation of a student to do accelerated work is another crucial variable. Students must want acceleration and need to understand the implications of it, regardless of the type employed. Not all students who are able to handle accelerated programs wish to participate in them, or find the approach a satisfying way to learn. Students should be consulted about program opportunities, with a competent adult explaining the relative advantages of such programs, yet noting that it may mean leaving friends who are age mates in a given classroom setting, extra work, and a greater challenge. For some students, acceleration would not be a choice. As long as a fair case is made, it seems prudent to allow students to decide for themselves; success depends on the motivation and commitment of students to succeed as well as their ability. Note that accelerative experiences are seldom appropriate for the underachieving gifted student, since the setting tends to increase the disparity between productive and nonproductive students and leads to heightened anxiety on the part of the underachiever.

4. *Consider acceleration for a group of gifted students rather than just one, regardless of treatment type.*

The extra supportive interaction and stimulation accruing from group accelerative experience is an important factor. Individual acceleration, whether it be in a content area or at a grade level, can be a lonely experience, at least initially, unless support systems are present in the school context. By accelerating groups of able learners rather than individually advancing them, cognitive growth is enhanced as well as social-emotional adjustment. The environment remains familiar in important dimensions; only learning expectations change.

Historically and currently, content acceleration almost always occurs for groups of students, probably accounting for the fact that it is the most common form of acceleration practiced. The program examples discussed earlier in this chapter also employ group acceleration regardless of the prototype chosen. Thus educators can offer the advantage of accelerative experiences to more students at less risk of minimal and short-term social isolation.

5. *Consider the need for additional program modifications beyond acceleration.*

As the program examples illustrate, acceleration is only one type of intervention for talented learners, and while one can argue that it is a necessary strategy to employ, it cannot be considered sufficient. There is a need to see a larger perspective. One does not choose acceleration *rather* than enrichment or counseling. The three interventions are inextricably linked in a confluent model that implies the fundamental importance of each to an ideal program for gifted students. Figure 13–1 illustrates the overlapping nature of such provisions at all levels of schooling and the types of options available within each basic type of provision. An accelerative provision may be in a content area or by an administrative arrangement of mixed-grade grouping to foster telescoping or grade skipping. Enrichment can be an intensification of the regular curriculum, such as debate or archaeology as focal points for language arts or science. Acceleration can also be an extension beyond the regular curriculum in the study of a foreign language during the elementary years. Counseling

Figure 13–1 A Model of Interlocking Provisions for Talented Learners at All Levels of Schooling

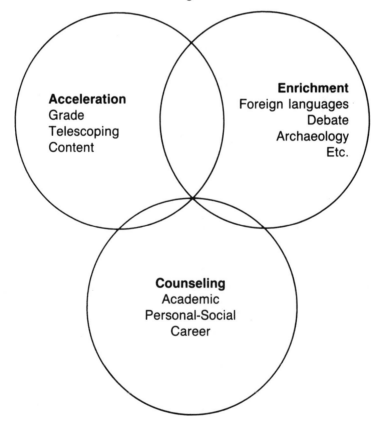

provisions can be socio-personal in nature, or they can focus on areas such as academic or career planning. Although the basic provisions remain fundamental to appropriate program intervention for talented learners, the extent and nature of each provision is based on individual learners' needs and on distinct capabilities.

6. *Consider carefully the criteria for the selection of a staff person to work with an accelerated student or group of students.*

Not all good teachers can work effectively in an accelerated program. There are specific qualities necessary to the success of teachers assigned to such programs:

- Approval and endorsement of the strategy of acceleration for able learners

    The attitude of the teacher toward acceleration is crucial. A teacher must enthusiastically embrace the idea of acceleration and find strategies to set classroom expectations at levels that honor it.

- Capability to adapt and modify a curriculum to provide accelerative experiences

    Teachers chosen to work with students in accelerated programs need to understand how to compress material, select key concepts for emphasis, and share knowledge systems with their students rather than merely double the homework amount or "cover" more material in class. While accelerative programs should be more challenging, they should not rob the student of inordinate amounts of time or lead to an increase in low-level work.

- Evidence of advanced knowledge and competency in the content dimension of the program

    Able learners demand teachers who know subject matter. This is especially true of accelerated learners, for their conceptual insights can easily take them into advanced thinking and work in a given area. A teacher must be able to recognize this "vertical intuitiveness" and apply it constructively in the context of teaching and learning. This is rarely possible for teachers with limited content expertise. Ideally, teachers who work with accelerated math programs in algebra should know calculus; literature teachers should know the Great Books of the Western World; and science teachers, recent developments and research findings relevant to their teaching area.

- Good classroom management abilities

    A teacher in an accelerated program must be very conscious of the differences within an accelerated group of learners. Some will be capable of moving very rapidly; others may wish to explore an area of interest in depth. Classroom environments should be flexible enough to accommodate such individual differences. Cluster grouping and regrouping within an accelerated program is essential. Teachers need to be able to work with various instructional strategies, including small group and individual instruction.

7. *Consider planning accelerative options through the formation of an articulation task force that spans preschool through college entry.*

Careful school district planning is necessary to effect positive accelerative experiences for students. This means bringing educators together from all levels of the community to discuss acceleration issues and develop a cooperative plan. Preschool educators and university educators should be involved from the beginning since early referral is an important aspect of any acceleration plan. Working out appropriate scope and sequence for accelerated curricula and reviewing logistical issues regarding early entrance and early exit options are important issues for such a task force to consider.

8. *Consider the development of specific written policies and procedures regarding the practice of acceleration at the local and state levels.*

In order to maximize curriculum and program flexibility, it may be appropriate to develop written policy statements regarding acceleration. Some policies currently in effect in local districts and some states actually impede or prevent students from taking advantage of acceleration. It is important that such antiquated restrictions are removed and more flexibility instated to ensure able students maximum opportunities in a given educational system. Provisions need to be considered for at least the following issues:

- continuous progress based on ability and performance, not age or grade, in individual curriculum areas
- early entrance to school
- appropriate credit and/or placement for advanced coursework taken off-campus, given validation or proficiency
- early involvement in college work through the College Board Advanced Placement Program or local arrangements with institutions of higher education

Through careful consideration of the eight decision rules just enumerated, educators can begin to put into widespread practice an intervention tool long supported by the research literature. The time for acceleration to become standard practice for talented learners has come.

References

American Association of Gifted Children. (1978). *On being gifted.* New York: Walker.

Barbe, W.B. (1954). A follow-up study of graduates of special classes for gifted children. *Dissertation Abstracts, 14,* 299.

Begle, E.G. (1976). *Acceleration for students talented in mathematics.* Stanford: Stanford University, Stanford Mathematics Education Study Group. (ERIC Document Reproduction Service No. ED 121 607).

Benbow, C.P., & Stanley, J.C. (Eds.). (1983). *Academic precocity: Aspects of its development.* Baltimore: The Johns Hopkins University Press.

Birch, J.W. (1954). Early school admission for mentally advanced children. *Exceptional Children, 21,* 84–87.

Bloom, B., & Sosniak, L. (1981). Talent development versus schools. *Educational Leadership, 39,* 86–94.

Cox, C.M. (1926). The early mental traits of three hundred geniuses. *Genetic Studies of Genius,* Vol. II. Stanford: Stanford University Press.

Daurio, S.P. (1980). Educational enrichment versus acceleration: A review of the literature. In W.C. George, S.J. Cohn, & J.C. Stanley (Eds.), *Educating the gifted, acceleration and enrichment.* Baltimore: The Johns Hopkins University Press, 13–53.

Flesher, M.A. (1945). Did they graduate too young? *Educational Research Bulletin, 24,* 218–221.

Fund for the Advancement of Education of the Ford Foundation (1953). *Bridging the gap between school and college.* New York: Research Division of the Fund.

Gallagher, J. (1969). Gifted children. In R.L. Ebel (Ed.), *Encyclopedia of education research* (4th ed.) (pp. 537–544). New York: Macmillan.

Gallagher, J. (1976). *Teaching the gifted child.* (2nd ed.). Boston: Allyn & Bacon.

Goldberg, M.M. (1958). Recent research on the talented. *Teacher's College Record, 60,* 150–163.

Hall, T. (1954). *Gifted children, the Cleveland story.* Cleveland: World.

Hauck, B.B., & Freehill, M. (1972). *Gifted case studies.* Dubuque, IA: William C. Brown.

Hobson, J.R. (1963). High school performance of underage pupils initially admitted to kindergarten on the basis of physical and psychological examinations. *Educational and Psychological Measurement, 23,* 199–170.

Hollingworth, L.S. (1929). *Gifted children: Their nature and nurture.* New York: Macmillan.

Klausmeier, H.J. (1963). Effects of accelerating bright older elementary pupils: A follow-up. *Journal of Educational Psychology, 54,* 165–171.

Kulik, J.A., & Kulik, C.C. (1984, October). Synthesis of research on effects of accelerated instruction. *Educational Leadership, 42,* 84–89.

Learned, W.S., & Wood, B.D. (1938). *The student and his knowledge.* New York: Carnegie Foundation for the Advancement of Teaching.

Miles, C.C. (1946). Gifted Children. In L. Carmichael (Ed.), *Manual of child psychology.* New York: John Wiley.

Montour, K.M. (1977). Three precocious boys: What happened to them? *Gifted Child Quarterly, 20,* 173–179.

Pressey, S.L. (1949). *Educational acceleration: Appraisal and basic problems*. Bureau of Educational Research Monographs (31). Columbus, OH: The Ohio State University Press.

Reynolds, M., Birch, J., & Tuseth, A. (1962). Review of research on early admission. In M. Reynolds (Ed.), *Early school admission for mentally advanced children*. Reston, VA: Council for Exceptional Children.

Roedell, W., Jackson, N., & Robinson, H. (1980). *Gifted young children*. New York: Teacher's College Press.

Terman, L.M., & Oden, M.H. (1947). *The gifted child grows up*. Stanford: Stanford University Press.

Worcester, D.A. (1956). *The education of children of above average mentality*. Lincoln: University of Nebraska Press.

14

Comments on "Acceleration"

Ned S. Levine, M.S.
Tucson Unified School District

I n her chapter on acceleration, Joyce Van Tassel-Baska presents a summative argument for the use and efficacy of acceleration as a means of successful and appropriate educational intervention in programming for the gifted child. She provides us with a review of the research literature that supports this approach while offering a smattering of the programs that actively employ the option. Finally, she claims that the use of acceleration "improves motivation . . . prevents the development of habits of mental laziness . . ." and is a time- and money-saving device for both the individual and the institution involved.

In order to accept such claims at their face value, we must first conclude that the accelerated program is (*i*) supported by the literature, (*ii*) a preferable alternative to regular educational programming, (*iii*) compatible with other program needs of the individual gifted child and the gifted population as a whole, and (*iv*) categorically different from the educational avenue offered the nongifted individual in both form and function.

The Literature

Let us begin with a review of the literature. In an attempt to dispel the prevailing myths concerning the permanent emotional and intellectual damage associated with acceleration, a summary of the supportive research is divided

197

into the following areas: early entrance, elementary school acceleration, high school acceleration, higher education acceleration, and eminent persons' acceleration.

Almost all the research conclusions cited reflect the prevailing "negative" attitude that, through this (as well as many other types of programming) variation, no *detrimental* effects were observed, either subjectively or objectively, over long periods of time. Acknowledgment is made by the studies quoted that there are in fact "short-term" emotional adjustments required of certain individuals and that there may be the category of "gifted underachievers" for which such an option is not an acceptable solution. These are important exclusions that will be addressed more fully.

Early entrance to the public or private school experience based on prerequisite academic and emotional (maturational) skills appears to be an open-and-shut case. It can be said that if academically capable, socially mature, underaged individuals are identified and then allowed to enter school and function at their ability and social level, they will maintain their academic and social level. In other words, early entrance will do them no harm. In addition, Hobson's longitudinal study upholds the hypothesis that successful early placement has additional benefits for the system in that the child becomes a more productive member of the institution as demonstrated by an increased involvement with rewards, honors, and extracurricular activities. The statement that is made in support of this type of placement is central to the entire issue of special practices in education of gifted learners, i.e., that one should place a person according to demonstrated readiness rather than just age. I do not believe that many would argue with that point (or could do so successfully). Instead, I believe the problems that students experiencing this and other similar accelerative advances must overcome are not only societal (as Van Tassel-Baska states) but are also problems created by institutions in implementing the practice of acceleration itself. Specifically, it is apparent from this and other research that acceleration is the answer for the child and the system that are in total agreement with each other. The child who accepts the system as is, and the system that accepts the child, will do just fine with this approach. They will meet each other's needs and consider one another successful in doing so.

Not all gifted children manifest their talent solely through an ability to procure knowledge at an accelerated pace. This assumption, a mainstay of the argument for acceleration as *the* educational intervention, may be traced back to the original definitions of giftedness provided by Galton (1883) and Catell (1890), where energy and the capacity for physical labor were the two determining qualities for intellectual levels. Recent definitions include identifying gifted and talented individuals who manifest exceptional creative, leadership, visual/performing arts, or interpersonal and intrapersonal abilities. Program decisions made solely on the evidence of academic superiority neglect the many other unique qualities of these groups.

A similar point can be made in looking at the practice of acceleration in the nation's elementary school programs. However, here it becomes more obvious that acceleration can and does take two separate avenues. One approach is simply to allow an individual to skip a grade. As an administrative decision, it is a clean, quick, and inexpensive procedure. The child is moved on to another body of knowledge to master after having demonstrated competency in the preceding skill levels. This is a successful conclusion if we all agree that knowledge is the mastery of a carefully delineated, sequential list of objectives. Education can then be thought of as an arcade game: the higher the score, the higher the level of achievement. There is no light but that at the end of the tunnel. Van Tassel-Baska herself complains that this limited concept of success is often the mistaken belief of the educators in the field, and yet it is the preferred application of the process.

Grade skipping is the approach most often used in place of a program for the gifted rather than in conjunction with other services. It appears that highly gifted individuals suffer least from this approach, and, if done with the proper preskill analysis and planned instruction, grade-skipping can avoid acquisition gaps in those subjects that require sequential learning (Gowan & Demos, 1964; Stanley, 1977). The research cited is anecdotal, employing, for the most part, a case study approach that is often subject to selective bias effect. Generalizations drawn from such research must be limited to the population selected. Here, as in the case of an early childhood admission approach, we must realize that we have preselected individuals who are well-adjusted high achievers and have submitted them to more of the same, then measured our success on the basis of whether or not they continued to prosper in the system. This was/is the original problem with the Terman studies (Jacobs, 1970).

The strongest support in the research is for advanced placement at the high school and/or precollege level. Although the author reviews only two anecdotal publications (one in the College Board Review and the other the American Association of Gifted Children's volume *On Being Gifted*) and alludes to nine others, one could find with relative ease other studies which conclude that, in the areas of mathematics and foreign language, acceleration is a well-received, successful alternative (e.g., Stanley, George, & Solano, 1977; Stanley, 1979b; Khatena, 1982). In addition, the recent conclusions of Benbow and Stanley (1983) are in favor of allowing radical acceleration of the highly gifted into and through colleges. These individuals require fewer resources and less time, expend less money, and enter their careers sooner, consequently becoming more productive members of their occupational fraternities (Nevin, 1977).

What Now, My Teacher? More of the Same

The next question concerns whether the practices of grade acceleration, telescoping, and content acceleration are preferable methods for meeting the needs of the gifted population.

It should be obvious that grade skipping, if done in accordance with the cautions outlined by the author and with those dictated by common sense, is one acceptable means of accelerating the learning experience to match the child's demonstrated potential. (Again, this applies to the academically gifted more than to any other group.) Perhaps we should explore for a moment why it is so infrequently employed.

First, consider the scenario that precedes grade skipping. The child must be recognized by at least two sources as having exceptional abilities in not just one area but many areas crucial to the school mission (e.g., mathematical and verbal precocity). It is not usually sufficient for just one source (such as the parent, the teacher, or the special services personnel) to acknowledge the individual. Most of the people involved in the educational decisions for that particular child must reach a consensus that the normal placement is inadequate for that individual. This would not be so difficult to accept were it not for the fact that the decision must be a public admission of this inadequacy demonstrated by the movement of the child from one environment to another.

In spite of all that is said about teachers as responsible, caring human beings whose prime mission is to perform for the good of society, teaching itself is still a solitary act. When a teacher closes his or her door, so to speak, the classroom is still a kingdom unto itself. It requires a confident person with sufficient administrative support to not only recognize but to acknowledge an inadequacy in programming abilities and to reach the conclusion that it would be best to move a child along past the teacher's level of instruction because there was not anything to be gained by remaining there.

Parents, too, must make public the fact that their child is unique and requires this special treatment. I would hazard the guess that more parents are steered away from this decision by nonsupportive school personnel than by their own fear of possibly ostracising their child (Stanley, 1977; Newland, 1976).

The second kind of acceleration presented is telescoping, described as the task of accomplishing more than one year's curriculum in one year. The author states that this practice is "appealing" to educators because it is rather simplistic to employ in that "curriculum specialists don't have to alter scope and sequence charts. They stay the same; the child merely covers material at a faster rate." If we continue to pursue the analogy that the term implies, we will readily see the objectionable characteristics of this practice. A telescope is an instrument for obtaining a visual representation of an object from a great distance, rendering it accessible where it would normally not be. In so doing, the telescope also greatly reduces our field of vision, producing what might be referred to as the "tunnel effect." We attain an extremely limited goal, ignoring all the universe between the object we seek and the mind's-eye view of the object.

In addition, telescoping has the adverse effect of creating within the individual the very change in effect that the practice seeks to avoid. Rather than recognize that an academically gifted individual requires less drill and practice and more opportunities for analytical, abstract applications of the knowledge to be mastered, this approach, as described, smacks of the "more is not better, more is simply more" syndrome. It has the probability of taking on the characteristics of busy-work. The results of this mentality can be seen in the misuse by educators of multilevel skills kits and the almost universal negative regard on the part of the gifted student with respect to these materials.

The only applicability telescoping would appear to have is in that situation where the institution is unwilling or unable to change a standard bill of fare for its special needs population. I cannot think of many instances when telescoping would be an appropriate practice. Perhaps it is naive of me to uphold the belief that an institution, by definition, is designed to serve the needs of its constituents. However, there may be a case where a small and/or elite population cannot be served for either economic or political reasons. Or, perhaps, there are times when the talent to serve this special group is lacking, in which case it would behoove the institution to allow the individual to consume what it has to offer as rapidly as possible and to seek satiation elsewhere.

In any case, telescoping will only work if it is consistently applied throughout the institution. If the game plan is unchanged from beginning to end (if an individual can complete a given task in less time and be properly and consistently rewarded), it should be an option, albeit of the lowest priority when choosing program formats. Again, it should be obvious that the gifted underachiever is out in the cold on this one due to his or her qualitative differences.

Both parents and educators have a mindset to overcome. The lock-step year and grade approach to education is what this generation has encountered most frequently in public schools. Few of us are familiar with the alternatives, such as the one-room schoolhouse or the more recent return to nongraded and multigraded instruction as exemplified by the IGE (Individually Guided Education) system developed through the Kettering Foundation and the Wisconsin R&D Center. The temporary out-of-level instruction of talent search programs, the extension services of some universities, or the IEP models proposed by Renzulli and Smith (1979) and Meeker (1979) are also examples of other structures to accomplish what Van Tassel-Baska classifies as content acceleration.

Content acceleration is defined as a continuous-progress program based on the evaluation of the skill and learning rate of the individual. Such programs are traditionally offered as advanced placement courses within or out of the normal school setting. This may be accomplished by using procedures mentioned before, such as the IEP plan or the IGE structure, as variance classes in the regular curriculum adapting the technique of ability grouping, or by completely "artificial" programs external to the school setting, such as those found in private institutions.

Is Acceleration a Preferable Alternative to Regular Educational Programming?

Educators must realize by now that alternative programming for the gifted is essential. However, just having a "program" is no guarantee that we are meeting the needs of this subgroup. The use of acceleration often takes the place of a regular and well-defined program. I heartily agree with Van Tassel-Baska and congratulate her on acknowledging the fact that acceleration employed in isolation and without the proper supportive services can be just as damaging as no program at all.

For acceleration to be successful, it must be offered on a continuing basis, be well coordinated both internally and externally (i.e., the program must have internal consistency and be integrated with all other services and requirements of the child), and must offer clearly defined, extrinsic rewards equal in value to the extra achievements expected. An accelerated program must also have clearly stated entry and exit criteria.

If one takes into consideration the previous discussion of limitations to grade skipping and telescoping, the answer to the question posed at the beginning of this section is a qualified "yes." Acceleration has merit as a preferred program for the highly gifted, academically successful achievers, and it will help the student to avoid some of the boredom and dissatisfaction of the lock-step approach to subject presentation. It does, however, often remove the necessity for the student to make any major decision beyond that of assuming the additional workload inherent in these programs. There is no question that the student must ask as to the direction of study or the applicability of the material. Success is determined by completing what is required, the next step being well defined. It is a self-serving approach.

Of the three approaches associated with this type of intervention, the most palatable is content acceleration. If established and implemented correctly it could be a boon for any bright child, not only for the highly gifted. Whether we look at management of the learning environment to facilitate pre-evaluation, planning, implementation, and assessment of the learning cycle (as in the IGE structure) or at the implementation of different learning outcomes for different students dictated by the use of an IEP prescription, we find the general consensus that a flexible program based on individually diagnosed needs is a godsend for most gifted students.

Is This Just Another Ride on the Merry-Go-Round?

Are we off on another tangent here, or is this practice compatible with the other programming suggested for the gifted? No, no tangent. Acceleration must be accompanied by (*i*) a change in expectations of the teacher and child, (*ii*) a change in material taught, (*iii*) a change in structure within and beyond the "parent" institution responsible for the child's program completion both to implement and to accept the recommendations of those who have developed alternative criteria for mastery, and (*iv*) a realization that acceleration serves only a limited need for a finite subgroup of the gifted population. As long as we accept these facts, we will not be wasting anyone's time.

Studies in learning theory reinforce the already known fact that any practice in isolation without the intervention of a means for transference to occur is useless. A special education teacher must address a specific shortfall in the environment in which performance is expected. Enrichment must offer some understandable bridge to regular program skills for the child to perceive it as anything other than an ultimate waste of time. The same must be said for accelerative experiences.

Is Acceleration Only for the Go-Getter?

As presently practiced, it would appear that acceleration is an intervention method only for the go-getter. Clark, in *Growing Up Gifted* (1983), quotes Stanley (1979a) as stating ". . . these programs are designed to serve highly able, achieving, and motivated students . . ." (p. 153):

> With more than 2,000 mathematically able boys and girls already identified, we do not have the time and facilities to look for latent talent or potential achievers, worthy though that pursuit surely is.

We leave that to the many persons who prefer to specialize in identification and facilitation of underachievers, "late bloomers," and the "disadvantaged gifted." (Stanley, p. 101)

I would hazard the guess that the opportunity for acceleration is also severely restricted in other settings as well. It is a shame that we are not willing to chance success for underachievers by offering some form of accelerated programming to them in hopes of overcoming the ennui with which they view the normal academic structure (Whitmore, 1980).

What Happens to the Talented and the Talents in Each of Us?

At the risk of oversimplifying, let us assume that one of the prevalent qualities of the gifted is impatience with the mundane in general and the repetitive specifically. Accelerative avenues within specified tasks suit that characteristic just fine and present a perfect solution to the problem.

But what about those individuals with a desire to delve into the true meaning and development of the knowledge they perceive? And what of those who have the ability to grasp with intuitive insights the information that others struggle so long to comprehend? What of those who could care less about the whys and wherefores, who understand instead the hows before anyone can explain to them the rest?

What does acceleration offer the truly talented and creative instead of more of the same sooner? In his summative research on the predictive validity of creativity testing and the effects of early creativity training upon later success in the marketplace, Torrance (1979) found that a significant number of creative individuals attribute their apparent success to the fact that they had or still have mentors to assist them in the process of self-directed learning. In *Educational Psychology of the Gifted,* Khatena (1982) also lends his support to this and other alternatives.

When considered in the context of the wealth of literature on possible alternatives for programming, Van Tassel-Baska's model of interlocking provisions for talented learners at all levels of schooling is an oversimplification of the adjustments and considerations that should be made in programming for the gifted and talented. In addition, it graphically places a disproportionate emphasis on acceleration. As drawn, a discrete part of the programming changes made to accommodate the accelerative approach are done in isolation, unrelated to the personal-social needs of the gifted student. Perhaps a pyramid (with the base representing the individual's personal and social needs, the sides representing the possible adjustments in form and function of the educational program, and the learner's peculiarities defining the interaction of the sides and the base) would be a more appropriate structure (Figure 14–1). The limits of each adaptation to the program would then be based on an evaluation of the length and breadth of the individual gifted learner's preparation and need, as opposed to Van Tassel-Baska's concept of looking for ways in which the gifted learner fits the program.

Is It Time for Acceleration to Become Standard Practice for Talented Learners?

Van Tassel-Baska is to be commended for acknowledging the need to exercise appropriate educational judgments in making placement decisions. Her recommendations that acceleration should be employed after considering the nature of the individual, the degree of giftedness, and the student's preferences for doing accelerated work are central to the issue and have, therefore, received the most response here. But is it really time for acceleration to become the standard practice for talented learners?

Acceleration must be kept in its proper perspective. Acceleration (by the author's own admittance and certainly substantiated by the literature) is accomplished by change either in the content of the material the gifted learner must master or in the method through which the learner must attain mastery, or, preferably, both. But it is only one of dozens of modifications that could and should be used in designing an effective program. As a tool, it has appropriate uses as well as inappropriate applications.

One is continuously confronted by the limited resources available to gifted individuals and with the finite amount of time that can be realistically consumed for the educational act when making program decisions. These restrictions force the truly important question of what is the best learning experience we can give to gifted learners.

My answer is an individual's response to a lifetime filled with pertinent and mundane experiences in education of the gifted. It has grown and developed from 12 years in a public education program for "superior-ability students" that was based almost entirely on an accelerated curriculum and on the subsequent early completion of both college and graduate studies. It has been tempered by 15 years of teaching in public and private institutions here and abroad and was honed by my own successes and failures throughout those periods.

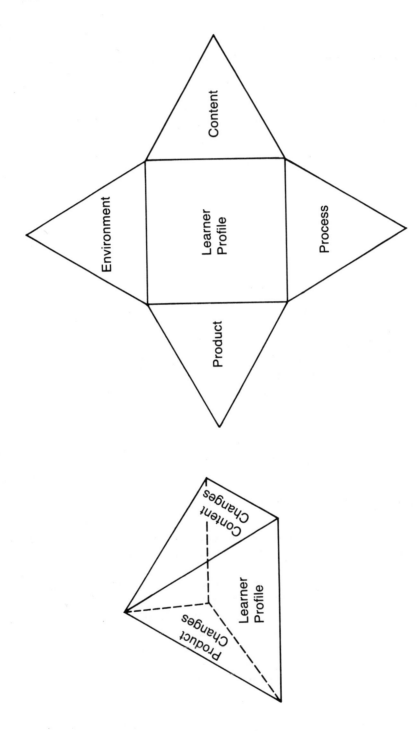

Figure 14–1 Curriculum Modifications Based on Learner Profile

Curriculum modification recommendations run the gamut of content-process-product-environment effectively with alterations specific to particular "body" types. Maker (1982) presents perhaps the best summary to date of the applicability of the more substantial suggestions. However, it is not my intention to deal here with the specifics but with the general, what we in education often euphemistically name the "goals."

Acceleration as presently practiced in the public school setting and in the private talent search programs maintains the rapid acquisition of a preselected bank of knowledge as its primary goal. It does not encourage creative thinking behaviors because it does not alter the process or the products a child may choose as a way to arrive at the end state. By defining success as narrowly as do the acceleration programs, the gifted learner is encouraged to become a passive recipient of the knowledge that the institution provides.

As educators of the gifted and talented, our goal should be to provide gifted students with a program that develops the ability to enter into a pertinent learning experience at any point in their lives. We should offer them the opportunity to be self-actualizing individuals in the true Rogerian sense. We should create for them and within them the perpetual stance that knowledge is a state of mind rather than a statement of facts. We should acknowledge readily that information has a limited applicability in time, and, rather than stress its acquisition as a goal, we should view it as merely the means to a temporary and specific end.

We should develop in individuals the competence to define and achieve success that relates to their definition of the real world. We should create people who are able to make decisions that further their personal development. We should encourage the differences rather than the similarities between us. If acceleration embraces these goals, it will gain my fervent support.

References

American Association of Gifted Children (1978). *On being gifted.* New York: Walker and Co.

Benbow, C.P., & Stanley, J.C. (Eds.). (1983). *Academic precocity: Aspects of its development.* Baltimore, MD: Johns Hopkins University Press.

Catell, J.M. (1890). Mental tests and measurements. *Mind, 15,* 373–380.

Clark, B. (1983). *Growing up gifted.* Columbus, OH: Charles E. Merrill Publishing Company.

Galton, F. (1883). *Inquiry into human faculty and its development.* London: Macmillan.

Gowan, J.C., & Demos, G.D. (1964). *The education and guidance of the ablest.* Springfield, IL: Charles C. Thomas.

Jacobs, J. (1970). Are we being misled by fifty years of research on our gifted children? *Gifted Child Quarterly, 14,* 120–123.

Khatena, J. (1982). *Educational psychology of the gifted.* New York: John Wiley & Sons.

Maker, C.J. (1982). *Curriculum development for the gifted.* Rockville, MD: Aspen Publishers.

Meeker, M.N. (1979). *Developing IEPs for the gifted and talented.* Los Angeles, CA: National/State Leadership Training Institute on the Gifted and Talented.

Nevin, D. (1977). Seven teenage math prodigies take off from Johns Hopkins on way to advanced degrees. *Smithsonian, 8* (October), 76–82.

Newland, T.E. (1976). *The gifted in socioeducational perspective.* Englewood Cliffs, N.J.: Prentice-Hall.

Renzulli, J.S., & Smith, L. (1979). *A guidebook for developing individualized educational programs (IEP) for gifted and talented students.* Mansfield Center, CT: Creative Learning Press.

Stanley, J.C. (1977). Educational non-acceleration: An international tragedy. Address to the 2nd World Conference on Gifted and Talented Children, University Center, University of San Francisco.

Stanley, J.C. (1979a). The case for extreme educational acceleration of intellectually brilliant youths. In J.C. Gowan, J. Khatena, and E.P. Torrance (Eds.), *Educating the ablest, A book of readings* (2nd ed.). Itasca, IL: F.E. Peacock Publishers.

Stanley, J.C. (1979b). The study and facilitation of talent in mathematics. In A.H. Parsons (Ed.), *The gifted and talented: Their education and development.* The Seventy-eighth Yearbook of the National Society for the Study of Education. Chicago, IL: Univ. of Chicago Press.

Stanley, J.C., George, W.C., & Solano, C.H. (Eds.). (1977). *The gifted and the creative: A fifty-year perspective.* Baltimore, MD: Johns Hopkins Univ. Press.

Torrance, E.P. (1979). *The search for satori and creativity.* Buffalo, NY: Beverly, Ltd.

Whitmore, J.R. (1980). *Giftedness, conflict, and underachievement.* Boston, MA: Allyn & Bacon.

15

Enrichment: An Educational Imperative for Meeting the Needs of Gifted Students

Kay Klausmeier
Tucson Unified School District

"Enrichment can be defined as the type of activity devoted to the further development of the particular intellectual skills and talents of the gifted child."
—James J. Gallagher (1975, p. 76)

In an effort to meet public demands for opportunities for gifted students in the 1950s and 1960s, "get-rich-quick" schemes were adopted by schools and individual teachers. Certain types of activities assumed to provide enrichment were quickly injected into the regular curriculum. In examining enrichment programs, Worcester (1956) found that many activities such as field trips, television programs, making collections, and survey courses in foreign language were casual, unsystematic, and superficial. Many educators recognized the inadequacy of merely offering special subjects or activities without developing academically relevant goals and objectives (Stanley, 1976) that were also related to "particular skills and talents of gifted students" (Gallagher, 1975).

In answer to the need for purposeful enrichment, a variety of curriculum models that provide teachers with techniques appropriate for enrichment within the regular classroom and in special programs have been developed. These models can be adopted by teachers using a variety of content to teach major concepts related to regular curriculum and to extend the learning beyond that curriculum.

209

Major Models for Enrichment

⨯Renzulli's Enrichment Triad

Perhaps the most familiar model is Renzulli's Enrichment Triad (1977), which consists of three types of enrichment: Type I, General Exploration; Type II, Group Training; Type III, Individual and Small Group Investigations of Real Problems. The first two types are for all children but the third is only for those who are self-motivated, show task commitment, and are actively engaged in investigating a real problem. Renzulli arrived at these attributes for the selection of students for Type III activities by studying successful or eminent adults.

The purpose of Type I activities is to expose all students to a variety of ideas, information, and attitudes concerning topics to stimulate interest. Renzulli suggests using resource centers in which both print and nonprint materials are available, conducting field trips, and having guest speakers. He would also encourage students to explore in any manner appropriate for expanding knowledge and generating interest.

More structured learning experiences that provide students with tools and systems for thinking and creating products characterize Type II activities. The purpose is to learn techniques and processes such as brainstorming, observation, categorization, and hypothesizing, which can be used in a variety of learning situations and which form a basis for methods of investigation in Type III activities.

Students who are motivated and committed participate in Type III investigations of real problems. Topics, designs of experiments or procedures for investigations, media for expression, products, and the environment in which investigations take place are chosen by the student. The teacher assists the student in acquiring necessary material and making arrangements and serves in general as a nonjudgmental consultant.

This model provides a broad framework for enrichment, but its effectiveness is more assumed than established through research (Maker, 1982). Also, the criteria for entering into the Type III activities (commitment, self-motivation) limit access to only a few, possibly highly conforming students if "task commitment" is interpreted as showing motivation for what the teacher wants a student to do. The progression of activities appears logical and as long as students can move back and forth among levels as needed, the Renzulli model is an easily adapted model in the regular classroom. However, if one examines the Revolving Door (Renzulli, Reis, & Smith, 1981), the concept of Type III activities that assumes students are only gifted when engaged in Type III investigations, the model loses depth and breadth in addressing the educational needs of the gifted.

⭑Creative Problem Solving

Another model widely applied as a means of enriching the regular curriculum is the Osborn (1963) and Parnes (1966) Creative Problem Solving (CPS) Technique. The assumption is made that by following a five-step process, individuals or groups can learn to be more creative and to solve problems more effectively. By taking known information and rearranging it, seeking variety, deferring judgment, developing and applying criteria to solutions, one can not only increase problem solving ability but arrive at better solutions.

The first two steps in the CPS process are to find the facts related to a situation or "problem" and then to find or identify the problem to be solved. Interestingly, different individuals or groups may find different problems based on the same facts. Thus, for example, given a real problem involving toxic waste, one group may define the problem as one of disposal, another as one of preventing manufacture. In the next two steps, groups propose a variety of ideas to solve the problem, set up criteria for selection of the best solution, and then use these criteria to choose the best solution. Finally, a plan is developed for carrying out the solution and gaining acceptance from those individuals it would affect or involve. The ideas, solutions, and plans may all be different but lead to the same result of eliminating the effects of the toxic waste.

The techniques used in Creative Problem Solving are applicable to all students. By its generality alone, it falls short of meeting a criterion of being qualitatively different for gifted students. The main advantage of CPS is its applicability to a variety of situations. Research has shown CPS to be effective across situations to solve problems (Biondi & Parnes, 1976; Torrance, 1972) and in developing divergent thinking including verbal fluency, flexibility, originality, elaboration, and sensitivity (Feldhusen & Kolloff, 1984). Given its broad applicability, emphasis on developing divergent thinking, and relative ease of teaching, it is relevant for inclusion in a repertoire of techniques for gifted students and can be implemented by regular classroom teachers.

Williams Total Creativity Program

The Total Creativity Program developed by Williams (1972) is based on a morphological model including curriculum (subject areas), teacher behaviors (strategies such as skills of search), and student behaviors of thinking and feeling (flexible thinking, imagination, evaluation). According to Williams, such "feelings" as intuition, fantasy, and imagination contribute to motivation, which is essential for creativity. Among the techniques teachers can use to promote creativity are provocative questions, paradoxes, analogies, discrepancies, visualization, and evaluation.

As an instructional system (Coleman, 1985), the Williams model and program provides teachers with a logical framework, sample lesson plans demonstrating methods and expected outcomes, checklists, and other assessments to aid teachers in information gathering on student behaviors before and after training.

The most obvious differences in Williams' model and other instructional models is that it addresses both cognitive and affective behaviors. Some of these feeling behaviors had previously been directly addressed only by separate creativity or counseling programs rather than recognized as a part of total behaviors related to learning. Although it was not originally developed for the gifted, Williams (1979) has suggested how the Total Creativity Program can be used within the Renzulli framework to meet the needs of gifted students.

Maker (1982) points out as disadvantages of the model that it does not directly meet the needs of gifted students, it lacks a comprehensive theory basis, and it lacks research. The Williams model is visually similar to Guilford's three-dimensional Structure of Intellect model (1967) but not conceptually as complex and integrated, nor does it follow Guilford's theory. Williams has used a variety of sources of theory and techniques to provide teachers with ways of enriching curriculum. No research has been done on the total model consisting of 18 strategies to determine if students make gains as a result of the program.

Taylor's Multiple Talent Approach

Taylor (1968) rejects the traditional intelligence and talent identification methods that identify only a fraction of students. He contends that as many as 60 percent of all children will score above the median in some ability. He proposes six types of talent: academic, creative, planning, communicating, forecasting, decision making. Based on previous research with adults, Taylor viewed creative problem solving and its reflection in work and creative products or performances as the result of combinations of talents, yet in schools academic talent has been the most prevalently developed talent. In studying his "talent totem pole" (1973), we see a varied profile of talents for each student. One student may be at the top of the totem pole in decision making and communicating but relatively low in academic and planning talents.

Taylor's model identifies elements within the talent areas that are evidence of special talent; however, it is not his purpose to search for giftedness, but rather to identify talents among large numbers of individuals. Although his approach has been effective in making educators aware of a broader spectrum of talent and possible characteristics among those with that talent, the model suffers from lack of a total approach and of a theory basis. However, many educators of the gifted note the real-world basis for the model which creates a profile of ability and talent rather than a single academic or IQ definition of ability and talent (Kaplan, 1974; Maker, 1982). These educators encourage development of programs that include the Taylor view of multiple talents.

Bloom's Taxonomy of Educational Objectives

Bloom's Taxonomy of Educational Objectives (1956) was developed in the era of broad curriculum reform in which behavioral objectives were used in curriculum planning and evaluation of outcomes. Bloom's taxonomy provided a hierarchical classification system for curriculum development from lower-level concepts to higher-level concepts. In the Bloom taxonomy, lower-order cognitive objectives must be mastered before higher-order ones; thus, knowledge must be mastered before comprehension and knowledge and comprehension objectives must be mastered and used in the next higher-order classification, application. Analysis, synthesis, and finally evaluation are mastered in cumulative, stepwise fashion.

Although not intended for education of gifted students, Bloom's taxonomy has been widely applied to curriculum materials for the gifted. The taxonomy has been treated as if it were a model for enrichment. It is a skeleton outline of objectives useful in examining and ordering curriculum, but it does not address specific needs of gifted students. Hierarchical models have come under attack recently as additional research on learning has been compiled. Research indicates that all individuals, especially those who are gifted, may not follow typical sequences of concept development or may do so quite rapidly (Sternberg, 1982); that concepts developed within one ability do not necessarily transfer to other abilities (Flavell, 1982); and that different representational languages affect performance (Siegler & Richards, 1982). Although Bloom's taxonomy is very useful, strict adherence to sequence may be inappropriate and even hinder development in gifted students.

Effectiveness of Models in Addressing Enrichment

All of the models cited above have contributed significantly to methods and systemization of providing curriculum enrichment. However, research on the effectiveness of comprehensive models for gifted students has generally been sparse. An exception has been creative problem solving and creative thinking programs. Results of studies with nongifted students have generally been not only positive in developing such creative behaviors as fluency, frequency, elaboration, originality, and problem solving (Feldhusen, Treffinger, & Bahlke, 1970; Torrance & Gupta, 1964), but also effective with gifted students (Feldhusen & Kolloff, 1984).

In the program used by Feldhusen and Kolloff with gifted students, a three-stage approach (Program for Academic and Creative Enrichment) was used: Stage I, basic thinking skills such as questioning, hypothesizing, and brainstorming; Stage II, a variety of strategies developed in previous programs for creative problem solving such as morphological analysis, synectics, attribute listing and then application to school, community, and national problems; Stage III, independent research and study skill development and practice based on individual interests and needs. The program was conducted as a pullout program one hour twice a week and taught by a trained resource teacher. The gifted students who participated in the program made significant advances in their verbal originality and figural originality as compared with gifted students who did not participate in the study.

Although research on creative problem solving has shown that these programs are effective, models still fall short of fulfilling the need for developing comprehensive, academically relevant goals and objectives for gifted students (Stanley, 1976) that also meet their enrichment needs related to their particular skills and talents (Gallagher, 1975). Perhaps more important, there is a need to re-examine the purpose of enrichment in light of current knowledge and educational trends. There are two immediate concerns:

- the identification of students who have potential, including the gifted handicapped, minorities, underachieving gifted, those with nontraditional talents and abilities and nontraditional means of expressing abilities
- the development of an integrated, longitudinal provision throughout the curriculum that allows for discovery and development of giftedness throughout grades and subject areas

The rationale for these two concerns is based on the new views of intelligence, creativity, and learning that have emerged as a result of two decades or more of research across a variety of disciplines.

New Views of Intelligence

Current theories of intelligence that are based on research in neurology, cognitive psychology, and information processing have critical implications for enrichment programs. Research across these disciplines has provided information about how individuals learn, the differences in abilities or talents within and between individuals, efficient methods of problem solving, and creative expression. Although no one theory has been universally accepted, there are a number of generally recognized findings from a variety of research approaches. The following are some of the major elements of these new views:

- Intelligence is multifaceted.
- Individuals may be gifted in only one or in more than one kind of intelligence.
- Intelligence is developed through experience as well as being genetically based.
- Intelligence, or at least efficient use of ability, can be increased or learned.
- Intelligence is dynamic; its functioning is dependent on interaction with the environment.
- Individuals who are expert in an area process information efficiently, using planning strategies, and evaluating and altering strategies to reach goals.
- Intelligence is expressed differently in different cultures.
- Intelligence and productive, creative behavior are linked.

Howard Gardner's (1985) synthesis of research has led him to conclude that there is a biological basis for existence of seven intelligences that can be identified as having distinctive mental processing elements. Additional elements may be held in common with other intelligences, but Gardner theorizes that evidence supports separate linguistic, musical, logical-mathematical, spatial, bodily-kinesthetic, and two personal intelligences (inter-personal and intra-personal). He has arrived at these through examination of research and through observation of idiot savants, brain-injured patients, geniuses, and precocious children.

Robert Sternberg (1982, 1983, 1985) has investigated intelligence by an information processing route. His research has led him to theorize a triarchic, three-part, view of intelligence: a practical or common-sense component; experience, which allows individuals to solve problems more quickly; and metacomponents (Sternberg, 1985). He has emphasized metacomponents such as planning and strategy selection as those that most distinguish the gifted. Planning, evaluation, and strategy selection, Sternberg believes, are the "cornerstones" of intelligence.

J.P. Das's (1979, 1984) work based on Luria's (1973) research on brain functioning postulates two methods of processing all information—simultaneously or successively. Das and his colleagues' research indicate that individuals across cultures process the same information differently based on the habitual experiences and aspects of the environment. Other elements necessary for intelligent behavior are an appropriate level of arousal or attention and planning behaviors. Planning is the highest level of functioning, involving selecting relevant information, organizing information, and evaluating and altering strategies. Individuals who have high planning ability are generally successful no matter whether they are artists or professionals such as lawyers.

Gardner, Sternberg, and Das, as well as researchers in neurology, agree that the brain and the ability to solve problems and think creatively develop with experience. Interaction with the learning environment is necessary for learning. Learning is dynamic, changing as a result of input. The implications for discovery and development of giftedness among special populations is particularly important. Neurological research has found that when one path is shut down by injury, other pathways are developed (Luria, 1973) to reach goals. Conceptual development and creative expression in the handicapped may be proceeding along pathways not currently assessed since most assessments use adaptations of tests standardized on nonhandicapped populations. Lack of exposure to certain culturally accepted and ingrained ways of perceiving and processing information will handicap minority groups and invalidate the use of many current tests of intelligence in other cultures.

One implication of Gardner's theory for identification of gifted students is that the elements or processing strategies associated with each intelligence need to be related to identifying giftedness in young children and then providing ways for the special enrichment needs of these students to be related to curriculum goals and objectives throughout the school years.

Sternberg's (1982) and Das's (1984) research provides strong support for the teaching of strategies, the use of open-ended questions, and the encouragement of differences rather than expecting one method of solution. Creative problem solving programs that develop these behaviors are compatible with current theories of intelligence.

Das emphasizes the need for appropriate levels of arousal that may be related to physical considerations as in hyperactivity and the need to minimize distractions. Appropriate levels of arousal may also be related to interest level and the use of materials and processes that activate thinking.

Next Steps

We appear to be on the threshold of major revisions in identifying gifted students. The verbal-spatial dichotomy and the single IQ score have been shown to be inadequate. The developmental-experiential nature of intelligence increases the importance of providing enrichment on a continuing, longitudinal basis throughout the school years. One comprehensive way of accomplishing this continual enrichment has been to examine the current curriculum goals and objectives and to extend them systematically and longitudinally providing enrichment that incorporates certain elements:

- methods for developing plans, strategies, and evaluation
- real-world experiences rather than contrived, possibly nongeneralizable or even impractical exercises
- enrichment for all intelligences
- provision for special populations and culturally different students

The major enrichment models have provided some appropriate techniques and management plans; however, none is comprehensive enough to be applied at every grade level and none addresses specific abilities in combination with techniques. As Maker (1985) has pointed out, "too often . . . the chosen model or models determine the goals rather than the goals determining the models used" (p. 9). In order to make enrichment relevant to individuals and curricula, each school district must examine its total program, asking how it can improve identification and in what ways enrichment can be accomplished at each grade level in elementary schools and in subject areas in secondary schools.

Maker (1985), working with teachers in Tucson, Arizona, has used a process for developing scope and sequence objectives for gifted programs. This process could be applied to developing enrichment scope and sequence.

Teachers first identified content goals, then examined teaching-learning models and selected the models useful in meeting the process goals:

Content goal: Present content related to broad-based issues, themes, or problems
Models: Jerome Bruner's Structure of a Discipline
Hilda Taba's Teaching Strategies
Process goal: Develop critical and higher level thinking skills
Models: Guilford's Structure of Intellect
Kohlberg's Discussions of Moral Dilemmas
Parnes's Creative Problem Solving Process
Product goal: Develop products that refine or challenge existing ideas, incorporate new and innovative ideas, and utilize techniques, materials, forms, and a body of knowledge in an innovative way.

Models: Renzulli's Enrichment Triad
Taylor's Multiple Talent Approach

After selecting the models, teachers developed outcome objectives that were specific and observable. Criteria for selecting which model would be used were clarity of the model's objectives, extent of the model's orientation to observable student outcomes, comprehensiveness in meeting the goal, ease with which each model could be combined with other models to provide a comprehensive listing of student outcomes related to a particular objective (Maker, 1985).

Tannenbaum (1983) has suggested an enrichment matrix format to help school districts develop a comprehensive program of enrichment. The matrix includes methods of acceleration and career exploration programs as well as cognitive and affective process modifications across content areas.

Tannenbaum proposes that within each subject area content adjustments would be listed according to the following categories: Telescoping Common Core, Expansion of Basic Skills, Programmatic Augmentation (honors program), Provisional Augmentation (based on particular teacher or student competencies or interests and including Renzulli Type III activities, Out-of-School Augmentation (career training, mentor programs, internships). For each content area, higher-level cognitive processes would be listed. Tannenbaum also recognizes the need for "teaching gifted children social and affective consequences of becoming a high-level producer or performer" (Tannenbaum, 1983, p. 438) by adding to each content area a provision for examining problems related to self-concept, friendship, career choice, and emotional development. The addition of this category recognizes not only the importance of social-emotional aspects of success in the real world but also that this is an area related to particular abilities in which some children will excel.

Maker and Tannenbaum's extensive efforts to combine curriculum, models, and needs of gifted students take time, organization, and desire on the part of teachers and administration. As Tannenbaum points out, however, in contrast to injecting activities on a periodic basis, developing "programmatic enrichment . . . takes a long time to plan, longer to implement, and much longer to fade" (Tannenbaum, 1983, p. 426).

The necessary elements for developing a comprehensive enrichment program are within the reach of the schools. The task remains for gifted program directors and curriculum directors to work together on curriculum task forces to provide a comprehensive enrichment plan that reaches far beyond the possibilities of individual classroom enrichment. A broader population of gifted students that has gone virtually unrecognized and unserved because of narrow definitions of giftedness can potentially be screened and served through implementation of enrichment throughout the curriculum. Districtwide provisions take the planning and development burden from individual teachers and can provide more expertise and opportunities for development and implementation of the program.

Perhaps through enrichment more teachers can make a difference to students who sit until they can sit no more and drop out. As an eleven-year-old boy from Michigan wrote about his feelings:

> All the time I just sat there,
> Sat there
> Waiting for something to happen.
>
> My teachers should have ridden
> with Jesse James
> My teachers should have ridden
> with Jesse James
> For all the time they stole from me.
>
> (Delisle, 1984, p. 71)

References

Biondi, A.M., & Parnes, S.J. (1976). *Assessing creative growth*, 2 vols. Great Neck, NY: Creative Synergetics Associates.

Bloom, B.S. (Ed.). (1956). *Taxonomy of educational objectives: Cognitive domain*. New York: David McKay.

Coleman, L.J. (1985). *Schooling the gifted*. Menlo Park, CA: Addison-Wesley.

Das, J.P. (1984). Intelligence and information integration. In J.R. Kirby (Ed.), *Cognitive strategies and educational performance* (pp. 13–31). New York: Academic Press.

Delisle, J.R. (1984). *Gifted children speak out*. New York: Walker.

Feldhusen, J.F., & Kolloff, P.B. (1984). The effects of enrichment on self-concept and creative thinking. *Gifted Child Quarterly, 2*: 53–57.

Feldhusen, J.F., Treffinger, D.J., & Bahlke, S.J. (1970). Developing creative thinking: The Purdue creativity program. *Journal of Creative Behavior, 4*, 85–90.

Flavell, H.H. (1982). Structures, stages, and sequences in cognitive development. *Minnesota Symposium on Child Psychology (Vol. 13)*. Hillsdale, NJ: Erlbaum.

Gallagher, J.J. (1975). *Teaching the gifted child*. Boston: Allyn & Bacon.

Gardner, H. (1985). *Frames of mind*. New York: Basic Books.

Guilford, J.P. (1967). *The nature of human intelligence*. New York: McGraw-Hill.

Kaplan, S.N. (1974). *Providing programs for the gifted and talented: A handbook*. Ventura, CA: Superintendent of Schools.

Luria, A.R. (1973). *The working brain: An introduction to neuropsychology*. (Basil Haigh, Trans.). New York: Basic Books.

Maker, C.J. (1982). *Teaching models in education of the gifted*. Rockville, MD: Aspen Systems.

Maker, C.J. (1985). *Developing scope and sequence in curriculum.* Manuscript submitted for publication.

Osborn, A.F. (1963). *Applied imagination* (3rd rev. ed.). New York: Charles Scribner's Sons.

Parnes, S.J. (1966). *Programming creative behavior.* Buffalo, NY: State University of Buffalo.

Renzulli, J.S. (1977). *The enrichment triad model.* Mansfield, Center, CT: Creative Learning Press.

Renzulli, J.S., Reis, S.M., & Smith, L.H. (1981). *The revolving door identification model.* Mansfield Center, CT: Creative Learning Press.

Siegler, R.S., & Richards, D.D. (1982). The development of intelligence. In R.J. Sternberg (Ed.), *Handbook of human intelligence* (pp. 901–971). New York: Cambridge University Press.

Stanley, J.C. (1976). Identifying and nurturing the intellectually gifted. *Gifted Child Quarterly, 20*(1): 66–75.

Sternberg, R.J. (1982). *Handbook of human intelligence.* New York: Cambridge University Press.

Sternberg, R.J. (1983). Components of human intelligence. *Cognition, 15,* 1–48.

Sternberg, R.J. (1985). *Human intelligence: The model is the message. Science, 230*(4730), 1111–1117.

Tannenbaum, A.J. (1983). *Gifted children: Psychological and educational perspectives.* New York: Macmillan.

Taylor, C.W. (1968). The multiple talent approach. *The Instructor, 77*(27), 142, 144, 146.

Taylor, C.W. (1973). Developing effectively functioning people—the accountable goal of multiple talent teaching. *Education, 94*(2),99–110.

Torrance, E.P., & Gupta, R. (1964). *Development and evaluation of recorded programmed experiences in creative thinking in fourth grade.* Minneapolis: Bureau of Educational Research, University of Minnesota.

Torrance, E.P. (1972). "Can we teach children to think creatively?" *Journal of Creative Behavior, 6,* 114–141.

Williams, F.E. (Ed.). (1972). A total creativity program. Englewood Cliffs, NY: *Educational Technology Publications.*

Williams, F.E. (1979). Williams' strategies orchestrating Renzulli's triad. *Gifted, Creative, and Talented, 9,* 2–10.

Worcester, D.A. (1956). *The education of children of above average mentality.* Lincoln: University of Nebraska Press.

16

Enrichment for the Future:

comments on "Enrichment"

Antoinette S. Ellis, B.A.
Portland State University
Michelle A. Ellis-Schwabe, M.A.
University of Arizona

This critique and analysis will attempt first to discuss and clarify the key difficulties we had with the body of Klausmeier's text and to fill in some presentational gaps or omissions, where possible. Second, in "Enrichment for the Future: Some Notes," we will briefly outline our conceptions of a broader base of student participation in enrichment programs and the necessity for the instructional techniques used by enrichment programs to be as inclusive as possible. We will discuss direct as well as implicit acceleration, activity and curricular adaptation, classroom environment modification, peer tutoring, and mentorships.

First, enrichment not only needs to be analyzed on the basis of its own merits and flaws but also in the light of a consideration of acceleration. In the wake of the formative three decades of enrichment's conceptualization and implementation, there have been left many unformalized approaches and unanswered questions. The field is subject to several major points of controversy at the present time. This would not seem necessarily, however, to preclude a serious analysis of the merits and/or flaws of enrichment as practiced currently and over the years. The analysis should begin with a description of enrichment that could give focus to possible "merits and flaws" to be analyzed. Although Gallagher's definition is quoted, we believe that the first task in criticizing or explaining enrichment for the gifted is to define the term itself.

Prior to an analysis of enrichment's merits and flaws, the reader might easily be willing to accept an apparently much-needed disclosure or better formula-

221

tion of a definition of the term "enrichment" itself. Unfortunately, this is not forthcoming. Certainly, the current definitions in the field are inadequate and we would like Klausmeier to offer a better alternative. We would also like to see her substantiate, interpret, and explain her conclusions more fully for the benefit of the reader.

It is our contention that there has been something of a growing consensus in the field building a viable and specific composite definition of enrichment as "the type of educative activity which goes above and beyond the regular curriculum (Renzulli, 1979; Stanley, 1976, 1981; Gallagher, 1975) in which particular attention is given to gifted students in individual needs, interests and learning styles as well as to integrated curricular modifications and content adaptations" (Gallagher, 1975; Renzulli, 1979; Maker, 1982; Clark, 1983). Needless to say, this definition implicitly "eschews" do-nothing, busywork, casual and academically irrelevant enrichment programs (Gallagher, 1975; Kaplan, 1975; Stanley, 1976, 1981; Renzulli, 1979; Maker, 1982; Khatena, 1983; Clark, 1983; Delisle, 1985).

It should further be noted that a similar and inclusive definition descriptive of enrichment is actually implicit in many suggestions for developing enrichment programs. Stated rather too inclusively to be handy but accurately representing current views, a summary of definitions might be as follows:

> An enrichment program is an individualized program of purposeful, content-based activities designed to extend the regular curriculum for gifted students to meet goals and objectives specified by and for particular school districts/schools considering both their resources and their student populations; these programs incorporate the use of methods and materials appropriate to the needs, interest and skills of the student(s) and are taught in a manner which maximizes the mode of instructional leadership.

Recognizing the fully ramified definitions developed by Gallagher (1975), Renzulli (1979), or others, or the composite definition given above, we believe some important merits and flaws in "enrichment" can be suggested.

First among possible merits seems to be that enrichment, where carefully formulated and systematically integrated and implemented, offers a program that is potentially easier to carry out within the educational setting than a highly articulated acceleration program might be; both parents and administrators appear to find the efforts toward an orderly and integrating enrichment experience for gifted children easier to understand and to support. Another positive feature is the inherent flexibility, without disruption of regular curricular progression or development, that enrichment programs can offer to creative and normal, along with gifted, students at times when it may be particularly appropriate for them. Finally, the student-sensitive outline of curricular modifications (including content, processes, and learning environment) provides positive opportunities to stimulate and encourage student interest in appropriate areas and fosters the creativity and independence that are often curtailed by regular academic procedures and potentially more curtailed under programs of direct acceleration.

Possible deficiencies in enrichment as defined above may continue to be (i) that still not enough is offered in the special program, as Stanley (1981) suggested, (ii) that scope and consequences overlap (Kaplan, 1975), and (iii) that individual needs may still outstrip or diverge too markedly from the coherent program provisions so that new learning or development does not result.

On the whole, Klausmeier's recommendations are acceptable with respect both to their insight into current enrichment program situations and their vision of significant steps to be taken toward strengthening programs and ameliorating insufficiencies. Her emphases on the needs for competent and feasible scope and sequence planning for enrichment programs, effective teaching, and widely available enrichment planning appear to be particularly important elements.

Enrichment programs that must address an audience of gifted children must be highly flexible and individualized in order to reach effectively the diverse and divergent individuals in the program. We believe that even the methods discussed by Klausmeier are not broad-based enough to bring into focus the great potential of differentiated enrichment programs for the present and future.

Two issues are at the focal point here: (i) participation in enrichment should be more broadly conceived, and (ii) a wider provision of educative techniques should be available as part of individualized enrichment. First, enrichment programs in which academically relevant and integrated contents are matched to individual interests, needs, flairs, and facilities, and in which teaching is especially marked by vital instructional leadership and facilitating instructional guidance, are programs not necessarily suited for the gifted alone (i.e., students with IQs of 130 or above). Generally, students with high creativity ratings do not score in a correspondingly exceptional range on conventional intelligence tests (Torrance, 1965), yet the very characteristics that may cluster in the profile of the creative child (independence, divergent thinking, intuition, originality, and productivity) may be the very center of the skills and proclivities the enrichment programs have been created to foster. For example, Renzulli's Triad uses, as a base for its selection of enrichment program participants, the "three-ring" conception of "above average though not necessarily superior general ability, task commitment and creativity" (Renzulli, 1979).

We agree wholly with Renzulli's broadening of the scope for selecting enrichment program students and further anticipate a future redefinition of "giftedness" reflecting these more inclusive and well-considered parameters, although, as Maker (1982) points out, there are important questions to be recognized concerning task commitment both from the point of view of its derivation and from the consideration of environmental preparation.

Further, there appears to be a subgroup of students who can be characterized as neither exceptionally creative nor intellectually superior but who, nevertheless, may become highly contributive individuals in our society. One must call to mind individuals of even immense creative power who were not early recognized as very much more than "problems" in their social or academic settings and who apparently "failed" in amassing accomplishments until some unanticipated "blossoming" happened (for example, Edison, Einstein, Darwin). In each case, of course, some particular youthful "fancy" appears to have been unexpectedly, and even unintentionally, parlayed into an enormous breakthrough of insight and understanding. It would seem to be period-provincial to assume that our present testing capacities and programming skills will assure us of picking out the "future contributors" at an early age for quality nurturance. Hence, we are in favor of conceptualizing enrichment programs much more broadly than they have been in the past—in order to, if you will, provide the small (curiosity-invoking) magnets to an unidentified little Einstein, the fascinating (and apparently nothing more) beetles and moths to an improbable little Darwin, or even small plastic gears to an unrevealed little Seymour Papert. Education's influence is great, its potential greater. We contend that the sweep of the net of enrichment cannot be allowed to be too narrow.

Second, to achieve even a part of their potential impact on the gifted, however variously defined or identified, it is obvious that many techniques of addressing the gifted are needed.

Although Klausmeier avoids any comparison of the relative benefits of acceleration and enrichment, it appears that such a comparison can reveal two significant points. First, enrichment may be conceived as essentially a horizontally progressive educational technique (enriching by broadening, diversifying, complexifying); however, careful analysis will reveal that one must necessarily recognize the possible accelerative vertical aspect of any such real progress along the "enriching" horizontal. While "acceleration" as a special educational program has distinct parameters of its own, the essence of acceleration (progressive movement along a sequential, hierarchical, academic continuum) is decidedly a possible implication of any achievement of enrichment. And, second, acceleration of this implicit kind and the possible consequential direct acceleration, or academic advancement, are both factors to be seriously considered in relation to enrichment programs. Acceleration is more surely a partner in enrichment than has been commonly recognized.

Further, we contend that, in addition to acceleration, the full array of activity and curricular adaptations and classroom environment modifications must be formally aligned with other potentially significant educative techniques such as peer tutoring and its adult-world model, mentorship activities, for use in enrichment programs.

Finally, it is certainly clear that it has been organizationally important for programs such as enrichment to be carefully defined and responsibly rationalized; however, the question of the scope and depth of the program must be as carefully considered and not be sacrified to organizational expediency. Enrichment is a vital new educational route that may well become a major educational thoroughfare in the years to come.

References

Clark, B. (1983). *Growing up gifted* (2nd ed.). Columbus, OH: Charles Merrill.

Gallagher, J.J. (1975). *Teaching the gifted child* (2nd ed.). Boston: Allyn & Bacon.

Kaplan, S.N. (1975). The should nots and shoulds of developing an appropriate curriculum for the gifted. In W.B. Barbe & J.S. Renzulli (Eds.), *Psychology and education of the gifted* (2nd ed.) (pp. 351–358), New York: Irvington.

Khatena, J. (1983). What schooling for the gifted? *Gifted Child Quarterly, 27,* 51–56.

Maker, C.J. (1982). *Teaching models in education of the gifted.* Rockville, MD: Aspen Publishers, Inc.

Renzulli, J.S. (1979). What makes giftedness? Reexamining a definition. In W.B. Barbe & J.S. Renzulli (Eds.), *Psychology and education of the gifted* (2nd ed.) (pp. 55–65). New York: Irvington.

Stanley, J.C. (1976). The case for extreme educational acceleration of intellectually brilliant youths. *Gifted Child Quarterly, 20,* 68–75.

Stanley, J.C. (1981). Rationale of the study of mathematically precocious youth during its first five years of promoting educational acceleration, In W.B. Barbe & J.S. Renzulli (Eds.). *Psychology and education of the gifted,* pp. 248–283.

Torrance, E.P. (1965). *Rewarding creative behavior.* Englewood Cliffs, NJ: Prentice-Hall.

17

Response to the Critique

Kay Klausmeier

E llis and Ellis-Schwabe insist that acceleration is a critical element in education of the gifted child and that it is a "partner in enrichment." I would agree in principle that the two are related, but I did not feel compelled to elaborate on the relationship in a discussion of enrichment. Acceleration deals with placement decisions based on evaluation of skill level and appropriateness of curriculum, whereas enrichment, as Ellis and Ellis-Schwabe suggest, relates to "complexifying, diversifying." Acceleration moves an individual to a higher level on the curriculum-skill continuum, while enrichment provides depth at that level. The issue is that enrichment should be at every level and should be qualitatively different. Enrichment is a process-topic-individual interaction designed to carry out educational goals and to meet individual student needs. The important point of a discussion of enrichment and acceleration is that the educational system needs to have the possibility for both in place throughout the curriculum and organizational structure in order to meet individual student needs.

IV

Policies, Program Development, and Evaluation:

what can we defend, and how should it be defended?

A s Seeley reminds us in Chapter 20, the word "defensibility" implies that we must be accountable for our practices in the field of education of gifted learners. Beyond this, we must also "guard against attack"; but guarding should not include defending practices just because we have developed them (and always believed they would work)! In this section, program development and evaluation are explored from several perspectives.

Feldhusen begins the section by providing an overview of the program development process and suggesting that those involved in initiating and implementing a program discuss various alternatives and their implications before beginning a program. He presents certain positions as being more defensible than others and outlines ways to design programs that include defensible practices. He agrees with the earlier consensus that a variety of program options (including both those labeled enrichment and those labeled acceleration) must be provided. Feldhusen reviews the works of several authors in this volume in the area of curriculum design, reminding us of the necessity to design a program that is "articulated across grade levels and among disciplines." The need for long-range planning by individual teachers as well as program developers and the coordination of this planning is evident from the discussion.

Healey's critique focuses on the need for cogent, well-defined policies that can be translated into practices and suggests that as educators we must succinctly articulate our positions. An obvious implication is that if we cannot state these policies clearly, they cannot be defended. Healey then makes his criticism constructive by presenting a series of policy statements based on an interpretation of Feldhusen's points of view. Further discussion of these explicitly stated policies could stimulate a thoughtful review of existing programs as well as offer a beginning point for the development of new services for gifted students. In light of the discussions by Seeley, Callahan and Caldwell, and Dinham and Udall, the existence of the sort of educational policy statements proposed by Healey could make an evaluator's task much easier. Since they advocate the involvement of evaluators in the program planning process, Callahan and Caldwell would probably suggest that evaluators assist in development of such clearly stated policies.

Seeley provides an overview of evaluation—its importance, how it is used and abused, essential elements, politics, and evaluation for defensibility. He reminds us of the importance of good evaluations, not just for ourselves (as a way to demonstrate the success of one program), but also the importance of good evaluations to the survival of the field of education for the gifted. Like Callahan and Caldwell, he suggests development of the evaluation design as the program is being formulated, but does not indicate the necessity for early involvement of those who will carry out the assessment. Finally, he states that the best defense of our programs includes demonstrating both relatedness and separateness. In other words, the program for gifted learners must be demonstrated to be "an integrated and meaningful part of the general education program," but distinctly different in certain ways.

Callahan and Caldwell's approach to evaluation is very different from the traditional viewpoint. The goal of evaluation is seen as assisting programs in their endeavor to be successful rather than giving an after-the-fact judgment of the worth of the program. They note a number of different purposes that can be served by the evaluation, all of which contribute to the aim of enhancing the defensibility of a program. In general, they seem to agree with Seeley (implicitly rather than explicitly) that we need to consider not only our own program and its success or failure, but also the impact our practices, successes, and failures may have on others.

Factors that would enhance the defensibility of a program, its replicability, and its value to the field include purposes which can be served by an appropriate (defensible) evaluation: (*i*) documentation of the need for the program, the case for a particular approach, the feasibility of a program, program implementation, and the results or impacts of the program; (*ii*) identification of program strengths and weaknesses; (*iii*) provision of data for in-progress revisions of the program; and (*iv*) explanation and description of the program to interested but uninformed audiences.

Callahan and Caldwell conclude by recommending that educators consider alternatives to the traditional "experimental" evaluation designs in which control and experimental groups are compared using "objective" and very quantitative measurements. These designs, according to Callahan and Caldwell, are often less objective than others because their biases "tend to be hidden in numbers, tests, and tables." Such designs are deemed incomplete because they neglect factors important in describing and judging the success of the program being evaluated.

Dinham and Udall agree that a model based in a naturalistic, qualitative philosophy is more appropriate for serving the needs of audiences for program evaluation. Generally, they decry the lack of true models available to the field, but describe a naturalistic approach, called the "responsive" model and used successfully in evaluations by Callahan, as one of the true models available. They differ from Callahan and Caldwell by emphasizing the importance of the audience and suggest that the purposes of evaluation are shaped entirely by the audiences and their needs. Callahan and Caldwell respond to this concern, however, by noting that although not so explicitly stated as in the Dinham and Udall article, their approach to evaluation is responsive to the needs of various audiences.

Participant attitudes and the political climate of the evaluation are discussed as important factors by Dinham and Udall as well as Seeley. Dinham and Udall then offer a discussion of the role of the evaluator and list some important criteria for selecting evaluators.

Finally, in the summary/conclusion of their essay, Dinham and Udall briefly note a point for which the editor has been waiting: defensible programs for the gifted ". . . show an internal consistency from definition to identification procedures through service delivery and program evaluation." Certainly, this need for consistency is implied in many other chapters in this volume, but never is the idea discussed in depth or its implications fully explained!

Since no one else has chosen to address the issue in depth, I will offer a few suggestions and raise a few questions based on the earlier discussions regarding definitions of giftedness. If one agrees that a program must be consistent from definition through evaluation (and I would add philosophy), then whether one chooses a "giftedness as productivity" concept (with qualitative differences existing only in adults, with learners perceived as different only in degree and thus only "potentially" gifted) or a "giftedness as developmental differences in the learner" concept will influence not only the identification process and the curriculum, but also the program evaluation.

Following the perspective of giftedness as adult productivity, the evaluation of the success of the selection process must demonstrate that the procedures used were effective in identifying students who were potentially productive. In fact, it must show that those who were selected for the program eventually became more productive than those who were not chosen for the program. Thus, the success of the program's identification procedures cannot be totally determined until 20 or 30 years later, when the students have reached adulthood! Certainly, one can collect data on the productivity of children in the program, but can we be certain that productive children become productive adults? or, conversely, that nonproductive children do not become productive adults? We cannot. In fact, there is some data to suggest that many children who do nothing in school become the most productive adults and that some of our most productive children stop producing as adults. The point is that the ultimate or true test of the effectiveness of identification within this concept of giftedness must come in the future, not now. What funding agency wants to wait 20 years for data on the success of a program?

Like the evaluation of identification procedures, the evaluation of the program design and curriculum must demonstrate that the students involved in the program did, in fact, become more productive, and that their productivity was a direct result of the program provided for them. This evaluation must show, for example, that the program provided instruction in needed skills to the learners, that these skills were generalized or transferred to the work setting, and that they enabled (or encouraged) greater productivity. Again, one can measure certain gains in the learner and assume that these gains are predictive of greater potential of the learner to become productive as an adult. However, this assumption would constitute a fairly shaky basis for an evaluation design.

On the other hand, if one conceptualizes giftedness as differences in the learner, an evaluator's task is much easier, and success can be demonstrated much more quickly. If the learner is viewed as having different interests, a different learning style, a different learning rate, or other differences that are evidenced now, evaluation of the identification process must demonstrate that the students who were selected for the program did, in fact, need a different program, and that the procedures used located all the students who needed a different program. This is quite a different task from demonstrating that students become productive adults.

Based on the conceptualization of gifted students as different learners, evaluation of the program and curriculum must demonstrate that the special program provided was more appropriate than the program previously provided for the student. The learner "developed better" or had his or her needs met more appropriately after placement in the special program. Changes could include higher achievement, better self-concept, higher creativity, better emotional or social adjustment, or other similar criteria. Progress (in areas deemed important) after placement in the program can be compared with progress before placement in the program to determine the appropriateness of the program for a particular learner or for a group of learners with similar characteristics. Basically, the evaluation needs to show that the learners did have needs not being met in the regular classroom and that the special program met these needs. Greater growth after placement than before is one sure way of demonstrating success.

In conclusion, it is necessary to develop comprehensive programs for the gifted that (1) provide a variety of options, (2) are coordinated and articulated, (3) are well-planned, (4) have clearly defined policies and procedures, (5) demonstrate success through well-designed, responsive evaluations, (6) have a sound theoretical base, and (7) respond to the needs of the community. We must also consider carefully the development of a program consistent in its philosophy, identification, service delivery, curriculum, and evaluation; and we must thoughtfully weigh the consequences of a particular philosophical position, following its logic in all aspects of program development, implementation, and evaluation. Two particular philosophical orientations have been used for illustrative purposes in the introductory sections for this volume. It is my belief that many issues discussed in the following section will have more meaning if the reader considers his or her own philosophical position and program while reading the following chapters.

18

Policies and Procedures for the Development of Defensible Programs for the Gifted

John F. Feldhusen, Ph.D.
Purdue University

P rograms of services for gifted and talented youth have evolved in cities and counties and as functions of state departments of education throughout the United States during the past 15 years. Some have reflected careful review and analysis of research, philosophical issues, and public policy, while others have grown in a desultory, thoughtless manner. Some have reflected clear goals of meeting the special needs of gifted and talented youth, while others seem to represent token efforts. In particular, the vast growth of part-time programs with resource teachers who often serve gifted and talented students for only a few hours per week illustrates rather obvious tokenism. In many or most of such programs no effort is made to modify the curriculum, teaching methods, or learning environment in the regular classroom where the gifted student spends the vast majority of time. Clearly, such limited approaches to serving the gifted reflect little review or analysis of research, philosophical issues, or public policy related to serving the needs of all youth.

In developing policies and plans, a number of issues should be addressed or considered by the planning committee. In this chapter I will set forth some of the major issues and propose some positions and approaches that seem to be more defensible than others. The issues to be addressed are as follows: (*i*) philosophical orientations, (*ii*) the target populations and the identification process, (*iii*) the planning-development process, (*iv*) clarifying needs and local conditions, (*v*) administrative mandate and leadership, (*vi*) program models, (*vii*) curriculum differentiations, (*viii*) articulation across grade levels and

235

among disciplines, (*ix*) selecting and training teachers, (*x*) inservice training needs, (*xi*) funding and financial constraints, and (*xii*) formative and summative program evaluation.

Philosophical Orientation

We are committed in the United States to the position that all youth have a right to a free public education. However, we are not in agreement concerning the form that education should take. To be fair or just, should it be the same for all youth at a given age or grade level? Or should it take cognizance of the special needs, characteristics, and abilities of each youth? While the latter position might be endorsed by a majority of school personnel, professional practice seems to say otherwise: third grade students are taught the third grade lesson. Individualization of offerings is rare. All students study the same lesson at the same time for the same amount of time.

One can distinguish three philosophical positions that provide a rationale for special services for the gifted and talented. First, we might agree that each student has a right to an education that is appropriate for his or her special individual characteristics and related needs. For example, gifted and talented youth have a need for education that is adjusted to their achievement levels in each subject and to the pace at which they are able to learn. They may be severely disturbed or bored with instruction that simply presents what they already know or that presents new skills and concepts at an inappropriately slow pace. Feldhusen and Wyman (1980, p. 15) offer the following list of special needs of the gifted and talented, all of which are based on observable characteristics and abilities.

1. Maximum achievement of basic skills and concepts.
2. Learning activities at appropriate level and pace.
3. Experience in creative thinking and problem solving.
4. Development of convergent abilities, especially in logical deduction and convergent problem solving.
5. Stimulation of imagery, imagination, spatial abilities.
6. Development of self awareness and acceptance of own capacities, interests, and needs.
7. Stimulation to pursue higher level goals and aspirations (models, pressure, standards).
8. Exposure to a variety of fields of study, art, professions, and occupations.

9. Development of independence, self direction and discipline in learning.
10. Experience in relating intellectually, artistically and affectively with other GCT students.
11. A large fund of information about diverse topics.
12. Access and stimulation to reading.

The major rationale for P.L. 94–142 is that an appropriate education must meet the special, individual needs of youth. While P.L. 94–142 pertains only to the education of handicapped and learning-disabled youth, there is also a need to provide educational services that recognize the special characteristics and related needs of gifted and talented students.

The second philosophical rationale for special program services is the assertion that all youth have a right to educational services that help develop their potential abilities to the highest level. This rationale clearly recognizes that potential differs because ability, health, energy, adjustment, and other factors differ in the individual. Some youth will have more potential because of their intelligence, musical aptitude, mechanical skill, or artistic talent and they have a right to an education that will enable them to develop their potentials to the highest possible levels. In practice this rationale implies that a fifth grade youngster who has superior motor capacities, as revealed in dance, is thereby reflecting high-level potential for success in ballet and should be given educational opportunities that sustain the accelerated state of development of these talents. The facilitation in youth is needed to enable high-level achievement in dance later in life.

A third rationale, one that now looms large among nations competing for positions in the world of commerce and politics, is that we must develop our gifted and talented youth so that they can serve the emerging talent needs of our nation's work force. We require creatively productive engineers, artists, teachers, scientists, architects, dentists, musicians, actors, and individuals in all areas of human endeavor. They must come from the ranks of gifted and talented youth. We are aware that other nations are striving to develop their pool of highly talented professionals, artists, and scientists and that we are trying to maintain our lead or, in some cases, keep up. In addition, states may strive to develop their pool of talented youth so that there will be an adequate pool of adult professionals, artists, and scientists to meet the states' developmental and competitive needs.

Open discussion and communication with all of the personnel in a school concerning the philosophical bases or barriers for special program services for gifted and talented youth is a desirable prelude to program development. Such open discussion should lead to a greater acceptance and understanding of program goals and/or a highlighting of pockets of resistance. For established programs a review and re-evaluation of the philosophical issues from time to time should serve to prevent the growth of opposition.

Target Population and Identification

Who are the youth who have need for special program services because of their superior or outstanding talents and abilities? How can we identify them and their special needs? How can we use the identification process to begin planning and providing a differentiated education for them? These are salient questions that are often ignored in the identification process. Instead, there is often an implicit assumption that our task in serving the gifted and talented is to find them, once and for all time, and programs will be self-defining.

With the Marland report in 1972 we stepped into the modern age and multi-talent conceptions of giftedness (p. 2):

> Gifted and talented children are those identified by professionally qualified persons who by virtue of outstanding abilities are capable of high performance. These are children who require differentiated educational programs and services beyond those normally provided by the regular school program in order to realize their contribution to self and society.
>
> Children capable of high performance include those with demonstrated achievement and/or potential ability in any of the following areas, singly or in combination.
>
> 1. General intellectual ability
> 2. Specific academic aptitude
> 3. Creative or productive thinking
> 4. Leadership ability
> 5. Visual and performing arts
> 6. Psychomotor ability

This definition, while subject to much criticism and possible preconceptions, nevertheless reminds us that giftedness is probably not a single unitary trait. Rather there might be a number of ways of being gifted or talented, and/or within gifted individuals there may be a number of talents, abilities, skills, conceptions of self, personality factors, interests, attitudes, motivations, and energy factors that constitute superior potential or giftedness.

School personnel and parents often seem to assume that giftedness is "born in" and fixed forever and that what is needed is to find the truly or really gifted child. Actually, giftedness is a set of abilities, traits, and characteristics that emerge through nurturance. Some children get off to a head start and remain ahead. A few have spurts later and seem suddenly to become gifted. But above all the abilities and skills of the gifted have been learned.

Human abilities emerge early in the first five years of life (Bloom, 1964) and their growth is facilitated by conditions at home and at school during the early years (Bloom & Sosniak, 1981). The Astor Program (Ehrlich, 1978) was designed especially to serve the needs of and facilitate growth in young gifted children. Many schools wait until the third or fourth grade to begin programs for the gifted and talented. Such a decision is really contradictory to our best knowledge. Programs for the gifted can best start at the preschool or kindergarten level, and there is much that parents can do at home to facilitate the development of giftedness from birth onward at home (White, 1975).

There are special problems of detecting and nurturing giftedness in atypical populations such as minority groups, handicapped individuals, rural youth, or the poor. Often the policies developed for school gifted programs pay no attention to the special needs of potentially gifted youth from atypical populations even though excellent guidance is available (Gallagher, 1975; Baldwin, Gear, & Lucito, 1978; Torrance, 1977; and Maker, 1977). In the planning and development process, as well as in later stages of program revision and updating, attention to the needs of special populations is essential to assure that the appropriate identification processes are used and that program services are provided to meet their special needs.

If the identification processes are focused too strongly on finding *the* gifted child, labeling is likely to follow. Cornell (1983) has demonstrated positive and negative effects of labeling children as gifted. Palmer (1983) suggested that the major impact of labels is the attributions or expectations associated with the labels. Gifted youth often abhor labeling (American Association for Gifted Children, 1978), but parents and school personnel persist in labeling youth as gifted while deploring or fearing the growth of a sense of elitism among them. In developing programs for gifted youth there should be explicit policy consideration of labeling procedures and the control or limitations that should be imposed.

A major issue in the identification of gifted and talented youth is how to find staff who are psychometrically competent to use tests, rating scales, observations, and related statistical procedures to identify and diagnose the needs of this population. The recent report by Richert et al. (1981) reveals relative chaos in the area of identification. Oftentimes the personnel assigned this task lack the necessary psychometric skills.

Finally, but most important, is the question of who to serve. Many schools have decided to limit their programs to the academic-intellectual area. Ease and convenience of identification is cited as one reason for such a decision.

Nevertheless, it seems much more defensible to consider potential talents in all areas of the curriculum. Thus, the following framework is proposed:

1. Academic-Intellectual

- Science
- Mathematics
- English
- Social Studies
- Languages
- Computers

2. Artistic-Creative

- Dance
- Music
- Drama
- Graphics
- Sculpture
- Photography

3. Vocational

- Home Economics
- Industrial Arts
- Agriculture
- Business

While the psychomotor area of athletics is not included in this framework, it seems likely that the varsity and intramural athletic programs in most schools provide abundant opportunities for identification and nurturance of talent in that area. The arts and the vocational areas should be a part of comprehensive programming for the gifted and talented (Milne, 1982). It is clear that some youth show superior talent in these areas and their talents should be nurtured. Furthermore, the charge of fostering elitism in gifted programs is exacerbated by the apparent assertion that giftedness can be shown only in the academic-intellectual areas.

Procedures for identification should, whenever possible, involve multiple inputs, but those inputs should bear a valid relationship to the types of giftedness being identified. Thus, a language arts achievement test, a verbal IQ, and a reading score may be valid identification scores for a program that seeks to identify and nurture verbal talents while these same scores would *not* be appropriate for identifying mathematical or artistic talent. Multiple inputs also means that in addition to test scores, ratings of observed behavior or products should be considered, and that such data should be secured not only from teachers but also from parents and potentially gifted youth themselves. Synthesizing data from the identification process calls for judgment. Numbers alone cannot determine a student's giftedness or special needs. Many schools have organized identification-differentiation committees to carry out the final process of selecting those youth who have superior talent and who need special program services.

The process of specifying the target populations for a gifted program and developing the identification-differentiation procedures is described by Tannenbaum (1983) as crucial in the establishment of a gifted program. The process should be reviewed frequently to make sure that those youth who need the services of a gifted program are being drawn in and provided for appropriately. Little harm will be done by drawing in false positives, but those potentially gifted youth who are left out by mistake may suffer irreparable lifelong damage.

Planning-Development Process

The planning-development process should be carried out by a knowledgeable committee under mandate from the board or the superintendent. Representation on the planning-development committee should include K-12 teachers, parents, and at least one administrator. The committee should continue to function after a program is in operation to ensure surveillance of implementation and to seek changes, additions, and innovations. The following outline might be used by the committee as a guide in the planning process:

1. Need for program
2. Philosophy of program
3. Goals (long-range, short-range)
4. Objectives (pupil, teacher, environmental)
5. Target groups
6. Screening and identification procedures
7. Administrative design(s)
8. Differentiated instruction
   A. Curriculum
   B. Teaching strategies

9. Amount of time spent by teachers in program
10. Articulation and coordination
11. Professional staff qualifications
12. Special education consultant services
13. Evaluation procedures
14. Budget

In carrying out its mandate the planning-development committee must deal with a number of the policy issues addressed in this chapter. To deal effectively and make wise decisions the committee members *must* be or become knowledgeable about the field of education of the gifted, they must know alternative program models from firsthand observation, they must have access to good consultants, and they must have adequate financial resources. The National/State Leadership Training Institute for the Gifted and Talented (316 W. 2nd Street, Suite PH-C, Los Angeles, CA 90012-3595) has published excellent resource material for such committees. Good consultants, speakers, inservice workshop leaders, and courses of instruction at colleges and universities seem to be abundantly available in the field. Excellent alternative program models are also available for visitation in many states. Many states also provide grant funds for program planning and development activities.

The planning-development committee is the focus of crucial policy matters and decision making. This committee will be the chief determiner of the success of a gifted program in meeting the special needs of gifted and talented youth.

Clarifying Needs and Local Conditions

One of the major functions of the planning-development committee is to determine local needs and conditions as the basis for program development. Needs assessment often refers to perceived local needs. A needs assessment may ask teachers, administrators, and parents about the number and types of gifted youth in the school, their special problems or needs, the difficulties teachers face in serving these youth, the services they see as being needed, and their reactions to some proposed program services. The needs assessment also typically tries to gauge the attitudes and opinions of the program constituents. The latter are likely to relate often to policy issues. Potential program goals and objectives can also be evaluated in a needs assessment.

The operational forms of needs assessment are typically rating scales or checklists, observation of classes, and interviews with various constituents.

Special technical assistance and some financial resources are needed to carry out an effective needs assessment.

Administrative Mandate and Leadership

Who will be in charge of the program for gifted and talented youth? What will the lines of authority be? Will the school board mandate that there be a program? Will the superintendent, assistant superintendents, curriculum coordinators, guidance personnel, psychologists, and other teachers support the program and offer assistance and leadership in its development?

Ideally, there will be one overall coordinator for a K-12 program, separate coordinators for the elementary and secondary levels if school size permits, and a clearly defined relationship of the program coordinators to the administration. The size of the school, of course, determines the overall budget available. In small schools the budget may not be large enough to warrant separate elementary and secondary coordinators. A critical policy problem arises when the role of the coordinator(s) must be defined in relation to building principals, other teachers who are not working in the gifted program, and support staff such as counselors or psychologists. Clearly, the usual line-staff hierarchy may not be applicable, but lines of authority must be specified. The coordinators of gifted programs may find themselves caught between refractory administrators and program goals. These issues can and must be addressed and resolved at the planning stage.

The brunt of the leadership task must inevitably fall upon the program coordinator. She or he must work with the planning-development committee, the administration, the program teachers, nonprogram teachers, and parents. The assignment is complex and calls for a high degree of leadership skill and knowledge of gifted program organization and services. The coordinator must provide the training and supervision to make the instructional program and curriculum achieve the specified goals and objectives.

Service Delivery Models

Ideal programs for the gifted and talented provide multiple services to meet the diverse needs of gifted and talented youth. We have used the term "multi-service programming" (Feldhusen, 1982) and Stanley (1979) has referred to it as the need for a smorgasbord. But the issue of selecting services remains and must be addressed by guiding policies that have been carefully considered.

Here such issues arise as how much and what kinds of acceleration, what forms or types of enrichment, how much individualization of instruction, the relationship between a pullout program and instruction in a regular classroom, and the amount of segregation-integration of gifted students with regular students.

The multiservice or smorgasbord approach to programming is essentially eclectic. It borrows the best from the Study of Mathematically Precocious Youth (Stanley, 1980), from The Revolving Door Model (Renzulli, et al., 1981), from the Individual Program Planning Model (Treffinger, 1981), and from various other models. It also uses as wide a variety of services as possible, drawn often from both in-school and out-of-school resources. In addition, an Individual Educational Program (IEP) or growth plan may be used to carry out the diagnosis-differentiation-prescription process.

The preeminent need of gifted and talented youth is for instruction and experiences at an appropriate cognitive level, pace, depth, and complexity to maintain a challenge and provide for continuous growth. Motivation to achieve, to learn, to investigate is the product of such appropriate instructional conditions. The second grader with reading ability at the fifth grade level will suffer under an instructional regimen that holds him or her to second grade level reading experiences. The mathematically gifted ninth grader being introduced to algebra will almost inevitably find the course simple and boring. If challenged, children learn, grow intellectually, and develop the necessary metacognitive skills needed for higher-level achievement.

Many program models stress the learning of process skills such as creativity, problem solving, independent research, critical thinking, and logic. An immediate criticism is that all youth need and can profit from instruction in the process skills. Nevertheless, it seems likely that gifted and talented youth have a special need for higher-level training in these process skills mainly because of their apparent link to adult creative production.

Weiss and Gallagher (1982) reviewed the research and descriptive reports on programs for the gifted and talented. They conclude that much of the work in this area reflects weak evaluation designs but that there is some evidence for the value or effectiveness of programs, especially in improving creative thinking skills. However, they note that there is little evidence for the transfer of such skills to other studies or activities in the lives of students. Further, they conclude that education of the gifted "remains a fertile and largely unexplored field" (p. 70).

Curriculum for the Gifted

The major new area of development in education of the gifted is curriculum. For about a decade the major foci of development were identification and program development. It often seemed that the curriculum was assumed to take care of itself. Many programs grew up then with piecemeal curricula drawn randomly from published and teacher-made sources. Pullout/resource room programs often seemed to have curricula that concentrated in the language arts, creativity, and independent research, with little attention to social studies, science, mathematics, or the arts. The major emphasis seems also to have been on the learning of process skills such as fluency, flexibility, originality, and elaboration (the divergent thinking operations, Torrance & Myers, 1970); analysis, synthesis, and evaluation (the Bloom cognitive skills, Bloom, 1956); research methods (Polette, 1982); logical and critical thinking (Halpern, 1984); and productive thinking, forecasting, decision making, communicating, and planning (the Talents Unlimited skills, Taylor, 1963). Specific content appeared in the curricula of gifted programs in relatively random fashion as a part of enrichment units of instruction. The exception, however, is the specified content of Advanced Placement courses (College Board, 1983) and the accelerated high school courses in science, mathematics, and English advocated by proponents of academic acceleration for gifted youth (Stanley & Benbow, 1982).

Kaplan (1979) presented an excellent model and guidelines for curriculum development in education of the gifted in the *Inservice Training Manual: Activities for Developing Curriculum for the Gifted and Talented*. The set of principles for a differentiated curriculum constitute one of the best guides available in the field (p. 5):

1. Present content that is related to broad-based issues, themes, or problems.
2. Integrate multiple disciplines into the area of study.
3. Present comprehensive, related, and mutually reinforcing experiences within an area of study.
4. Allow for the in-depth learning of a self-selected topic within the area of study.
5. Develop independent or self-directed study skills.
6. Develop productive, complex, abstract, and/or higher level thinking skills.
7. Focus on open-ended tasks.
8. Develop research skills and methods.
9. Integrate basic skills and higher level thinking skills into the curriculum.
10. Encourage the development of products that challenge existing ideas and produce "new" ideas.
11. Encourage the development of products that use new techniques, materials, and forms.

12. Encourage the development of self-understanding, i.e., recognizing and using one's abilities, becoming self-directed, appreciating likenesses and differences between oneself and others.
13. Evaluate student outcomes by using appropriate and specific criteria through self-appraisal, criterion referenced and/or standardized instruments.

A major new influence on curriculum development in education of the gifted was Maker's text *Curriculum Development for the Gifted* (1982). Maker stresses the need for curriculum for the gifted to be qualitatively different and based on their specific characteristics and needs. She proposes that in developing curriculum for the gifted attention must be paid to the content, to process/method issues, to the products of learning activities, and to the structure of the learning environment. A number of topics must be addressed (p. 10):

Content
  A. abstractness
  B. complexity
  C. variety
  D. organization
  E. economy
  F. study of people
  G. methods

Process/Method
  A. higher level thought
  B. open-endedness
  C. discovery
  D. proof/reasoning
  E. freedom of choice
  F. group interaction
  G. pacing
  H. variety

Product
  A. real problems
  B. real audiences
  C. evaluation
  D. transformation

Learning Environment
  A. student centered
  B. openness

    C. accepting
    D. complex
    E. high mobility

Van Tassel-Baska (1984, p. 58) developed a concise set of seven guiding principles for curriculum development for the gifted:

1. The content of curricula for the G/T should focus on and be organized to include more elaborate, complex, and in-depth study of major ideas, problems, and themes that integrate knowledge within and across systems of thought.
2. Curricula for the G/T should allow for the development and application of productive thinking skills to enable students to reconceptualize existing knowledge and/or generate new knowledge.
3. Curricula for the G/T should enable them to explore constantly changing knowledge and information and develop the attitude that knowledge is worth pursuing in an open world.
4. Curricula for the G/T should encourage exposure to selection and use of specialized and appropriate resources.
5. Curricula for the G/T should promote self-initiated and self-directed learning and growth.
6. Curricula for the G/T should provide for the development of self-understanding and the understanding of one's relationship to persons, societal institutions, nature and culture.
7. Evaluations of curricula for the G/T should be conducted in accordance with prior stated principles, stressing higher-level thinking skills, creativity, and excellence in performance and products.

This set of guidelines is noteworthy in several ways. The first guideline stresses the study of major ideas, problems, and themes that serve to integrate knowledge across systems of thought. The sixth guideline is also unique in suggesting that the pursuit of self-understanding in the gifted should focus on self in relation to other people, institutions, nature, and culture.

Curricula for the gifted and talented should be planned on a K-12 basis. That is, there must be appropriate learning experiences across the K-12 spectrum. There is, however, no way to specify a curriculum by grade level for all gifted youth because of differences in their levels and types of precocity. Some mathematically gifted youth are ready for algebra in sixth grade, some first graders who are verbally precocious are ready for fourth grade level reading experiences, and some artistically talented fourth graders are ready for high school level art instruction. K-12 curriculum planning means chiefly that opportunities are available for accelerated, integrative, and intellectually complex learning experiences when the student is ready.

Some uniformities are possible. Many verbally gifted youth should have introductory foreign language learning experiences in elementary school and formal language instruction beginning in the seventh grade. High school mathematics and science courses should be opened to mathematically gifted youth as much as three years ahead of the norm for grade level. Special Advanced Placement or honors courses should provide college level or accelerated challenges to gifted youth with content that is complex, integrative, and oriented to process thinking skills. Grouping at the elementary level and emphasis in secondary honors classes on problem solving, inquiry, creativity, and conceptual learning can also provide the proper challenges for the gifted. In the arts quite similar concepts are appropriate.

Above all, in designing curriculum for the gifted, it is essential that they be challenged to strive for high-level goals, for new understanding and creative excellence in all their studies. Creative production is best viewed as a process of first mastering the skills or understanding of what is already known in a field and then leaping beyond or creating the new concept, performance, work invention, or product. Gifted youth must work at these higher levels constantly seeking a better way or idea.

Articulation Across Grade Levels and Among Disciplines

Programs for the gifted and talented have evolved in elementary schools in total isolation from programs at the middle school and high school levels. In many cases there are programs at the elementary level only. Some schools offer pullout/resource room programs at the elementary level emphasizing language arts experiences while the junior high program stresses math acceleration and the high school program offers honors classes in several subjects. Thus, in many schools there is near chaos in the diversity of provisions at the different levels or discontinuity of services from level to level.

One excellent program for the gifted and talented in Indiana has provided articulated services across all grade levels, K-12, and across the disciplines of mathematics, science, language arts, and graphic and performing arts. The program also offers supplementary but integrated experiences on Saturday mornings. There has been much attention to the development of curricula in Gary, and much work is in progress. Teachers of the gifted are required to take training that prepares them for curriculum development activities. Outside specialists in the various disciplines have worked with the Gary staff for a number of years in developing the curriculum.

The purpose of a curriculum is to have a systematic plan for instructional activities and materials to achieve specified goals and objectives. Articulation is concerned with continuity and mutual reinforcement over time and across disciplines. The math and science curricula can be coordinated with the social studies, language arts, and arts curricula in the study of major concepts and themes. Feldhusen (1980) served as Editor and Van Tassel-Baska as Project Coordinator in a curriculum project aimed at developing interdisciplinary units of instruction for K-8 gifted youth, focusing on the major themes of reasoning, signs and symbols, change, and problem solving. The units are designed for three broad levels: primary, intermediate, and junior high. The four basic disciplines of social studies, mathematics, science, and language arts are used as content. The units are designed to help gifted youth achieve integrated, high-level understanding of the four themes. They have been used successfully in many gifted programs and represent the several dimensions of articulation. The purpose of articulation is to achieve consistent, high-level goals for the gifted with integrated learning experiences.

Selecting and Training Teachers

Teachers of the gifted and talented should be gifted and talented in the areas in which they attempt to instruct gifted and talented youth. It is, of course, extremely difficult to determine the level of artistic talent or mathematical ability necessary to teach the gifted. Obviously, it will differ according to the level of maturity of the gifted student. But it will be a level that should be decidedly superior to the level of ability or talent of teachers of average youth at that grade level.

Gallagher (1975) summarized research on the desirable characteristics of teachers of the gifted. Most of the evidence comes from studies of the perceptions of gifted youth, their parents, and teachers concerning desirable teacher characteristics. Seeley (1984) provides the following list as a summary of such research:

1. mature, experienced, self-confident
2. highly intelligent
3. avocational interests which are intellectual
4. high achievement needs
5. favorable attitudes toward the gifted
6. sense of humor

7. systematic
8. creative and flexible
9. broadly knowledgeable
10. hard working
11. understands and accepts individual differences
12. is a facilitator rather than director

In addition to the stable, entry characteristics of teachers of the gifted there is a concern for the competencies they should have when teaching this specific population. Such lists naturally vary by grade level and discipline. Seeley (1984), however, suggests that the following are basic competencies:

1. higher cognitive teaching and questioning
2. curriculum modification strategies
3. ability to develop curriculum
4. diagnostic-prescriptive teaching skills
5. student counseling strategies

Teachers of the gifted and talented should be role models, mentors who can inspire youth to higher-level goals, to strive for excellence. It seems clear that they should possess some special personal characteristics, appropriate competencies, and above all superior talent or ability in their teaching areas.

Inservice Training Needs

Inservice training is essential for developing and sustaining the teaching capabilities of staff members who work with gifted and talented youth. The five competencies listed earlier as essential for teachers of the gifted require intensive training efforts and frequent renewal work. Programs that group gifted youth full time at the elementary level or by discipline at any level can concentrate most of the inservice education on those teachers and their discipline areas. However, in such programs, counselors, administrators, and other teachers need some inservice to educate them about the nature and purpose of the gifted programs.

Pullout/resource room programs present special problems for inservice training. Obviously, much of the inservice effort must focus on the resource room teachers. Such efforts, and indeed most inservice training, should focus on the development of competencies and strategies for working with the gifted. But in pullout/resource room programs there is also a special need to work with the regular classroom teachers to help them develop the specific skills needed to work with their gifted students, including an appropriate individualized education program (IEP) (Butterfield et al., 1979). Renzulli (1981) has suggested procedures to help the regular classroom teacher compact and bypass some teaching activities so that gifted and talented youth can also participate in enrichment and accelerated learning experiences. Clearly, such activities call for special competencies, not ordinarily possessed by regular classroom teachers.

Regular classroom teachers can be taught to deal with many of the higher-level thinking skills in their own classrooms. In one school, the coordinator has used inservice to train a cadre of regular classroom teachers in how to work with the gifted and average youth in their regular classrooms in teaching the four creative thinking skills of fluency, flexibility, originality, and elaboration and the four affective skills of curiosity, risk taking, complexity, and imagination. In another project, classroom teachers are taught to work with gifted youth in the regular classroom on independent research projects. These are illustrations of programs in which inservice has been used to train regular classroom teachers to work with the gifted in a support role.

All teachers who work directly with the gifted need inservice experiences in curriculum development. Curricula should be determined by the staff of a program, but the teachers may not possess the necessary competencies or knowledge for appropriate curriculum development. Above all they need to learn how to implement the principles of curriculum development for the gifted listed earlier. There are also new concepts emerging in the field at all times that require continuing inservice efforts.

The role of the counselor is an emerging one in programs for the gifted (Van Tassel-Baska, 1983). Counselors need special training for their work with the gifted. They and other professionals in education of the gifted can profit most from graduate courses that provide in-depth training and up-to-date knowledge about working with the gifted. Courses in curriculum development, counseling, identification and evaluation, teaching higher-level thinking skills, and program evaluation can also provide the competencies that staff need to work with the gifted and talented.

Funding and Financial Constraints

Funding patterns for gifted programs differ from state to state and community to community. Formula funding and a state mandate mean that there is no choice in many communities; there must be a program. In other states and communities formula funds may be available but there is no mandate. Finally, there are the states that offer no financial aid for gifted programs and impose no mandate; the community must do it on its own if it chooses to have a program.

Pullout programs at the elementary level and special supplementary seminars at the secondary level are the most likely extra-cost programs. Full-time, self-contained classes at the elementary level and grouping by subject at the secondary level generally involve no extra cost per se since the children simply exchange one class for another. If class size is reduced to facilitate better responsiveness to individual needs, however, costs may be increased. Of course, in all types of programs there will be extra costs for the coordinators or administrative leaders, inservice training, and special materials. Program consultants and evaluators would also require additional expenditures.

Programs for the gifted seem to get higher-priority status in the budgets of large city schools than in small and/or rural communities. There is probably more egalitarianism and fear of elitism in small, rural communities. Individual differences are more readily accepted and encouraged in the city, and special talent or ability is more prized. Thus, the budget for gifted programs is often more generous in larger city school districts. Of course, it may also be the case that the budget in a large city school district *is* larger and more easily revised or modified to serve the gifted program.

Special personnel are needed to develop and serve in gifted programs. In larger districts there ought to be coordinators for the elementary, middle school, and high school level; one or more specially trained counselors; and specially trained teachers for resource rooms, seminars etc. Thus, additional budget allocations are needed, but they can be trimmed to fit the school size and program requirements.

Formative and Summative Program Evaluation

Weiss and Gallagher (1982) concluded from their review of the literature on education of the gifted that program evaluations have been poorly designed and that trained evaluators are scarce. They also suggest that there is a great need for formative evaluation. During the last decade there has been a frenetic development of gifted programs in the United States but very little attention to the operational quality or the effects of those programs on gifted students. Program developers have lacked the necessary skills to conduct good formative and summative evaluation, and the agencies providing support have frequently not demanded sound evaluation. A typical program evaluation calls for a consultant to spend a day or two visiting the program, reading documents and talking with personnel. A summary, general evaluation is then produced, based on no hard data or at best some attitudinal evaluations.

The field of education of the gifted needs formative evidence that gifted programs are operating as planned and successfully. Morale among all staff should be positive, and there should be good administrative support for the operations of the program. From a summative point of view there should be evidence that students achieve the immediate cognitive and affective objectives of the program. In pullout/resource room programs there should be evidence that basic skills and achievements are up to the expected levels in relation to students' abilities. And in the longer range there should be evidence that achievements at the elementary level contribute to success at the high school level and so on upward.

Are the creative thinking skills learned in a pullout program transferred and used later in the regular science or social studies class? Are independent study skills learned at the elementary and junior high level used in high school and college? In the largest sense, are skills and knowledge learned in the gifted program contributing to creative productivity beyond school? Is the program producing high-level achievers, inventors, artists, writers, scientists, politicians, teachers, etc? These are long-range questions that can only be answered by programs that operate for longer periods of time and that follow graduates beyond school.

Renzulli's (1975) *Guidebook for Evaluating Programs for the Gifted and Talented* offers excellent direction for conducting evaluations of gifted programs. In this book Renzulli also offers a wealth of instruments for program evaluation. In a report from the Educational Improvement Center, Sewell, New Jersey, Richert, Alvino, and McDonnel (1981) also offer information about a large number of instruments that, while presented as resources for identification of the gifted and talented, can be used in program evaluation.

Personnel in education of the gifted should develop the expertise or should use appropriate consultants to design effective formative and summative evaluations of gifted programs. Continued funding of programs can be assured with evidence that the program is functioning as intended and that gifted and talented students are achieving program objectives. Unfortunately, some programs go unevaluated because program personnel are defensive or unwilling to face possible realities. Well-designed evaluations can detect program strengths and weaknesses and pave the way to more successful programs.

Summary

In this discussion of policies and procedures for the development of defensible programs for the gifted, philosophical issues and orientation were presented as a first major consideration. Next the problem of defining or specifying the target populations was discussed along with some problems in identifying the gifted and talented. The planning and development processes were discussed as a function of the appropriate committee for the task. Next came a closely related discussion of needs assessment and clarification of local conditions as bases for program development. There then followed a review of issues related to the local mandate and administrative leadership, consideration of alternative program models and alternative services, curriculum differentiation and articulation across grade levels and among disciplines, selecting and training teachers, and inservice training needs. Funding of programs and financial constraints were presented as issues reflecting state-by-state and community differences. Finally, the problems of program evaluation were presented as crucial in the design and defense of quality programs for the gifted and talented.

References

American Association for Gifted Children. (1978). *On being gifted*. New York: Walker.

Baldwin, A.Y., Gear, G.H., & Lucito, L.J. (1978). *Educational planning for the gifted*. Reston, VA: Council for Exceptional Children.

Bloom, B.S. (1956). *Taxonomy of educational objectives*. Handbook 1, Cognitive domains. New York, NY: David McKay.

Bloom, B.S. (1964). *Stability and change in human characteristics*. New York: John Wiley.

Bloom, B.S., & Sosniak, L.A. (1981). Talent development. *Educational Leadership, 39,* 86–94.

Butterfield, S.M., Kaplan, S.N., Meeker, M., Renzulli, S.J., Smith L.H., & Treffinger, D.J. (1979). *Developing IEPs for the gifted/talented*. Los Angeles: Leadership Training Institute on the Gifted and the Talented.

College Board. (1983). *A guide to the advanced placement program*. New York: Author.

Cornell, D.G. (1983). Gifted children: The impact of positive labeling on the family system. *American Journal of Orthopsychiatry, 53,* 322–335.

Ehrlich, V.Z. (1978). *The Astor program for gifted children*. New York: Teachers College, Columbia University. A technical report.

Feldhusen, J.F. (Ed.). (1980). *Concept curriculum for the gifted*. Matteson, IL: Region I South Area Service Center for The Gifted.

Feldhusen, J.F. (1982). Meeting the needs of gifted students through differentiated programming. *Gifted Child Quarterly, 26,* 37–41.

Feldhusen, J.F., & Wyman, A.R. (1980). Super Saturday: Design and implementation of Purdue's special program for gifted children. *Gifted Child Quarterly, 24,* 15–21.

Gallagher, J.J. (1975). *Teaching the gifted child*. Boston: Allyn & Bacon.

Halpern, D.F. (1984). *Thought and knowledge: An introduction to critical thinking.* Hillsdale, NJ: Lawrence Erlbaum Associates.

Kaplan, S.N. (1979). *Inservice training manual: Activities for developing curriculum for the gifted/talented*. Los Angeles: Leadership Training Institute on the Gifted and Talented.

Maker, C.J. (1977). *Providing programs for the gifted handicapped.* Reston, VA: Council for Exceptional Children.

Maker, C.J. (1982). *Curriculum development for the gifted.* Rockville, MD: Aspen Systems.

Marland, S.P. (1972). *Education of the gifted and talented: Report to The Congress of the United States by the U.S. Commissioner of Education.* Washington, DC: U.S. Government Printing Office.

Milne, B.G. (1982). *Vocational education for gifted and talented students.* Columbus, OH: National Center for Research in Vocational Education.

Palmer, D.J. (1983). An attributional perspective on labeling. *Exceptional Children, 49,* 423–429.

Polette, N. (1982). *Three Rs for the gifted.* Littletown, CO: Libraries Unlimited.

Renzulli, J.S. (1975). *A guidebook for evaluating programs for the gifted and talented.* Los Angeles: Leadership Training Institute for the Gifted and the Talented.

Renzulli, J.S., Reis, S.M., & Smith L.H. (1981). *The revolving door identification model.* Mansfield Center, CT: Creative Learning Press.

Richert, E.S., Alvino, J.J., & McDonnel, R.C. (1981). *National report on identification.* Sewell, NJ: Educational Improvement Center-South.

Seeley, K. (1984). Facilitators for gifted learners. In J.F. Feldhusen (Ed.), *Toward Excellence in Gifted Education.* Denver: Love.

Stanley, J.C. (1979). The study and facilitation of talent for mathematics. In A.H. Passow (Ed.), *The gifted and the talented: Their education and development.* The Seventy-eighth Yearbook of The National Society for the Study of Education (pp. 169–189). Chicago: University of Chicago Press.

Stanley, J.C. (1980). On educating the gifted. *Educational Researcher, 9,* 8–12.

Stanley, J.C., & Benbow, C.P. (1982). Educating mathematically precocious youth: Twelve policy recommendations. *Educational Researcher, 11,* 4–9.

Tannenbaum, A.J. (1983). *Gifted children: psychological and educational perspectives.* New York: Macmillan.

Taylor, C.W. (1963). Multiple talent approach. *The Instructor, 27,* 142, 144–146.

Torrance, E.P. (1977). *Discovery and nurturance of giftedness in the culturally different.* Reston, VA: Council for Exceptional Children.

Torrance, E.P., & Myers, R.E. (1970). *Creative learning and teaching.* New York, NY: Dodd, Mead & Co.

Treffinger, D.J. (1981). *Blending gifted education with the total school program.* Williamsville, NY: Center for Creative Learning.

Van Tassel-Baska, J. (Ed.) (1983). *A practical guide to counseling the gifted in a school setting.* Reston, VA: Council for Exceptional Children.

Van Tassel-Baska, J. (1984). Appropriate curriculum for the gifted. In J.F. Feldhusen (Ed.), *Toward Excellence in Gifted Education.* Denver: Love.

Weiss, P., & Gallagher, J.J. (1982). *Report on education of gifted, Volume II: Program effectiveness, education of gifted and talented students: A review.* Chapel Hill, NC: Frank Porter Graham Development Center.

White, B. (1975). *The first three years of life.* Englewood Cliffs, NJ: Prentice-Hall.

19

Creating a Gifted Ghetto from the Principle of 'No Policy':

a reply to "Policies and Procedures"

William C. Healey, Ph.D.
University of Arizona

In his chapter, "Policies and Procedures for the Development of Defensible Programs for the Gifted," John Feldhusen synthesizes many of the issues confronting the profession of gifted education. Also, he suggests that he would attempt to resolve many of these issues through the formulation of appropriate policies and procedures.

Although he uses the issues to discuss numerous concepts and recommended practices, he frequently fails to translate his values and observations into explicit statements of preferred policy or procedure. This lack of specificity, unfortunately, leaves readers with some uncertainty about how his views would be represented in such statements. On the other hand, Professor Feldhusen may have been deliberate in his approach by reasoning that policy makers should be free to interpret his ideas into whatever statements they judge to be situation appropriate.

In my opinion, Professor Feldhusen might have advanced the field of gifted education further by boldly and consistently articulating precise proposals of policy and procedure for all to see and evaluate in comparison with their own beliefs. In stating such an opinion, however, one is reminded of Haskins' and Gallagher's admonition that "arguments of invited experts often go beyond the limited fields of competence in which their prestige has been earned" (1981, p. 4).

The topic of policy and procedure formulation forces each potential policy maker to stretch his or her expertise by assessing a set of issues that has rather broad and interrelated social, political, economic, and educational implications. Each of us, I suspect, would prefer to analyze the issues, propose policy, and project the possible implications of policy implementation with the round-table assistance of a legislative researcher, a policy analyst, philosopher, futurist, artist, sociologist, economist, historian, and computer-assisted statistician. Their collective wisdom could be helpful to anyone facing the need to generate appropriate, intelligent policies, comprehend the range of policy making that is needed, or predict the potential impact that each policy would have on all affected parties. One could expect these individuals to posit various equations of potential policies and their projected impact. Then, such equations should be subjected to linear regression or the logit regression technique for analysis, depending on how the choices of policy were specified.

In the immediate absence of such broad expertise, this invited reply to Feldhusen begins with a statement of the obvious. *The United States has no public policy that supports the special education of gifted and talented children.* Consequently, no common goal exists for the 50 states and 15,000 school districts in the country to establish policies and procedures governing special programming for children with exceptionally high intellectual, artistic, or leadership abilities. To many educators and parents, the absence of a national (or is it federal) policy is a disgrace. Others, including some school superintendents, teachers, politicians, and members of the general public, still believe in the historic myths that have been perpetrated on the gifted, not the least of which is the assumption that bright and creative children will fare well in spite of an ordinary, if not inept, regular educational program.

Unfortunately, Feldhusen presents no data to refute the aforementioned concept. Also, he offers no evidence to support an assertion that gifted education makes a positive difference in the achievement of exceptional children or that it, ideally, benefits the nation. In fact, Weiss and Gallagher (1982) found limited research evidence that is persuasive in showing the benefits of special programming.

In the absence of these data, Feldhusen has had to construct a compelling rationale for the enactment of public policy and procedures from his "logic of ideology." He simply concludes, as an ideologue, that logic exists in having special programs, and proceeds to tell the reader about the history and practices of gifted education in a partial prescription for ideological action. Further, he suggests that open discussions within the schools will foster acceptance or highlight pockets of resistance toward the goals and objectives in a proposed program for gifted and talented children. By saying nothing more about resistance, he fails to alert the reader to a crucial step that should be taken by any sophisticated policy maker.

Policy development or change requires careful preparation that includes understanding the opposition and designing tactics for handling contrasting ideologies. The proponent of policies supporting gifted education cannot ignore the fact that other individuals or groups, who inevitably enter into the politics of policy making, will have their own ideologic beliefs and values that do not support special education of an intellectual elite or the creatively advanced. They, too, feel strongly that their position serves the public interest. They would not, most likely, concur with Feldhusen's contention that the public schools have a responsibility to provide a gifted dancer in fifth grade with the quality and intensity of training that she would need for later success as a professional ballerina.

As an example of such opposition, parents and a few educators in 1984 vehemently argued that the University High School for gifted learners in Tucson, Arizona, should be closed down and the students integrated into the regular classes of Tucson High School. They alleged inequality of opportunity and a loss of financial and curricular resources from Tucson High to University High. The debate, ironically, surfaced just as the state legislature mandated special programming for the gifted in all public schools. This local confrontation subsequently was settled through a compromise by having school officials retain the gifted program, but move it from a special school into another regular high school in the district.

Many statements of opposition to gifted education have been expressed in the last three decades, both locally and nationally. Although Feldhusen cited the Marland Report of 1972 as a "modern age" concept of giftedness, it represented federal policy for less than ten years and completely disappeared by action of the Reagan Administration.

The "pro" and "anti" gifted education groups probably would be described by the political scientist as participants in the *pluralist* model of public policy formulation. The model is predicated on James Madison's observation that American politics is driven by thousands of interest groups. Indeed, to provide or not provide "gifted education" is, first and foremost, a political issue. Second, it is an economic issue, and finally it becomes a socioeducational debate among groups and individuals with divergent points of view.

Unfortunately, many of Feldhusen's statements in advocating for policy on behalf of the gifted and talented can be challenged as the mere assumptions of a well-meaning altruist. Also, while his ideology is revealed in a set of beliefs, these beliefs are never transformed into specific statements of policy. In fact, his focus on the need for policies and procedures becomes blurred when he addresses some issues that have little to do with the formulation of basic policies and procedures (i.e., professional differences about human abilities or curricular components). Perhaps his recommendations would be more constructive if they were summarized as a set of principles from which he or others could recommend or establish policies and procedures. For example, liberals and conservatives might subscribe to the principle, extending from the Constitution's Fifth Amendment, that gifted children and their parents should have a guaranteed right to due process in determining appropriate educational plans for the gifted. The articulation of such a principle might find general support among most politicians, citizens, and educators. The next step would be to translate the principle into a specific policy. Finally, the policy would be made operational with a set of procedures to be followed by school personnel in complying with the guarantee.

To illustrate how additional concepts and principles involving "preferred practices" in gifted education might be presented as explicit policy proposals, some of Feldhusen's points of view, if interpreted correctly in this critique, are represented below as "first draft" policy statements.

1. *All children and youth, including the gifted and talented, shall be afforded an appropriate education at public expense.*

   This policy would be akin to the one that was established federally for the handicapped in the Education for All Handicapped Children's Act, as amended in 1975 by Public Law 94-142. Feldhusen suggests that the right to an appropriate education was the major rationale for Public Law 94-142 and that such rights should be extended to the gifted and talented. He does not address the need for such a basic policy. However, neither constitutional nor compulsory attendance law affords the gifted and talented a right to a free, appropriate education. He implies that the values of such a policy should be regarded as being absolute and beyond the need for justification by stating a closely related position that is represented below in policy statement 2.

2. *Gifted and talented children and youth shall be provided with regular, special, and related educational services (from preschool through high school) that are designed to meet their psychoeducational needs and help develop their abilities to the highest possible level during their enrollment in school.*

   Feldhusen says that the gifted and talented have a right to special services that "will enable them to develop their potentials to the highest possible levels." Although similar wording may be found in some school district policy manuals, schools have not been held to such a policy. Interestingly, the court case of *Battle v. Commonwealth of Pennsylvania* (1980, p. 278) ruled as follows:

   > It is beyond dispute that although an educational system ideally should provide the opportunity for its students to develop their fullest potential, even the best systems are incapable of achieving this goal. This position was taken one step

further in a 1980 statement by the National School Boards Association (NSBA). The NSBA petition, submitted to the court in an amicus curiae brief, denied that public education has ever guaranteed that children will reach their full potential (Larsen, Goodman, & Glean, 1981).

Policies, like the one above, must stand the test of feasibility. Which policy should we support: the one by Feldhusen, the court, or the NSBA?

3. *The philosophy, goals, objectives and procedures of the program(s) for gifted and talented children and youth shall be presented in a comprehensive, written plan for public comment and discussion at least once anually at a publicly announced open meeting.*

Feldhusen believes that open discussion and communication concerning "the philosophical basis and barriers for special program services" are a desirable prelude to program development. The policy statement above captures the spirit of his belief and adds specificity to it for purposes of developing implementation procedures.

4. *Formal procedures shall be followed for the early referral, screening, and comprehensive assessment of potentially gifted and talented children and youth.*

Feldhusen indicates that certain implicit assumptions and problems surround the process of identifying the gifted and talented. Policy statements 4 and 5 lay the foundation for establishing appropriate identification procedures.

5. *Assessments of potentially gifted and talented children and youth shall be selected and conducted by specially qualified personnel in a reliable manner that is culturally and linguistically appropriate to each individual who is to be assessed.*

Feldhusen contends correctly that personnel need special preparation and that policies must accommodate for the appropriate assessment of "atypical populations."

The intent of policy statements 6–9 should be clear and will not be discussed in regard to Feldhusen's policy recommendations.

6. *No children or youth shall be excluded indiscriminately from the program(s) for the gifted and talented because of their minority status, handicapping*

DEFENSIBLE PROGRAMS FOR THE GIFTED

condition, creed, sex, or religious convictions if they meet the eligibility criteria and have parent or guardian approval for participation.

7. *The classification process shall not result in stigma or undue expectations imposed by school personnel.*

8. *Parents or guardians shall be notified and provided with an opportunity to approve or reject any proposed assessment or placement of their child or youth who is being considered for the gifted and talented program(s).*

Further policies in regard to the nature of the notice and approval process should be developed to complement statement 8.

9. *The program(s) shall be coordinated and staffed by supervisors, curriculum specialists, teachers, assessment personnel, counselors, and others who are specifically qualified to work with the gifted and talented*

10. *Teachers shall be gifted in intellectual ability or have special talent according to their respective roles and shall demonstrate, through formal evaluation, competent performance as a teacher of the gifted or talented.*

This proposed policy is derived directly from Feldhusen's first statement in his section on teacher selection. To require, by policy, that teachers be intellectually gifted or show special talent consistent with their assigned roles may be appropriate, but it probably would be highly controversial. Although the issue has been debated among experienced educators of the gifted and talented, few have been bold enough to advocate for the implementation of this policy. Even if teacher unions and other groups accepted the concept, they most likely would insist that the policy requires (a) a definition of "gifted" and "talented" teachers and (b) procedures that would utilize agreed-upon criteria for teacher selection and subsequent evaluation.

11. *Individualized educational plans shall be written for all gifted and talented pupils at least annually and as dictated by their development and achievement.*

Feldhusen addresses the need for this policy, but he does not discuss the procedures that would be required to effect it. Conceptually, the policy is appropriate. Operationally, school districts may be reluctant to adopt it unless they can avoid the implementation problems that were experienced in complying with an equivalent policy under Public Law 94-142.

12. *A comprehensive curriculum shall be designed and articulated throughout the program(s) in a manner that represents the research on effective teaching and learning for gifted and talented pupils.*

Feldhusen discusses many issues involved with the design and coordination of curricula in programs for the gifted and talented. The above policy statement attempts to establish a means to achieve the ends that Feldhusen envisions.

The following three policies are not discussed, but they are presented with the intent of capturing other values or principles expressed by Feldhusen. They are stated in an explicit manner that should allow readers to determine if they subscribe to Feldhusen's beliefs.

13. *Due process protections shall be afforded to all parents, guardians, and pupils participating in the program(s) for the gifted and talented.*

14. *Specially designed program(s) of counseling and instruction shall be made available to all parents and guardians in a manner that is appropriate to the age and levels of instruction for their children and youth in the gifted and talented program(s).*

15. *An advisory committee consisting of school administrators, teachers, parents, and experts associated with the gifted and talented program(s) shall be established to recommend policy to the Board of Education.*

Obviously, these proposed policies are neither inclusive nor detailed enough in some instances to be totally appropriate. However, they simulate the process that must take place if Feldhusen's concepts are to be converted into policy statements that would guide the education of the gifted and talented. Certainly, the drafting of potential policy statements forces all of us to test our beliefs and assess how our principles would be represented by policy. When policy statements are drafted, they frequently, if not generally, create additional issues that must be resolved.

As a first step, Navarro (1984) suggested that educators and others must "understand the politics of an issue in all of its rich interest-group and ideological diversity. This also means identifying the special interest players in the game together with their lobbying strategies and tactics . . . this entails using the 'logic of ideology' not only to identify the contrasting ideological principles, but also to probe the underlying values, beliefs and assumptions that often put well-meaning liberals and conservatives on opposite sides of the policy fence" (p. 281).

The second step is economic analysis. Who benefits and who pays for the implementation of the procedures that must accompany the new policy? Finally, the third step uses the political and economic analyses to reconstruct well-conceptualized policies and procedures that can be evaluated separately for their impact in making the special interest group—as well as the school, state, or nation—better off.

Determining the appropriateness of a policy and the correctness of its procedures is a difficult, controversial, and pragmatic act. Such pragmatism does not require compromise in one's principles, but it helps to replace blind ideology with realism.

Nationally, the issue of creating special educational policy and procedural opportunities for gifted and talented children remains unresolved in a rich diversity of opinion. At the state and local levels, the "pro-gifted education bloc" has experienced some success by influencing the enactment of policy that requires or enables school districts to do something "special" in identifying and educating gifted and, occasionally, talented children. However, the ambivalent and "anti-gifted education" blocs have, in a quiet but often effective manner, frequently thwarted the creation of a gifted and talented educational policy. When federal, state, and local educational agencies fail to establish policies for the special education of the gifted and talented, they essentially are supporting a policy that these children will be educated in the regular class. Such unwritten policies, in practice, relegate the gifted and talented too often to an unchallenging, lock-step curriculum that, for them, is exile in an educational ghetto.

References

Battle v. the Commonwealth of Pennsylvania, 629 F.2d 269 (3rd Cir. 1980).

Haskins, R., & Gallagher, J. (Eds.). (1981). *Models for analysis of social policy: An introduction.* Norwood, NJ: Ablex.

Larsen, L., Goodman, L., & Glean, R. (1981). Issues in the implementation of extended school year programs for handicapped students. *Exceptional Children, 47,* 256–265.

Navarro, P. (1984). *The policy game.* New York: John Wiley.

Weiss, P., & Gallagher, J. (1982). *Report on education of gifted, volume II, program effectiveness, education of gifted and talented students: A review* (A technical report). Chapel Hill, NC: Frank Porter Graham Child Development Center.

20

Evaluation for Defensible Programs for the Gifted

Kenneth R. Seeley, Ph.D.
University of Denver

E valuation is often the orphan child of program management. Too often an afterthought, evaluation has a bad name because it is not done well or at the right time. This chapter will present many ideas of what evaluation is and is not. Furthermore, the chapter will provide some models and insights for creating program evaluation that contribute highly to defensible programs for the gifted.

Before defining evaluation and discussing its importance, some assumptions need to be made explicit. While it is true that programs for gifted children have some unique features, there is no need to create wholly new approaches to evaluating them. The discussion in this chapter is based on the assumption that there already exist excellent practices in educational evaluation that are very appropriate for gifted programs. There is no need to reinvent the wheel. This is not to say that the unique features of these programs are to be ignored. Rather, good evaluation is sensitive to any unique aspects of a program. Special evaluation problems that deal specifically with gifted programs will be discussed later in the chapter.

Evaluation Defined

The simplest definition of evaluation is a process of examining actions and events according to some predetermined standards for the purpose of making decisions. Thus, we have three components: examination, determination of standards, and decision making.

The process of examining actions and events involves many activities including data gathering, data analysis, and data reporting. This examination may be broad in scope or very narrow. It typically goes beyond educational measurement. There are some decision makers who would evaluate the success of a program purely on the grounds of test scores. This is not evaluation. It is measurement only and very narrow measurement at that. So, for the purposes of our discussion, the assumption is made that the examination piece of evaluation is broad based involving many activities that transcend pure measurement.

Evaluation implies attention to predetermined standards that guide the examination of actions and events. These are value-related standards with a strong accent on "value." The actions and events being evaluated in education are value laden and certainly any evaluation is also valued-based. The notion that evaluation is somehow neutral and scientific is pure fantasy. Just as values are inextricably tied to education, they are also imbedded in any process to examine education. The predetermined nature of these standards is essential to guiding the examination process. Evaluation is not an open-ended hunting expedition. The examination should tell us how close we came to some predetermined standard in order to make a decision.

Decision making is the final part of the definition of evaluation. Gorton (1980) defines decision making as ". . . a process influenced by information and values, whereby a perceived problem is explicitly defined, alternative solutions are posed and weighted, and a choice made that subsequently is implemented and evaluated" (p. 229). Evaluation should provide the information, the problem definition, and alternatives for the decision maker. Decision making and evaluation should maintain close interaction for effective development of any organization. In summary, then, it can be said that decision making is both the end result and the purpose of evaluation.

This chapter will examine evaluation as a process and a product. By design, it will present distinct points of view regarding many aspects of evaluation related to the main theme of this book: creating defensible programs for the gifted. The presentation of these viewpoints will be decidedly biased rather than balanced. In that there is a critique to follow, the reader can receive some balance through this format.

The chapter will be divided into five major areas following this section. These are: (*i*) evaluation and its importance, (*ii*) the uses and abuses of evaluation, (*iii*) essential elements of good evaluation, (*iv*) the politics of evaluation, and (*v*) evaluation for defensible programs.

Ultimately, this chapter will attempt to develop a better understanding of evaluation as something that is not only useful and "doable," but of utmost importance to the survival of programs for gifted children. Evaluation is the tool of defensibility. Where this tool is used skillfully, programs for the gifted will survive.

The Importance of Evaluation

Whenever a special group of learners is identified for some differentiated educational experience or program, we generally refer to this as a "categorical program." Such programs are funded by category from local, state, or federal education budgets. Categorical programs are usually line items in these budgets, requiring a periodic appropriation from a school board or legislature. Examples of categorical programs are vocational education, special education, education of the gifted, and early childhood education, to name but a few. Because these programs usually require special appropriations of funds (rather than being included in a general education appropriation), they entail a higher degree of accountability. One school official complained that he spends ten hours per week keeping track of data for handicapped children to get $100,000 a year from the state government, and yet he merely signs an annual attendance report for the same state government to receive $25 million. Why all the work for so little money? Such is the nature of categorical funding: Careful evaluation is required to meet the high expectancy for accountability.

In most states, programs for the gifted are categorical programs with annual appropriations from state legislatures. At the local level, boards of education usually fund gifted programs categorically. Each year we must defend our programs and justify their continued existence by presenting evidence of success and/or need. This evidence requirement is facilitated by program evaluation data. Often the future survival of a program for gifted children depends on the quality of the evaluation. There are certainly other factors that contribute to survivability, but evaluation is a process that results in a product that has the greatest impact on decision makers.

Our discussion of gifted programs as categorical indicated that there are high accountability demands. This helps justify the importance of evaluation from an administrative point of view. However, evaluation is also important to the teachers and staff who work with gifted children daily. Unfortunately, evaluation is too often viewed as outside the concern of teachers. Somehow, administrators or consultants are the people who should worry about evaluation. This perception can have many negative consequences, not the least of which is to shift decision making further away from the program. Practitioners should work hard to be a part of the evaluation process if they are committed to their programs. This observation may seem like rhetoric to some, but it is clearly better to be a part of the examination and standard-setting process of evaluation than to leave it to those with little or no investment in the program. Keep in mind that there is no neutral or scientific evaluation. The bias of practitioners close to the program should be a part of the evaluation. Who knows better where the problems are? Who knows better what the standards and values should be?

Evaluation is important to administrators and to practitioners when viewed as the vehicle for decision making. Obviously, some decisions are made impulsively or intuitively rather than being based on evaluation data. However, major decisions in education are usually data based, and even impulsive decisions can be reversed given good data. The task, then, is to get good data that addresses progress toward standards to assist in decision making. How formal this process is depends on the nature and scope of the evaluation and the level of decision making. Evaluation for decision making happens constantly on an informal level such as deciding which books to order or which teacher should be assigned to a particular school. These are important decisions, but they do not require a formal evaluation plan. They do require the use of evaluation information to be most effective.

If we think of evaluation in both formal and informal terms, it increases in its importance. In the ideal world, there would be an evaluation data bank for most decisions. In the real world our evaluation information is usually limited because of a scarcity of resources. We will probably have "good" evaluation data only on a small piece of our total program at any point in time. Therefore, what evaluation we can do is that much more important, particularly when decisions will be made about a program's future.

Abuses of Evaluation

Too often evaluation is viewed as esoteric or threatening or just some academic "gymnastic." When viewed as any or all of these things, evaluating loses its importance and effectiveness.

If evaluation is seen as esoteric by practitioners or decision makers, then it probably did not involve these people or did not address real needs. The blame for this must lie with the evaluator and those whose program is being evaluated. Practitioners must demand involvement in the evaluation of their program. Evaluators should want those closest to the program involved. If this does not happen, then evaluation is usually esoteric and meaningless.

Evaluation as a threat is a common abuse when planned as a punitive exercise. Whenever we measure in the human domain, we raise anxiety. This is to be expected as a part of any evaluation. However, the abuse of evaluation occurs when the threat is real and punitive. Decision makers will design an evaluation with the purpose of gathering data to eliminate a program. Such an abuse usually is a muckraking expedition to look for every weakness while ignoring strengths. It often establishes predetermined standards so high or unrealistic that the program is doomed to fail.

The final or common abuse of evaluations is the "academic gymnastic." Someone in the administrative hierarchy decides that a program should be evaluated because of some pressure or request for information from a superior. What usually ensues is a poorly designed series of evaluation activities with little or no funding. Often the evaluation is planned after the program is over or nearing its end, asking all involved if they liked what happened. Usually, people do like what happened and the evaluation reports survey data from parents, students, or teachers. This leads to rounds of self-congratulatory accolades. Such abuse of evaluation is obviously open to the "academic gymnastic" criticism. Just as with the esoteric evaluation, the results are meaningless.

These abuses of evaluation have given it a "bad name" in education. However, the importance of evaluation is too great to have it dismissed from consideration because of abuses in the past. The next section will present good evaluation practices that will go far to prevent these abuses.

Essential Elements of Good Evaluation

Renzulli (1975) presents five essential purposes of a good evaluation:

1. To discover whether and how effectively the objectives of a program are being fulfilled.
2. To discover unplanned and unexpected consequences that are resulting from particular program practices.
3. To determine the underlying policies and related activities that contribute to success or failure in particular areas.
4. To provide continuous in-process feedback at intermediate stages throughout the course of a program.
5. To suggest realistic, as well as ideal, alternative courses of action for program modification. (p. 6)

If we fulfill these five purposes, we have the basis for a good evaluation. Keeping in mind that the overall purpose of evaluation is decision making, one can relate Renzulli's five points to that end. When we know how effectively we met the program's objectives, we can make decisions about where we need improvement. The second purpose is a bit more elusive for evaluators. In management jargon it is "cost benefit" when there is a positive unplanned consequence. This is often overlooked in evaluation of gifted programs. A cost benefit analysis can reveal many positive spinoffs of gifted programs for nongifted children, parents, teachers, and community members that were not originally planned. This analysis helps justify programs. However, there are sometimes unplanned consequences that are not positive. These should also be examined in a good evaluation. One common unexpected consequence of a pullout gifted program is that the gifted students will not want to come to the program because they have to make up all the work in their regular classes. This double work penalty often drives students away from the special program. Side effects need to be examined in any evaluation.

In fulfilling the third of Renzulli's purposes we attempt to find the causes of the conditions discovered by the evaluation. Too often we obtain and report good evaluation data and infer incorrectly. If, for instance, we find that 80 percent of the students did not like the special unit on John Steinbeck, we might infer that the topic was not of interest or it was poorly presented. However, the real reason may have been that there were not enough books in the school library and the students had a difficult time finding the materials to keep up with the assigned readings. A good evaluation must go beyond "what" and attempt to find out "why." The evaluation must also answer "why" for successes as well as failures. In defending programs for the gifted, we must know why something works well. This knowledge helps form the theoretical base for special programs.

The "continuous in-process feedback" is commonly referred to as formative evaluation. During the operation of a program, it is important to monitor activities and make "mid-course" corrections as needed. This need for continual examination would appear obvious to most. If something is not working well, then it is changed. What often happens, however, is that decisions to change are not noted for the purposes of evaluation. Changing a schedule or reassigning a teacher can have a great impact on the measured effectiveness of a program. A plan for formative evaluation should be in place to monitor and record these decisions during the operation of the program.

The fifth and final purpose given by Renzulli is to provide information for decision making. As defined earlier, decision making is both the end result and the purpose of evaluation. Renzulli suggests that we should have evaluation information that provides both realistic and idealistic alternatives for decision makers. What is real and what is ideal may be perceived differently by different audiences. For parents of gifted students, having a total full-time program for the gifted may be their real expectancy, but this may be considered "ideal" by school officials. Evaluators must be very sensitive to their audience when generating alternatives for decision makers. This is not to suggest that recommendations should be distorted. Rather, making a recommendation from evaluation data for program modification requires that some attention be given to the potential impact of each course of action.

Renzulli's *Guidebook for Evaluating Programs for the Gifted and Talented* presents a good overview of major approaches to evaluation. Readers may want to refer to this source book for ideas. The bias of this writer is toward the approach suggested by Provus (1969) and Sjogren (1970). These authors provide an excellent basis for quality evaluation approaches using an input-process-output model. Historically, evaluation has focused on outcomes. Certainly, the abuse of standardized measures to make program decisions reflects this approach to evaluation. The fact, for instance, that 80 percent of the sixth graders score at the 40th percentile in mathematics is only an outcome measure using one instrument. Evaluation must examine the inputs, processes, and outputs of the sixth grade mathematics program if the purposes stated earlier in this section are to be achieved.

The input stage of evaluation describes the existing conditions or context of the evaluation. These important input variables must be identified and measured for their impact. They might include financial inputs, number and quality of staff assigned, number and quality of students, facilities, organizational and community structures, and other preexisting conditions.

Information about the processes of a program helps accomplish the formative evaluation and provides some reasons for outcomes. An evaluator must have a clear understanding of what goes on in a program if the outcome data are to have any meaning. If we want to answer those "why" questions about our program, then we must examine the processes.

Finally, the evaluation must address the outcomes or outputs of the program. An essential element of outcome evaluation is the use of multiple measures. Typically, this includes attitudes, skills, perceptions, and knowledge. Further evaluation of outcomes should demonstrate relationships among inputs and the relationship of the processes to the outcome. Sometimes this evaluation can be direct, but it often must be done by inference. However, evaluators do not like to admit that they don't know why a certain outcome resulted. We must move to legitimate ignorance when it comes to outcome evaluation. If we really have no idea why something resulted, we should say so instead of inventing explanations. Such care in reporting outcomes will greatly enhance decision making.

Politics of Evaluation

As discussed earlier, gifted programs are categorical and subject to high accountability demands. Categorical programs are also politically unpopular with general school administrators. Superintendents of schools are constantly saying "Just give us the money and we will take care of the kids." They want no strings attached. Categorical programs are expensive to administer, time consuming to operate and supervise, and, worst of all, they have a vocal constituency of advocates.

An underlying political theme in categorical educational programs is that they come into being because of a failure or weakness in the existing general educational program. School officials do not like to hear that they are not meeting the needs of a group of children appropriately. In all fairness, we must have some empathy for school officials who face a constant barrage of requests from various groups to create special programs or services. These range from sex education and fine arts to prayer and religion in the school. Now, in march a group of advocates for gifted children and school officials ask themselves "Isn't the regular curriculum good for anyone?" The answer to that question varies depending on your perspective. In any case, we must recognize the political "given" that categorical programs are inherently unpopular with general school administrators.

In viewing the politics of evaluation in a climate of unpopular categorical programs, it is urgent to take the pulse of those who surround the program being evaluated. This climate reading will greatly enhance the process for any evaluator. Perhaps there are some of those dynamics discussed under abuses of evaluation.

Four areas relate to the politics of evaluation: (i) the audience, (ii) timing, (iii) cost benefit, and (iv) reporting. The general climate was discussed above and certainly overlays these four areas.

The nature and extent of an evaluation is largely determined by the audience(s). The political dimension is likewise greatly affected by the audience. If the evaluation is for the teachers and administrators in the gifted program only, there is a very different political climate than when the audience is the superintendent and school board. Politically, the evaluator must assess the motivations, values, and attitudes of the audience. If the evaluation is to determine whether the program should be cut or expanded, the political tone needs very careful attention in design and reporting. If, however, the intent of the evaluation is just fine tuning a program that is well supported, the job is much less politically loaded.

The second political dynamic is timing. The best time to design the evaluation is when the program is being formulated. Unfortunately, evaluation is usually added on after the program has been operating and when concerns are raised about effectiveness. Timing needs to be addressed for both when to do the evaluation and when to report it. Programs for the gifted are typically evaluated too soon. One year of operation is not enough time for a good summative evaluation of a gifted program. Three years is closer to the ideal for making substantive decisions about the effectiveness of a program. Certainly, formative or ongoing evaluation should be in place. However, evaluators must attempt to expand the time dimension in order to provide a good summative evaluation.

Timing of the evaluation report can be of great political importance. If the report is to be given to a school board, this should be done at a time when other agenda items are not controversial, if possible. For instance, if the board is in conflict about teacher negotiations or a major reorganization of the administrators, it would be best to delay the evaluation report so it can be received in the best possible climate. Similarly, if the superintendent has just had a negative confrontation with the parents of the gifted group, timing might dictate some delay in the report. Even if the report is generally positive, a negative political climate can distort the outcome. Many evaluators would say timing is everything.

The third area of political concern is cost benefit. This can be extremely positive and is too often overlooked in an evaluation. Gain scores and survey data from program participants can be good, but cost benefit data is the "frosting on the cake." Those who make important decisions about programs for the gifted are typically general administrators or board members who are concerned with the implementation of the total school district program. Cost benefit data can show how the gifted program enhances the regular curriculum. It can also demonstrate good community relations through such activities as mentorships or community-based research projects. These are extremely important in gaining and maintaining political support. At the school building level, cost benefit data can convince principals that the gifted class not only provides a special service to a small group of students, but also that the spinoffs enhance the total educational enterprise. These programs raise the top so that regular teachers can see a continuum that addresses maximums, not just minimum mastery. Independent projects of gifted students can result in high-quality products that expand and enrich the curriculum for all students in the building. These are but a few of the cost benefits of providing programs for the gifted. They need to be a part of any good evaluation.

The final political concern is the evaluation report. Of particular importance is the format and presentation to the audience. The content of the report should be relevant, credible, and understandable. However, it is worthless unless it is effectively communicated to the audience. Too often evaluation reports are lengthy tomes of data summaries and interpretive narration. While much of this is necessary as reference material, the evaluator should provide a brief executive summary at the outset of the report to provide an overall impression of the program's effectiveness. Case studies and personal vignettes also help in communicating the evaluation information.

The presentation of the evaluation report is also politically sensitive. Timing was discussed earlier and is very important. How the presentation is done and by whom is also important. Involving gifted students in the reporting is often an excellent way to communicate the program evaluation. Some portions of the evaluation can even be performed by the students themselves. Rather than just serving as respondents, gifted students can design and implement a survey of other students, parents, or teachers to provide input about their program. Basic statistical concepts can be mastered this way, and students can also learn opinion polling. If gifted students are involved in the evaluation process and its presentation, the positive political impact on administrators and/or board members is tremendous. Visual aids such as video tape and student products also enhance the presentation of the evaluation report. Evaluation need not be a dry stack of paper to wade through. The report and its presentation should be made lively and imaginative while providing substantive information for decision making. The medium may not be the entire message when it comes to evaluation, but it certainly enhances understanding and support for special education for the gifted.

Attention to political dimensions of evaluation is not intended here as a subversive activity. Rather it is an exhortation to sensitivity when reporting human interactions to those who make decisions about the nature and extent of those interactions. Because education of the gifted is value loaded for most audiences, care must be taken in assessing and accommodating to the political climate. The rewards for this level of sensitivity are both good evaluation practice and the evolution of more effective programs for gifted students.

Evaluation for Defensible Programs

As discussed earlier, there is an inherent unfairness in the high accountability demands of categorical educational programs. We must acknowledge this as a reality and use evaluation effectively to be accountable for what we do in educating gifted students. The concept of defensibility goes beyond accountability. It implies a guarding against attack as well as a need to justify a program. The guardianship of gifted programs seems to fit our current "orphan" status as an education specialty. We must assume this task with effective tools used skillfully to avoid our demise. There are many educators who believe that special provisions for the gifted are a frill and inconsistent with a society of egalitarian values. Evaluation for defensibility must confront the high accountability demands as well as the attacks from educators and the community.

Evaluation procedures can make a bad program look good and a good program look bad. The cornerstone of evaluation to provide defensible programs for the gifted must be efficacy. If an evaluation uncovers real weaknesses we must avoid our temptation to overlook these data in the name of defending the concept of a differentiated program for the gifted. Too often we assume our guardianship task so vociferously that we are blinded by our advocacy and as a result defend activities that are not efficacious or effective. We have good reason to feel paranoid and defensive. However, we can lose everything if we defend activities that good evaluation tells us are less than effective.

How, then, can we use evaluation as the tool of defensibility in a climate of constant attack by nonbelievers? The answer lies in finding common ground in the general education endeavor. The evaluation must exploit the special nature of gifted students and their education but also cast the program as an integrated and meaningful part of the general education program. This may seem to be a paradox. We must defend the need for differentiated programs while at the same time demonstrate our relatedness to the overall educational enterprise. Essentially, this entails a two-part approach to defensibility rather than a juxtaposition. Evaluation data can serve these two needs well by making explicit the examination of differentiation and integration. This two-pronged approach is very helpful in attaining the goal of defensibility.

A final comment on defensibility is intended to close this discussion on a positive note. The national climate for excellence in education provides us the perfect opportunity to develop programs for gifted students. Perhaps at no other time in recent history since the post-Sputnik era of the late 1950s have we been in a better period to advocate for the gifted. Armed with good data, we can demonstrate to decision makers that programs for the gifted are an inherent part of the quest for excellence. To ignore this group of learners is to continue mediocrity at a time of national concern with education. Our task of defensibility is now a bit easier in a climate that nurtures excellence. We must capitalize on this national interest and demonstrate both the efficacy and effectiveness of our programs for the gifted.

> The virtues which flower in any society are the virtues which the society nourishes. The qualities of mind and character which stamp a people are the qualities which that people honor, the qualities they celebrate, the qualities they recognize instantly and respect profoundly . . . . When an institution, organization or nation loses its capacity to invoke high individual performance, its great days are over. (Gardner, 1961, p. 193)

References

Gardner, J.W. (1961). *Excellence.* New York, NY: Harper & Row.

Gorton, R.A. (1980). *School administration and supervision.* Dubuque, IA: W.C. Brown.

Provus, M. (1969). Evaluation of ongoing programs in the public school systems. In R.W. Tyler (Ed.), *Educational evaluation: New roles, new means*. Sixty-eighth Yearbook of the National Society for the Study of Education, Part II. Chicago: Univ. of Chicago Press.

Renzulli, J. (1975). *A guidebook for evaluating programs for the gifted and talented*. Ventura, CA: County Superintendent of Schools.

Sjogren, D. (1970). Measurement techniques in evaluation. In C.F. Paulsen (Ed.), *Strategy for evaluation design*. Portland, OR: Oregon State System of Higher Education.

21

Defensible Evaluations of Programs for the Gifted and Talented

Carolyn M. Callahan,
Ph.D.
Michael S. Caldwell, Ph.D.
University of Virginia

For the past decade the focus in the area of programs for the gifted and talented has been on the development of defensible identification criteria, defensible curricula, and defensible administrative designs. Only passing attention has been given to the evaluation of programs and then only as such evaluations were required by local school boards or other funding agents who requested data to support the claims of the programs.

A common proposition in gifted education is that program evaluation efforts are often inappropriate and/or ill-conceived and, thus, do not serve the cause. As with many assumptions and beliefs that are widely held, there is more than a little truth to that proposition, i.e., where there is smoke there is fire. However, one might look at the issue from another perspective and suggest that evaluation has become a "whipping boy" (or girl) and that one cannot expect that program evaluations can (by providing evidence of success) make up for programs that are ill conceived and/or poorly implemented and that, in fact, have not had significant impact. Nor can program evaluators be expected to evaluate that which cannot be identified, defined, or described by those who are responsible for the program. In other words (if you can stand one more old adage), evaluation cannot be expected to make a silk purse out of a sow's ear.

In truth, claimants on both sides of this issue can make a case, depending on the particular program or program evaluation that is examined. There are, indeed, many inappropriate evaluations and there are, indeed, many ill-defined, indefensible, and inadequate programs. But, rather than belabor the mistakes of the past, our purpose in this chapter will be to examine noteable developments in the field of program evaluation over the past decade that have potential to carry us to a point where program evaluation will no longer be viewed as inappropriate or even counterproductive for programs for the gifted. Because these new approaches are based on interweaving the evaluation design process with the program design process they not only serve to make evaluation more effective but are also useful tools in alleviating many of the design and implementation problems faced by programs for the gifted.

Six of the major themes that have characterized recent developments in the field of program evaluation will form the underlying basis of the discussions to follow. These themes will be addressed and elaborated upon through the discussion of general issues and problems faced in making the evaluation of programs for the gifted defensible, understandable, and useful. The themes to be considered are:

1. Program evaluation is an integral part of program planning and design. Both the evaluation design and the program design will be enhanced if planning for evaluation occurs simultaneously with planning for identification, curriculum, teacher training, etc.
2. The problems and issues encountered in carrying out the evaluation of gifted programs are not sufficient cause to justify failure to evaluate. The problems are not insurmountable and new models, new approaches to instrumentation, and new procedures for data analysis provide options that can be successfully incorporated into effective program evaluation.
3. Evaluation as a process is changing in purpose and scope.
4. Evaluation is not simply judging the worth of a program.
5. New developments in the field of evaluation have potential usefulness in the evaluation of programs for the gifted.
6. Evaluation is what you make it.

Problems and Issues

The problems and issues involved in constructing defensible program evaluations for programs for the gifted fall into four general categories: communication, purpose, program description, and comparison and value judgment issues and problems.

Communication

Communication is a perennial problem in the design of effective evaluations, but it seems to be magnified in the evaluation of programs for the gifted because of the nature of the programs themselves. The unique goals and objectives of such programs, the unusual nature of program delivery systems, the specialized vocabulary used to communicate purposes, etc., form the basis for an extensive laundry list of problems that have plagued the external evaluator in coming to a clear understanding of exactly what the program is about and that have deceived the internal evaluator into believing that the program is clearly defined when, in fact, the program lacks definition.

Rather than list all of the compendium of problems that have resulted from poor communication (see Renzulli, 1975; Callahan, 1983; and Callahan & Caldwell, 1984) suffice it to say that any such list might begin with misunderstandings of the intended goals of the program and consequent choice of inappropriate instruments to assess those goals and might end with a completely incomprehensible evaluation report or one that provides the decision maker with little or no useful data for subsequent decisions.

There are many reasons for poor communication. They range from arrogance on the part of the evaluator to the lack of a specified purpose on the part of the program administrator who attempts to describe the program to be evaluated. Patton (1981) contends that one of the reasons for poor communication is that the roles assumed by evaluators are often counterproductive to successful evaluation. For example, he describes the "baseball player" evaluator who wants you to believe that he is really one of your team and that his only aim is to help you make gifted children happy, productive students. If you start out believing this role, you are often disappointed when the evaluator turns up criticisms of the program or fails to demonstrate the results you count on him or her to deliver. The evaluator should not perceive the role as being one of the team but rather as a resource to the team or one who can deliver valuable data and information—the scout for the team, not the pitcher.

Patton also describes the evaluator who wears a suit of mirrors so that you will see this person as a reflection of yourself, never revealing true biases or beliefs and again giving you a false sense of security about support for the program. Evaluators should clearly state any biases and values that might relate to the program so that their work can be judged in light of those biases. Of course, no one is completely objective and all planning, instrument selection, and data analysis will reflect biases. The "astronaut" evaluator, according to Patton, tries to impress you with knowledge of the latest and most sophisticated data analysis techniques and computer equipment so that there will be good reason why you don't understand the results presented in the final report. The effective evaluator does not seek to impress you with statistics or technology but with clearly explained, well-justified approaches to assessment and data analysis. The "knight in shining armor" is the evaluator who delights in pointing out all the flaws in your program but uses the armor to ensure that no criticism will ever fall on him. A more reasonable evaluator will recognize your humanness and be willing to subject the evaluation process to scrutiny. The "military issue evaluator" is one of the most dangerous of all. This person speaks with great authority and tries to influence the way you run your program in accord with the demands of the evaluation design. An evaluator should never run the program or assume a command role. The "prostitute evaluator," according to Patton, is willing to give you any results your heart desires but fails to deliver information that represents the true status of your program. Finally, the "ghostly evaluator" is one who you hardly ever see but who you feel lurking about, working behind your back, and shaking skeletons out of the closet. This person is often heard to say, "Trust me, I'll help you." In contrast, effective evaluation is based on mutual trust and an evaluation that is carried out in an open and frank manner.

These represent only a few of the roles discussed by Patton that inhibit effective communication. They were described as if they applied only to external evaluators or evaluation consultants, but any individual who undertakes an internal evaluation either from a department of evaluation within a school division or as a representative of the program can easily fall into these roles in dealing with program staff. Further, internal evaluators are often plagued by a variation of the communication problem—not being able to see the forest for the trees. That is, internal evaluators often come to the task of evaluation with some preformed notions of what the program is (or should be), which often blinds them to the realities of the program or leads them to believe they know and understand things that are really unknowns.

To their credit, professional evaluators have become increasingly aware of the problems presented by the assumptions of the roles described. However, the burden of ensuring that evaluators do not assume meaningless or counterproductive facades remains with the program administrator. It is important always to keep in mind that the evaluator's function is to be a resource to the program, not a judge or a burden. The evaluator—internal or external—should be held accountable to the program just as the program is accountable to its clientele.

Evaluators have no corner on the market when it comes to problems with communication. Communication problems often stem from the program staff and the difficulties they may have in describing and defining the goals, objectives, activities, and anticipated outcomes of the programs. The field of the education of the gifted has become falsely secure in the use of jargon to express its intents. For example, the words "higher-level thinking skills" roll off the tongues of educators of the gifted like honey and with complete confidence that everyone will understand exactly what is meant. What a surprise to discover that several leading group intelligence tests claim to measure higher-level thinking skills! What a further surprise when the evaluator proposes using one of those tests to assess the effectiveness of the program, convinces an administrator that such a test is appropriate, and then fails to find significant changes as a result of program implementation. Not only is it often difficult to ascertain the intent of programs, it is often difficult to even ascertain the day-to-day operational or instructional activities or the lines of responsibility within the program because they have never been articulated and defined.

Often the excuse is given that these communication problems arise because the program is "so unique" or "so different" that others couldn't be expected to understand. In addition, program administrators will often claim that there are simply no words to describe it. The most fitting translation of these comments is "we don't really know what it is that we are doing." Any program that exists has boundaries and activities, and uses resources. These must be clearly defined for effective program operation. If this task cannot be accomplished for the evaluator it is unlikely that the program has a clear plan of operation.

The solutions to communication problems are very complex. To ensure effective communication it is imperative that the evaluator and the consumer of evaluation are both aware of the purpose of the evaluation. In addition, the evaluator should always be willing to broaden the traditional conceptions of evaluation. These may sound like simple steps in developing effective evaluation plans, but the changing conceptions of the purpose of evaluation have led to confusion in the minds of many.

Purpose

From the time that Scriven (1967), Stufflebeam (1968), and Stake (1967) first began exploring the concept of evaluation as the process of gathering data for the purpose of decision making, the scope of the field of program evaluation has expanded considerably. Prior to that time evaluation paradigms had closely mimicked research paradigms and both evaluators *and* those evaluated tended to think only in terms of very reductionistic and outcome-oriented questions such as these: Did the students become more creative as a result of this instructional program? Are teachers teaching any differently because of this staff development program?

Although such outcome variables legitimately remain one of the foci of evaluation efforts, recently expanded conceptions of evaluation are directed toward the goals of providing information that is of greater utility to the program being evaluated, such as increasing communication and addressing those issues fundamental to program planning for the gifted and talented. With these revised notions of the purpose of evaluation we have found new answers to the question, What is it, exactly and specifically, that program evaluation is supposed to do?

Documentation of the need for the program. One of the first questions that should be asked in program evaluation is, Why implement this program in the first place? Silly question? Not at all. All too often program planners and developers fail to ask this question and then proceed to develop programs that are either redundant or not based on the needs of the population they seek to serve.

In evaluating programs for the gifted the first purpose is to document that there, in fact, exists a population that can be called gifted and talented and that the needs of that group (those to be served by the program) were not being served prior to implementation of the program. Further, the evaluation should determine whether the population identified as having a need is actually being served by the program that has been developed. Unfortunately, the current attention to the gifted and talented has had both positive and negative influences on the creation of new programs. For example, the common belief is that once a strong academic program has been established then one should turn to developing programs for students who are gifted in the fine and performing arts. One school district following this line of reasoning began to develop a program for high school students with particular talents in these areas when, in fact, the high school already had the following organizations in place: an orchestra, a drama club, a choral society, a marching band, a jazz combo, an oratorical society, and a mime troup. One might reasonably question the necessity of initiating a separate program in the fine and performing arts. At the other extreme we find schools that seek to develop programs for those who are gifted in the fine and performing arts when there is no regular school program in the arts that can serve as a basis for screening and identification.

Documentation of the case for a particular approach. What makes us believe that a particular approach for serving the gifted and talented is the most appropriate one at this time and in this situation? What arguments are there that the approach we have selected is the one that will best meet the needs of the gifted group we identified? The evaluation that addresses these questions will seek to document the cases for curricular approaches, administrative arrangements or approaches, staff development plans, etc. For example, the evaluator might ask, Can it be demonstrated that the Individualized Programming Planning Model (Treffinger, 1981) will best meet the needs of the students we have identified as gifted? or, Will a pullout program be effective given our geography or our philosophy of education? or Is systemwide staff development for teachers the logical first step in program development or should we begin with administrator inservice?

Addressing and answering these questions during the planning stages will help prevent making crucial planning errors that could result in the failure of the program to meet its goals or even to exist at some time in the future. For example, one school district had planned to bus students to a resource room centrally located in the district. This would have meant that some students would spend over an hour on the bus going to and from the center—a waste of valuable instructional time. An administrator new to a particular school district proposed a pullout program unaware that one of the underlying assumptions of the school district (not stated or verbalized) was that every effort must be made not to remove students from the regular classroom setting.

At this stage in program evaluation, one is examining the *logic* of the decision-making process and seeking information on the consistency of arguments, plans, and decisions. The most appropriate time for evaluators to attend to this purpose of evaluation (including the purpose of documenting need discussed above and the feasibility discussed in the following section) is during the planning and development stages of the program. Unfortunately, most program developers are inclined to consider evaluation after the major program decisions have been made and the program has been in operation for some time—often after major errors have been made and often too late to provide data that will enhance, or sometimes save, a program.

Documentation of the feasibility of a program. Closely related to the purposes described thus far is that of documenting the feasibility of implementing the program. In this aspect of program development the evaluator asks, What makes you believe that, given the available resources, the program can be implemented as described and intended? For example, is it feasible to expect that all classroom teachers will have the skills to implement a cluster-group program when there is no provision for staff development? Is it feasible to expect teachers to be willing to continue in a position as itinerant teacher when they must spend half of every day in a car going from school to school and must carry all materials from building to building? (One might also ask if this is an efficient and effective use of staff.)

Note that all of the preceding purposes of evaluation occur prior to the actual implementation of the program. In short, some of the greatest potential contributions of program evaluation involve providing information for making program decisions during the planning phase. In our opinion, the traditional concept of program evaluations as an "end-of-project" activity has been and continues to be one of the single most serious problems in this field. This is especially true if one perceives a major goal of program evaluation as assisting programs in their endeavor to be successful rather than as merely rendering an after-the-fact judgment of the worth of the program.

Documentation of program implementation. A major function of the complete program evaluation is to document whether the program is being implemented as intended—or whether it is even being implemented at all. Does the program exist in practice as well as on paper and, if so, to what degree is implementation congruent with documentation? Many fine programs exist as documents that have been submitted to school boards and/or other funding agents. However, it is not at all uncommon to find that the instruction in the classroom or even the administrative arrangements bear little resemblance to the written documentation. Examples of questions that might evolve in serving this purpose of evaluation include: Are classroom teachers and resource teachers really developing individualized educational plans for each identified gifted child? (In one school district, where the gifted program specifically called for an IEP for each gifted student, the teachers were mimeographing their classes' IEPs. In another school district where specific direction had been given that selection and consequent IEP construction was to be based on students' individual achievement, the activities listed had little or no relationship to the students' specific abilities and achievements.) Are the selection committees *truly* using multiple criteria for identification or does a multiple regression analysis show that the IQ score is really the determining factor in identification? (More than one school district that had invested considerable time, effort, and money in collecting additional data found that the actual process was subverted by the individual belief among identification/selection committee members that the IQ was paramount.) Does the teacher who is presumably implementing the Enrichment Triad Model (Renzulli, 1975) really design exploratory activities based on student interest or are these activities based more on teacher interest and/or availability of instructional packages?

The reasons for finding that a program is or is not being implemented as described are multiple. In the first place, it is very important for program administrators to identify what is really happening in a program. Very often the activities in the classroom have little or no resemblance or connection to the stated (written) goals and objectives of the program. This should be of great concern to administrators accountable for ensuring that those goals are achieved. The incongruency between written documentation and actual implementation can occur for many reasons. It may be that the program proposal was written by a central office administrator who knew very little about education of the gifted and talented and then it was abandoned when someone with expertise began to run the program. It may be that teachers attended a particularly inspiring inservice and then went back to their classrooms and began to implement the ideas. It may be that experience over several years has led to the evolution of a program and this change has not been recorded. When incongruency is discovered, it should *not* automatically be assumed that program implementation should be modified—it is possible that the documentation needs to be modified to reflect the program as it exists in fact.

A second reason for documenting the fact that a program is being implemented as intended is that most instruments selected to measure student achievement are based on the stated program goals, objectives, and instructional plan. As an extreme example, if a school has stated that its goals for the gifted program are the development of higher-level thinking skills and creativity and the program consists of rapid acceleration, it is unlikely that the instruments chosen to assess the goals will reflect the changes actually achieved by the program.

Identification of program strengths and weakness. One of the most obvious but often overlooked purposes that can be served by an effective program evaluation is the identification of program strengths and weaknesses. When program evaluation is solely a process of judging whether or not the program has achieved its goals, it fails to help the program administrator and staff identify those aspects of the program that contributed to or interfered with effective program implementation. Discovering after two years of instruction that the students have not significantly improved their scores on tests of creativity or higher-level thinking skills is of little use if program personnel do not have information that will help them modify the program to better achieve that goal. It is of potentially great value to ask; What parts of the program *appear* to be working and what parts of the program *do not appear* to be working?

Questions that might be answered when this purpose of evaluation is served include: Are the teachers cognizant of the needs of the gifted and do they use appropriate instructional strategies to meet those needs? (It is highly unlikely that teachers who do not know how to meet the needs of the gifted will be successful in implementing a program for that population.) Is there a curriculum plan? Is that plan defensible as a differentiated curriculum? Does that curriculum plan address the goals and objectives of the program? (In far too many cases there is no curriculum plan except for that which exists in the mind of a resource room teacher. Often there is no plan for scope and sequence, which results in the repetition of activities and instruction for the *same* goals and objectives at the *same* level of sophistication year after year.) Do the buses deliver the children on time? (In one school district teachers believed that principals were sabotaging their program by delaying buses when, in reality, a mechanical failure in several buses was causing delay.)

Provision of data for in-progress revisions of the program. When program strengths and weaknesses are identified, it is necessary to make the needed revisions as soon as possible. During program evaluation it is thus important to ask, What are those aspects of the program that need to be changed *and* what are some of the alternatives to be considered? For example, as part of an evaluation that sought to identify causes for a lack of success of gifted students in independent study, evaluators discovered that many students lacked the skills of creative problem solving that would have helped them identify topics for study, alternative sources of information, and alternatives when their initial plans for carrying out the independent study were thwarted. The evaluators were able to suggest instructional materials for remediating this problem by consulting other programs for the gifted that had addressed this issue. (Note: Some program evaluation "purists" might suggest that, in this example, the program evaluator had shifted roles and has become, in fact, a substantive consultant to the program. While we are aware of the potential conflicts in such a situation, our conception of the primary purpose of program evaluation as being to assist the program to be successful dictates that we should accept such a risk.) In another case a program that seemed to be instructionally sound was receiving considerable criticism. Evaluators were able to identify poor communication with parents and principals as a deficit in program implementation and to suggest several vehicles of communication that were favored by both groups.

Again, the reader should note that the immediately preceding purposes force the evaluator into the process of program evaluation from the beginning of the planning phase. This is in contrast to the traditional conception which limits program evaluators to making final judgments about the worth of a program. Instead these purposes are integral to our conception of evaluation which calls for assisting the program in achieving success.

Documentation of the results or impact of the program. Documentation of the results or impact of a program traditionally received the most attention. And in evaluations of gifted programs that stressed results or looked at the achievement of program goals as the only focus, the tendency was to look only at stated student outcome variables rather than at other potential outcomes, impacts, or results of program evaluation. Such evaluations failed to consider impacts on program staff, regular school personnel, parents, community, the institution/school system or unintended, but significant student outcomes. Certainly, gifted students and the impact of the program on their achievement is, and should remain, of major concern. After all, that is our purpose in developing these programs in the first place.

Accordingly, questions asked to serve this purpose of evaluation should continue to focus on such issues as "Has the program improved the higher-level thinking skills or critical thinking skills of the students?" "Are the students more creative as a result of the instruction that has been provided?" "Have underachieving gifted students improved their classroom achievement?" But questions addressing other potential outcomes should also be considered. For example: Did teachers change their instructional strategies as a result of the staff development program? (Of what use is it really to ask teachers whether they enjoyed the inservice, found it useful, etc.? By the time such information is gathered the staff development program has little use for the data and, in addition, there is little evidence that such responses correlate to changed behavior.) Are administrators, support staff, other teachers supportive and contributing to the program? Does the community view the program as beneficial? Is the total educational program provided by the school benefited or hindered by the program? Does the program have any negative impacts (e.g., on self-concept or peer relationships)?

Explanation and description of the program to interested but uninformed audiences. The final goal of defensible program evaluations to be discussed in this chapter is the documentation of the resources, activities, and impacts/ results of the program for funding agents, potential adopter or adapters of the program, and/or interested persons such as parents, community groups, central administration staff, principals, regular teaching staff, other school personnel, etc. Each of these groups would fall under the category of evaluation consumers that Renzulli (1975) would call Prime Interest Groups. That is, each of these groups has a potential interest in knowing exactly what the program was all about, what resources were expended, and what the outcomes of that process were—albeit for different reasons and with a different focus in each case.

Funding agents are, of course, interested in knowing whether the outcomes warrant the expenditure of the monies they provided. They will want to know whether gifted students are doing things, learning things, and accomplishing goals they would not accomplish without the program. Potential adopters or adapters would be interested in knowing whether the program could be implemented in their schools with the same outcomes. What preconditions would be necessary? (For example, must there be an existing program in music and art? Is a special site necessary? Are special materials required? Must there be an individually guided program already in place in the regular classroom? Is special training needed for staff? How much? What kind? Where is it obtained?)

If each of the purposes discussed above were to be considered and incorporated at the onset of both program and evaluation designs, both the evaluator and the program planner would have a clearer picture of the program intent and the expectations for what the evaluation can be expected to yield. In addition, there will be a greater likelihood of improved communication, more useful evaluation reports, and more satisfied consumers of evaluation.

Program Description

A significant step in improving the evaluation process is to ensure that the evaluation includes a thorough program description or statement of the object of program evaluation. The evolution of evaluation practice has been impacted by active interaction between the evaluation process and the program development process to the point where program description is now used as a means of improving both the program planning process and the evaluation design process. Essentially, program description is a process whereby the evaluator and program staff describe all of the resources used in the program, program activities, and the anticipated program outcomes (and on some occasions potential unintended outcomes). This description usually incorporates both written descriptions and graphic representations showing the relationships between these variables (Yavorsky, 1984). It is one of the most overlooked stages of program evaluation, but one that can be most valuable. Why is this process considered so valuable?

It is not possible to evaluate what you cannot describe. The most important reason for program description is that it is simply not possible to evaluate what you cannot describe. For example, if the curriculum cannot be completely described, it is not possible to select appropriate assessment instruments. To tell an evaluator that the goals of the program include "creativity development" is not at all sufficient. There are literally hundreds of definitions of creativity involving personality variables, product variables, and process variables. The instruments that measure these variables are as diverse as the definitions and strategies that might be used to develop the construct. In order for the evaluator to make appropriate choices about the assessment strategy to be used, he or she must have more complete understanding of the accepted definition of the concept and of the strategies used in instruction. As a further example, if administrative functions cannot be described, it is impossible to identify sources of administrative inadequacy. If materials do not arrive on time, who is at fault? If appeals are not handled appropriately, who is responsible?

Standards. A full and accurate program description also provides a standard against which to make comparisons. If a curriculum for the gifted is described as the IPPM Model or the Enrichment Triad Model and the component parts of those models can be described, then the evaluator can determine whether the model has been adequately implemented by comparing what is actually carried out in the classroom with the model's standards—How many IEPs were completed? Did the students actually complete "real-life products"? Such descriptions provide standards for judging whether needed resources were actually provided and expended appropriately, whether program activities were implemented as described, and whether program goals were attained.

One criterion of a sound program evaluation is the degree to which the program received a fair test. There have been documented instances (Rossi & Freeman, 1982) in which evaluations have been conducted on the basis of program documents when, in fact, the program was never implemented! Small wonder that the evaluations showed no program impacts. One might wonder how many potentially useful educational testaments have been discarded because they have not been implemented as intended and, therefore, have not had a "fair test."

An operational plan. One of the most useful benefits of completing a full program description is that it provides an operational plan for the program management and staff as well as information about the program for the evaluator. When one is asked to identify all of the resources, activities, and expected outcomes of a program, it becomes very obvious when there are activities for which no outcome is expected or when there are anticipated outcomes for which no resources are allotted or activities planned. It is useful in helping staff identify exactly what inputs (resources) are available, and what activities must be accomplished (e.g., identification, curriculum planning, staffing, staff development) in order to achieve intended outcomes. In addition, an operational plan will often also suggest the order of implementation as it becomes clear that the outcomes of one activity are inputs or resources for the next activity. For example, it is necessary to have a plan for identification before one can begin appropriate training for identification and selection committees (a factor often overlooked resulting in confusing and inapplicable inservices addressing all possible alternatives in identifying the gifted).

A basis for attributing outcomes. When a program description is completed it will illustrate the relationships between various components, resources, activities, and outcomes of a program. Thus, when an outcome is achieved or not achieved it is possible to trace back through the activities and resources to identify those that did or did not contribute to the outcome. For example, if instruction does not achieve the desired outcomes it may be the result of inappropriate identification procedures, lack of appropriate inservice for teachers, inappropriate staff selection, etc. In one gifted program, teachers were extremely disappointed when few of the students were successful in completing their Type III activities of the Enrichment Triad Model. Examination of the identification procedures revealed that only student aptitude (IQ) was a factor in the selection process. Since it is assumed that students who are successful in completing these activities are characterized as having above-average ability, creativity, and task commitment, the problem and possible solutions became immediately apparent.

A mechanism for checking perceptions. Forcing program staff and management to provide a specific outline of the program is an avenue for those individuals to cross-check their perceptions of the program to ensure that they have a consistent understanding of the program. Often such cross-checking will reveal significant differences or lack of understanding, as when one teacher who may have attended a workshop on creativity may feel that the development of creativity means the development of creative thinking processes and an appropriate attitude, whereas another teacher may feel that it means the generation of creative products.

The value of an accurate and comprehensive program description cannot be overstated. We have encountered numerous instances in which differing perceptions of program staff have actually resulted in activities that were counterproductive to the program.

Trouble spots. Experience is one of the most valuable assets an evaluator and program planner can apply in ensuring that the evaluation design will monitor areas that traditionally have been problems in programs for the gifted. Pullout programs, for example, always have the potential for problems with coordination with the regular school program and curriculum. They also have the potential for causing student problems (e.g., pressure to make up missed classroom work, peer interaction problems, teacher resentment problems). Very often facilities present problems as well. A teacher once developed a unit on ecology that was extremely impressive on paper, but school policy prohibited the students from leaving the building during class time—an obvious problem.

Generation of evaluation concerns. Just as the description brings to light potential trouble spots to be considered in the evaluation, it also suggests other areas that should be of concern in the evaluation design. Each set of resources, activities, and outcomes should be examined to determine whether data should be gathered to judge the degree to which the resources exist, the activities have been implemented, or outcomes have been attained. If identification is part of a gifted and talented program, its standards and the proper implementation of the process becomes an area of concern. If staff training is a crucial component of the gifted program, then one should be concerned about the adequacy of training.

Explanation of the program. As we have noted, outside audiences often have a vested interest in a particular program. A program description allows those parties to identify the specific purposes, resources, activities, and outcomes of the program.

Comparisons and Value Judgments

How are you? How was breakfast? How successful is your program? Each time we are asked one of these questions we implicitly ask the question, Compared with what? Evaluation by definition involves a value judgment and value judgments involve the use of relative terms such as good/bad and adequate/inadequate. While several of these terms may appear to be absolute, a careful analysis reveals that, in fact, a comparison is implicit. For example, the assignment of a value of good or bad to the question "How are you?" carries very little meaning in the absence of asking and answering the implied question, "Compared with what?" I may be well compared with yesterday, but miserable compared with my usual state.

In the field of education answers to this question are typically translated into norm-referenced or criterion-referenced models. The norm-referenced model answers the comparison question by stating, "Compared with other programs like it or compared with no program at all." The criterion-referenced model answers this question by stating, "Compared with the criteria (standards) of what a good program should be." In the first instance we are comparing the object of evaluation with others like it and in the second we are comparing the object of the evaluation with some "absolute" criterion or standard. It is important to note that the concept of criterion-referenced comparison is less pure or absolute than some would have us believe. While it is true that the actual comparison of the object of the evaluation with the criterion/standard is absolute, i.e., the standard is either met or it is not met, where does the standard come from in the first place? Generally, the substance of the standards are not generated in a vacuum, but rather grow out of experience with other objects or events of a similar nature. In other words, the concept of an "ideal" program is heavily influenced by experiences with one or more real programs and, thus, the concept is, in fact, norm referenced.

Similarly, it is important to give careful consideration to the issue of setting the level at which the standard is applied. That is, the cutoff score that divides good from bad, adequate from inadequate, etc., is as important as the actual substance of the standard. For example, it may be decided that the criterion (substance of the standard) will be increased performance on measures of critical thinking. How much increase will be accepted as evidence of having attained the criterion? Where will those levels come from if not from experiences with individuals or programs and with the development of what it is "reasonable" to expect in terms of a minimum level of performance relative to the standard. Again, this is a norm-referenced notion if one's perception grows out of experiences with some other group of similar students. Unfortunately, in the field of education for the gifted, both the substance of the standards and the appropriate level of standards are not easily identified. The goals of programs for the gifted are not the same as those of the regular curriculum and the levels of performance that might be expected of gifted students on the sorts of goals that are stated have not been established as they have been for an average student. How do we know, for example, how many points student scores should increase on the fluency subscale of the Torrance Tests of Creative Thinking with one year of effective instruction?

We are faced with somewhat of a quandary and must, therefore, be especially careful in the program description to carefully identify standards and to consider ways to establish appropriate cutoff scores if criterion-referenced models are to be used. Certainly, there are problems with both norm-referenced and criterion-referenced approaches to program evaluations in the field of education of the gifted and talented. Some of these problems have been discussed in depth by Callahan (1983) and some alternative strategies were proposed for implementing quasi-experimental solutions to these problems. It is, of course, possible to design program evaluations that contain norm-referenced *and* criterion-referenced questions. However, it is important that the evaluator and program staff recognize the differences because these differences have implications for the types of information required to answer the evaluation question and the manner in which the findings of the evaluation are reported and interpreted. It is also important that arbitrary criterion standards not be established. If at all possible, empirical data should be collected or existing norms for gifted students should be consulted in setting these standards.

Alternatives in Evaluation Design

In addressing the problems and issues of program evaluation in gifted programs, it has generally been expected that the questions will lend themselves to an experimental design solution comparing a control and an experimental group using objective and very quantitative outcome measures. However, several of the purposes of evaluation, discussed in this chapter, simply are not served well by such approaches and on many of the occasions when certain purposes could be served by such an approach the circumstances are not such that an evaluation design of that nature is possible (see Callahan, 1983).

Evaluators have come to recognize that strict experimental paradigms are antiseptic, incomplete, and often detached from the purposes of program evaluation. Evaluators have begun to explore numerous alternatives and have looked in many different fields for metaphors that might be adapted to the evaluation of educational programs. Scriven (1981) has described a procedure similar to that used by Ralph Nader in product evaluation; Gephart (1981) used the paradigm of watercolor painting, and Della-Piana (1981) looked to film criticism for a model. Cost analysis, law, architecture, geography, philosophy are other areas that are discussed in a series of books devoted to looking at alternatives to traditional design (Smith, 1981a; Smith, 1981b).

If program evaluation designs are to adequately serve programs as intended, then the designs should document the nature of the programs and the happenings of the programs within their natural settings and then describe program effects through an analysis of these observations. Models that approach evaluation in this manner have been characterized as "naturalistic." Many varieties of this general category have evolved since Guba proposed it in 1978 (Guba, 1978). Unfortunately, these models have often been considered and labeled qualitative and subjective and, therefore, often have been regarded as less than "scientific." This is unfortunate for a number of reasons. First, experimental design paradigms are not necessarily more quantitative and are often *less* objective. Biases in experimental design are, in fact, more dangerous because they tend to be hidden in numbers, tests, and tables. Second, naturalistic models often incorporate the use of both quantitative and qualitative data.

The characteristics of naturalistic models of evaluation are:

1. They all have a phenomenological base.
2. They focus on description and understanding.
3. They have as their purpose the discovery and verification of propositions.
4. They take a holistic view of the system or program being evaluated.
5. They work from an emergent, variable design mode.
6. They deal with multiple realities.
7. They consider values as an important set of variables to consider. (Guba, 1978)

For purposes of illustrating the contrast of naturalistic techniques to traditional means of making comparisons and judgments about programs, we will review Eisner's (1979) connoisseurship model and Guba's (1981) investigative journalism model.

Connoisseurship

Elliot Eisner's model for educational evaluation suggests a new approach both to the design of evaluation and to the presentation of evaluation results. Using the terms *educational connoisseurship* and *educational criticism* to describe the process, he bases his thinking on parallel artistic concepts. Accordingly, he suggests that many of the processes and outcomes of educational programs cannot be broken down into either specific behavioral objectives or test items that the statistician can use a basis for value judgments—just as a sculpture or a painting or a film is a holistic piece of work so is the educational process a holistic entity. Therefore, rather than pursue a reductionistic approach of breaking down everything into its finer parts, he suggests that we consider the approaches used by art critics, literary critics, and film critics.

In brief (and the process is a very complex one that merits considerable study for appropriate implementation) the process involves (1) close examination by *an educational connoisseur* of the holistic nature of an activity to *disclose* its meanings to the public, (2) using our knowledge of the activity at its best *and* under given circumstances to judge the worth of a given program, and (3) *extensive* observation of classrooms, instruction, and other activities by knowledgeable consultants. Eisner further suggests that the traditional form of representation used to report evaluation results is often too restrictive and that we consider alternatives such as films (e.g., *High School*), slides and photographs, music, literary narrative (hardly the stuff of most evaluation reports), and enactments as alternatives to statistics and charts.

Should you challenge this model as not objective because of the inherent bias of observers, Eisner (as well as other nontraditional evaluators) does not believe that *any* evaluation or evaluator is really value free or unbiased. By virtue of the evaluation questions asked, selection or framing of an instrument, or other choices, we choose the values that are reflected.

Investigative Journalism

In looking for and developing models that satisfy the requirements of naturalistic/observational evaluation, Guba (1981) sought models that met the following conditions:

1. included a wide range of data collection methodologies
2. used data collection methodologies that would not interact with or be reactive with the program

3. used content and context analysis (examining both program documents and program context as well as program implementation)
4. relied on observation of actions as well as atmosphere in terms of emotions, obvious value clues, and nonverbal clues
5. used interview for the purposes of acquaintance with issues, focusing of issues, and verification of propositions
6. relied on structural corroboration—building a case on a series of reliable and supporting facts to convince a jury that an argument is sound or that a judgment is warranted (or is not warranted as might be the case)

Guba's model of investigative journalism includes all of these features and is characterized by the steps of tracking (looking at an activity that has normal patterns of functioning for abnormalities), key interviews, use of files and documents, triangulation (using many sources and types of data to lead to the same proposition), circling, shuffling and filing, aborting and/or reporting, and followthrough verification.

Both this model and the connoiseurship model require the same care and exactness as an experimental design, but have the advantage of richness and thoroughness of reporting not possible with a plan that calls for the selection of experimental and control groups, pre- and posttesting, controlling extraneous variables, and statistical comparisons of means. Although those steps may form some part of the procedures called naturalistic evaluation, they are only elements of the verification process, not the focus of the approach. [Many other models of naturalistic evaluation exist and more details of their applicability to gifted programs can be found in Barnette's (1984) contribution to the *Journal for the Education of the Gifted.*]

These evaluation models have been described only briefly here and they certainly have shortcomings as well as benefits (e.g., cost, degree of expertise required for implementation, credibility in a world where the test of significance has been the predominant test of worth. Nonetheless, this brief introduction to the characteristics of the naturalistic approach should demonstrate its potential for serving the many purposes of evaluation that will most benefit programs for gifted students and thus the students themselves.

Summary

The focus of this chapter has been to suggest that program evaluation (or program managers when seeking a program evaluator) should consider the wide range of purposes that a program evaluation might serve—as opposed to merely seeking answers to program impact questions usually related to student outcome behaviors. Such program evaluations will require consideration of less traditional approaches but have the potential for providing useful information during the planning and implementation phases of the gifted and talented program as well as providing richer descriptions of the programs for potential adopters or adapters.

References

Barnette, J.J. (1984). Naturalistic approaches to gifted and talented program evaluation. *Journal for the Education of the Gifted, 7*(1), 26–37.

Callahan, C.M. (1983). Issues in evaluating programs for the gifted. *Gifted Child Quarterly, 27*(1), 3–7.

Callahan, C.M., & Caldwell, M.S. (1984). Using evaluation results to improve programs for the gifted and talented. *Journal for the Education of the Gifted, 7*(1), 60–74.

Della-Piana, G.M. (1981). Film criticism. In N.L. Smith (Ed.), *New techniques for evaluation* (pp. 274–285). Beverly Hills: Sage.

Eisner, E.W. (1979). *The educational imagination: On the design and evaluation of school programs.* New York: Macmillan.

Gephart, W.J. (1981). Water-color painting. In N.L. Smith (Ed.), *Metaphors for evaluation.* Beverly Hills, CA: Sage Publications.

Guba, E.G. (1978). Toward a methodology of naturalistic inquiry in educational evaluation. *CSE Monograph Series in Evaluation, 8.*

Guba, E.G. (1981). Investigative journalism. In N.L. Smith (Ed.), *New techniques for evaluation* (pp. 167–262). Beverly Hills: Sage.

Patton, M.Q. (1981). *Creative education.* Beverly Hills: Sage.

Renzulli, J.S. (1975). *Working draft: A guidebook for evaluating programs for the gifted and talented.* Ventura, CA: Office of the Ventura County Superintendent of Schools.

Rossi, P.H., & Freeman, H.E. (1982). *Evaluation: A systematic approach* (2nd ed.). Beverly Hills: Sage.

Scriven, M. (1967). The methodology of evaluation. In R.E. Stake (Ed.), *Curriculum Evaluation* (American Educational Research Association Monograph Series on Evaluation, No. 1). Chicago: Rand McNally.

Scriven, M. (1981). Product evaluation. In N.L. Smith (Ed.), *New techniques for evaluation* (pp. 121–166). Beverly Hills: Sage.

Smith, N.L. (Ed.). (1981a). *Metaphors for evaluation: Sources of new methods.* Beverly Hills: Sage.

Smith, N.L. (Ed.). (1981b). *New techniques for evaluation.* Beverly Hills: Sage.

Stake, R.E. (1967). The countenance of educational evaluation. *Teachers College Record, 68,* 523–540.

Stufflebeam, D.L. (1968). *Evaluation as enlightenment for decision-making.* Columbus, OH: Evaluation Center, Ohio State University.

Treffinger, D.J. (1981). *Blending gifted education with the total school program.* Williamsville, NY: Center for Creative Learning.

Yavorsky, D.K. (1984). *Discrepancy evaluation: A practitioner's guide.* Charlottesville, VA: University of Virginia, Curry School of Education Evaluation Research Center.

22

Evaluation for Gifted Education: Synthesis and Discussion

Sarah M. Dinham, Ph.D.
Anne J. Udall, M.A.
University of Arizona

The best educational program for gifted students integrates evaluation functions from student identification to curriculum planning and teacher appraisal to program accountability. Both the Callahan and Caldwell article and Seeley's appropriately consider evaluation as integral to programs for the gifted. They imply that the program itself and its evaluation component are improved if planned and conducted as one.

Evaluation is an essential part of an excellent—a defensibly excellent—program for gifted students, as it is for all educational programs. While education of the gifted is unique in its constituencies and educational strategies, its evaluation needs are not. The educator concerned with evaluation of programs for the gifted will find useful material not only in sources on evaluation of programs for the gifted specifically, but also should turn for the most current theories, the most defensible evaluation strategies, to the general literature of program evaluation.

This chapter discusses Seeley's and Callahan and Caldwell's contributions as well as the contributions of the extensive literature on program evaluation and offers a synthesis of evaluation principles and practices for education of the gifted. It (1) reviews educational evaluation's myriad definitions and purposes to illustrate the variety of needs evaluation serves; it then reviews (2) the climate in which evaluation occurs, (3) the variety of procedural approaches in past and current use, and (4) the elements of one illustrative approach, responsive evaluation, including (5) the evaluator's multiple roles.

Definitions and Purposes

Among the many professional terms suffering from rapid changes of definition, "evaluation" is especially vexing because it is used widely both in education and in the general lay vocabulary. Before "evaluation" took on its present meaning in education of the gifted, the term was used principally for diagnostic assessment practices usually involving individual measurement and clinical judgment, for example, in programs for the gifted or psychological recommendations. Simultaneously, the notion of personnel evaluation for teachers—of gifted students and others—gained attention, the term "evaluation" taking on meanings varying from "surveillance" to "systematic appraisal of job performance."

In the 1970s when "evaluation" took on a special meaning, various definitions gave rise to various models for conducting evaluation. For example, early evaluation models emphasized attainment of established program objectives (Tyler, 1969). The importance of examining unintended outcomes and providing feedback for mid-program correction was proposed early (Scriven, 1967). Conceptions of decision-oriented evaluation significantly advanced the field's thinking (Stufflebeam et al., 1971); Seeley's chapter in this volume rests on this view. The definition of evaluation varied from model to model; through the years the definitions have moved from emphasizing the object(s) being evaluated—the program—toward emphasizing those who need the evaluation, the audience(s) for the findings. Today the *definition* of evaluation is a matter of less consequence; more important is addressing evaluation's *purpose*.

Evaluation is changing in purpose and in scope, as Callahan and Caldwell point out. In recent years the trend from decision-oriented models toward models addressing multiple purposes for multiple audiences has resulted in varied and flexible evaluation design alternatives, discussed later in this chapter, and procedures drawing on naturalistic as well as traditional scientific models. The newest developments in evaluation do indeed, as Callahan and Caldwell point out, have great potential.

Callahan and Caldwell conclude their chapter with an important point: that evaluation today serves a wide range of purposes. As Seeley points out, evaluation is seen today not only as a product (some speak of "an" evaluation document as "an" evaluation), but as a process as well. The evaluation process, serving many purposes, may be "defined," as Callahan and Caldwell's sixth theme implies, in any way that is useful. "Useful" as a cue for defining evaluation is imbedded in two contexts: the need and the audience. Evaluation is defined by its purpose: to meet the varied needs of multiple audiences.

Evaluation's Audiences

The purpose of evaluating a program for the gifted is to meet the needs of audiences who have an interest in the program and/or its evaluation. In discussing views of evaluation some years ago, Stake said "I prefer to think of ways that evaluation can provide a service, and be useful to specific persons. For an evaluation to be useful the evaluator should know the interests and the language of his audiences. During an evaluation study, a substantial amount of time may well be spent in learning about the . . . needs of the persons for whom the evaluation is being done" (1975, p. 13).

An educational program for the gifted has many audiences: parents, district administrators, program teachers, school counselors, the board of education, and officials in state and federal agencies responsible for categorical programs, as Seeley mentions. These audiences' needs for evaluation vary; the program evaluation should be designed to meet them.

Identifying the audiences themselves is a crucial early step in implementing evaluation. Usually, one or more audiences will commission the evaluation; other audiences' needs must nonetheless be identified and met for the evaluation (and hence the program itself) to be broadly credible. Guba and Lincoln offered examples of audiences for a program's evaluation (1981, pp. 307–308). Among them are several that pertain to the program's origins, a matter particularly important in programs for the gifted:

1. The program's developer(s)
2. Providers of program funds
3. Those who originally identified the needs the program addresses
4. Those who contracted for the evaluation

The most obvious audiences would be those concerned with the program's planning and/or implementation:

1. The program's teachers and other staff
2. The school district's administrators
3. Administrators peripherally concerned with the program, such as building principals

Also included in the broad definition of audiences are many not directly concerned with the program's planning or implementation, but important to the program itself:

1. Direct and indirect beneficiaries such as students and parents
2. Those who might suffer indirect side effects, for example, able students not meeting the program's inclusion criteria

Audiences should be the focus of the evaluation. Audiences' needs—their conceptions of the program, their desire for information, for accountability, for alternatives, for assurance—shape the evaluation's purposes.

Needs Served by Evaluation

As the audiences for the gifted programs are multiple and diverse, so too are the needs the evaluation will serve. In their chapter Callahan and Caldwell list a useful array of illustrative needs for evaluation of educational programs for the gifted: appraising alternative approaches, documenting program implementation, discerning program strengths and weaknesses, aiding in program revision, documenting program impacts/results, and informing others about the program.

Renzulli's (1975) requirements for good evaluation provide another sample list of needs that an evaluation might serve: discovering fulfillment of program objectives, discerning program consequences, determining contributions to program success/failure, providing in-process feedback, suggesting modifications. Seeley suggests one central purpose for evaluation: "examining actions and events according to some predetermined standards for the purpose of making decisions." However, all three examples—Callahan and Caldwell's, Renzulli's, and Seeley's—ignore the evaluation audience. All three propose to substitute their own definitions of needs.

Evaluation's purposes are formed by the intersection of audiences and their needs, as illustrated in Figure 22–1. No outsider can legitimately mandate what the particular audiences' needs might or should be. Evaluation of a program for gifted students will typically address several needs for several audiences, but seldom all conceivable needs for all possible audiences.

At worst, evaluations miss the mark altogether. The evaluation of a program for the gifted might be planned to meet needs imagined by the program director or evaluator when the audiences' needs are none of those but several others. For example the program director might imagine that cost-outcome analysis is the most crucial evaluation when in fact the program's teachers need an evaluation to review program alternatives or modifications. An evaluator bent on program improvement might not recognize that the State Department of Education's accountability mandate would more likely be met by program census and outcome studies than by formative curriculum monitoring.

An evaluation failing to address the specific audiences' specific needs is no evaluation indeed. Empty exercises embellished with administrative or scientific trappings are worse than no evaluations at all, for they insult both the program and the spirit of evaluation.

Figure 22–1 Illustrative Purposes for Program Evaluation

	Sample Audiences				
	Adminis- trators	Board of Education	Counseling Staff	Director of Gifted Program	Education Committee, State Legislature
Needs: Account- ability					4
Baseline testing			5		
Cost- outcome		1			
Documenting enrollment					
Effect on district	2				
Feedback to improve program				3	
etc.					

Illustration 1: Cost-outcome analysis for Board of Education

Illustration 2: Administrators' assessments of program effects on other programs in the building or districtwide

Illustration 3: Formative evaluation: Provide feedback to program director for improving program

Illustration 4: Provide testimony to legislature regarding compliance with state-mandated guidelines for program documentation

Illustration 5: Information for counselors to use in selection of participants and program placement

The Evaluation Climate

An evaluation meeting specific audiences' specific needs takes place in a specific setting. Unique to that setting are important influences that shape the evaluation. These "human factor" influences, as Guba and Lincoln (1981) call them, create the evaluation's climate, inevitably affecting the evaluation proceedings. Although both Seeley and Callahan and Caldwell indirectly mention some human factor influences surrounding evaluation, the influences are important enough to be discussed directly. In evaluation of programs for the gifted, two features of the evaluation's climate deserve special attention: the participants' attitudes and the setting's politics.

Attitudes

Many writers, including Seeley and Callahan and Caldwell, have described the reactions attending announcement, implementation, or reporting of an evaluation (e.g., Posavac & Carey, 1985). Evaluation may be greeted with enthusiasm, more likely with caution, often with misunderstanding, perhaps with disappointment or with weary resignation. At worst, program participants may sabotage the evaluation efforts.

The origins for these reactions are complex. Abuses of evaluation practice (some of which Seeley mentions) explain some of the negative attitudes. For example, using evaluation as a punitive measure guarantees mistrust and hostility. Other reasons for resistance to evaluation include the perception of evaluation as the same as traditional research (Callahan & Caldwell, 1984), lack of understanding (Banner, Doctors, & Gordon, 1975), lack of visible policy impact (Cronbach et al., 1981), lack of relevant findings (Leviton & Hughes, 1981), limited focus (Weiss, 1975), and the fear that negative findings will detrimentally affect the program (Banner, Doctors, & Gordon, 1975).

Even a well-planned evaluation addressing these concerns will undoubtedly take place in an uneasy climate. Since evaluation—which observes and draws conclusions—includes elements of judgment, that judgment, even when done in the most constructive manner, will always create a certain degree of anxiety. Moreover, whenever evaluation is undertaken, not only will it disrupt individual calm; evaluation by its very mission disrupts the institutional status quo.

The Political Context

As Seeley's and Callahan and Caldwell's chapters illustrate, one cannot discuss evaluation without discussing politics. Social, economic, and personal interactions among people create the political climate for any endeavor; because evaluation is an interactive undertaking, there will always be politics where there is evaluation. Seeley's article and many other sources as well have examined the role of politics in evaluation's climate (Cohen, 1970; Cronbach et al., 1981; Hendrickson & Barber, 1980; House, 1972; Myers, 1981; Sjoberg, 1975; Sroufe, 1977; Weiss, 1973, 1975). In fact, Cronbach et al.

have pointed out that a theory of evaluation is as much a theory of political interaction as it is a theory of determining facts (1981, p. 3).

Weiss (1975) described three ways politics influence evaluation. First, in education of the gifted, a complex political climate already surrounds the program, a reflection of the community and its needs. This existing political climate, which shapes the decision to initiate the program, exerts continuing influence. The decision to evaluate some aspect(s) of the program emerges from this milieu, and will—in turn—influence the evaluation. Cronbach et al. observed that "time and again, political passion has been a driving spirit behind a call for rational analysis" (1981, p. 4).

Second, Weiss noted that evaluation results feed into the political arena, influencing subsequent decisions about the program for the gifted. Guba and Lincoln (1981) concur, observing that evaluation is always disruptive of the prevailing political climate (p. 299). Evaluators are themselves often caught in the political context; the evaluators have political influence even when they do not seek it, and often their professional conclusions will not substitute for the political process (Cronbach et al., 1981, p. 3).

And finally, Weiss pointed out that evaluation itself has a political stance, and both implicitly and explicitly will make political statements about programs. Evaluation seeks to understand events and activities in order to guide the future, in contrast with accountability, which takes a backward view in order to determine blame or praise; in fact a demand for accountability has been called a sign of the system's pathology (Cronbach et al., 1981, p. 4).

Every educational situation will have its own unique political context, but most programs for the gifted will share, to some extent, certain common political climatic elements. Seeley discusses some of these common factors in his paragraphs on categorical programs. Educators of the gifted are very familiar with other pressures as well, such as ambivalent community attitudes toward serving gifted students and the usually vocal, dominant parent support groups. When evaluating programs for the gifted one must be aware of both the general, the political context of evaluation, and the particular, the political history of education for gifted students.

The evaluation climate, a rich tapestry of individual and community viewpoints, surrounds all evaluations. The situation's politics and the attitudes of involved individuals will dramatically influence all stages of an evaluation. But evaluation should not be dismissed because of its complex climate; instead, awareness of these "human factors" is a precondition to conducting an effective evaluation (Weiss, 1975).

The evaluation climate for programs for the gifted can be improved by several direct means. Most basically, as Weiss (1973) and Callahan and Caldwell have said, many evaluation difficulties can be eliminated if programs are clearly conceptualized and designed at the outset. Vague goals, poor communication, and an inadequate evaluation component unnecessarily increase the complexities of climate. Careful program design, coupled with an evaluation plan responsive to its audience, would begin to address many political and attitude problems. Political and attitude climates are also improved with sound communication patterns established by the evaluator.

The evaluation model presented in the following sections of this chapter not only responds to audiences' needs but also accepts and builds on the multiple realities of the evaluation climate.

Implementing Evaluation

Models

Over the past 20 years many "models" have been advanced for conceptualiz-ing and/or conducting evaluation. The evaluation literature contains an astonishing assortment of acronyms and titles for evaluation—for example the CIPP model (Stufflebeam et al., 1971), goal-free evaluation (Scriven, 1973), Tyler's (1969) classic objectives-based evaluation, the countenance model (Stake, 1967), utilization focused evaluation (Patton, 1978), and many others.

Many of these conceptualizations are not complete enough to meet the criteria for a model. Nevo pointed out that many "approaches" have been " . . . unduly referred to as models . . . " (1983, p. 117). Snow defines "model" as " . . . well developed descriptive analogies used to help visualize, often in a simplified or miniature way, phenomena that cannot be easily or directly observed. Each model is thus a projection of a possible system of relationships among phenomena, realized in verbal, material, graphic, or symbolic terms" (1976, p. 81). By this definition, an evaluation model would show a well-developed theoretical base; in addition, the evaluator would design a thorough evaluation supported by the underlying theory. One is hard pressed to find evaluation models that meet Snow's criteria. Education of the gifted, a field searching for evaluation techniques, has also fallen into the trap of labeling as an evaluation "model" a conceptual approach or a set of conve-nient procedures (e.g., Park & Buescher, 1982; Rimm, 1982).

The history of evaluation has been characterized not by true models but by two types of thinking. On the one hand, there are myriad evaluation approaches, each reflecting viewpoints about the nature of reality but lacking the specificity required for evaluation planning. For example, Seeley bases his chapter on the "input-process-output" approach, and Callahan and Caldwell discuss the emerging connoisseurship and investigative approaches to evalua-tion. On the other hand, the field has seen scores of clever and useful procedures developed separately from overall purposes and lacking a conceptual base. The classic experimental (or as a compromise, quasi-experimental) approach was predominant in early evaluations; proposals that these are ideal approaches may still be found in the general evaluation literature (e.g., Nunnally, 1975; Rossi & Freeman, 1982) and in the evaluation literature for gifted education as well (Payne & Brown, 1982).

In short, there is a substantial need for evaluation models that not only rest in a well-defined philosophy, but also offer specificity for planning evaluations that will reflect both the fluidity of audiences' needs and the practicalities of the evaluation climate. One model that shows great promise is the responsive model, which Callahan and Caldwell mention. The responsive model has a strong base in naturalistic paradigms, and Stake (1975), Guba and Lincoln, (1981), and other major proponents have also developed practical steps for its implementation.

Responsive evaluation is distinguished by its concept of evaluation's purpose, the purpose stated previously in this chapter: meeting audiences' needs. This qualitative model rests philosophically in post-positivist (or some would say phenomenological) paradigms, rather than the positivism of traditional psychological research paradigms (Stainback & Stainback, 1984). Its practice is defined by the perceptions and needs of those whom the evaluation serves. Indeed, all components of the evaluation situation are acknowledged as contextual and interactive, characterized by many varying perceptions, opinions, beliefs, and values. Because human behavior is significantly influenced by the setting in which it occurs, responsive evaluation requires an understanding of the framework in which subjects interpret their views, thoughts, feelings, and actions (High, Udall, & Dinham, 1984). Responsive evaluation rests in naturalistic approaches, approaches distinguished from experimental inquiry chiefly by lack of constraints upon both antecedent variables and possible outputs (Guba & Lincoln, 1981, p. 79), both of which are generated from the context.

Seeley, Callahan and Caldwell, and others, have discussed many of the problems in evaluating a program for gifted students, including accurately measuring program goals and finding appropriate research designs (Callahan, Covert, Aylesworth, & Vance, 1981; Callahan, 1983; Renzulli, 1975). Because the responsive model is adaptable and comprehensive, it seems especially suited for evaluating programs for gifted students (Barnette, 1984). Two recent evaluations of programs have used the responsive model with great success (Callahan, 1980; LeCompte, 1981).

Components of a Responsive Evaluation

With the responsive model, because audience needs define evaluation procedures, there can be no "cookbook" for conducting the evaluation. Most often the evaluation's components will not be stages to be implemented one by one; instead, the components will interact. The evaluation procedure will include *planned* recycling among these components. Figure 22–2 illustrates the major components of the responsive model and gives examples of the recursive process.

Figure 22–2 shows that the entire evaluation process is interactive, occurring (1) within the evaluation climate. Initially some audience(s) will (2) determine needs for an evaluation, and (3) negotiate with or select an evaluator(s) who will, in turn, (4) help reclarify the identified needs. The needs determine strategies for the (5) evaluation techniques, including establishing a timeline and determining methodology.

Once evaluation strategies have been outlined, the evaluator will (6) identify the tactics, the sources of information that will address the audiences' needs. Information collection, a component that might have begun at earlier stages, is redefined and refined for the particular audiences' particular needs. For example, some evaluations of programs for gifted students examine student gains; others assess various audiences' satisfaction or track students into college to determine long-term effect.

Measuring gifted student gains has been a major source of concern for evaluators of programs for the gifted (Ganopole, 1982; Park & Buescher, 1982; Renzulli, 1975), as there are many difficulties, including low ceilings on standardized tests, lack of tests for assessing cognitive and creative skills, and regression toward the mean. As a result of these problems the evaluator may need to adapt or develop specialized instruments to assess program effects; there is some promising literature in this area (Archambault, 1984; Aylesworth, 1984; Delisle, 1984; Reis, 1984).

Specialized instruments may be developed for the particular evaluation, and (7) multiple sources of information—both quantitative and qualitative—are collected. These data may come from standardized tests, surveys, budget information, policy documents, memos, and interview findings.

An illustration of the relationship between identified evaluation needs and sources of information appears in Exhibits 22–1 and 22–2. Exhibit 22–1 displays the needs identified for one gifted program evaluation and the types of information to address each need. One major need from Exhibit 22–1, assessing program goals' attainment, is illustrated in Exhibit 22–2.

Both during and after data collection, the data are (8) analyzed with techniques appropriate for the type of information considering the audiences' needs. Naturalistic methods often require the analytic techniques being developed for qualitative data (Miles & Huberman, 1984).

Those who emphasize the importance of utilizing evaluation results point out the obvious: an evaluation without impact is no evaluation. The role of communication throughout evaluation, which Callahan and Caldwell discuss

Figure 22–2 Major Components of the Responsive Model

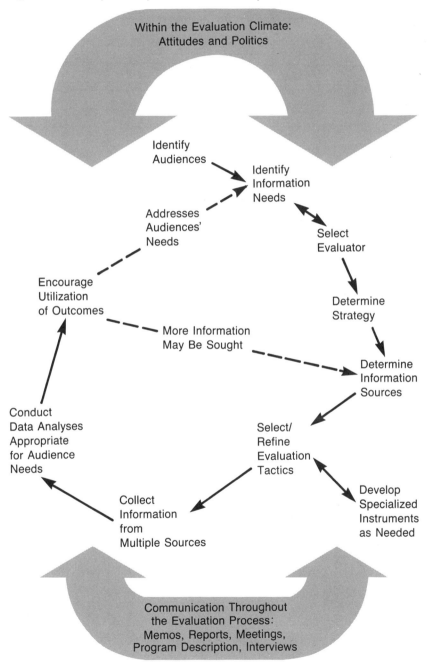

Exhibit 22–1 Evaluation Questions and Sources of Information for Answering Them

Sources of Information	DELIVERY		CURRICULUM			METHOD	DEVELOPMENT			ATTITUDES		
	1. What is the best way to serve district's gifted?	2. How can the program consolidate itself?	3. How will you implement curriculum scope and sequence?	4. Is the curriculum qualitatively different?	5. How are the students benefiting?	6. Is the identification method effective?	7. How many children are being served?	8. How can communication be improved?	9. How can staff development be encouraged?	10. What are the attitudes toward the program?	11. What are student attitudes toward the program?	12. How do parents feel?
1. Review of state law	x					x						
2. Review of district philosophy statement	x		x									
3. Demographic statistics	x						x					
4. Interview principals	x	x		x	x			x		x		
5. Review current practices elsewhere	x			x				x	x			
6. Review referral steps						x						
7. Classroom observation			x	x	x					x	x	

IDENTIFIED NEEDS

8. Teacher logs		x	x	x		
9. Student logs	x	x	x	x		x	x
10. Student questionnaires	x						
11. Parent questionnaires	x	x		x		x	x
12. Teacher questionnaires	x	x	x	x	x	x	
13. Unit plans	x	x		x			
14. Standardized tests	x	x	x	x			
15. Other tests	x	x	x	x			
16. Self-concept scales		x		x			
17. Learning environment scales		x		x			
18. Curriculum Guide	x						
19. GATE Curriculum Guide		x					

Source: Adapted from *A Proposal for Evaluating the Gifted Program in Tucson Unified School District* by M.H. High, A.J. Udall, and S.M. Dinham (1984). Available from A.J. Udall, University of Arizona Department of Special Education.

Exhibit 22–2 Evaluation of Program Goals

QUESTION 5: How are students benefiting from the gifted program?

Types of Information	PROGRAM GOALS										
	Present broad-based interdisciplinary content	Understand/know methodologies of disciplines	Understand roles of individuals in change	Develop concepts/skills in district curriculum guide	Develop critical and higher-level thinking skills	Develop affective behaviors for creative processes	Develop convergent and divergent skills of creativity	Develop products	Encourage development of self-actualization	Develop independence and self-direction	Encourage sound relationships
1. Unit plans	x	x	x							x	
2. Student journals	x	x	x				x	x	x	x	
3. Student product review			x			x	x	x		x	
4. Classroom environment scale										x	
5. Classroom observation					x	x	x	x		x	x
6. Cognitive skills				x	x						
7. Something about myself				x		x			x		
8. Piers-Harris Self-Concept Scale									x		

Source: Adapted from *A Proposal for Evaluating the Gifted Program in Tuscon Unified School District* by M.H. High, A.J. Udall, A.J. Udall, and S.M. Dinham (1984). Available from A.J. Udall, University of Arizona Department of Special Education.

at length, is critical. While Seeley discusses the final report, it is but a small part of a good evaluation. Planned (9) communication, including informal and formal reporting, takes place throughout a responsive evaluation; not only is the style of communication critical but the many forms of communication are all essential: memos, meetings, the program description, interviews, and formal written reports are all important communication modes.

Several other important points about (10) utilization of evaluations bear special attention as well: the timing of evaluation findings and their relevance to each audience, effective coordination during the evaluation and in targeting interim and concluding findings, and the involvement of the audience in the evaluation. The extensive literature on evaluation utilization discusses human resistance to change, communication of evaluation findings, various levels and types of evaluation utilization, evaluation qualities that bring about implementation of findings and recommendations, and roles of the evaluator and the audience (Cox, 1977; Guba & Lincoln, 1981; Patton, 1978; Smith, 1982). In a well-conducted evaluation, evaluation results will be utilized naturally because these issues have been considered.

As Figure 22–2 demonstrates, the ten components of the evaluation process are cyclical. For example, evaluation findings influence the program, its climate, and eventually subsequent evaluation needs and procedures. Ideally, as Callahan and Caldwell point out, evaluation is but an initial step in program implementation. At present this ideal is a rarity; most evaluations are initiated after a program has been functioning for some time. The benefits of early evaluation planning are obvious. Once the initial evaluation is begun, a continuous evaluation process can be integrated into the ongoing program.

The Evaluator

The evaluator as a person (or a team) is an important element in evaluating any program for gifted students. The complex evaluation climate places high demands on the evaluator. The evaluator is not only responsible for directing the evaluation but is often the instrument of evaluation; the evaluator consults with the audience(s), helps refine needs, collects a major portion of the data, and reports both informally and formally throughout the evaluation. The roles of evaluators, their competencies, and selection are therefore crucial matters.

The Evaluator's Role

During the course of an evaluation the evaluator will play many roles. Although Callahan and Caldwell mention some roles an evaluator should not play, there are many roles evaluators will find themselves taking during the course of an evaluation. The ability to understand these various roles and adapt swiftly will often determine the success of the evaluation. Myers (1981) outlines these roles:

1. Political sensor: accurately assessing the political climate
2. Political participant: establishing close working relationships with program personnel and other audiences
3. Sleuth: determining not only the written goals, objectives, and needs but the covert ones as well
4. Methodologist: selecting appropriate methodology for the evaluation
5. Counselor-educator: educating program personnel and other audiences about evaluation
6. Communicator: communicating effectively with program staff and others during the entire course of the evaluation
7. Salesperson: selling the evaluator, the evaluation plan, and the findings.

These various roles often overlap; an evaluator will be playing several roles at once.

Necessary Competencies

Certain attributes have been advanced as mandatory for a program evaluator. Some of the general evaluation literature discusses these questions (Anderson & Ball, 1980; Cronbach et al., 1981; Guba & Lincoln, 1981). For evaluation of programs for the gifted some of the most pertinent are:

1. Strong interpersonal and communication skills, including speaking and writing skills, and interviewing and observing skills
2. Knowledge of measurement, statistical analysis, qualitative and quantitative research methods, and alternative evaluation designs
3. Knowlege of the field where the evaluation is taking place, for example gifted education
4. Professional and ethical sensitivity
5. Management and organizational skills

In addition, since evaluation includes many subtle questions of values and ethics, the evaluator is often confronted with ethical questions and decisions resting on values. At times, evaluators may find their beliefs conflicting with evaluation needs or findings. They may find difficult strictures on confidentiality, may find themselves in complicated professional relationships with various audiences, or may need to confront their own personal biases as they interpret data and/or report findings. Anderson and Ball (1980) discuss many of these issues at length.

Evaluator Selection

In the responsive model there are no predetermined criteria for selecting an evaluator; audience needs define the selection. Guba and Lincoln (1981) discuss the selection process at length. They advocate use of evaluation teams, no matter how small the undertaking, in order to provide validation of results and rigor as well as credibility and breadth of talents.

The evaluator will be selected either internally—for example, from the program staff itself or the school district—or externally. Either choice carries both benefits and liabilities in costs, political advantages and disadvantages, technical knowledge, biases, values, and credibility.

Summary

The objective of this chapter was to provide a comprehensive overview of the role of evaluation in creating defensible programs for gifted students. Defensible programs are characterized by a sound underlying theoretical base, reflect the community they serve, are evolving constantly, and show an internal consistency from definition to identification procedures through service delivery and program evaluation. Defensible evaluation procedures are not separate from defensible programs—one ensures the other. This chapter offers a synthesis of defensible evaluation principles and practices for education of the gifted incorporating Seeley's and Callahan and Caldwell's contributions as well as ideas from education for the gifted and general evaluation literature.

This chapter proposes that there is no one single definition of evaluation. Evaluation is defined by its purpose: to meet the varied needs of multiple audiences. These needs, whatever they may be, should be the focus of the evaluation. Because there exist any number of needs an evaluation might meet, there may be any number of purposes. Evaluation purposes are formed by the intersection of audiences and their needs; an evaluation failing to address the specific audiences' specific needs is no evaluation indeed.

Identifying the audience(s) is a crucial early stage in evaluation. An evaluation audience will vary, depending on the context of the program, but may include teachers, parents, administrators or school board, as well as others.

All evaluations are surrounded and influenced by several important factors—most important, the participants' attitudes and the politics of the setting. Whenever evaluation is undertaken, it disrupts not only individual calm but the institutional status quo as well. In addition, the politics surrounding an evaluation—both the decision to evaluate and the evaluation itself—will dramatically influence the program. Awareness of the complexities of the evaluation climate is a precondition for conducting a successful evaluation.

Educators of gifted students, along with others in evaluation, have fallen into the habit of labeling both general viewpoints and convenient evaluation practices as "models." Yet most supposed "models" lack the depth of a strong theoretical base combined with thorough evaluation techniques. There is a substantial need for evaluation models that not only rest in a well-defined philosophy, but also reflect the variety of needs of evaluation audiences and accept the practicalities of the evaluation climate. The responsive model shows great promise, especially since it seems strongly applicable to programs for the gifted.

The role, competencies, and selection of the evaluator are crucial. The evaluator will play many different roles during the evaluation, roles requiring numerous competencies. Audience and program evaluation needs will determine evaluator selection, be it an internal or external selection.

As yet, educational programs for the gifted have not been fully accepted by the communities they serve. Society's ambivalent attitudes toward their most capable members have created tremendous pressure on programs. One hears constant demands for justification of funding, identification procedures, and service delivery models. In an age of declining funds, this pressure can grow.

It is not enough to point to the call for education for the gifted found frequently in national reports. Successful, defensible programs for the gifted will speak for themselves. A solid evaluation component meeting the needs of program audiences must be an integral part of any program for the gifted if it is to be labeled defensible.

References

Anderson, S.B., & Ball, S. (1980). *The profession and practice of program evaluation.* San Francisco: Jossey-Bass.

Archambault, F. (1984). Measurement and evaluation concerns in evaluating programs for the gifted and talented. *Journal for the Education of the Gifted, 7*(1), 12–25.

Aylesworth, M. (1984). Guidelines for selecting instruments in evaluating programs for the gifted. *Journal for the Education of the Gifted, 7*(1), 38–44.

Banner, D.K., Doctors, S.I., & Gordon, A.C. (1975). *The politics of social program evaluation.* Cambridge, MA: Ballinger.

Barnette, J.J. (1984). Naturalistic approaches to gifted and talented program evaluation. *Journal for the Education of the Gifted, 7*(1), 26–37.

Callahan, C.M. (1980). *Evaluating a local gifted program*. Paper presented at the Annual Meeting of the American Educational Research Association, Boston. (ERIC Document Reproduction Service No. ED 195 189)

Callahan, C.M. (1983). Issues in evaluating programs for the gifted. *Gifted Child Quarterly, 27,* 3–9.

Callahan, C.M., & Caldwell, M.S. (1984). Using evaluation results to improve programs for the gifted and talented. *Journal for the Education of the Giftd, 7*(1), 1984.

Callahan, C.M., Covert, R., Aylesworth, M., & Vance, P. (1981). Evaluating a local gifted program: A cooperative effort. *Exceptional Children, 48,* 157–163.

Cohen, D.K. (1970). Politics and research: Evaluation of social action programs in education. *Review of Educational Research, 40,* 213–238.

Cox, G.B. (1977). Managerial style: Implications for the utilization of program evaluation information. *Evaluation Quarterly, 1*(3), 499–508.

Cronbach, L.J., Ambron, S.R., Dornbusch, S.M., Hess, R.D., Hornik, R.C., Phillips, D.C., Walker, D.F., & Weiner, S.S. (1981). *Toward reform of program evaluation.* San Francisco: Jossey-Bass.

Delisle, J.R. (1984). Quasi-experiments in gifted education: A confounding problem. *Journal for the Education of the Gifted, 8(1),* 151–155.

Ganopole, S.J. (1982). Measuring the educational outcomes of gifted programs. *Roeper Review, 5*(1), 4–7.

Guba, E.G., & Lincoln, Y.S. (1981). *Effective evaluation: Improving the usefulness of evaluation results through responsive and naturalistic approaches.* San Francisco: Jossey-Bass.

Hendrickson, L., & Barber, L. (1980). Evaluation and politics: A critical study of a community school program. *Evaluation Review, 4,* 769–878.

High, M.H., Udall, A.J., & Dinham, S.M. (1984, May). *A proposal for evaluating the gifted program in Tucson Unified School District.* (Available from Anne J. Udall, University of Arizona Department of Special Education)

House, E.R. (1972). The politics of evaluation in higher education. *Journal of Higher Education, 45,* 618–627.

LeCompte, M.D. (1981). *Evaluation of the Vanguard Program: A new approach to assessment of programs for the gifted and talented.* Paper presented at the Annual Meeting of the Southwest Educational Research Association, Dallas. (ERIC Document Reproduction Service No. ED 204 938)

Leviton, L.C., & Hughes, E.F.X. (1981). Research on the utilization of evaluations: A review and synthesis. *Evaluation Review, 5,* 525–548.

Miles, M.B., & Huberman, A.M. (1984). *Qualitative data analysis: A sourcebook of new methods.* Beverly Hills: Sage.

Myers, C.J. (August, 1981). *Successfully managing the politics of evaluation through role versatility.* (Available from Dr. Chris Myers, Legal and Evaluation Services, Tucson Unified Tucson: Tucson Unified School District, Tucson, Arizona)

Nevo, D. (1983). The conceptualization of educational evaluation: An analytical review of the literature. *Review of Educational Research, 53,* 117–128.

Nunnally, J.C. (1975). The study of change in evaluation research: Principles concerning measurement, experimental design, and analysis. In E.L. Struening & M. Guttentag (Eds.) *Handbook of evaluation research* (Vol. 1). Beverly Hills: Sage.

Park, B.N., & Buescher, T.M. (1982). Evaluating programs for the gifted through student self-documentation. *Roeper Review, 5*(1), 15–17.

Patton, M.Q. (1978). *Utilization-focused evaluation.* Beverly Hills: Sage.

Payne, D.A., & Brown, C.L. (1982). The use and abuse of control groups in program evaluation. *Roeper Review, 5*(1), 11–14.

Posavac, E.J., & Carey, R.G. (1985). *Program evaluation* (2nd ed.). Englewood Cliffs, NJ: Prentice-Hall.

Reis, S.M. (1984). Avoiding the testing trap: Using alternative assessment instruments to evaluate programs for the gifted. *Journal for the Education of the Gifted, 7*(1), 45–59.

Renzulli, J. (1975). *A guidebook for evaluating programs for the gifted and talented.* Ventura, CA: Office of the Ventura County Superintendent of Schools.

Rimm, S. (1982). Evaluation of gifted programs—As easy as ABC. *Roeper Review, 5*(1), 8–10.

Rossi, P.H., & Freeman, H.E. (1982). *Evaluation: A systematic approach* (2nd ed.). Beverly Hills: Sage.

Scriven, M.S. (1967). The methodology of evaluation. *AERA Monograph Series on Curriculum Evaluation, 1.*

Scriven, M.S. (1973). Goal-free evaluation. In E.R. House (Ed.), *School evaluation: The politics and process.* Berkeley: McCutchan.

Sjoberg, D. (1975). Politics, ethics, and evaluation research. In E.L. Struening & M. Guttentag (Eds.), *Handbook of evaluation research* (Vol. 2). Beverly Hills: Sage.

Smith, N.L. (1982). *Communication strategies in evaluation.* Beverly Hills: Sage.

Snow, R.E. (1976). Theory construction for research on teaching. In R. Travers (Ed.), *Second Handbook of Research on Teaching.* Chicago: Rand McNally.

Sroufe, G.E. (1977). Evaluation and politics. In J.D. Scribner (Ed.), *The politics of evaluation.* Chicago: The University of Chicago Press.

Stainback, S., & Stainback, W. (1984). Broadening the research perspective in special education. *Exceptional Children, 50,* 400–408.

Stake, R.E. (1967). The countenance of educational evaluation. *Teachers College Record, 68,* 523–540.

Stake, R.E. (Ed.). (1975). *Evaluating the arts in education: A responsive approach.* Columbus, OH: Charles Merrill.

Stufflebeam, D.L., Foley, W.J., Gephart, W.J., Guba, E.G., Hammond, R.L., Merriman, H.O., & Provus, M.M. (1971). *Educational evaluation and decision making.* Itasca, IL: F.E. Peacock.

Tyler , R.W. (Ed.) (1969). *Educational evaluation: New roles, new means.* Chicago: University of Chicago Press.

Weiss, C.H. (1973). Where politics and evaluation research meet. *Evaluation, 1,* 37–45.

Weiss, C.H. (1975). Evaluation research in the political context. In E.L. Struening, & M. Gutentag (Eds.), *Handbook of evaluation research* (Vol. 1). Beverly Hills: Sage.

23

A Response to "Evaluation for Gifted Education"

Carolyn M. Callahan
Michael S. Caldwell

The basic premises of Dinham and Udall's discussion of the evaluation process and the various approaches that can be used to make the evaluation process a productive one are sound and worthy of consideration by evaluators and consumers of evaluation. However, there are several points on which we would quarrel with the interpretation of both our chapter and the work of other authors and "model builders." To suggest that the Renzulli and Callahan and Caldwell approaches to evaluation "ignore the evaluation audience" and the needs of that audience is to miss a fundamental element of those works. First, Renzulli went to great lengths to solicit input from groups that he identifies as "Prime Interest Groups." In fact, his Input Questionnaire notion and interviews with Prime Interest Groups (p. 54) are based on a direct attempt to determine which evaluation questions are considered important by audiences that have a vested interest in the program. His Key Features Matrix also emphasizes the need to attend to information needs of selected audiences.

We also do not attempt to prescribe needs of audiences, but rather our intention is to suggest a broad range of possible purposes of evaluation and needs of audiences through example. These examples were not intended to be exhaustive or limiting to the evaluator or to the programs being evaluated. The description of the program, if carried out as described, would, in and of itself, lead program evaluators and staff to identify areas of concern to the consumers of the program and the evaluation information.

Several other concerns raised by Dinham and Udall are also reflected in our article, if not quite as directly as in the synthesis chapter. For example, the suggestion that evaluators often focus on inappropriate evaluation questions is addressed in our article in the suggestion to do a careful and complete program description to verify program components, activities, and outcomes. If program evaluation questions are derived from a true description of the program that reflects the concerns of the audiences involved, then the likelihood that the generation of evaluation questions will meet the needs of the audiences will be greatly enhanced. Further, the stated purpose of providing information to interested audiences will ensure the inclusion of the needs of funding agents.

V

Defensible
Programs for
Gifted Students:

what are they?

The purpose of this final section is to synthesize and summarize the various points of view of the authors who have contributed to this volume regarding the central issue of defensibility. Obviously, not all authors agree about what practices are defensible and what practices are not. However, the intent of this chapter is to note areas of agreement as well as areas in which opposing points of view have been presented. Finally, questions and concerns not addressed by the authors will be noted, as will new questions and new directions suggested or implied in the material.

The content of the chapter will be organized around the key questions presented in the introduction to this volume. These questions were provided to authors writing about a particular issue. Some chose to respond directly to the questions while others did not. All were given the freedom to include whatever ideas, issues, questions, and answers they viewed as important and related to the topic. Another set of queries could be labeled "questions we should have asked, but did not!" Hindsight, as usual, provided a better perspective than foresight. The final synthesizing question, "What are the most important elements of a defensible program for the gifted?" is answered in an attempt to present a summary and synthesis of the many ideas discussed.

Any attempt to summarize the ideas of others carries with it the danger that ideas will be misinterpreted or misrepresented. To guard against this possibility, all authors were given the opportunity to note any problems with interpretation of their ideas.

Is "qualitatively different" a key concept in defining defensible programs for the gifted?

The first author, Foster, addresses the question more directly than some others, when he says ". . . defining qualitative differences among individuals has been a lynchpin idea of the gifted movement for quite some time." However, his major point is that the "gifted movement" has used an inappropriate metaphor for the concept of qualitative differences, a point to which we shall return in answering the next question.

The next author, Berliner, agrees that "qualitatively different" is a key concept and that qualitative differences in learners imply a need for differences in curriculum, school organization, instruction, and teacher education. He states ". . . if the gifted are seen as different, then they must also be seen as requiring unique ways to be taught. Viewed in this light, the gifted, along with the learning disabled, the blind, the deaf, and the retarded are *special* children in need of *special* education by a *specially* trained teacher." He also notes, however, that even if one holds the viewpoint that the gifted are merely quantitatively different or possess "more" of certain traits, schools must still respond by providing appropriate programs to accommodate these differences, speeding up mastery of the basic curriculum, providing challenges not included in "customary mathematics" or "ordinary literature," and developing an organizational structure that allows ungraded or continuous progress in areas of giftedness.

A different idea, also presented by Berliner, is that more important than the "degree" versus "kind" conception of giftedness as a key concept is one's conception of the etiology of giftedness. He posits that if only genetic and physiological factors are considered causes of giftedness, then "schools are irrelevant as change agents," and if only environmental factors are viewed as causes, all children should be treated the same and provided with the "best" education for the gifted. If, however, one believes that giftedness is the result of an interaction of genetic, physiological, and environmental factors (as is believed by most individuals), then schools must accept their serious role in the development of existing aptitudes of students. Schools must recognize that differences in capacity exist, *and* they must realize the importance of their role in either inhibiting or facilitating the development and expression of abilities.

Feldhusen agrees with this point of view and goes even further to propose that "giftedness is a set of abilities, traits, and characteristics that emerge through nurturance," and that ". . . above all the abilities and skills of the gifted have been learned." He generally assumes an environmentalist's point of view, but suggests that these gifted characteristics emerge as early as ages one through five years.

Clearly, the authors in this volume agree that regardless of how one defines giftedness or the concept "qualitatively different," it is a key idea in programs for the gifted and historically has been important as well. Separating the concept from its various applications and the many contexts in which it has been used is difficult, though, and no authors chose to examine it in this way. We will see later, however, that "appropriate" is a concept that must be combined with qualitatively different in defining programs and curricula.

Are gifted individuals qualitatively different from individuals who are not gifted?

Again, Foster is the first author to address this question, and his answer is that clearly some individuals are qualitatively different from others, but he seems to prefer eliminating the words "gifted" and "not gifted" from the question. He defines qualitative difference as "the attainment of individual excellence in the form of an innovative, productive life of outstanding proportions—an achievement attained by few." Further, he uses the term "genius" and states that it is "the outcome of a life of innovation and productivity that in some fashion changes the way in which we view our human condition." According to Foster, we have used the metaphor of giftedness in a way that implies that a "gift" of genetic endowment initially sets one apart and defines a person as qualitatively distinct. This is inappropriate, argues Foster, because research on initial psychological traits shows only quantitative differences, not qualitative ones. He believes that qualitative differences develop from "an open-ended interaction of multiple factors: general human capacity, environmental opportunity, universal patterns of human development, and intentional and accidental learning."

In support of his belief that inherent psychological traits show only qualitative differences between individuals, Foster selectively reviews research indicating that there are numerous quantitative differences between gifted learners and other learners. In his critique of Foster's article, Berliner suggests that the data cited by Foster showing various quantitative differences can be used to support the belief that the gifted are qualitatively different. He believes that "the gifted are 'different' [qualitatively different] *because* they are 'more' [quantitatively different]." By employing a mathematical system called catastrophe theory, which states that quantitative differences in a phenomenon eventually result in a qualitative difference, one can explain the differences between individuals as differences of kind as well as degree. Catastrophe theory has been used in several areas of the behavioral sciences to predict when several quantitative differences (e.g., a dog that is becoming more enraged and more afraid) will result in a qualitative change (e.g., the dog fights or runs away). Applying this model to giftedness suggests that when we consider psychological factors such as ability, motivation, and creativity separately, we can place each person along a continuum of quantitative differences on each factor. However, Berliner says "when *more* of these attributes are possessed in some unique configuration a catastrophe occurs—the person goes from bright to gifted, or achievement oriented to gifted, or creative to gifted." Thus, a change in the state, or quality, has occurred.

Although not directly addressing the question, Maker cites research not considered by Foster when he asserts that "The only significant indications regarding such a condition [gifted children are qualitatively different] relate to a form of developmental acceleration, at best a transient difference eventually ameliorated by time." In fact, studies cited by Maker have shown that not all individuals "catch up" with the gifted in cognitive development. A significant percentage of the general population never achieves a level of development that permits the use of formal operational reasoning, for instance. In her introduction to the section, Maker also presents the argument that if one views differences between the developmental stages described by Piaget as qualitative ones (which is the general consensus of theorists and researchers), then the fact that gifted children move through developmental stages more rapidly and are at a higher developmental level than their less able peers makes them qualitatively different from their age mates.

Silverman's views on the subject are quite different, although generally supportive of the hypothesis that there are definite differences between gifted people and those who are not gifted and that these differences can be observed in learners. She does not directly address the question of whether these are differences in degree or kind, but suggests that the two differing viewpoints about the nature of qualitative differences reflect masculine and feminine concepts of giftedness.

The consensus of opinion seems to be that certain individuals are indeed, qualitatively different, whether the label used is "gifted," "productive," "genius," or something else. However, a definite difference of opinion does exist regarding when certain differences of degree or magnitude become differences in kind, regarding the role of quantitative differences in producing these qualitative differences, and the role of sex differences in the process. If, as Berliner and Maker suggest, quantitative differences result in immediate qualitative differences, then certain children (and learners of all ages) are qualitatively different from other learners. If, as Foster suggests, these quantitative differences only result in qualitative ones after one has demonstrated or achieved a life of productivity, then only adults and a few highly exceptional children are qualitatively different. If Foster's point of view is accepted, and if one is convinced by the literature on adult accomplishments of women, then the obvious conclusion is that very few females are qualitatively different from other females.

*Must one conclude that gifted individuals are qualitatively different in order
to justify the provision of a qualitatively different curriculum?*

The answer to this question seems to be an unequivocal "it depends"! How
the question is answered depends on one's definitions of giftedness, qualitative
differences as they apply to individuals, and qualitative differences as they
apply to the curriculum.

If one's definition of giftedness, as suggested by Berliner, includes the
viewpoint that giftedness is genetically determined, then schools play no part
in the development of talents and abilities. If one believes that giftedness is
determined solely by the environment, then all students should be treated in
the same way so that they will all become gifted. On the other hand, if one
believes that giftedness is determined by the interaction of genetic, environmental, and physiological factors, then schools are obliged to select certain
children as having a greater genetic endowment or physiological factors that
may interact with certain environmental factors to produce outstanding
achievement and to provide the qualitatively different environment necessary
to enable the development of giftedness.

Berliner also suggests that if one defines giftedness as quantitative differences or differences in degree, this view would also imply different
educational provisions. Because the learner acquires information more rapidly
than others, he or she should be encouraged to master the curriculum more
rapidly than most, which necessitates a change in school organization to allow
continuous progress. Because gifted learners possess this greater ability to
master the basic curriculum, they need challenges other than ordinary mathematics or basic science. Both the change in school organization to allow
continuous progress and the change in curriculum to add new challenges can
certainly be considered qualitative differences.

With regard to the definitions of qualitative differences in individuals and
curriculum, what seems important to many authors is the consistency between
one's concepts. If qualitative differences in individuals are described in a
particular way, then the qualitatively different curriculum provided for them
must be consistent with this description of the individuals the program is
designed to serve. The most obvious distinction in the definitions of
qualitative differences in individuals in this volume is that, on one view,
learners are qualitatively different and in the other view, only productive adults
are qualitatively different. In her introductions to the various sections, Maker
explains that each of these definitions leads to different interpretations of a
qualitatively different curriculum. For example, if learners are different, then
the curriculum is designed to accommodate those differences now, and if the
learner is expected to become different later, the curriculum is designed to

develop abilities that will be needed at some time in the future or will enable the person to become different.

Linda Silverman's viewpoint on this issue, however, is unlike that of other authors. She contends, and presents a strong case for her belief, that by adopting the view that only adults who have achieved a high level of recognized productivity are gifted (i.e., by equating giftedness with eminence), we penalize gifted girls more than gifted boys, and destroy or limit their chances to achieve at a high level. Silverman's point of view is that if educators would view giftedness as qualitative differences in learners, or as "developmental advancement," they would "enable more gifted girls to be identified and nurtured before their gifts dwindle to the vanishing point."

Interestingly enough, Silverman's suggestions for educators present a different view of the connection or consistency between one's definition of qualitative differences in the learner and qualitative differences in the curriculum. Because girls are often treated differently from boys at home and in classrooms, according to Silverman (and many other writers), girls hide or possibly lose their abilities by the time they are in junior high school and at this point, become "qualitatively different" from gifted boys with respect to cognitive, emotional, and social traits. During elementary school, then, gifted girls should be treated in much the same way as gifted boys. However, after junior high school, they may need to be treated quite differently because of their differing characteristics, so that they can overcome the many barriers they face and the negative influences of a male-oriented society.

Borland supports this point of view. He wishes, however, that Silverman would emphasize overall changes designed to prevent the loss of female talent that occurs when gifted girls fail to become gifted women, rather than focusing on ways to modify our identification procedures so that more girls are admitted to programs for the gifted at middle and high school. Essentially, I think, he would recommend a greater focus on curricular changes as well as changes in the way adults, in general, interact with gifted girls. Perhaps he would even suggest large-scale social changes. Presumably, these changes would be qualitative rather than quantitative.

Like Borland, Fox recommends emphasis on changes in the curriculum to make it more appropriate for gifted girls. Her suggestion that gifted girls do not "learn as much" from their educational experiences would lead one to hypothesize that a different type of curriculum is necessary, and even perhaps that different teaching strategies need to be used with boys and girls at an early age. However, she concludes by suggesting that Silverman's recommendations for parents and educators at the end of the chapter should be the major emphasis of the reader.

In summary, the answer to the question posed at the beginning of this section seems to be that there is a definite connection between one's definition of qualitative differences in people and the provision of a qualitatively different curriculum. The question is complicated, however, by the issue of whether one considers qualitative differences as occurring in the learner or in the adult, and the nature of these differences. It seems safe to conclude that consistency between one's definition of the term "qualitative difference" as it applies to individuals and curricula is the most important element in the answer to this question.

What is the most defensible definition of giftedness—one that views qualitative differences as existing in children or one that views such differences as existing only after one becomes an eminent or productive adult?

Several authors in this volume present convincing arguments favoring a definition of giftedness that views giftedness or qualitative differences as existing in children (or learners) rather than as a quality one can determine only after significant productive contributions have been made. Although their perspectives and reasons are somewhat different, the conclusions are much the same. Berliner argues that learners are different qualitatively *because* they possess differences in degree, and Maker suggests that they are different in kind from their age mates as a result of their movement through cognitive developmental stages more rapidly. Both suggest that viewing giftedness in terms of qualitative differences in learners enables educators of the gifted to make a better case for the provision of special services to gifted children.

Borland and Silverman, perhaps, present the case for the "giftedness as learner differences" perspective better than other authors, though for somewhat different reasons. Silverman, as noted earlier, views the two perspectives as masculine and feminine. According to Silverman, the "masculine view is that the true test of ability is the quantity, quality, and influence of one's accomplishments in adult life" and that ". . . the feminine view is primarily concerned with the impact of developmental differences on a child's immediate needs." Her suggestion is that adoption of the "male" point of view causes gifted women and girls to be penalized. She further suggests that defining giftedness, or by implication qualitative differences, in terms of adult productivity has limited utility for teachers and parents because ". . . trying to guess which children will be the most influential adults is a bizarre game of chance." Borland supports this point of view, but prefers not to categorize definitions according to gender, and calls Silverman's "masculine" definition a "national-resources" perspective and her "female" definition a "special-educational" perspective. The national-resources definition is characterized as such because it has as its basis the selection of individuals who can "be exploited" for the national good. The special educational definition has as its basis an *educational need* that is not being met by the regular curriculum.

Borland's arguments, though more convincing, are like Maker's in the introductory sections. One aspect of Borland's case concerns the problems inherent in predicting which children will become eminent adults. The lives of these eminent adults are studied, their early characteristics are determined, and today's children are required to exhibit these traits in order to be placed in a special program. Borland sums up the problems with assuming that such characteristics will predict success with the comment "Yesterday's context could very likely not be valid for defining tomorrow's giftedness." Another point concerns the fact that children are qualitatively different from adults, and one should not expect a direct connection or "an exact isomorphism" between traits of eminent adults and children who are "potentially eminent."

Like Berliner, Borland also argues that national-resources definitions remove the focus from the real source of the problem and its solution, which is the school. Educators can modify the curriculum, change the organizational structure of the school, and use teaching strategies that enable students to learn better, learn more, learn more pleasantly, and be more productive—as children. We cannot even predict the future, much less change it for a student.

A different argument against the national-resources viewpoint, focusing more on the ways these definitions are implemented, is that they tend to favor those who are advantaged, who are well-adapted and working up to capacity in the regular classroom. Often those who demonstrate the greatest educational "need" because they are not performing as well in the classroom as their ability scores would predict (e.g., gifted underachievers, gifted nonconformers) are exluded from such programs.

Finally, an interesting compromise between the two definitions—or perhaps an integration of the two—is proposed by Silverman in her response to the critiques. She suggests that a "special educational" definition may be more appropriate for preschool and elementary programs while a "national-resources" definition may be best for secondary programs. This idea makes a great deal of sense to me for several reasons, and seems worthy of serious consideration. First, a "special educational" definition for early programs would allow many students who have demonstrated high abilities, and perhaps low motivation or other characteristics showing a lack of "fit" with the system, to be included in special programs. This early stimulation and challenge could mean the difference between "turning on" and "turning off" to education in later years. A definition based on need would also recognize the difficulties inherent in attempting to predict adult productivity in young children.

On the other hand, adopting a national-resources definition at the secondary level would allow students who have demonstrated high achievement, high motivation, high creativity, and/or high productivity without correspondingly high ability scores to be served in a program. At this age, prediction of adult productivity would be much less difficult than at earlier ages. The students have had many more opportunities to demonstrate the leadership qualities, motivation, persistence, achievement, creativity, and productivity that are indicators of future productivity. As is often the case, a compromise definition that incorporates the best reasoning and most important ideas from opposing points of view may be more appropriate than an either-or approach.

Are gifted females qualitatively different from gifted males?

Although this question was not asked, it was answered unequivocally by Silverman in her discussion of the phenomenon of giftedness in girls and women. Gifted females are definitely qualitatively different from gifted males, according to Linda Silverman. In light of the general discussion of giftedness by Foster and Berliner, Silverman's evidence indicates that differences of ability between males and females are not largely hereditary, but rather exist because of cultural and environmental differences (e.g., sex-role expectations, treatment by adults) between boys and girls. These differences can be identified in many areas: performance on intelligence tests, performance on tests of achievement, achievement motivation, and expectations for success. Interestingly enough, with regard to timing, the point at which differences in treatment result in qualitative differences between boys and girls, as presented by Silverman, is around the age of 14, or when they are in junior high school. There appear to be fewer differences between boys and girls until that time, but later differences, and differences between men and women, seem to be much greater.

Using catastrophe theory as an explanation for this phenomenon seems quite logical, and it even seems possible to identify the precise age at which certain quantitative differences become qualitative—or perhaps the age at which no perceivable differences in ability become real qualitative differences.

Borland agrees with Silverman's contention that the different treatment of gifted girls causes them to become different, but he goes beyond her thesis to posit the hypothesis that not only do gifted girls *appear* less competent than their formerly equal-ability male counterparts, but also they *are* less competent: "unequal treatment of inherently equal groups results in unequal competence in some areas. . . ." Because this lower competence is real rather than an artifact caused by a desire to hide one's ability in order to be more socially acceptable, the problem is much more serious than it otherwise would be.

Fox, in contrast, does not answer the question of whether gifted women or girls are different from gifted men or boys. She questions some of Silverman's conclusions, citing as one of her reasons the fact that there is a paucity of research comparing boys and girls who are gifted. Thus, many conclusions are based on research with the general population. Another reason for her skepticism is that she has a different perspective from Silverman regarding certain psychometric issues. Although Fox questions some of the reasons used to support Silverman's conclusions that there are as many gifted females as males, she focuses on explanations of different performance based on differential treatment of the two groups.

Her final conclusion emphasizes a point about which few would quarrel, and indeed that many of us have stated in other contexts: differences are not necessarily deficits, and the fact that many differences have been found between men and women does not suggest that either is inherently inferior or inherently superior. However, if differences result in deficits or perceived deficits, then something is wrong and we must do what we can to change it!

What constitutes a qualitatively different (and appropriate) curriculum?

The first author to discuss qualitative differences in the curriculum is Kaplan. She notes that the key issue is not whether the need for a differentiated curriculum exists, but what should be its nature. When providing guidelines for educators to determine the nature of differentiated curriculum, Kaplan also reminds us that differentiation is not enough: the curriculum must also be appropriate for gifted students. In addition, she places into perspective the many viewpoints assumed by authors writing on the subject.

Various individuals have attempted to conceptualize curriculum that is appropriately differentiated for the gifted, approaching the issue from perspectives such as the following: societal, programmatic, discrepancy, model-specific, trait-related, curricular-related. To take into account these points of view, Kaplan suggests a multistage definition that includes various perspectives and responds to the multiple environments in which gifted students learn. These stages are (i) *reflective* of the context; (ii) *generic*, in that broad ends and multiple means are included; (iii) *comparative*, in that certain standards are met; (iv) *diagnostic*, in that the specific needs of the population are met; and (v) *selective*, in that self-selected needs of the learner are met. Finally, a list of criteria is provided for judging the appropriateness of a differentiated program for the gifted:

1. Directed by a philosophical point of view or theory
2. Adheres to the principles of continuity and sequence
3. Provides for vertical and horizontal experiences without overemphasis on either
4. Integrates models and strategies selectively without overdependence on any
5. Responds to the population and is not followed in a lock-step manner
6. Accommodates the range of learning and teaching styles of students and teacher

7. Provides for basic instructional variables
8. Communicates objectives and learning experiences clearly and precisely
9. Responds to each learner's needs, interests, and abilities.

Ward, while suggesting that Kaplan's parameters are helpful, proposes the use of Passow's definition of differentiation. This perspective is similar to that labeled by Kaplan as "societal" in that it focuses on providing gifted individuals with learning opportunities that will enable them to make outstanding contributions to society. The definition also includes elements of the perspective labeled by Kaplan as "trait-related" because it focuses on opportunities needed to nurture talents and assumes that when these talents are nurtured and the individual makes outstanding contributions, personal satisfaction will result. By comparison, the definition Ward proposes takes into account only two perspectives Kaplan suggests one consider.

Ward then provides examples of his own principles for differentiating the curriculum: administrative adaptations should not constitute the uniqueness of the program; instruction should "match" the broader capacities of the students in both pace and complexity; evaluation of student achievement and objectives should be at an equally high level; and content taught to gifted students should "extend into the general nature of all the chief branches of knowledge." Thus, he has rejected a "programmatic" view of differentiation and has provided principles that illustrate aspects of both "trait-related" and "curricular-related" definitions. With regard to the five stages of defining a differentiated curriculum outlined by Kaplan, Ward has provided three more principles (in addition to the seven proposed by the Leadership Training Institute's Curriculum Council) educators can follow in their development and evaluation of a differentiated curriculum for gifted students.

As Kaplan indicates in her description of the various types of definitions of differentiation, Maker generally assumes the "curricular-related" point of view as she describes ways the basic curriculum should be modified or adapted (in the areas of content, process, product, and learning environment) to make it more appropriate for gifted students. From this particular perspective, however, Maker recommends modifications that meet two basic criteria: (i) build upon and extend the characteristics that make the children different, both as a group and as individuals (a "trait-related" definition); and (ii) take into account, or prepare students for, their probable social roles (a "societal" definition). Like Ward, in Chapter 11 Maker provides recommendations that relate most to the "comparative" stage of curriculum differentiation. Unlike Ward, however, Maker supplies specific examples of learning activities illustrative of the recommended principles.

In Chapter 11 Maker focuses on the integration of what is called "significant" content with processes in the teaching of gifted students. The emphasis of her discussion is that teaching can and should accomplish the dual function of developing important conceptual understandings and enhancing thinking skills. Her chapter is in some ways a reaction to many current practices in programs for the gifted that are in Kaplan's "should not" category of differentiation practices: "popularized curriculum," different curriculum, and (most important) "disjointed curriculum."

Schiever provides a further elaboration of the "comparative" stage of curriculum differentiation from the "curricular-related," "trait-related," and "societal" viewpoints by demonstrating how the principles that Maker advocates can be incorporated into the teaching process. She supplies a well-articulated plan for developing a year's curriculum that meets the principles that Maker outlines. At the same time, Schiever demonstrates how the various stages of differentiation (reflective, generic, comparative, diagnostic, selective) outlined by Kaplan could be addressed. She ends by comparing the principles of curriculum differentiation advocated by Kaplan in another publication with the principles that Maker outlines in Chapter 11 and elsewhere.

Taking Schiever's lead, and as a way of examining the chapters in this volume addressing differentiation of the curriculum for the gifted, it seems apropos to suggest that the reader examine the "comparative" principles advocated by various contributors. In addition to the four authors who directly addressed the issue of curriculum differentiation (Kaplan, Ward, Maker, and Schiever), others who explored ideas related to the topic should be included in any comparison (e.g., Van Tassel-Baska, Levine, Klausmeier, Ellis and Ellis-Schwabe, and Feldhusen). The seven principles proposed by the curriculum council of the Leadership Training Institute and included in Kaplan's chapter can provide the basis for such a comparison:

1. The content of curricula for the gifted/talented should focus on and be organized to include more elaborate, complex, and in-depth study of major ideas, problems, and themes that integrate knowledge with and across systems of thought.
2. Curricula for the gifted/talented should allow for the development and application of productive thinking skills to enable students to reconceptualize existing knowledge and/or generate new knowledge.
3. Curricula for the gifted/talented should enable them to explore constantly changing knowledge and information and develop the attitude that knowledge is worth pursuing in an open world.
4. Curricula for the gifted/talented should encourage exposure to, selection, and use of appropriate and specialized resources.
5. Curricula for the gifted/talented should promote self-initiated and self-directed learning and growth.

6. Curricula for the gifted/talented should provide for the development of self-understandings and the understanding of one's relationship to persons, societal institutions, nature, and culture.
7. Evaluations of curricula for the gifted/talented should be conducted in accordance with prior stated principles, stressing higher-level thinking skills, creativity, and excellence in performance and products.

What the reader will find, in making this comparison, is that there is very little disagreement among the various authors on the fundamental principles proposed by the Leadership Training Institute. Differences that exist are mainly in the specific ways each author recommends that the principles be implemented in a program for gifted students. There are also differences in the relative emphasis placed on each concept as curricular recommendations are made. Many ideas and suggestions for implementing these basic principles have been provided in this volume.

To justify a program for the gifted, must one be able to state that the curriculum would not be good for, or could not be used with students who are not gifted?

This question was initially included because it is often asked of program developers and implementers. Frequently, critics and would-be attackers of programs directly suggest or imply that educators of the gifted must justify or defend their "special" educational programs for the gifted by *proving* that the curriculum and/or teaching strategies advocated for or employed in the special program would not be good for all children! Renzulli (1977) also followed this line of reasoning when he proposed that his Type I and Type II Activities (which, he reasoned, cannot be defended as only appropriate for gifted students) be implemented in the regular classroom and that Type III Activities (seen, in his view, as only appropriate for students identified as possessing traits that suggest they may become productive adults) be reserved for a special program for the gifted. The question is also relevant to program development because educators are forced to examine their beliefs about differences in learners, the type of curriculum being provided for all learners, and possible needs not being met by the regular curriculum. Practices advocated for gifted learners must also be scrutinized carefully to determine their appropriateness.

Interestingly enough, even though this question was posed to several authors, none chose to address it directly! Only a few thoughts were offered by the editor in the introduction to a section. However, some authors did indirectly offer answers that would have the same result as that proposed by the editor.

Certain authors have indirectly addressed the question by proposing that to defend its use one would not need to prove that a curriculum designed for gifted learners would not be good for or could not be used with students who are not gifted. The crucial factors involved in defending practices (including the curriculum) included in *any* special program, regardless of the population are (*i*) appropriate for the identified learners, (*ii*) necessary for the identified population, and (*iii*) different from what is currently provided for all learners. In other words, one must demonstrate that the curriculum being provided for the identified special learners is meeting a certain need(s).

If, by examining the special curriculum being provided for students who are gifted (or learning disabled, or having reading problems), other educators decide that the curriculum or certain elements of it should be incorporated into the general curriculum, we should be pleased rather than upset! If they go even further and actually incorporate these changes, then educators in the special program can focus on other needs and continue to employ techniques that cannot be used effectively in the usual classroom setting. This answer is consistent with the recommended definition of giftedness as one that incorporates current "educational need" as it relates to the current school organization, curriculum, and the instructional strategies employed.

What makes acceleration a defensible (and appropriate) approach in programs for the gifted?

There seems to be general agreement among the various authors about the practice of acceleration: it has certain advantages for certain gifted learners when put into practice appropriately and combined with techniques to accommodate learner needs or learning styles. There is, as stated earlier by the editor, a difference in emphasis or focus of the authors in this volume.

Kaplan, the first to discuss acceleration, lists as one of the requirements for curriculum to be appropriate for gifted students that it "provides for vertical and horizontal experiences without overemphasizing one type of curricular option over another." Ward refers to acceleration in conjunction with complexity in the second proposition listed in his critique: ". . . the instruction of the gifted should be characterized by a pace and a level of complexity which are best suited to their broader capacities." Van Tassel-Baska concludes "acceleration must be the recommended framework around which schools facilitate education of talented learners." Thus, she would seem to place more emphasis on acceleration as an overall strategy than would other authors. One of the programs described in Van Tassel-Baska's chapter as an example of the prototype "grade acceleration" would be considered by many as "homogeneous grouping" rather than acceleration since students are grouped according to ability in each subject. Acceleration seems to be a component of the program, but ability grouping seems to be the general framework.

Despite her conclusion that acceleration should be the framework, Van Tassel-Baska states very clearly that acceleration must be combined with other strategies to provide a comprehensive program: ". . . while one can argue that it [acceleration] is a necessary strategy to employ, it cannot be considered sufficient." She recommends enrichment, counseling, and acceleration as the major components of any program. Other supportive, and necessary, components for a successful accelerative program, according to Van Tassel-Baska are the following: attention to affective needs, peer interaction through intellectual discussions, reorganization of the curriculum according to higher-level skills and concepts, ". . . materials that organize subject matter according to its structural or thematic nature," diverse strategies and experiences, careful consideration of the learners to receive acceleration, acceleration of groups rather than individuals, carefully selected teachers, careful planning and articulation of experiences, and written policies and procedures.

Levine generally agrees with Van Tassel-Baska, but adds different requirements for the successful use of acceleration: change in expectations of the teacher and child, change in what is taught, change in structure inside and outside the "parent" institution so that the alternative program is accepted, a realization that acceleration serves a limited need for a "finite subgroup of the gifted population," that it be offered on a continuing basis, well-coordinated with other services, internally consistent, and carry with it clearly defined rewards that equal the extra expectations.

Levine also recommends more narrow parameters for defining the usefulness of acceleration in two ways. First, he suggests that grade acceleration and content acceleration are useful practices, but that telescoping has limited usefulness because it is generally defined as teaching the same curriculum only covering it more rapidly, which suggests no changes in teaching methods or depth and breadth of concepts taught. Another limitation is the numbers and types of students with whom acceleration should be employed. Levine states that it is apparent from research and practice that ". . . acceleration is the answer for the child and the system who are in total agreement with each other" and that as presently practiced, it is only for the "go-getter." He also discusses some characteristics of gifted individuals that would not be nurtured by an accelerated curriculum and concludes that acceleration tends to focus on acquisition of knowledge as a goal rather than as a means to an end. Educators, according to Levine, need to develop in gifted children the attitude that knowledge is a "state of mind rather than a statement of facts."

With regard to students who can be served appropriately by acceleration, Van Tassel-Baska and Levine agree that acceleration is appropriate for certain types of learners. Van Tassel-Baska presents seven decision rules for the practice of acceleration, three of which pertain to student characteristics. She recommends acceleration for students who learn rapidly, who are high achievers, and who are interested in (and motivated to) participate in such programs. As discussed earlier, Levine also adds agreement between the "system" and the child and the child being a "go-getter," which can be seen as elaborations of Van Tassel-Baska's third criterion—interested in participating.

In summary, acceleration is a defensible practice in education of gifted learners because it has demonstrated certain results: (*i*) improvement in motivation, confidence, and scholarship; (*ii*) prevention of "mental laziness;" (*iii*) facilitation of early completion of professional training; (*iv*) reduction in the cost of education; and (*v*) increase in time for adults to be productive in their careers. Acceleration is only defensible, however, if it is implemented with learners who can benefit most from it and who desire this approach, if it is combined with other intervention strategies that take into account the whole child and a variety of learning characteristics, and if it is well-planned, articulated, and coordinated with other services both within and outside the system, clearly defined with appropriate policies and procedures, and implemented by the "right" teachers.

What makes enrichment a defensible and appropriate approach in programs for the gifted?

The first, and most important, requirement for enrichment to be defensible is that it be clearly defined. A myriad of educational practices can be labeled enrichment, and many of them cannot be defended as either necessary or appropriate for gifted students. Klausmeier focuses on definitions by Gallagher and Stanley, emphasizing that enrichment must include comprehensive, academically relevant goals and objectives and that it must be devoted to development of the particular intellectual skills and talents of gifted students. She further elaborates from this perspective and adds that, in determining or devising appropriate enrichment, we must carefully consider new theories and research on intelligence, must take into account the needs of special populations of gifted students, and must provide for systematic and longitudinal development of giftedness. Educators must examine current goals and objectives and new information about giftedness and must develop enrichment programs that address the concerns outlined by Gallagher and Stanley. Some examples of new elements needed in enrichment programs are (*i*) methods for developing high-level activities such as planning and evaluation, (*ii*) real-world experiences rather than contrived, possibly nongeneralizable activities, and (*iii*) enrichment for all intelligences. Ellis and Ellis-Schwabe stress the need for an individualized program that is purposeful, content-based, designed to extend the regular curriculum, and taught in a manner that "maximizes the mode of instructional leadership."

In addition to being clearly defined and meeting the conditions outlined above, an enrichment program is appropriate and can be defined if it is implemented well. Klausmeier stresses that content must be meshed with processes, an idea the reader has encountered before in Maker's and Schiever's articles. Ellis and Ellis-Schwabe heartily agree with this component. Another important aspect of an enrichment program, discussed by Klausmeier, is that it would be defined according to individual needs over a long period of time and that it should be an instructional consideration rather than an administrative format. As readers may recall, Ward has also stressed that acceleration and enrichment are best thought of as curricular issues. Authors (other than the editor in the introduction to the section, and Kaplan and Van Tassel-Baska) do not emphasize that enrichment should be combined with acceleration to be effective. Certainly, this idea is mentioned in passing by several authors, but it is not stressed to the same extent as is combining acceleration with enrichment.

Ellis and Ellis-Schwabe propose a definition that integrates ideas from several authors: "the type of educative activity that goes above and beyond the regular curriculum in which particular attention is given to gifted students in individual needs, interests, and learning styles as well as to integrated curricular modifications and content adaptations." Kaplan's discussion of the concepts of appropriateness and differentiation would be especially helpful in this context as well. The criteria Kaplan includes for both concepts should be applied in judging enrichment provisions and would be helpful to those involved in developing definitions of enrichment to fit a specific situation. Ellis and Ellis-Schwabe suggest that enrichment can be made more defensible as an educational practice if (*i*) the students to whom it is offered include students other than gifted students as traditionally defined by an IQ score (e.g., creative children, children having problems in the traditional classroom) and (*ii*) a wider variety of educative techniques, such as peer tutoring and mentorships, are included.

Enrichment as a concept does have some problems, the greatest of which is probably the difficulty in defining it, both in general and in particular situations. Other difficulties include distinguishing it from regular education, developing a scope and sequence that shows how the enriching activities are interrelated among themselves as well as how they build upon the regular curriculum, making decisions about the type and amount of content necessary to ensure new learning, and finding the resources (both human and financial) that enable teachers and other educators to provide the type and amount of enrichment experiences students need. Although this is not listed as a major flaw by the various authors, it seems necessary to note here that there is very little data from research available to support the various claims made for the benefits of enrichment. The reader may have questioned why so little research was cited in either of the chapters on the subject of enrichment while numerous studies were employed to build the case for acceleration. I am not suggesting that there is none, but I am calling attention to the fact that there is very little.

Despite the problems inherent in its use, enrichment offers many benefits. These are discussed by writers asked to address enrichment as well as those writing about acceleration and the general curriculum for gifted students:

1. It may be potentially easier to carry out than a highly articulated acceleration program.
2. Parents and administrators may perceive enrichment as a more acceptable alternative than acceleration.
3. Challenging materials and content may be included in the curriculum for gifted students without disrupting the regular curriculum's progression.
4. Student creativity and individual interests, which may be curtailed by the regular curriculum or by a highly accelerated program, can be stimulated and developed through appropriate enrichment.
5. Some of the affective goals of programs for the gifted can best be met through inclusion of materials and activities not provided through the usual curriculum.

How does one justify the expenditure of additional funds or reallocation of existing resources for a program for gifted students?

This question could be considered the most fundamental one, or the first to be answered when considering a program. Basically, the question is "How can people be convinced that a program is needed?"

Convincing program administrators, school boards, and others in the community that a special program for gifted students is needed is not easy. Many individuals believe that such programs are not necessary in the first place, and even if needed, are elitist. How can one justify giving even more advantages to those who are already ahead of the rest of the population? Seeley notes that as "categorical" programs, services for gifted students have an inherent bias to overcome. Such programs generally are established because of a failure or a weakness in the existing program—or at least this is the perception of general school administrators. Indeed, one of the arguments proposed for justifying the provision of special services (and the core of one of the leading definitions of giftedness) is that some students have educational needs that are not being met by the standard or usual educational program.

Healey also reminds us that to develop or change public policy, we must prepare our arguments carefully. This preparation includes understanding the opposition and designing tactics for handling ideologies that are different from or in conflict with the policies we wish to establish. He continues by pointing out that whether or not special education is provided for gifted students is ". . . first and foremost, a political issue. Second, it is an economic issue, and finally, it becomes a socioeducational debate among groups and individuals with divergent points of view." Thus, anyone desiring to establish special programs must first assess the political and economic climate and then determine attitudes of those surrounding the program to understand what arguments and/or evidence might be most convincing to opponents of the idea.

Feldhusen discusses three philosophical positions that can be assumed in developing answers to the question of how to justify a program for the gifted. The first is that each individual, regardless of abilities or other characteristics, has a right to an education appropriate to his or her characteristics and needs. This is essentially the "special educational" definition and rationale presented earlier by Berliner, Maker, Borland, and Silverman. Examination of educational policy and statutes related to education, however, reveals that in the nation and in most (if not all) states, all children are guaranteed a free education, while only exceptional children are guaranteed a free, *appropriate* education. Gifted children are assured of an appropriate education only if they are included in the state's or nation's definition of exceptional children. Certainly, the argument that children should have an appropriate education is an important one, but we must recognize that use of this line of reasoning may not always be successful in convincing various audiences of the value of a special program for gifted students.

A second philosophical position suggested by Feldhusen is that all children have the right to services that develop their abilities to the highest level so their "potential" can be fulfilled. Since there are obviously differences in potential, the educational services must be different. Healey, however, cites court cases and policy statements of national organizations that show there is little or no public support for helping children realize their full potential. On the other hand, if one examines the educational philosophy and goal statements of many public school districts, one would find statements such as this very clearly included as goals of the educational program. Even if there are no state or national policies or statutes supporting the school's responsibility to help students realize their full potential, there may be local goals or policies that are clearly in agreement with this perception of the school's responsibility. Such policies can then be a part of arguments to support programs for gifted students.

Readers have certainly heard the third philosophical position: As a nation, state, and community, we need to develop our gifted and talented students so they can contribute to the good of everyone. For many individuals, this seems to be the most convincing argument, and one can certainly see its potential when examining historically the cycles of national interest in providing special programs for gifted students. The greatest support for such programs has been evidenced during times of national crisis. Developing nations often view their gifted youth as their only hope for survival and become actively engaged in recruitment and education of these children. As we have discussed earlier, use of this argument, or, rather, defining giftedness in this way, also leads to the greatest difficulties in demonstrating success.

Putting these arguments into the context of Healey's statement that whether or not a program for gifted students is provided is first a political then an economic issue, then a socioeducational debate reveals that Seeley's comments could be characterized mainly in terms of the politics of a situation, as could Feldhusen's third argument (the national-resources definition of giftedness). Another suggestion made by Seeley is that we capitalize on the current political climate of emphasis on and interest in excellence. How can one achieve excellence without providing appropriate services for one's most promising students? Feldhusen's first two arguments may be more appropriate as a part of a socioeducational debate. Certainly, there are many other political issues that could be discussed and many political tactics one could employ, but no authors chose to address this question. Space does not permit a full consideration of the issue, so I would simply suggest careful consideration and use of the very successful methods used by our counterparts in special education who have advocated special services for handicapped students.

Economic issues have not been discussed except by Feldhusen in his review of the possible public funding patterns for programs. Since there is very little federal money available for establishing programs or conducting research related to gifted students, most funding must come from states or local communities. Again, no authors chose to address this issue, and it requires more development than I can provide in this chapter. It seems to me, however, that we need to be exploring different avenues for funding, especially private agencies, business, and industry. Such organizations and agencies have a vested interest in talent development and could become excellent partners with public and private educational agencies.

Finally, in socioeducational debates about the pros and cons of programs for gifted students, proponents can include arguments of the type discussed by Feldhusen: an individual's right to an appropriate education and to an education that develops that individual's "full potential." Many of the suggestions made by Callahan and Caldwell can be helpful in developing answers in advance to arguments of those who are opposed to programs for the gifted. If evaluators are involved in the program planning process, for example, they can assist in collecting data to document the fact that a population needing special services does exist, that this population is not insignificant, and that its needs are not being met by existing programs. Data can also be collected to document the feasibility of a proposed program.

Perhaps the best advice presented in this volume for those who wish to justify the provision of special services is to assess the various factors in the educational climate (e.g., political, economic, socioeducational) and be prepared to answer a variety of concerns by providing data and logical arguments to support the need for such a program. Obviously, this is not novel advice! However, the various authors in this volume have supplied numerous suggestions for specific techniques not usually employed to assess the climate and prepare a supportive case.

What policies, procedures, and arrangements will facilitate or inhibit the development of a program for the gifted that is defensible?

The answers to this question will be presented in three sections: (1) methods for program development (i.e., the *process* of program development), (2) policies that need to be established, and (3) standards for program operation. Since program evaluation and the methods for conducting it are related to both this question and the following one, evaluation issues related to program development and operation will be discussed in this section while issues related to continuing an established program will be the subject of the following section.

Program Development

Feldhusen addresses numerous issues, and makes many recommendations concerning the character of a program development process that can result in a defensible program. First, he recommends that a knowledgeable committee consisting of teachers, parents, and at least one administrator be responsible for program development and continual review. Callahan and Caldwell would recommend an evaluator either as a member of the committee or a consultant to it. This group would then have several tasks, including the following (among others):

1. Conduct a careful review and analysis of research, philosophical issues, and public policy. (Feldhusen)
2. Conduct open discussions of philosophical bases and barriers to special programs. (Feldhusen)

3. Conduct a needs assessment (Feldhusen) or document that a population exists whose needs are not being met by the present program (Callahan and Caldwell, Seeley).

4. Develop clearly stated policies with assistance from "a legislative researcher, a policy analyst, a philosopher, a futurist, an artist, a sociologist, an economist, a historian, and a computer-assisted statistician." (Healey)

5. Define the population to be served. (Feldhusen, Callahan and Caldwell, Healey, Seeley)

6. Develop clearly stated goals for meeting special needs. (Feldhusen, Callahan and Caldwell, Healey, Seeley)

7. Develop a clearly stated plan for identification, delivery of services, staff development, articulation of the curriculum and other services with the regular curriculum K-12, and for systematic assessment of all aspects of the process and the program. (Feldhusen, Callahan and Caldwell, Seeley)

Policies

Since Healey has developed a series of policy statements that are based on the ideas presented in Feldhusen's chapter, the reader is referred to Healey's discussion for a specific listing of recommended policies from those authors. The policies include statements relating to the provision of appropriate, special services; development of a written, comprehensive plan available for public scrutiny and periodic discussion; establishment of formal procedures for identification that are appropriate for all, including those from special groups; notification of parents; staffing by qualified individuals; individualized programs; articulated comprehensive curricula; and due process procedures. Perhaps the most controversial of these is Feldhusen's recommendation that teachers of gifted students be gifted and talented in the areas in which they attempt to instruct gifted students.

Additional policies suggested by Feldhusen and other authors include provisions for formative and summative evaluations to be conducted and used as the basis for program revision and justification. This evaluation should be broad-based, should include a variety of audiences, and should employ designs other than traditional experimental ones.

Program Operation Standards

Obviously, policies result in particular procedures. Thus, this section is in part a result of the preceding one. However, certain procedures that authors in this volume have recommended may be implied, though not explicitly, by the policy statements in Healey's article. One could also consider many of the procedures listed in this section as standards by which one's program can be judged. They, of necessity, reflect the wisdom and values of the authors in this volume.

1. Extensive, ongoing inservice and staff development should be provided, and even required, for all individuals who will contribute either directly or indirectly to the education of gifted students. This includes regular classroom teachers and central administration staff as well as those directly involved.
2. When a pullout program is the primary method of service delivery, modification of the regular curriculum and teaching methods are essential to providing a comprehensive, appropriate program for gifted students.
3. Special programs or provisions for gifted students should begin at the preschool and primary level and should continue throughout high school.
4. Definitions of giftedness should include a variety of types of ability.
5. Identification procedures should contain multiple means of assessment and must be consistent with the definition(s) of giftedness.
6. Decisions should be based on professional judgments of need rather than numbers (such as an IQ score).
7. A program coordinator is needed to ensure quality, continuity, and articulation of the program.
8. A wide variety of services is necessary.
9. A curriculum scope and sequence should be available.
10. The program evaluation procedures must be clear, consider a variety of audiences, be comprehensive, provide data for in-progress revision of the program, and provide data showing clearly where changes are necessary.

Since evaluation was a major focus of three chapters in the last section of this volume, and it has not been discussed previously in this chapter, it deserves additional comments. Callahan and Caldwell's philosophy is that a major goal of evaluation is to assist programs in being successful rather than to make after-the-fact judgments of worth. Seeley sees evaluation as a tool for making decisions (which, of course, could occur prior to program implementation as well as after). Dinham and Udall emphasize the multiple purposes of evaluation, suggesting that it is defined by its purpose: "to meet the varied needs of multiple audiences." Thus, an important first step in implementing evaluation is identifying the audience(s). Following this identification, one must then determine the needs of audiences that can be met through program evaluation. In addition, the climate of the program, or the setting in which evaluation occurs, must be carefully considered.

As all authors have noted, either directly or indirectly, a clearly conceptualized and described program is necessary before a good evaluation can be designed. A thorough evaluation cannot "make up" for a poorly conceived, ambiguous program design. Two related purposes of evaluation, however, are to contribute to the development of a program design and to provide data to assist in clarifying or describing that program. For example, a usual target for evaluation is student change (learner outcomes). Often, these changes are predicated on the sometimes false assumption that teachers are using the methods they are supposed to be using. Further, this assumption rests on the sometimes faulty assumption that staff development efforts have been successful! In other words, the evaluation can provide data to indicate (*i*) whether staff development efforts resulted in actual changes in the behavior of teachers (not simply whether inservice was enjoyed or "perceived as useful" since such results show little or no correlation to changed behavior), (*ii*) what teaching methods and curricula are actually being implemented in classrooms, and (*iii*) student outcomes that may be attributed to the program.

All authors suggest that readers investigate and become familiar with the variety of "models" for evaluation available in both the general literature and the literature specifically related to programs for the gifted. Adaptations and modifications of models or approaches can be made to fit the audiences, needs, climate, and program. Dinham and Udall caution us about the widespread use of the word "model," however, reminding us that some methods do not meet the criteria necessary to warrant a label of model. Most "models," based on their analysis, are at best conceptual approaches or at worst, sets of convenient procedures. Models are more easily defended because of their strong base and consistent, well-developed procedures.

All authors have their favorite models or approaches. Seeley likes the input-process-output approach because it considers conditions and contexts (input), the procedures and strategies used in the program (process), and finally, the results of the program (output). Callahan and Caldwell prefer naturalistic models because they seem more appropriate for accomplishing the purposes of program evaluation, are less biased, and include both quantitative and qualitative data. Dinham and Udall also prefer a naturalistic model, the responsive model, because of its well-defined procedures, its strong conceptual base, its recognition of the interactive nature of components of the situation being evaluated, and its responsiveness or adaptability to the differing characteristics of these components.

Regardless of the model or approach used, communication is critical, according to all authors. Planned communication should occur frequently, and should include a recognition of the many problems discussed by Callahan and Caldwell. The responsibility for more effective communication rests with both the program staff and the evaluator. Evaluators and program administrators should recognize the various roles assumed by evaluators and the problems resulting. They should also recognize the problems resulting from lack of clarity, feelings of threat, and use of jargon on the part of those involved in the program. Attention to these and other issues discussed at length by the authors in this volume should ensure an evaluation design that is defensible in and of itself, and one that contributes to the defensibility of the program for gifted students.

How can the continued operation of a program for gifted students be justified?

Seeley's definition of evaluation as "a process of examining actions and events according to some predetermined standards for the purpose of making decisions" provides a useful context for answering this question. In light of other discussions in this volume, it is clear that evaluation can have many purposes and that making decisions about the continued operation of a program is one of its very important goals.

This question could be interpreted very narrowly, and the answer of "yes" or "no" could be considered the major outcome of a program evaluation. Thus, the question becomes "Should the program continue?" However, considering the opinions of various authors in this volume leads to a broader conception of the question, so that a "yes, and . . ." or "no, but . . ." answer is provided. As the authors have stated numerous times and in many ways, the results of a good evaluation should not only provide data to support continuation of a program but also to suggest *how* the program should be continued. As Seeley has noted, evaluation is the tool of defensibility, and if we use it successfully, we can ensure the survival of programs for the gifted both nationally and locally.

It can safely be said that the first step toward justifying a program's continued operation is to conduct a good, comprehensive evaluation that addresses the concerns of audiences involved with its continuation, especially those responsible for allocating funds and making decisions. Sounds logical, doesn't it? Evaluation needs, also, to show how improvements can make the program more effective or suggest new directions for the future. Furthermore, the evaluation can be even more successful, according to some authors, if certain results are clear. Feldhusen notes that evaluation should demonstrate that the program is operating as planned and is operating successfully. Factors considerd a part of successful operation are such components as positive morale, administrative support, achievement of students in basic skills and in areas addressed by the program's objectives. According to Feldhusen, the evaluation should also demonstrate that student achievement at each level contributes to success at the next level and that creative and productive thinking skills taught in the special program transfer to behavior in the regular curriculum. Finally, he mentions in passing the need for programs to demonstrate their contribution to students' success beyond school. Are the program's graduates becoming high-level producers?

Seeley takes a different approach and suggests that we not only emphasize the special nature of the students and their education, but also demonstrate how the program is "an integral and meaningful part of the general education program." Related to this perception of the program is the collection of convincing data that demonstrate how the program for gifted students enhances the regular curriculum or program through development of good community relations, raising expectations for performance of all children, enhancing instruction for all bright children, or emphasizing the development of thinking skills in all students. He notes that the independent projects of gifted students can call attention to the higher quality one can expect from other students as well.

Finally, Seeley cautions us against the temptation to overlook weaknesses in our programs. Good evaluations should uncover sources of weakness and suggest practices that need to be discontinued or changed. If programs for the gifted are to survive and grow, we must not "assume our guardianship task so vociferously that we are blinded by our advocacy and as a result defend activities that are not efficacious or effective."

A very clear indication of numerous reviews of literature and research is that there is too little information available that clearly demonstrates the effectiveness of special programs for gifted students. Positive results of well-designed comprehensive program evaluations as well as experimental, comparative studies are essential if the field of education for the gifted is to continue to justify its existence.

What are the elements of a defensible program for gifted students?

In an attempt to synthesize the diverse perspectives presented in this volume and develop standards that can be used to assess a program's defensibility, I have developed a list of criteria that can be applied to the various components of a program. Merging diverse perspectives can often result in development of abstract concepts that are useful because of their wide range of applicability. Such fusion can also result in criteria that are so general they are meaningless. My hope is that the abstractness of the following principles will widen their scope of applicability and that the descriptions provided and the specific examples (throughout this volume) from which they were drawn will ensure their usefulness.

Appropriate

All phases of a program must meet the criterion of appropriateness. Definitions must be appropriate for the context or climate, and identification procedures must be appropriate for the population served by a program. Appropriateness of the curriculum, teaching strategies, and services has been discussed extensively and is a key to differentiating programs for gifted students. Finally, the methods and models for program evaluation must be appropriate for the context, the audience, and the program.

Articulated

All aspects of a defensible program are articulated, both internally and externally. Within the program, all available services for each student and for groups of students fit together well so that all needs are served without duplication. In addition, the services, and even more important, the curriculum is coordinated and articulated with the regular educational program and curriculum to ensure that valuable skills are not missed and that overlap is avoided. Services provided within a program or within a school system are also articulated within a larger educational community, including preschools, museums, colleges, universities, and other agencies. Program planning and evaluation efforts should include careful designs to ensure coordination of various aspects of the educational program.

Clear

Clarity is essential. No aspect of a program can afford ambiguity or sloppiness. Definitions should clearly specify what giftedness is, and should lead to procedures for identification that are also explicit. Policies governing the program should be precisely stated, and the goals for the program should be unambiguous. Services, curriculum, and assessment procedures should be carefully and clearly described. The relationship between special and regular educational services should be definite as should the differences between these services.

Consistent

Internal consistency characterizes a defensible program for the gifted (or any defensible program, for that matter). Identification procedures must be compatible with the definition, and the curriculum must match the needs/characteristics of the students who are being served as well as be carefully designed to reach the established goals of the program. Methods for evaluation must also be in accord with all other aspects of the program. Finally, the various components of a comprehensive plan for services must spring from an underlying conceptual/philosophical base and must be compatible with each other and with the underlying concept.

Comprehensive

This criterion relates to most aspects of the program, but should not be used to imply that all children should receive services or that schools must provide services to every possible type of giftedness. Comprehensiveness is most important in its application to identification methods, services, curricular adaptations, student assessment, and program evaluation. Multiple methods, a variety of sources, and assessment over a long period of time contribute to the comprehensiveness of identification procedures. A continuum of services with varied provisions for acceleration, enrichment, counseling, support services, mentorships, and other opportunities is evidence that a program is comprehensive in its offerings. The curriculum is extensive if it provides for variations in learner needs such as rate, style, entering level, and interests. It must also provide challenge, appropriate depth, and breadth to accommodate many different learners and levels of abstractness needed by learners at various developmental stages. Evaluation and assessment are comprehensive when they consider multiple audiences and audience needs, include a variety of techniques, involve all those concerned with the program, and consider multiple outcomes.

Responsive

To be defensible, a program for gifted students must be responsive. The definition of giftedness must be responsive to the needs and concerns of the local community, the state, and the nation. As long as public funds are being spent on education, educators must respond to the needs of the public. Program developers must assess the needs of the general community as well as the needs and concerns of the educational community. These concerns must then be addressed through program goals, policies, and services. The curriculum and teaching strategies must result from a recognition of individual characteristics and learning needs and must be changed when necessary. Evaluation of the program must be accountable to various audiences and must be used to make appropriate modifications. Thus, the evaluation must respond to the program and the program to the evaluation.

Unique

Any categorical or special program must be unique. It must be identifiably different from the existing services provided to all children. Of course, it must be integrated with other services, but uniqueness is still important. Descriptions of giftedness should establish clear differences between those who need special services and those who do not, and identification procedures must verify these differences. The curriculum must build upon the regular curriculum, but must be distinctive, either in content, processes, products, learning environment, or all of these areas. Justification for a program need not include assurance that certain provisions would not be useful with other populations of children, but it must demonstrate with certainty that these provisions are not currently a part of the general educational program.

Valid

Validity of the underlying philosophical and theoretical bases of programs is of primary concern in the establishment of programs for the gifted. All other aspects of a program must also meet this criterion. The validity of instruments used in assessment of students is of primary concern as is the validity of instruments used in program evaluation. The success of teaching techniques and curricular adaptation must be verifiable as well, and convincing evidence must be provided. Not only must we supply evidence for the validity of individual programs, but we must, as a group, prove that the idea of special education for gifted students is a valid one.

INDEX

The Editor and Contributors

C. June Maker is Associate Professor of Special Education at The University of Arizona. In this capacity, she is responsible for the development and coordination of graduate degree concentrations in education of the gifted at both the master's and doctoral levels. She holds national offices in several organizations for the gifted. Her publications are on the subjects of curriculum development for the gifted, teaching models in education of the gifted, the gifted handicapped, teacher training, the development of talents in exceptional children, and teaching learning disabled students. She has been a coordinator of a graduate program at the University of New Mexico, a teacher, a regional supervisor for a state department of education, an administrative intern in the Federal Office for the Gifted, and has consulted with numerous local school districts, state departments of education, and other public and private agencies both in the United States and abroad. She holds degrees from the University of Virginia (Ph.D.), Southern Illinois University (M.S.), and Western Kentucky University (B.S.).

David C. Berliner is Professor of Educational Psychology in the Division of Educational Foundations and Administration at the University of Arizona. Since receiving his Ph.D. from Stanford University, he has served in several capacities, including Director for Research at the Far West Laboratory and Head of the Educational Psychology Department at the University of Arizona. Dr. Berliner reviews manuscripts for numerous journals and serves as consulting editor for many others. His publications number in the hundreds and cover topics related to education and psychology. Currently he is president of the American Educational Research Association.

James H. Borland is an Adjunct Assistant Professor of Education at Teachers College, Columbia University, where he received his Ph.D. in Special Education in 1981. He is also co-director of the Center for the Study and Education of the Gifted and the Hollingworth Preschool for the Gifted. He has served as a consultant and speaker on Gifted Education for numerous organizations and school districts over the past 8 years. Dr. Borland has been a teacher of the gifted, a teacher of handicapped students, and a social worker. He currently serves as co-editor of a forthcoming book series on the psychology and education of the gifted.

Michael S. Caldwell received his Ph.D. from Ohio State University in 1965. He has been Associate Dean for Research and Instruction and is currently Director of both the Bureau of Educational Research and the Evaluation Research Center in the Curry School of Education, University of Virginia. Dr. Caldwell has directed and been extensively involved with numerous research and evaluation projects dealing with teacher evaluation and research and evaluation for gifted and talented children. His writings and publications reflect this involvement.

Carolyn M. Callahan received her Ph.D. from the University of Connecticut in 1973. Since that time she has been at the University of Virginia, where she is currently an Associate Professor in the Curry School of Education and Director of the Summer Enrichment Program. Her publications cover a wide range of topics in education of the gifted. A past president of the Association for the Gifted, Dr. Callahan also serves on the editorial boards of *Roeper Review, Exceptional Children,* and *Teaching Exceptional Children.*

Sarah M. Dinham is an Associate Professor of Educational Psychology at the University of Arizona. Her interests are educational evaluation, postsecondary academic affairs, and education in professional fields. She holds a Ph.D. from Michigan State University in Educational Research and Educational Psychology. Dr. Dinham's accomplishments include research on teaching, higher education, architectural education, and evaluation.

Antoinette S. Ellis is a freelance writer and is currently completing her Ph.D. in Education with a concentration in creativity at Portland State University. She received her undergraduate degree in 1960 and completed 2 years of graduate work in philosophy at Bryn Mawr College. For 10 years she was employed as a writer/editor in the Computer Technology Program, Northwest Regional Educational Laboratory in Portland, Oregon, where she co-authored and edited several textbooks and numerous sets of curriculum materials.

Michelle A. Ellis-Schwabe completed her doctorate in Educational Psychology in 1986. Her major field is School Psychology with minors in Special (Gifted) Education and Educational Administration. She holds undergraduate degrees in Psychology and Dance from the University of Washington and a Master's in Special Education from the University of Oregon. She has had 5 years of teaching and therapy experience and is presently employed as Special Education Director/Therapist in a residential treatment facility for emotionally handicapped adolescents.

John F. Feldhusen is Professor and Chairman of the Educational Psychology Section, Purdue University, and Director of the Purdue Gifted Education Resource Institute. A past president of the National Association for Gifted Children, he was also named a Distinguished Scholar of the Association in 1984. Dr. Feldhusen is a Fellow of the American Psychology Association, a past editor of *The Educational Psychologist,* and is currently Editor of *The Gifted Child Quarterly.*

William Foster is a faculty member in the Graduate School of Education at Rutgers University. He is presently Director of the Center for Individual Development in the Department of Educational Psychology. Dr. Foster's interests focus on the psychology of excellence. He has recently published in *Gifted Child Quarterly* and *The Journal of Counseling and Development.* Dr. Foster has served on the advisory board of the Council for Exceptional Children— Talented and Gifted, the Governmental Advisory Board for the Gifted and Talented in New Jersey, and the Research Committee for the National Association of Gifted Children.

Lynn H. Fox is a consultant with the Harrison Group, Inc., in St. Petersburg, Florida. Her research interests are primarily in sex differences in mathematical achievement and education, particularly mathematics education for the academically gifted. She holds a B.S.Ed. with specialization in mathematics and an M.Ed. in Educational Psychology from the University of Florida. Her M.A. and Ph.D. are in Developmental and Educational Psychology from the Johns Hopkins University. She has received research grants from the Spencer Foundation, the Robert Sterling Clark Foundation, and the National Institute of Education, and she has served on the SAT Advisory Committee for the College Board and as a consultant to the Ford Foundation. Dr. Fox is a co-editor of several books and the author of numerous journal articles and book chapters about the academically talented.

William C. Healey is a Professor of Special Education at the University of Arizona and directs the personnel preparation program in special education administration. He has been instrumental in creating policies and programs for the gifted and talented as a former teacher, assistant superintendent, state director of special education, national professional organization program director, and assistant dean for research and graduate studies. He currently serves as an editorial board member, *Topics in Gifted Education;* Member, the Association for the Gifted; and Advisory Board Member, Arizona Association for the Gifted and Talented.

Sandra N. Kaplan is the Associate Director of the National/State Leadership Training Institute on the Gifted and the Talented. She has served as a consultant in gifted education to state, regional, and local education agencies. Dr. Kaplan has authored articles and books in gifted and general education.

Kay L. Klausmeier is currently a school psychologist in Tucson and a graduate student in the Department of Special Education at the University of Arizona. She holds an M.A. in counseling and guidance and an Ed.S. in special education and school psychology. As a teacher in regular, gifted, and learning disabilities programs she became interested in students who had exceptional abilities but were underachievers. Ms. Klausmeier's current research interests are K-12 and college gifted underachievers and the relation of information processing styles and higher level thinking skills.

Ned S. Levine is currently the Curriculum Director for Science, Health, and Physical Education in Tucson, Arizona's largest school district. Among other experiences in his 16 years in teaching, he has served as the director of the gifted and talented program in an urban school district. Mr. Levine has authored many articles, program documents, and federally funded proposals. His honors include both academic and service-related awards.

Shirley W. Schiever is a doctoral candidate at the University of Arizona majoring in Special Education with a focus on the gifted. She has taught in the regular classroom and a resource room for gifted students and has coordinated a district-wide program for gifted students. Curriculum issues and the use of teaching and learning models are prime interests and the topics of her dissertation. She is President of the Arizona Association for the Gifted and Talented. Other professional affiliations include the National Association for Gifted Children; the Council for Exceptional Children, Talented and Gifted Division; and the World Council for Gifted and Talented Children.

Kenneth R. Seeley is Director of Program Development for the Clayton Foundation in Denver, Colorado. He is also Adjunct Professor in gifted education at the University of Denver. He has served as Editor of *The Journal for the Education of the Gifted* and was an executive board member of The Association for the Gifted. Dr. Seeley has published and done research in the areas of evaluation, giftedness and delinquency, and program administration.

Linda Kreger Silverman is a psychologist and has been an Assistant Professor in Gifted Education at the University of Denver for the past 8 years. She continues to teach at the University of Denver while providing services to gifted students and their parents. She has worked extensively in the field of gifted education since 1962 and is currently completing textbooks on developmental approaches to gifted education and on educating gifted/handicapped learners. Her research includes the exceptionally gifted, underachievement, emotional development of gifted adults, counseling needs of gifted adolescents, teaching strategies for the gifted, self-concept, assessment of giftedness in infancy, gifted females, and gifted/handicapped children. She is presently investigating the relation between early ear infections and underachievement. In addition to these responsibilities, Dr. Silverman lectures, teaches, and consults in many parts of the country.

Anne J. Udall is currently a teacher of gifted learning disabled students in the Tucson Unified School District, a program that she designed, implemented, and refined during the past 4 years. She is completing her doctoral studies in special education and educational psychology at the University of Arizona. In her professional areas of interest—program evaluation, gifted handicapped individuals, curriculum development, and instructional theory—she has completed research, written articles and book chapters, conducted workshops, developed instructional programs, and evaluated programs.

Joyce Van Tassel-Baska initiated and developed the Midwest Talent Search Project in 1981 and has served as its director since that time. She was formerly the director of a Chicago-area regional gifted center and also served as the director of gifted programs for Illinois. She has been coordinator of gifted programs for the Toledo, Ohio public school systems and a teacher of gifted high school students in English and Latin. She has worked as a consultant on gifted education in more than 35 states and for key national groups. She currently serves on the editorial board for *The Journal for the Education of the Gifted* and *Gifted Child Quarterly* and is past president of The Association for the Gifted of the Council for Exceptional Children. She was recently elected to the Board of Directors of the National Association of Gifted Children and is on the education council of the National Business Consortium on the Gifted and Talented. Dr. Van Tassel-Baska has also served as visiting instructor in gifted education at several universities. Her major research interests are on the disadvantaged gifted as a special population and effective curricular interventions with the gifted. She holds B.A., M.A., M.Ed., and Ed.D. degrees from the University of Toledo.

Virgil S. Ward, who was retired as of June 1986 from the University of Virginia's School of Education after 30 years of affiliation, continues to specialize in the psychological fields of human intelligence, cognition, and life-span development. In the field of education, Dr. Ward pursues his career-long interest in theory and its underlying relations to educational issues, projects, and institutional programs. His most active areas of research, publication, and consultative service are theories and systems of lifetime education and differential education for the gifted.